Table of Contents

Preface. xv
Foreword. xxi

1. Building Web Apps with WordPress. 1
What Is a Website? 1
What Is an App? 1
What Is a Web App? 1
Features of a Web App 2
Why Use WordPress? 3
You Are Already Using WordPress 4
Content Management Is Easy with WordPress 4
User Management Is Easy and Secure with WordPress 4
Plugins 5
Flexibility Is Important 5
Frequent Security Updates 6
Cost 6
.NET App 6
WordPress App 7
Responses to Some Common Criticisms of WordPress 7
When Not to Use WordPress 10
You Plan to License or Sell Your Site's Technology 10
There Is Another Platform That Will Get You "There" Faster 10
Flexibility Is NOT Important to You 11
Your App Needs to Be Highly Real Time 11
WordPress as an Application Framework 11
WordPress Versus MVC Frameworks 12
Anatomy of a WordPress App 15
What Is SchoolPress? 15
SchoolPress Runs on a WordPress Multisite Network 15

The SchoolPress Business Model   15
Membership Levels and User Roles   16
Classes Are BuddyPress Groups   16
Assignments Are a Custom Post Type   16
Submissions Are a (Sub)CPT for Assignments   17
Semesters Are a Taxonomy on the Class CPT   17
Departments Are a Taxonomy on the Class CPT   17
SchoolPress Has One Main Custom Plugin   17
SchoolPress Uses a Few Other Custom Plugins   18
SchoolPress Uses the StartBox Theme Framework   18

2. WordPress Basics. 21
WordPress Directory Structure   21
Root Directory   22
/wp-admin   22
/wp-includes   22
/wp-content   22
WordPress Database Structure   23
wp_options   23
Functions Found in /wp-includes/option.php   24
wp_users   26
Functions Found in /wp-includes/…   27
wp_usermeta   30
wp_posts   34
Functions found in /wp-includes/post.php   34
wp_postmeta   38
Functions Found in /wp-includes/post.php   38
wp_comments   42
Functions Found in /wp-includes/comment.php   42
wp_commentsmeta   46
Functions Found in /wp-includes/comment.php   47
wp_links   49
wp_terms   50
Functions Found in /wp-includes/taxonomy.php   50
wp_term_taxonomy   53
/wp-includes/taxonomy.php   53
wp_term_relationships   54
Extending WordPress   55

3. Leveraging WordPress Plugins. 57
The GPLv2 License   58
Installing WordPress Plugins   58

05/07

UNIVERSITY OF
WOLVERHAMPTON

:h

ss

Harrison Learning Centre
City Campus
University of Wolverhampton
St Peter's Square
Wolverhampton
WV1 1RH
Telephone: 0845 408 1631
Online renewals: www.wlv.ac.uk/
lib.myaccount

an

Telephone Renewals: 01902 321333 or 0845 408 1631
Please RETURN this item on or before the last date shown above.
Fines will be charged if items are returned late.
See tariff of fines displayed at the Counter.   (L2)

Beijing · Cambridge · Farnham · Köln · Sebastopol · Tokyo

Building Web Apps with WordPress

by Brian Messenlehner and Jason Coleman

Printed in the United States of America.

Published by O'Reilly Media, Inc., 1005 Gravenstein Highway North, Sebastopol, CA 95472.

O'Reilly books may be purchased for educational, business, or sales promotional use. Online editions are also available for most titles (*http://my.safaribooksonline.com*). For more information, contact our corporate/institutional sales department: 800-998-9938 or *corporate@oreilly.com*.

Editors: Meghan Blanchette and Allyson MacDonald	**Indexer:** Ellen Troutman
Production Editor: Nicole Shelby	**Cover Designer:** Randy Comer
Copyeditor: Charles Roumeliotis	**Interior Designer:** David Futato
Proofreader: Amanda Kersey	**Illustrator:** Rebecca Demarest

April 2014:   First Edition

Revision History for the First Edition:

2014-04-07:   First release

See *http://oreilly.com/catalog/errata.csp?isbn=9781449364076* for release details.

ISBN: 978-1-449-36407-6

[LSI]

Building Your Own Plugin   59
File Structure for an App Plugin   60
   /adminpages/   61
   /classes/   61
   /css/   62
   /js/   63
   /images/   63
   /includes/   63
   /includes/lib/   64
   /pages/   64
   /services/   65
   /scheduled/   65
   /schoolpress.php   65
Add-Ons to Existing Plugins   66
Use Cases and Examples   66
   The WordPress Loop   66
   WordPress Global Variables   67
   Action Hooks   77
   Filters   78
Free Plugins   79
   All in One SEO Pack   79
   BadgeOS   79
   Custom Post Type UI   80
   Posts 2 Posts   80
   Members   81
   W3 Total Cache   81
Premium Plugins   81
   Gravity Forms   81
   Backup Buddy   82
   WP All Import   82
Community Plugins   82
   BuddyPress   82

4. Themes.   95
Themes Versus Plugins   95
   When Developing Apps   95
   When Developing Plugins   96
   When Developing Themes   97
The Template Hierarchy   97
Page Templates   99
   Sample Page Template   99
   Using Hooks to Copy Templates   102

When to Use a Theme Template   103
Theme-Related WP Functions   103
  Using locate_template in Your Plugins   104
Style.css   106
  Versioning Your Theme's CSS Files   106
Functions.php   108
Themes and Custom Post Types   108
Popular Theme Frameworks   108
  WP Theme Frameworks   109
  Non-WP Theme Frameworks   110
Creating a Child Theme for StartBox   111
Including Bootstrap in Your App's Theme   111
Menus   113
  Nav Menus   113
  Dynamic Menus   114
Responsive Design   115
  Device and Display Detection in CSS   115
  Device and Feature Detection in JavaScript   116
  Device Detection in PHP   118
  Final Note on Browser Detection   122
Versioning CSS and JS Files   123

5. Custom Post Types, Post Metadata, and Taxonomies. 125
Default Post Types and Custom Post Types   125
  Page   125
  Post   125
  Attachment   126
  Revisions   126
  Nav Menu Item   126
Defining and Registering Custom Post Types   126
  register_post_type($post_type, $args);   127
What Is a Taxonomy and How Should I Use It?   135
  Taxonomies Versus Post Meta   135
  Creating Custom Taxonomies   137
  register_taxonomy($taxonomy, $object_type, $args)   137
  register_taxonomy_for_object_type($taxonomy, $object_type)   141
Using Custom Post Types and Taxonomies in Your Themes and Plugins   141
  The Theme Archive and Single Template Files   142
  Good Old WP_Query and get_posts()   142
Metadata with CPTs   145
  add_meta_box($id, $title, $callback, $screen, $context, $priority,
    $callback_args)   146

Custom Wrapper Classes for CPTs   148
    Extending WP_Post Versus Wrapping It   150
    Why Use Wrapper Classes?   151
    Keep Your CPTs and Taxonomies Together   151
    Keep It in the Wrapper Class   152
    Wrapper Classes Read Better   154

6. Users, Roles, and Capabilities. **155**
Getting User Data   156
Add, Update, and Delete Users   158
Hooks and Filters   161
What Are Roles and Capabilities?   162
    Checking a User's Role and Capabilities   163
    Creating Custom Roles and Capabilities   164
Extending the WP_User Class   166
Adding Registration and Profile Fields   168
Customizing the Users Table in the Dashboard   172
Plugins   174
    Theme My Login   174
    Hide Admin Bar from Non-Admins   174
    Paid Memberships Pro   174
    PMPro Register Helper   174
    Members   175

7. Other WordPress APIs, Objects, and Helper Functions. **177**
Shortcode API   177
    Shortcode Attributes   178
    Nested Shortcodes   179
    Removing Shortcodes   180
    Other Useful Shortcode-Related Functions   180
Widgets API   181
    Before You Add Your Own Widget   182
    Adding Widgets   182
    Defining a Widget Area   186
    Embedding a Widget Outside of a Dynamic Sidebar   188
Dashboard Widgets API   188
    Removing Dashboard Widgets   189
    Adding Your Own Dashboard Widget   191
Settings API   193
    Do You Really Need a Settings Page?   194
    Could You Use a Hook or Filter Instead?   194
    Use Standards When Adding Settings   196

Ignore Standards When Adding Settings	196
Rewrite API	197
Adding Rewrite Rules	198
Flushing Rewrite Rules	199
Other Rewrite Functions	200
WP-Cron	202
Adding Custom Intervals	204
Scheduling Single Events	204
Kicking Off Cron Jobs from the Server	205
Using Server Crons Only	206
WP Mail	207
Sending Nicer Emails with WordPress	207
File Header API	209
Adding File Headers to Your Own Files	211
Adding New Headers to Plugins and Themes	212

8. Secure WordPress.	**215**
Why It's Important	215
Security Basics	216
Update Frequently	216
Don't Use the Username "admin"	216
Use a Strong Password	217
Examples of Bad Passwords	217
Examples of Good Passwords	218
Hardening Your WordPress Install	218
Don't Allow Admins to Edit Plugins or Themes	218
Change Default Database Tables Prefix	218
Move wp-config.php	219
Hide Login Error Messages	220
Hide Your WordPress Version	220
Don't Allow Logins via wp-login.php	221
Add Custom .htaccess Rules for Locking Down wp-admin	221
Backup Everything!	222
Scan Scan Scan!	223
Useful Security Plugins	223
Spam-Blocking Plugins	223
Backup Plugins	224
Scanner Plugins	224
Login and Password-Protection Plugins	225
Writing Secure Code	225
Check User Capabilities	226
Custom SQL Statements	227

Data Validation, Sanitization, and Escaping 227
Nonces 232

9. JavaScript, jQuery, and AJAX. **237**
What Is AJAX? 237
What Is JSON? 237
jQuery and WordPress 238
 Enqueuing Other JavaScript Libraries 238
 Where to Put Your Custom JavaScript 239
AJAX Calls with WordPress and jQuery 240
Managing Multiple AJAX Requests 244
Heartbeat API 246
 Initialization 246
 Client-side JavaScript 247
 Server-side PHP 248
 Initialization 248
 Client-side JavaScript 249
 Server-side PHP 250
WordPress Limitations with Asynchronous Processing 251
Backbone.js 251

10. XML-RPC. **255**
wp.getUsersBlogs 255
wp.getPosts 256
wp.getPost 257
wp.newPost 259
wp.editPost 259
wp.deletePost 260
wp.getTerms 261
wp.getTerm 261
wp.newTerm 262
wp.editTerm 263
wp.deleteTerm 263
wp.getTaxonomies 263
wp.getTaxonomy 264
wp.getUsers 264
wp.getUser 265
wp.getProfile 265
wp.editProfile 266
wp.getCommentCount 266
wp.getPageTemplates 267
wp.getOptions 267

wp.setOptions	267
wp.getComment	268
wp.getComments	269
wp.deleteComment	269
wp.editComment	270
wp.newComment	270
wp.getMediaLibrary	271
wp.getMediaItem	271
wp.uploadFile	272
wp.getPostFormats	273
wp.getPostType	273
wp.getPostTypes	273

11. Mobile Apps with WordPress. **275**
App Wrapper	275
iOS Applications	275
Enrolling as an Apple Developer	276
Building Your App with Xcode	277
App Distribution	280
iOS Resources	280
Android Applications	281
AndroidManifest.xml	282
activity_main.xml	283
Creating an APK file	284
Getting Your App on Google Play	285
Android Resources	285
Extend Your App	285
AppPresser	286
Mobile App Use Cases	286

12. PHP Libraries, External APIs, and Web Services. **289**
Imagick	290
MaxMind GeoIP	290
Google Maps JavaScript API v3	292
Directions	293
Distance Matrix	293
Elevation	293
Geocoding	293
Street View Service	293
Practical App	293
Google Translate	296
Google+	297

People	297
Activities	297
Comments	297
Moments	297
Amazon Product Advertising API	298
Request Parameters	298
Operations	299
Response Groups	300
Twitter REST API v1.1	301
Set Up Your App on Twitter.com	302
Leverage a PHP Library	303
Facebook	304
Pictures	304
Search	305
Permissions	305
Building an Application	306
Leverage What's Out There	306
Twilio	306
Microsoft Sharepoint	307
We Missed a Few	309
13. Building WordPress Multisite Networks.	**311**
Why Multisite?	311
Setting Up a Multisite Network	312
Managing a Multisite Network	313
Dashboard	314
Sites	314
Users	314
Themes	315
Plugins	315
Settings	316
Updates	317
Multisite Database Structure	317
Network-Wide Tables	317
Individual Site Tables	319
Shared Site Tables	320
Multisite Plugins	320
WordPress MU Domain Mapping	320
Blog Copier	321
More Privacy Options	321
Multisite Global Search	321
Multisite Robots.txt Manager	321

Basic Multisite Functionality   321
$blog_id   321
is_multisite()   322
get_current_blog_id()   322
switch_to_blog($new_blog)   322
restore_current_blog()   323
get_blog_details($fields = null, $get_all = true)   323
update_blog_details($blog_id, $details = array())   325
get_blog_status($id, $pref)   325
update_blog_status($blog_id, $pref, $value)   325
get_blog_option($id, $option, $default = false)   326
update_blog_option($id, $option, $value)   326
delete_blog_option($id, $option)   327
get_blog_post($blog_id, $post_id)   327
add_user_to_blog($blog_id, $user_id, $role)   327
create_empty_blog($domain, $path, $weblog_title, $site_id = 1)   328
Functions We Didn't Mention   328

14. Localizing WordPress Apps.   329
Do You Even Need to Localize Your App?   329
How Localization Is Done in WordPress   330
Defining Your Locale in WordPress   330
Prepping Your Strings with Translation Functions   331
__($text, $domain = "default")   331
_e($text, $domain = "default")   331
_x($text, $context, $domain = "default")   332
_ex($title, $context, $domain = "default")   333
Escaping and Translating at the Same Time   333
Creating and Loading Translation Files   333
Our File Structure for Localization   334
Generating a .pot File   335
Creating a .po File   336
Creating a .mo File   337
Loading the Textdomain   337
Localizing Nonstring Assets   339

15. Ecommerce.   341
Choosing a Plugin   341
Shopping Cart Plugins   341
Membership Plugins   343
Digital Downloads   344
Payment Gateways   344

Merchant Accounts   345
SSL Certificates and HTTPS   346
   Installing an SSL Certificate on Your Server   346
   SSL with Paid Memberships Pro   348
   SSL with Jigoshop   349
   WordPress Login and WordPress Admin over SSL   350
   WordPress Frontend over SSL   350
   SSL on Select Pages   351
   Avoiding SSL Errors with the "Nuclear Option"   355
Setting Up Software as a Service (SaaS) with Paid Memberships Pro   357
The Software as a Service Model   357
   Step 0: Figure Out How You Want to Charge for Your App 357
   Step 1: Installing and Activating Paid Memberships Pro 358
   Step 2: Setting Up the Level   359
   Step 3: Setting Up Pages   361
   Step 4: Payment Settings   362
   Step 5: Email Settings   363
   Step 6: Advanced Settings   364
   Step 7: Locking Down Pages   365
   Step 8: Customizing Paid Memberships Pro   367

16. WordPress Optimization and Scaling. 377
Terms   377
Origin Versus Edge   378
Testing   379
   What to Test   379
   Chrome Debug Bar   381
   Apache Bench   384
   Siege   390
   Blitz.io   391
W3 Total Cache   391
   Page Cache Settings   393
   Minify   395
   Database Caching   395
   Object Cache   395
   CDNs   396
   GZIP Compression   396
Hosting   396
   WordPress-Specific Hosts   397
   Rolling Your Own Server   397
Selective Caching   410
   The Transient API   411

Multisite Transients   414
Using JavaScript to Increase Performance   414
Custom Tables   416
Bypassing WordPress   418

Index. 419

Preface

As we write this, WordPress powers 20% of the Internet, and that number is growing. Many developers want to do more with their WordPress sites but feel that they need to jump ship to a more traditional application framework like Ruby on Rails, Yii, Zend, or Codeigniter to build "real" web apps. This sentiment is wrong, and we're here to fix it.

Despite starting out as a blogging platform and currently existing primarily as a content management system, WordPress has grown into a flexible and capable platform for building web apps. This book will show you how to use WordPress as an application framework to build *any* web app, large or small.

Who This Book Is For

This book will be most useful for WordPress developers looking to work on heavier applications and PHP developers with some WordPress experience looking for a PHP-based application framework.

Commercial plugin and theme developers, or anyone working on large distributed WordPress projects, will also find the concepts and techniques of this book useful.

If you are a PHP or language-agnostic developer using another framework and jealous of the large library of WordPress plugins and themes, you may be surprised to learn how well WordPress can work as a general application framework. Reading and applying the lessons in this book could change your work life for the better.

We assume that readers have an intermediate understanding of general PHP programming. You should also have a basic understanding of HTML and CSS, and familiarity with MySQL and SQL queries. Basic understanding of JavaScript and jQuery programming will help with the JavaScript and AJAX chapter and related examples.

Who This Book Is Not For

This book is not for people who want to learn how to use WordPress as an end user. There will be brief introductions to standard WordPress functionality, but we assume that readers have already experienced WordPress from a user's perspective.

This book is not meant for nonprogrammers. While it is possible to build very functional web applications by simply combining and configuring the many plugins available for WordPress, this book is written for developers building their own plugins and themes to power new web apps.

This book will not teach you how to program but will teach you how to program "the WordPress way."

What You'll Learn

Our hope with this book is that you will learn the programming and organizational techniques and best practices for developing complex applications using WordPress.

Chapter 1 defines what we mean by "web app" and also covers why or why not to use WordPress for building web apps and how to compare WordPress to other application frameworks. We also introduce SchoolPress, the WordPress app that we use as an example throughout the book.

Chapter 2 covers the basics of WordPress. We go over the various directories of the core WordPress install and what goes where. We also explain each database table created by WordPress, what data each holds, and which WordPress functions map to those tables. Even experienced WordPress developers can learn something from this chapter and are encouraged to read it.

Chapter 3 is all about plugins. What are they? How do you make your own plugins? How should you structure your app's main plugin? When should you leverage third-party plugins or roll your own?

Chapter 4 is all about themes. How do themes works? How do themes map to views in a typical model-view-controller (MVC) framework? What code should go into your theme, and what code should go into plugins? We also cover using theme frameworks and UI frameworks and the basics of responsive design.

Chapter 5 covers custom post types and taxonomies. We go over the default post types built into WordPress, why you might need to build your own, and then how to go about doing that. We also cover post meta and taxonomies, what each is appropriate for, and how to build custom taxonomies and map them to your post types. Finally, we show how to build wrapper classes for your post types to organize your code utilizing object-oriented programming (OOP).

Chapter 6 covers users, roles, and capabilities. We show how to add, update, and delete users programmatically, and how to work with user meta, roles, and capabilities. We also show how to extend the WP_User class for your user archetypes like "customers" and "teachers" to better organize your code using OOP techniques.

Chapter 7 covers a few of the more useful WordPress APIs and helper functions that didn't fit into the rest of the book but are still important for developers building web apps with WordPress.

Chapter 8 is all about securing your WordPress apps, plugins, and themes.

Chapter 9 covers using JavaScript and AJAX in your WordPress application. We go over the correct way to enqueue JavaScript into WordPress and how to build asynchronous behaviors in your app.

Chapter 10 covers the XML-RPC API for WordPress and how to use it to integrate WordPress with outside apps.

Chapter 11 covers how to use WordPress to power native apps on mobile devices by creating app wrappers for iOS and Android.

Chapter 12 covers some third-party PHP libraries, services, and APIs that are often used in web apps and how to integrate them with WordPress.

Chapter 13 covers WordPress multisite networks, including how to set them up and things to keep in mind when developing for multisite.

Chapter 14 covers localizing your WordPress plugins and themes, including how to prep your code for translation and how to create and use translation files.

Chapter 15 covers ecommerce. We go over the various types of ecommerce plugins available and how to choose between them. We then go into detail on how to use Word-Press to handle payments and account management for software as a service (SaaS) web apps.

Chapter 16 covers how to optimize and scale WordPress for high-volume web apps. We go over how to test the performance of your WordPress app and the most popular techniques for speeding up and scaling sites running WordPress.

About the Code

All examples in this book can be found at *https://github.com/bwawwp*. Please note that these code examples were written to most clearly convey the concepts we cover in the book. To improve readability, we often ignored best practices for security and localization (which we cover in Chapter 8 and Chapter 14 of this book) or ignored certain edge cases. You will want to keep this in mind before using any examples in production code.

The sample app SchoolPress can be found at *http://schoolpress.me*, with any open sourced code for that site available at *https://github.com/bwawwp/schoolpress*.

Conventions Used in This Book

The following typographical conventions are used in this book:

Italic
> Indicates new terms, URLs, email addresses, filenames, and file extensions.

`Constant width`
> Used for program listings, as well as within paragraphs to refer to program elements such as variable or function names, databases, datatypes, environment variables, statements, and keywords.

`Constant width bold`
> Shows commands or other text that should be typed literally by the user.

`Constant width italic`
> Shows text that should be replaced with user-supplied values or by values determined by context.

 This element signifies a tip, suggestion, or general note.

 This element indicates a warning or caution.

Using Code Examples

This book is here to help you get your job done. In general, if example code is offered with this book, you may use it in your programs and documentation. You do not need to contact us for permission unless you're reproducing a significant portion of the code. For example, writing a program that uses several chunks of code from this book does not require permission. Selling or distributing a CD-ROM of examples from O'Reilly books does require permission. Answering a question by citing this book and quoting example code does not require permission. Incorporating a significant amount of example code from this book into your product's documentation does require permission.

We appreciate, but do not require, attribution. An attribution usually includes the title, author, publisher, and ISBN. For example: "*Building Web Apps with WordPress* by Brian Messenlehner and Jason Coleman (O'Reilly). Copyright 2014 Brian Messenlehner and Jason Coleman, 978-1-449-36407-6."

If you feel your use of code examples falls outside fair use or the permission given above, feel free to contact us at *permissions@oreilly.com*.

Safari® Books Online

 Safari Books Online is an on-demand digital library that delivers expert content in both book and video form from the world's leading authors in technology and business.

Technology professionals, software developers, web designers, and business and creative professionals use Safari Books Online as their primary resource for research, problem solving, learning, and certification training.

Safari Books Online offers a range of product mixes and pricing programs for organizations, government agencies, and individuals. Subscribers have access to thousands of books, training videos, and prepublication manuscripts in one fully searchable database from publishers like O'Reilly Media, Prentice Hall Professional, Addison-Wesley Professional, Microsoft Press, Sams, Que, Peachpit Press, Focal Press, Cisco Press, John Wiley & Sons, Syngress, Morgan Kaufmann, IBM Redbooks, Packt, Adobe Press, FT Press, Apress, Manning, New Riders, McGraw-Hill, Jones & Bartlett, Course Technology, and dozens more. For more information about Safari Books Online, please visit us online.

How to Contact Us

Please address comments and questions concerning this book to the publisher:

O'Reilly Media, Inc.
1005 Gravenstein Highway North
Sebastopol, CA 95472
800-998-9938 (in the United States or Canada)
707-829-0515 (international or local)
707-829-0104 (fax)

We have a web page for this book, where we list errata and any additional information. You can access this page at *http://oreil.ly/building-apps-wp*.

To comment or ask technical questions about this book, send email to *contact@bwawwp.com*.

For more information about our book and online examples see our website at *http://bwawwp.com.*

Find us on Facebook: *http://facebook.com/bwawwp*

Follow us on Twitter: *http://twitter.com/bwawwp*

Follow us on Instagram: *http://instagram.com/bwawwp*

Acknowledgments

Thanks to Jason Coleman and Matt Mullenweg; I could not have written this book without them. I would like to thank Meghan Blanchette and Allyson MacDonald for staying on top of things at O'Reilly Media, and thanks to our technical reviewers. I am thankful of my wife and best friend, Robin Messenlehner, and my children Dalya, Brian Jr., and Nina Messenlehner, for supporting me and my efforts to write this book. I would also like to acknowledge my business partners and friends Brad Williams, Lisa Sabin-Wilson, and the entire WebDevStudios.com team for building the best WordPress development and design shop on earth! And last but not least, I love you, Mom!

— Brian Messenlehner

Thanks to my coauthor Brian for asking me to write this book with him. Thanks to our editors Meghan and Allyson for keeping us on track and helping us to stay true to our original vision. Thanks to our great technical editors Peter MacIntyre and Pippin Williamson for reviewing our code and writing and providing valuable feedback. Thanks to Frederick Townes for his feedback and contributions to our chapter on optimization and scaling. Thanks to everyone in the WordPress community who answered all of my random tweets and may or may not have known they were helping me to write this book. Thanks to my wife, Kim, for supporting me as always during yet another adventure in our life. Thanks to my daughter, Marin, for missing me when I was away to write, and my son, Isaac, for constantly asking me if I had "finished the book yet." Last but not least, thanks to my family who have always supported my writing: Mom, Dad, Jeremy, and Nana Men are all excited to be the first nonprogrammers to read *Building Web Apps with WordPress.*

— Jason Coleman

Foreword

The web is evolving and WordPress is no different. What started out as a blogging platform has grown into a powerful content management system that powers more websites on the internet today than any other platform. WordPress is endlessly flexible, allowing you to build any type of application you can dream of. Whether it's a native mobile app for locating a local business or an e-commerce desktop app with membership capabilities, WordPress has the ability not only to power these apps, but to drastically reduce the development time to do so.

Brian and Jason are leading the charge in changing how we think about app development. Their knowledge and experience will help guide you through the process of building powerful web applications using the internet's most popular development framework, WordPress.

The future of the internet is web apps and WordPress is making it easier than ever to create that future. Code on!

— Brad Williams, Co-Founder of WebDevStudios

## CHAPTER 1

Building Web Apps with WordPress

Let's start by defining what a web app is and how it differs from a website or a web service.

In reality, this book will help you build anything with WordPress: websites, themes, plugins, web services, and web apps. We chose to focus on web apps because they can be seen as super websites that make use of all of the techniques we'll cover.

There are many people who believe that WordPress isn't powerful enough or meant for building web apps, and we'll get into that more later. We've been building web apps with WordPress for many years and know that it absolutely is possible to build scalable applications using WordPress.

In this chapter, we'll cover why WordPress is a great framework for building web apps. We'll also cover some situations where using WordPress *wouldn't* be the best way to build your web app.

What Is a Website?

You know what a website is. A website is a set of one or more web pages, containing information, accessed via a web browser.

What Is an App?

We like the Wikipedia definition: "Application software, also known as an application or an app, is computer software designed to help the user to perform specific tasks."

What Is a Web App?

A web app is just *an app run through a web browser.*

Please note that with some web apps, the browser technology is hidden, for example, when integrating your web app into a native Android or iOS app, running a website as an application in Google Chrome, or running an app using Adobe AIR. However, on the inside of these applications is still a system parsing HTML, CSS, and JavaScript.

You can also think of a web app as *a website, plus more application-like stuff.*

There is no exact line where a website becomes a web app. It's one of those things where you know it when you see it.

What we *can* do is explain some of the features of a web app, give you some examples, and then try to come up with a shorthand definition so you know generally what we are talking about as we use the term throughout the book.

 You will see references to SchoolPress while reading this book. SchoolPress is a web application we are building to help schools and educators manage their students and curricula. All of the code examples are geared toward functionality that may exist in SchoolPress. We will talk more about the overall concept of SchoolPress later in this chapter.

Features of a Web App

The following are some features generally associated with web apps and applications in general. The more of these features present in a website, the more appropriate it is to upgrade its label to a web app.[1]

Interactive elements

A typical website experience involves navigating through page loads, scrolling, and clicking hyperlinks. Web apps can have links and scrolling as well, but will tend to use other methods of navigating through the app.

Websites with forms offer transactional experiences. An example would be a contact form on a website or an application form on the careers page of a company website. Forms allow users to interact with a site using something more than a click.

Web apps will have even more interactive UI elements. Examples include toolbars, drag and drop elements, rich text editors, and sliders.

---

1. Many of the ideas in this section are influenced by these blog posts: "What is a Web Application?" by Dominique Hazaël-Massieux (*http://bit.ly/wiawa*) and "What is a Web Application?" by Bob Baxley. (*http://bit.ly/wiawa2*)

Tasks rather than content

Remember, web apps are "designed to help the user to perform specific tasks." Google Maps users get driving directions. Gmail users write emails. Trello users manage lists. SchoolPress users comment on class discussions.

Some apps are still content focused. A typical session with a Facebook or Twitter app involves about 90% reading. However, the apps themselves present a way of browsing content different from the typical web browsing experience.

Logins

Logins and accounts allow a web app to save information about its users. This information is used to facilitate the main tasks of the app and enable a persistent experience. When logged in, SchoolPress users can see which discussions are unread. They also have a username that identifies their activity within the app.

Web apps can also have tiers of users. SchoolPress will have admins controlling the inner workings of the app, teachers setting up classes, and students participating in class discussions.

Device capabilities

Web apps running on your phone can access your camera, your address book, internal storage, and GPS location information. Web apps running on the desktop may access a webcam or a local hard drive. The same web app may respond differently depending on the device accessing it. Web apps will adjust to different screen sizes, resolutions, and capabilities.

Work offline

Whenever possible, it's a good idea to make your web apps work offline. Sure, the interactivity of the Internet is what defines that "web" part of web app, but a site that doesn't stop working when someone drives through a tunnel will feel more like an app.

Emails can be drafted offline in Gmail. Evernote will allow you to create and edit notes offline and sync them to the Internet when connectivity comes back.

Mashups

Web apps can tie one or more web apps together. A web app can utilize various web services and APIs to push and pull data. You could have a web app that pulls location-based information like longitude and latitude from Twitter and Foursquare and posts it to a Google Map.

Why Use WordPress?

No single programming language or software tool will be right for every job. We'll cover why you may *not* want to use WordPress in a bit, but for now, let's go over some situations where using WordPress to build your web app *would* be a good choice.

You Are Already Using WordPress

If you are already using WordPress for your main site, you might just be a quick plugin away from adding the functionality you need. WordPress has great plugins for ecommerce (Jigoshop), forums (bbPress), membership sites (Paid Memberships Pro), social networking functionality (BuddyPress), and gamification (BadgeOS).

Building your app into your existing WordPress site will save you time and make things easier on your users. So if your application is fairly straightforward, you can create a custom plugin on your WordPress site to program the functionality of your web app.

If you are happy with WordPress for your existing site, don't be confused if people say that you need to upgrade to something else to add certain functionality to your site. It's probably not true. You don't have to throw out all of the work you've done on WordPress already, and all of the following are great reasons to stick with WordPress.

Content Management Is Easy with WordPress

WordPress was developed first as a blogging platform, but through the years and with the introduction of custom post types (CPTs) in version 3.0, it has evolved into a fully functional content management system (CMS). Any page or post can be edited by administrators via the dashboard, which can be accessed through your web browser. You will learn about working with CPTs in Chapter 5.

WordPress makes adding and editing content easy via a WYSIWYG editor, so you don't have to use web designers every time you want to make a simple change to your site. You can also create custom menus and navigation elements for your site without touching any code.

If your web app focuses around bits of content (e.g., our SchoolPress app is focused on assignments and discussions), the Custom Post Types API for WordPress (covered in Chapter 5) makes it easy to quickly set up and manage this custom content.

Even apps that are more task oriented will typically have a few pages for information, documentation, and sales. Using WordPress for your app will give you one place to manage your app and all of your content.

User Management Is Easy and Secure with WordPress

WordPress has everything you need for adding both admin users and end users to your site.

In addition to controlling access to content, the Roles and Capabilities system in WordPress is extensible and allows you to control what *actions* are available for certain groups of users. For example, by default, users with the contributor role can *add* new posts, but can't *publish* them. Similarly, you can create new roles and capabilities to manage who has access to your custom functionality.

Plugins like Paid Memberships Pro can be used to extend the built-in user management to allow you to designate members of different levels and control what content users have access to. For example, you can create a level to give paying members access to premium content on your WordPress site.

Plugins

There are over 27,000 free plugins in the WordPress repository (*http://wordpress.org/plugins/*). There are many more plugins, both free and premium, on various sites around the Internet. When you have an idea for an extension to your website, there is a good chance that there's a plugin for that, which will save you time and money.

There are a handful of indispensable plugins that we end up using on almost every site and web application we build.

For most websites you create, you'll want to cache output for faster browsing, use tools like Google Analytics for visitor tracking, create sitemaps, and tweak page settings for search engine optimization (SEO), along with a number of other common tasks.

There are many well-supported plugins for all of these functions. We suggest our favorites throughout this book; you can find a list of them on this book's website (*http://bwawwp.com/plugins/*).

Flexibility Is Important

WordPress is a full-blown framework capable of many things. Additionally, WordPress is built on PHP, JavaScript, and MySQL technology, so anything you can build in PHP/MySQL (which is pretty much anything) can be bolted into your WordPress application easily enough.

WordPress and PHP/MySQL in general aren't perfect for every task, but they are well suited for a wide range of tasks. Having one platform that will grow with your business can allow you to execute and pivot faster.

For example, here is a typical progression for the website of a lean startup running on WordPress:

1. Announce your startup with a one-page website.
2. Add a form to gather email addresses.
3. Add a blog.
4. Focus on SEO and optimize all content.
5. Push blog posts to Twitter and Facebook.

6. Add forums.

7. Use the Paid Memberships Pro plugin to allow members to pay for access.

8. Add custom forms, tools, and application behaviors for paying members.

9. Update the UI using AJAX.

10. Tweak the site and server to scale.

11. Localize the site/app for different countries and languages.

12. Launch iOS and Android wrappers for the app.

The neat thing about moving through the path is that at every step along the way, you have the same database of users and are using the same development platform.

Frequent Security Updates

The fact that WordPress is used on millions of sites makes it a target for hackers trying to break through its security. Some of those hackers have been successful in the past; however, the developers behind WordPress are quick to address vulnerabilities and release updates to fix them. It's like having millions of people constantly testing and fixing your software, because that's exactly what is happening.

The underlying architecture of WordPress makes applying these updates a quick and painless process that even novice web users can perform. If you are smart about how you set up WordPress and upgrade to the latest versions when they become available, WordPress is a far more secure platform for your site than anything else available. Security is discussed in more detail in Chapter 8.

Cost

WordPress is free. PHP is free. MySQL is free. Most plugins are free. Hosting costs money. But depending on how big your web application is and how much traffic you get, it can be relatively inexpensive. If you require custom functionality not found in any existing plugins, you may need to pay a developer to build it. Or if you are a developer yourself, it will cost you some time.

Let's compare building a simple web application on top of WordPress to building a simple .NET web application from scratch:

.NET App

1. IIS — Pay for License

2. SQL Server — Pay for License

3. .NET developers typically cost more than PHP developers.

4. Pay to construct a solid database schema.

5. Pay to create helper functions for moving data in and out of your database.

6. Pay to create a login process for your users.

7. Pay to develop any custom functionality you require.

8. Security! You have no idea how your app will hold up against the Internet, but you're going to pay to try to make your app as secure as possible.

WordPress App

1. Apache — $0

2. MySQL — $0

3. PHP developers typically cost less than .NET developers and are way cooler! This is a fact.

4. WordPress has a proven database schema and is ready to go.

5. WordPress has a ton of helper functions for interacting with the database, and in most cases you can utilize CPTs and taxonomies to store and categorize your data without much code.

6. WordPress already has a solid login process.

7. You can gain most functionality you require from free third-party plugins. If any custom development is required, it would only be for niche functionality that doesn't already exist.

8. Security! WordPress is running on about 20% of all websites on the Internet. You can bet that it is one of the securest platforms (don't make your admin password "password").

In short, you can build any size application on top of WordPress and nine times out of 10, it will cost less money and take less time to develop than on any other platform.

Responses to Some Common Criticisms of WordPress

There are some highly vocal critics of WordPress who will say that WordPress isn't a good framework for building web apps, or that WordPress isn't a framework at all. With all due respect to those with these opinions, we'd like to go over why we disagree. Here are some common criticisms:

WordPress is just for blogs. Many people believe that since WordPress was first built to run a blog, it is only good at running blogs.

Statements like this were true a few years ago, but WordPress has since implemented strong CMS functionality, making it useful for other content-focused sites. WordPress is now the most popular CMS in use, with over 50% market share.[2]

Figure 1-1 shows a slide from Matt Mullenweg's "State of WordPress" presentation from WordCamp San Francisco 2013. The upside-down pyramid on the left represents a circa 2006 WordPress, with most of the code devoted to the blog application and a little bit of CMS and platform code holding it up. The pyramid on the right represents the current state of the WordPress platform, where most of the code is in the platform itself, with a CMS layer on top of that, and the blog application running on top of the CMS layer. WordPress is a much more stable platform than it was just a few years ago.

Figure 1-1. Diagrams from Matt Mullenweg's "State of WordPress" presentation in 2013. WordPress wasn't always so stable.

The Custom Post Types API can be used to tweak your WordPress install to support other content types besides blog posts or pages. This is covered in detail in Chapter 5.

WordPress is just for content sites. Similar to the "just for blogs" folks, some will say that WordPress is just for content sites.

WordPress is the clear choice for any content-related website. However, as we'll go over in detail in this very book, WordPress is a great framework for building more interactive web applications as well.

The main feature allowing WordPress to be used as a framework is the plugins API, which allows you to hook into how WordPress works by default and change things. Not only can you use the thousands of plugins available in the WordPress repository and elsewhere on the Internet, you can use the plugins API to write your own custom plugins to make WordPress do anything possible in PHP/MySQL.

WordPress doesn't scale. Some will point to a default WordPress install running on low-end hosting, note how the site slows down or crashes under heavy load, and conclude that WordPress doesn't scale.

---

2. W3Tech (*http://bit.ly/w3techs*) has regular surveys on the use of different content management systems.

This statement is provably false. WordPress.com runs on the same basic software as any WordPress site and at the time of this writing is somewhere between the 13th most- and 22nd-most-visited website in the world.[3]

The issues with scaling WordPress are the same issues you have scaling any application: caching pages and data and handling database calls more rapidly. We can learn by how large sites like WordPress.com, TechCrunch, and the *New York Times* blogs have scaled on WordPress. Similarly, most of the lessons learned scaling PHP/MySQL applications in general apply to WordPress as well. Scaling WordPress apps is covered in detail in Chapter 16.

WordPress is insecure. Like any open source product, there will be a trade-off with regard to security when using WordPress.

On the one hand, because WordPress is so popular, it will be the target of hackers looking for security exploits. And because the code is open source, these exploits will be easier to discover.

On the other hand, because WordPress is open source, you will hear about it when these exploits become public, and someone else will probably fix the exploit for you.

We feel more secure knowing that there are lots of people out there trying to exploit WordPress and just as many people working to make WordPress secure against those exploits. We don't believe in "security through obscurity" except as an additional measure. We'd rather have the security holes in our software come out in the open rather than go undetected until the worst possible moment.

Chapter 8 will cover security issues in more detail, including a list of best practices to harden your WordPress install and how to code in a secure manner.

WordPress plugins are crap. The plugin API in WordPress and the thousands of plugins that have been developed using it are the secret sauce and in our opinion the number one reason that WordPress has become so popular and is so successful as a website platform.

Some people will say, "Sure, there are thousands of plugins, but they are all crap."

OK, some of the plugins out there are crap. But there are a lot of plugins that are most definitely not crap.

Paid Memberships Pro, developed by our coauthor Jason Coleman, is not crap. Using Paid Memberships Pro to handle your member billing and management will allow you to focus your development efforts on your app's core competency instead of how to integrate your site with a payment gateway.

---

3. Quantcast top sites (*http://www.quantcast.com/top-sites*) and Alexa top sites (*http://www.alexa.com/topsites*)

A lot of plugins do something very simple (e.g., hiding the admin bar from nonadmins), work exactly as advertised, and don't really have room for being crap.

Even the crappy plugins can be fixed, rewritten, or borrowed from to work better. You may find it easier sometimes to rewrite a bad plugin instead of fixing it. However, you're still further ahead than you would be if you had to write everything yourself from scratch.

No one is forcing you to use WordPress plugins without vetting them yourself. If you are building a serious web app, you're going to check out the plugin code yourself, fix it up to meet your standards, and move on with development.

When Not to Use WordPress

WordPress isn't the solution for every application. Here are a few cases where you *wouldn't* want to use WordPress to build your application.

You Plan to License or Sell Your Site's Technology

WordPress uses the GNU General Public License, version 2 (GPLv2), which has restrictions on how you distribute any software that you build with it. Namely, you cannot restrict what people do with your software once you sell or distribute it to them.

This is a complicated topic, but the basic idea is if you are only selling or giving away *access* to your application, you won't have to worry about the GPLv2. However, if you are selling or distributing the underlying source code of your application, the GPLv2 will apply to the code you distribute.

For example, if we host SchoolPress on our own servers and sell accounts to access the app, that doesn't count as distribution, and the GPLv2 doesn't impact our business at all.

However, if we wanted to allow schools to install the software to run on their own servers, we would have to share the source code with them. This would count as an act of distribution. Our customers would be able to legally give our source code away for free even if we had initially charged them for the software. We'd have to use the GPLv2 license, which wouldn't allow us to restrict what they do with the code after they downloaded it.

There Is Another Platform That Will Get You "There" Faster

If you have a team of experienced Ruby developers, you should use Ruby to build your web app. If there is a platform, framework, or bundle that includes 80% of the features you need for your web app and WordPress doesn't have anything similar, you should probably use that other platform.

Flexibility Is NOT Important to You

One of the greatest features of a WordPress site is the ability to change parts of your website to better fit your needs quickly. For example, if Facebook "likes" stop driving traffic, you can uninstall your Facebook connect plugin and install a Google+ one.

Generally, updating your theme or swapping plugins on a WordPress site will be faster than developing features from scratch on another platform.

However, in cases where optimization and performance are more important than being able to quickly update the application, programming a native app or programming in straight PHP, is going to be the better choice.

For example, if your app is going to do one simple thing (say just display the current time), you will want to build your app at a lower level. Similarly, if you have Facebook's resources, you can afford to build everything by hand and use custom PHP-to-C compilers to shave a few milliseconds off your website load times.

Your App Needs to Be Highly Real Time

One of the potential downsides of WordPress, which we will get into later, is its reliance on the typical web server architecture. In the typical WordPress setup, a user visits a URL, which hits a web server (like Apache) over HTTP, kicks off a PHP script to generate the page, and then returns the full page to the user.

There are ways to improve the performance of this architecture using caching techniques and/or optimized server setups. You can make WordPress asynchronous by using using AJAX calls or accessing the database with alternative clients. However, if your application needs to be real-time and fully asynchronous (e.g., a chatroom-like app or a multiplayer game), you have our blessing to think twice about using WordPress.

Many WordPress developers, including Matt Mullenweg, the founder and spiritual leader of WordPress, understand this limitation. It is very likely that the WordPress core will be updated over time to work better for real-time asynchronous apps (the Heartbeat API released in version 3.6 of WordPress is a good step in this direction), but currently you're going to face an uphill battle trying to get WordPress to work asynchronously with the same performance as a native app or something built using Node.js or other technologies specifically suited to real-time applications.

WordPress as an Application Framework

Content management systems like WordPress, Drupal, and Joomla often get left out of the framework discussion, but in reality, WordPress (in particular) is really great for what frameworks are supposed to be about: quickly building applications.

Within minutes, you can set up WordPress and have a fully functional app with user signups, session management, content management, and a dashboard to monitor site activity.

The various APIs, common objects, and helper functions covered throughout this book allow you to code complex applications faster without having to worry about lower-level systems integration.

Figure 1-2 shows that right triangle from Mullengweg's 2013 "State of WordPress" presentation depicting a stable WordPress platform with a CMS layer built on top and a blogging application built on top of the CMS layer.

The reality is that the majority of the current WordPress codebase supports the underlying application platform. You can think of each WordPress release as a application framework with a sample blogging app bundled in.

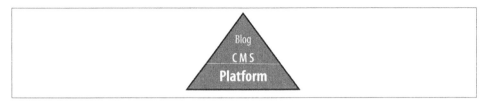

Figure 1-2. The WordPress platform.

WordPress Versus MVC Frameworks

MVC stands for model-view-controller and is a common design pattern used in many software development frameworks. The main benefits of using an MVC architecture are code reusability and separation of concerns. WordPress doesn't use an MVC architecture, but does in its own way encourage code reuse and separation of concerns.

I'll explain the MVC architecture very briefly and how it maps to a WordPress development process. This section should help readers who are familiar with MVC-based frameworks understand how to approach WordPress development in a similar way.

Figure 1-3 describes a typical MVC-based application. The end user uses a *controller*, which manipulates the application state and data via a *model*, which then updates a *view* that is shown to the user. For example, in a blog application, a user might be looking at the recent posts page (a view). The user would click a post title, which would take the user to a new URL (a controller) that would load the post data (in a model) and display the single post (a different view).

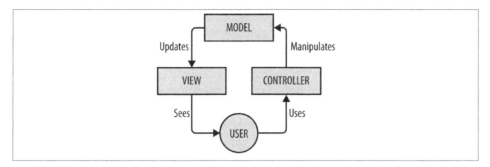

Figure 1-3. How MVC works

The MVC architecture supports code reusability by allowing the models, views, and controllers to interact. For example, both the recent posts view and the single posts view might use the same post model when displaying post data. The same models might be used in the frontend to display posts and in the backend to edit them.

The MVC architecture supports separation of concerns by allowing designers to focus their attention on the views, while programmers focus their attention on the models.

You could try to use an MVC architecture within WordPress. There are a number of projects to help you do just that; however, we think trying to strap MVC onto WordPress could lead to issues unless the WordPress core were to officially support MVC. Instead, we suggest following the "WordPress Way," as outlined in this book.

Still, if you are interested…

MVC plugins for WordPress

- WP MVC (*http://bit.ly/wp-mvc*)
- Churro (*http://bit.ly/churro-plugin*)
- Tina MVC (*http://bit.ly/tina-mvc*)

There are a couple of ways to map an MVC process to WordPress.

Models = plugins

In an MVC framework, the code that stores the underlying data structures and business logic are found in the models. This is where the programmers will spend the majority of their time.

In WordPress, plugins are the proper place to store new data structures, complex business logic, and custom post type definitions.

This comparison breaks down in a couple of ways. First, many plugins add view-like functionality and contain design elements. Take any plugin that adds a widget to be used in your pages. Second, forms and other design components used in the WordPress dashboard are generally handled in plugins as well.

One way to make the separation of concerns more clear when adding view-like components to your WordPress plugins is to create a "templates" or "pages" folder and put your frontend code into it. Common practice is to allow templates to override the template used by the plugin. For example, when using WordPress with the Paid Memberships Pro plugin, you can place a folder called "paid-memberships-pro/pages" into your active theme to override the default page templates.[4]

Views = themes

In an MVC framework, the code to display data to the user is written in the views. This is where designers will spend the majority of their time.

In WordPress, themes are the proper place to store templating code and logic.

Again, the comparison here doesn't map one to one, but "views = themes" is a good starting point.

Controllers = template loader

In an MVC framework, the code to process user input (in the form of URLs or $_GET or $_POST data) and decide which models and views to use to handle a request are stored in the controllers. Controller code is generally handled by a programmer and often set up once and forgotten about. The meat of the programming in an MVC application happens in the models and views.

In WordPress, all page requests (unless they are accessing a cached *.html* file) are processed through the index.php file and processed by WordPress according to the Template Hierarchy. The template loader figures out which file in the template should be used to display the page to the end user. For example, use search.php to show search results, single.php to show a single post, etc.

The default behavior can be further customized via the WP_Rewrite API (covered in Chapter 7) and other hooks and filters.

Codex information on the Template Hierarchy (*http://bit.ly/temp-hier*) is available online; the Template Hierarchy is covered in more depth in Chapter 4.

For a better understanding of how MVC frameworks work, the PHP framework Yii (*http://bit.ly/yii-guide*) has a great resource explaining how to best use their MVC architecture.

---

4. This technique for overriding plugin templates is covered in Chapter 4.

For a better understanding of how to develop web applications using WordPress as a framework, continue reading this book.

Anatomy of a WordPress App

In this section, we'll describe the app we built as a companion for this book: School-Press. We'll cover the intended functionality of SchoolPress, how it will work and who will use it, and—most importantly for this book—how each piece of the app will be built in WordPress.

Don't be alarmed if you don't understand some of the following terminology. In later chapters, we will go over everything introduced here in more detail. Whenever possible, we'll point to the chapter of this book that corresponds to the feature being discussed.

What Is SchoolPress?

SchoolPress is a web app that makes it easy for teachers to interact with their students outside of the classroom. Teachers can create *classes* and invite their students to them. Each class has a forum for ad hoc discussion and also a more structured system for teachers to post *assignments* and have students turn in their work.

The working app can be found on the SchoolPress website (*http://schoolpress.me*). The SchoolPress source code can be found on GitHub (*https://github.com/bwawwp/school press*).

SchoolPress Runs on a WordPress Multisite Network

SchoolPress runs a multisite version of WordPress. The main site at schoolpress.me hosts free accounts where teachers can sign up and start managing their classes. It also has all of the marketing information for separate school sites on the network, including the page to sign up and checkout for a paid membership level.

Schools can pay an annual fee to create a unique subdomain for their school, like *yourschool.schoolpress.me*, that will house classes for their teachers and offers finer control and reporting for all classes across the entire school. Details on using a multisite network with WordPress can be found in Chapter 13.

The SchoolPress Business Model

SchoolPress uses the Paid Memberships Pro, PMPro Register Helper, and PMPro Network plugins to customize the registration process and accept credit card payments for schools signing up.

Schools can purchase a unique subdomain for their school for an annual fee. No other SchoolPress users pay for access.

When school admins sign up, they can specify a school name and slug for their subdomain (`myschool.schoolpress.me`). A new network site is set up for them and they are given access to a streamlined version of the WordPress dashboard for their site.

The school admin then invites teachers into the system. Teachers can also request an invitation to a school that must be approved by the school admin.

Teachers can invite students to the classes they create. Students can also request an invitation to a class that must be approved by the teacher.

Teachers can also sign up for free to host their classes at `schoolpress.me`. Pages hosted on this subdomain may run ads or other monetization schemes. Details on how to setup ecommerce with WordPress can be found in Chapter 15.

Membership Levels and User Roles

Teachers are given a Teacher membership level (through Paid Memberships Pro) and a custom role called "Teacher" that gives them access to create and edit their classes, moderate discussion in their class forums, and create and manage assignments for their classes.

Teachers do not have access to the WordPress dashboard. They create and manage their classes and assignments through frontend forms created for this purpose.

Students are given a "Student" membership level and the default "Subscriber" role in WordPress. Students only have access to view and participate in classes they are invited to by their teachers. Details on user roles and capabilities can be found in Chapter 6. Details on using membership levels to control access can be found in Chapter 15.

Classes Are BuddyPress Groups

When teachers create "classes," they are really creating BuddyPress groups and inviting their students to the group. Using BuddyPress, we get class forums, private messaging, and a nice way to organize our users.

The class discussion forums are powered by the bbPress plugin. A new forum is generated for each class, and BuddyPress manages access to the forums. Details on leveraging third-party plugins like BuddyPress and bbPress can be found in Chapter 3.

Assignments Are a Custom Post Type

Assignments are a custom post type (CPT), with a frontend submission form for teachers to post new assignments. Assignments are just like the default blog posts in WordPress, with a title, body content, and attached files. The teacher posting the assignment is the author of the post.

WordPress has built-in post types like posts and pages and built-in taxonomies like categories and tags. For SchoolPress, we are creating our own CPTs and taxonomies. Details on creating custom post types and taxonomies can be found in Chapter 5.

Submissions Are a (Sub)CPT for Assignments

Students can post comments on an assignment, and they can also choose to post their official submission for the assignment through another form on the frontend.

Submissions, like assignments, are also CPTs. Submissions are linked to assignments by setting the submission's `post_parent` field to the ID of the assignment it was submitted to. Students can post text content and also add one or more attachments to a submission.

Semesters Are a Taxonomy on the Class CPT

A custom taxonomy called "Semester" is set up for the group/class CPT. School admins can add new semesters to their sites. For example, a "fall 2013" semester could be created and teachers could assign this semester when creating their classes. Students can then easily view a list of all fall 2013 classes to browse through.

Departments Are a Taxonomy on the Class CPT

A custom taxonomy called "Department" is also set up for the group/class CPT. This is also available as a dropdown for teachers when creating their classes and allows for a browsable list of classes by department.

SchoolPress Has One Main Custom Plugin

Behind the scenes, the custom bits of the SchoolPress app are controlled from a single custom plugin called SchoolPress. This — the main plugin — includes the definitions for the various custom post types, taxonomies, and user roles. It also contains the code to tweak the third-party plugins SchoolPress uses like Paid Memberships Pro and BuddyPress.

The main plugin also contains classes for school admins, teachers, and students that extend the WP_User class and classes for classes, assignments, and submissions that wrap the WP_Post class. These (PHP) classes allow us to organize our code in an object-oriented way that makes it easier to control how our various customizations work together and will make it easier to extend our code in the future. These classes are fun to work with and allow for the code that you see in Example 1-1.

Example 1-1. Possible user log-in events

```
if($class->isTeacher($current_user))
{
    //this is the teacher, show them teacher stuff
    //...
}
elseif($class->isStudent($current_user))
{
    //this is a student in the class, show them student stuff
    //...
}
elseif(is_user_logged_in())
{
    //not logged in, send them to the login form with a redirect back here
    wp_redirect(wp_login_url(get_permalink($class->ID)));
    exit;
}
else
{
    //not a member of this class, redirect them to the invite page
    wp_redirect($class->invite_url);
    exit;
}
```

Creating custom plugins is covered in Chapter 3. Extending the WP_User class is covered in Chapter 6.

SchoolPress Uses a Few Other Custom Plugins

Occasionally a bit of code will be developed for a particular app that would also be useful on other projects. If the code can be contained enough that it can run outside of the context of the current app and main plugin, it can be built into a separate custom plugin.

An example of this would be the force-first-name-last-name plugin that was a requirement for this project. It didn't require any of the main plugin code to run and is useful for other WordPress sites outside of the context of the SchoolPress app.

SchoolPress Uses the StartBox Theme Framework

The main schoolpress.me site runs on a customized StartBox child theme. If a school signs up for a premium subdomain, it can choose from a variety of StartBox child themes; it also has the ability to change any of the theme's colors, fonts, and logos to better fit its branding.

All themes use a responsive design that ensures the site will look good on mobile and tablet displays as well as desktop displays.

The code in the StartBox theme (*http://wpstartbox.com*) is very strictly limited to display-related programming. The theme code obviously includes the HTML and CSS for the site's layout, but also contains some simple logic that integrates with the main SchoolPress plugin (like the preceding branching code). However, any piece of code that manipulates the custom post types or user roles or involves a lot of calculation is delegated to the SchoolPress plugin.

## CHAPTER 2

WordPress Basics

WordPress was first developed in 2003 and was created primarily as blogging software. By the release of version 3.5, the image of Wordpress had changed from blogging software to a versatile CMS (content management system) and the word "blog" was actually removed from the description of the software and in most places in the source code. Today, it has evolved to become the largest platform on the web and is used on about 20% of all the websites on the Internet.

There are a couple of reasons WordPress has gained so much popularity over the years. The first is that WordPress is open source software and has an entire community of people who are invested in improving it and continually contributing new code to extend its functionality. WordPress users, developers, and designers are always thinking of new creative ways to use WordPress and creating plugins for these new features, which are then made available to the community.

Another reason WordPress has been so successful is the fact that it is an extremely flexible CMS and can be used to power all different types of websites. Developers are constantly exploring innovative new ways to use the software, including using it to build web applications, which is the focus of this book.

 We are going to assume that you already know how to use Word-Press, and have already installed the latest version somewhere. If this is your first time using WordPress, you should check out the book *WordPress for Dummies*. Not saying you're a dummy or anything, but everyone has to start somewhere.

WordPress Directory Structure

Let's take a quick top-level look at the folders and files that are included within a typical WordPress install.

Root Directory

In the root directory, there are a few core WordPress files. Unless you are digging around in the core WordPress code looking for hooks to use or certain functionality, the only file you may need to ever alter is *wp-config.php*. You should never, ever, ever, ever[1] alter any other core WordPress files. Hacking core is a bad idea because you won't be able to upgrade WordPress when a new version becomes available without overriding your changes. The only directory you should need to interact with is *wp-content* because it contains your plugins, themes, and uploaded files.

Any time you find yourself wanting to hack a core WordPress file, think again. There is probably a hook you could use to accomplish the same goal. If there isn't a hook available to do what you need, add one and try to get it added to core. The core WordPress developers are very responsive about adding in new hooks and filters.

/wp-admin

This directory contains core directories and files for managing the WordPress admin interface. Another key file in this directory is *admin-ajax.php*, which all AJAX requests should be run through. AJAX is covered in Chapter 9.

/wp-includes

This directory contains core directories and files for various WordPress functionality.

/wp-content

This directory contains subdirectories for the plugins and themes you have installed on your site and any media files you upload to your site. If you create a plugin that needs to store dynamic files of its own, it is a best practice to place them somewhere in the *wp-content* folder so they are included in a content backup.

The following directories are subdirectories of the *wp-content* directory.

/wp-content/plugins

Any WordPress plugin you install on your WordPress site will be located in this directory. By default, WordPress comes with the Hello Dolly and Akismet plugins.

---

1. ... ever, ever, ever ...

/wp-content/themes

Any WordPress themes you install on your WordPress site will be located in this directory. By default, WordPress comes with the Twenty Eleven, Twenty Twelve, Twenty Thirteen, and Twenty Fourteen themes.

/wp-content/uploads

Once you start uploading any photos or files to your media library, you will start seeing this directory being populated with those uploaded files. All uploaded media is stored in the *uploads* directory.

/wp-content/mu-plugins

In WordPress, you can force the use of any plugin by creating a *mu-plugins* directory inside of the *wp-content* directory. This directory does not exist unless you create it. The "mu" stands for "must use," and any plugin you put in the *mu-plugins* folder will automatically run without needing to be manually activated on the admin plugins page. In fact, you won't even see any must use plugins listed there.

Must use plugins are especially useful on multisite installs of WordPress so you can use plugins that your individual network site admins won't be able to deactivate.

WordPress Database Structure

WordPress runs on top of a MySQL database and creates its own tables to store data and content. Below is the database schema created by a default install of WordPress. We have also included some basic information on built-in WordPress functions for interacting with these tables. If you can grasp the database (DB) schema and get comfortable with the list functions in this chapter, you can push and pull any data into and out of WordPress.

> The following table names use the default prefix of wp_. This prefix can be changed during the WordPress installation, and so the exact table names of your WordPress install may vary.

wp_options

The wp_options table stores any sitewide data for you. This table stores the name, description, and admin email that you entered when running a typical install. This table will also come prepopulated with a few records that store the various default settings within WordPress. Table 2-1 shows the database structure for the wp_options table.

Table 2-1. DB schema for `wp_options` table

Column	Type	Collation	Null	Default	Extra
option_id	bigint(20)		No	None	AUTO_INCREMENT
option_name	varchar(64)	utf8_general_ci	No		
option_value	longtext	utf8_general_ci	No	None	
autoload	varchar(20)	utf8_general_ci	No	Yes	

Functions Found in /wp-includes/option.php

The following functions can all be found in *wp-includes/option.php*:

add_option($option, $value = ', $deprecated = ', $autoload = yes)

First checks if an option_name exists before inserting a new row:

- $option—A required string of the option_name you would like to add.
- $value—An optional mixed variable of the option_value you would like to add. If the variable passed is an array or object, the value will be serialized before storing in the database.
- $deprecated—This parameter was deprecated in version 2.3 and is not used anymore.[2]
- $autoload—An optional Boolean used to distinguish whether to load the option into cache when WordPress starts up. Set to yes or no. The default value is no. This can save you a DB query if you are sure you are going to need this option on every page load.

update_option($option, $newvalue)

Updates an existing option but will also add it if it doesn't already exist:

- $option—A required string of the option_name you would like to update/add.
- $newvalue—An optional mixed variable of the option_value you would like to update/add.

get_option($option, $default = false)

Retrieves the option_value for a provided option_name:

---

2. The third parameter for add_option, which was deprecated in 2.3, used to be a "description" string that was stored along with the option in the wp_options table.

- $option—A required string of the option_name you would like to get.

- $default—An optional mixed variable you would like to return if the op
tion_name you provided doesn't exist in the table. By default, this parameter is false.

delete_option($option)

Deletes an existing option from the database permanently:

- $option—A required string of the option_name you would like to delete.

 Most of the code examples in this book are not fully functional code. They are basic theoretical examples of how to use the functions we are talking about. You can follow along with most of the code examples if you like in a custom plugin or your theme's *functions.php* file.

Example 2-1 demonstrates some of the basic functions for interacting with the wp_op tions table.

Example 2-1. Adding, updating, getting, and deleting records in the wp_options table

```php
<?php
// add option
$twitters = array( '@bwawwp', '@bmess', '@jason_coleman' );
add_option( 'bwawwp_twitter_accounts', $twitters );

// get option
$bwawwp_twitter_accounts = get_option( 'bwawwp_twitter_accounts' );
echo '<pre>';
print_r( $bwawwp_twitter_accounts );
echo '</pre>';

// update option
$twitters = array_merge(
        $twitters,
        array(
                '@webdevstudios',
                '@strangerstudios'
        )
);
update_option( 'bwawwp_twitter_accounts', $twitters );

// get option
$bwawwp_twitter_accounts = get_option( 'bwawwp_twitter_accounts' );
echo '<pre>';
print_r( $bwawwp_twitter_accounts );
echo '</pre>';
```

```
// delete option
delete_option( 'bwawwp_twitter_accounts' );


/*
The output from the above example should look something like this:
Array
(
    [0] => @bwawwp
    [1] => @bmess
    [2] => @jason_coleman
)
Array
(
    [0] => @bwawwp
    [1] => @bmess
    [2] => @jason_coleman
    [3] => @webdevstudios
    [4] => @strangerstudios
)
*/
?>
```

wp_users

When you log in to WordPress with your username and password, you are referencing data stored in this table. All users and their default data are stored in the wp_users table. Table 2-2 shows the database structure for the wp_users table.

Table 2-2. DB schema for wp_users table

Column	Type	Collation	Null	Default	Extra
ID	bigint(20)		No	None	AUTO_INCREMENT
user_login	varchar(60)	utf8_general_ci	No		
user_pass	varchar(64)	utf8_general_ci	No		
user_nicename	varchar(50)	utf8_general_ci	No		
user_email	varchar(100)	utf8_general_ci	No		
user_url	varchar(100)	utf8_general_ci	No		
user_registered	datetime		No	0000-00-00 00:00:00	
user_activation_key	varchar(60)	utf8_general_ci	No		
user_status	int(11)		No	0	
display_name	varchar(250)	utf8_general_ci	No		

Functions Found in /wp-includes/...

The following functions are found in */wp-includes/pluggable.php* and */wp-includes/user.php*:

wp_insert_user($userdata)

Inserts a new user into the database. This function can also be used to update a user if the user ID is passed in with the $user_data. $userdata is a required array of field names and values. The accepted fields are:

- *ID*—An integer that will be used for updating an existing user.
- *user_pass*—A string that contains the plain-text password for the user.
- *user_login*—A string that contains the user's username for logging in.
- *user_nicename*—A string that contains a URL-friendly name for the user. The default is the user's username.
- *user_url*—A string containing the URL for the user's website.
- *user_email*—A string containing the user's email address.
- *display_name*—A string that will be shown on the site. Defaults to the user's username. It is likely that you will want to change this, for appearance.
- *nickname*—The user's nickname. Defaults to the user's username.
- *first_name*—The user's first name.
- *last_name*—The user's last name.
- *description*—A string containing content about the user.
- *rich_editing*—A string for whether to enable the rich editor. `False` if not empty.
- *user_registered*—The date the user registered. Format is Y-m-d H:i:s.
- *role*—A string used to set the user's role.
- *jabber*—User's Jabber account.
- *aim*—User's AOL IM account.
- *yim*—User's Yahoo IM account.

wp_create_user($username, $password, $email)

This function utilizes the prior function `wp_insert_user()` and makes it easier to add a new user based on the required columns:

- $username—A required string of the username/login of a new user.
- $password—A required string of the password of a new user.

- $email—A required string of the email address of a new user.

wp_update_user($userdata)

This function can be used to update any of the fields in the wp_users and wp_userme ta (covered next) tables tied to a specific user. Note that if a user's password is updated, all of his cookies will the cleared, logging him out of WordPress:

- $userdata—A required array of field names and values. The ID and at least one other field is required. These fields are the same ones accepted in the wp_in sert_post( ) function.

get_user_by($field, $value)

This function returns the WP_User object on success and false if it fails. The WordPress User class is found in */wp-includes/capabilities.php* and basically queries the wp_user table like so:

```
SELECT * FROM wp_users WHERE $field = $value;
```

The WP_User class also caches the results so it is not querying the database every time it is used. The class also figures out the roles and capabilities of a specific user, which we will go over in more detail in Chapter 6:

- $field—A required string of the field you would like to query the user data by. This string can only be id, slug, email, or login.
- $value—A required integer or string of the value for a given id, slug, email or login.

get_userdata($userid)

This function actually utilizes the previous function get_user_by( ) and returns the same WP_User object:

- $userid—A required integer of the user ID of the user you would like to get data for.

wp_delete_user($id, $reassign = *novalue*)

You guessed it: this function deletes a user and can also reassign any of their posts or links to another user:

- $id—A required integer of the ID of the user you would like to delete.

- $reassign—An optional integer of the ID you would like to reassign any post or links from the deleted user to. Example 2-2 demonstrates some of the basic functions for interacting with the `wp_users` table.

Example 2-2. Working with the `wp_users` table

```php
<?php
// insert user
$userdata = array(
    'user_login'    => 'brian',
        'user_pass'     => 'KOO3gT7@n*',
        'user_nicename' => 'Brian',
        'user_url'      => 'http://webdevstudios.com/',
        'user_email'    => 'brian@schoolpress.me',
        'display_name'  => 'Brian',
        'nickname'      => 'Brian',
        'first_name'    => 'Brian',
        'last_name'     => 'Messenlehner',
        'description'   => 'This is a SchoolPress Administrator account.',
        'role'          => 'administrator'
);
wp_insert_user( $userdata );

// create users
wp_create_user( 'jason', 'YR529G%*v@', 'jason@schoolpress.me' );

// get user by login
$user = get_user_by( 'login', 'brian' );
echo 'email: ' . $user->user_email . ' / ID: ' . $user->ID . '<br>';
echo 'Hi: ' . $user->first_name . ' ' . $user->last_name . '<br>';

// get user by email
$user = get_user_by( 'email', 'jason@schoolpress.me' );
echo 'username: ' . $user->user_login . ' / ID: ' . $user->ID . '<br>';

// update user - add first and last name to brian and change role to admin
$userdata = array(
        'ID'         => $user->ID,
        'first_name' => 'Jason',
        'last_name'  => 'Coleman',
        'user_url'   => 'http://strangerstudios.com/',
        'role'       => 'administrator'
);
wp_update_user( $userdata );

// get userdata for brian
$user = get_userdata( $user->ID );
echo 'Hi: ' . $user->first_name . ' ' . $user->last_name . '<br>';

// delete user - delete the original admin and set their posts to our new admin
// wp_delete_user( 1, $user->ID );
```

```
/*
The output from the above example should look something like this:
email: brian@schoolpress.me / ID: 2
Hi: Brian Messenlehner
username: jason / ID: 3
Hi: Jason Coleman
*/
?>
```

wp_usermeta

Sometimes you may want to store additional data along with a user. WordPress provides an easy way to do this without having to add additional columns to the users table. You can store as much user metadata as you need to in the wp_usermeta table. Each record is associated to a user ID in the wp_user table by the user_id field. Table 2-3 shows the database structure for the wp_usermeta table.

Table 2-3. DB schema for wp_usermeta table

Column	Type	Collation	Null	Default	Extra
umeta_id	bigint(20)		No	None	AUTO_INCREMENT
user_id	bigint(20)		No	0	
meta_key	varchar(255)	utf8_general_ci	Yes	NULL	
meta_value	longtext	utf8_general_ci	Yes	NULL	

get_user_meta($user_id, $key = '', $single = false)

Gets a user's meta value for a specified key:

- $user_id—A required integer of a user ID.
- $key—An optional string of the meta key of the value you would like to return. If blank then all metadata for the given user will be returned.
- $single—A Boolean of whether to return a single value or not. The default is false and the value will be returned as an array.

There can be more than one meta key for the same user ID with different values. If you set $single to true, you will get the first key's value; if you set it to false, you will get an array of the values of each record with the same key.

update_user_meta($user_id, $meta_key, $meta_value, $prev_value = '')

This function will update user metadata but will also insert metadata if the passed-in key doesn't already exist:

- $user_id—A required integer of a user ID.
- $meta_key—A required string of the meta key name for the meta value you would like to store. If this meta key already exists, it will update the current row's meta value, if not it will insert a new row.
- $meta_value—A required mixed value of an integer, string, array, or object. Arrays and objects will automatically be serialized.
- $prev_value—An optional mixed value of the current metadata value. If a match is found, it will replace the previous/current value with the new value you specified. If left blank, the new meta value will replace the first instance of the matching key. If you have five rows of metadata with the same key and you don't specify which row to update with this value, it will update the first row and remove the other four.

 This function relies on the update_metadata() function located in */wp-includes/meta.php*. Check it out!

add_user_meta($user_id, $meta_key, $meta_value, $unique = false)

Yup, this function will insert brand-new user meta into the wp_usermeta table. We don't use this function often anymore because we can just use update_user_meta() to insert new rows as well as update them. If you want to ensure that a given meta key is only ever used once per user, you should use this function and set the $unique parameter to true:

- $user_id—A required integer of a user ID.
- $meta_key—A required string of the meta key name for the meta value you would like to store.
- $meta_value—A required mixed value of an integer, string, array, or object.
- $unique—An optional Boolean, which when set to true will make sure the meta key can only ever be added once for a given ID.

delete_user_meta($user_id, $meta_key, $meta_value = '')

Deletes user metadata for a provided user ID and matching key. You can also specify a matching meta value if you only want to delete that value and not other metadata rows with the same meta key:

- $user_id—A required integer of a user ID.

- $meta_key—A required string of the meta key name for the meta value you would like to delete.

- $meta_value—An optional mixed value of the meta value. If you have more than one record with the same meta key, you can specify which one to delete by matching the meta value. It defaults to nothing, which will delete all meta rows with a matching user_id and meta_key.

Example 2-3 demonstrates some of the basic functions for interacting with the wp_user name table.

Example 2-3. Working with the wp_username table

```php
<?php
// get brian's id
$brian_id = get_user_by( 'login', 'brian' )->ID;

// add user meta - unique is set to true. no polygamy! only
    one wife at a time.
add_user_meta( $brian_id, 'bwawwp_wife', 'Robin Jade Morales Messenlehner', true);

// get user meta - returning a single value
$brians_wife = get_user_meta( $brian_id, 'bwawwp_wife', true);
echo "Brian's wife: " . $brians_wife . "<br>";

// add user meta - no 3rd parameter/unique. can have as many kids
    as wife will let me.
add_user_meta( $brian_id, 'bwawwp_kid', 'Dalya' );
add_user_meta( $brian_id, 'bwawwp_kid', 'Brian' );
add_user_meta( $brian_id, 'bwawwp_kid', 'Nina' );

// update user meta - this will update brian to brian jr.
update_user_meta( $brian_id, 'bwawwp_kid', 'Brian Jr', 'Brian' );

// get user meta - returning an array
$brians_kids = get_user_meta( $brian_id, 'bwawwp_kid' );
echo "Brian's kids:";
echo '<pre>';
print_r($brians_kids);
echo '</pre>';

// delete brian's user meta
delete_user_meta( $brian_id, 'bwawwp_wife' );
delete_user_meta( $brian_id, 'bwawwp_kid' );
```

```php
// get jason's id
$jason_id = get_user_by( 'login', 'jason' )->ID;

// update user meta - this will create meta if the key doesn't exist for the user.
update_user_meta( $jason_id, 'bwawwp_wife', 'Kimberly Ann Coleman' );

// get user meta - returning an array
$jasons_wife = get_user_meta( $jason_id, 'bwawwp_wife' );
echo "Jason's wife:";
echo '<pre>';
print_r($jasons_wife);
echo '</pre>';

// add user meta - storing as an array
add_user_meta( $jason_id, 'bwawwp_kid', array( 'Isaac', 'Marin' ) );

// get user meta - returning a single value which happens to be an array.
$jasons_kids = get_user_meta( $jason_id, 'bwawwp_kid', true );
echo "Jason's kids:";
echo '<pre>';
print_r($jasons_kids);
echo '</pre>';

// delete jason's user meta
delete_user_meta( $jason_id, 'bwawwp_wife' );
delete_user_meta( $jason_id, 'bwawwp_kid' );

/*
The output from the above example should look something like this:
Brian's wife: Robin Jade Morales Messenlehner
Brian's kids:
Array
(
    [0] => Dalya
    [1] => Brian Jr
    [2] => Nina
)
Jason's wife:
Array
(
    [0] => Kimberly Ann Coleman
)
Jason's kids:
Array
(
    [0] => Isaac
    [1] => Marin
)
*/
?>
```

wp_posts

Ah, the meat of WordPress. The `wp_posts` table is where most of your post data is stored. By default, WordPress comes with posts and pages. Both of these are technically posts and are stored in this table. The `post_type` field is what distinguishes what type of post a post is, whether it is a post, a page, a menu item, a revision, or any custom post type that you may later create (custom post types are covered more in Chapter 5). Table 2-4 shows the database structure for the `wp_posts` table.

Table 2-4. DB schema for wp_posts table

Column	Type	Collation	Null	Default	Extra
ID	bigint(20)		No	None	AUTO_INCREMENT
post_author	bigint(20)		No	0	
post_date	datetime		No	0000-00-00 00:00:00	
post_date_gmt	datetime		No	0000-00-00 00:00:00	
post_content	longtext	utf8_general_ci	No	None	
post_title	text	utf8_general_ci	No	None	
post_excerpt	text	utf8_general_ci	No	None	
post_status	varchar(20)	utf8_general_ci	No	Publish	
comment_status	varchar(20)	utf8_general_ci	No	Open	
ping_status	varchar(20)	utf8_general_ci	No	Open	
post_password	varchar(20)	utf8_general_ci	No		
post_name	varchar(200)	utf8_general_ci	No		
to_ping	text	utf8_general_ci	No	None	
pinged	text	utf8_general_ci	No	None	
post_modified	datetime		No	0000-00-00 00:00:00	
post_modified_gmt	datetime		No	0000-00-00 00:00:00	
post_content_filtered	longtext	utf8_general_ci	No	None	
post_parent	bigint(20)		No	0	
guid	varchar(255)	utf8_general_ci	No		
menu_order	int(11)		No	0	
post_type	varchar(20)	utf8_general_ci	No	Post	
post_mime_type	varchar(100)	utf8_general_ci	No		
comment_count	bigint(20)		No	0	

Functions found in /wp-includes/post.php

The following functions are found in *wp-includes/post.php*.

wp_insert_post($postarr, $wp_error = false)

Inserts a new post with provided post data:

- $postarr—An array or object of post data. Arrays are expected to be escaped; objects are not.
- $wp_error—An optional Boolean that will allow for a WP_Error if returned `false`.

The defaults for the parameter $postarr are:

- *post_status*—Default is *draft*.
- *post_type*—Default is *post*.
- *post_author*—Default is current user ID (`$user_ID`). The ID of the user who added the post.
- *ping_status*—Default is the value in the *default_ping_status* option. Whether the attachment can accept pings.
- *post_parent*—Default is 0. Set this for the post it belongs to, if any.
- *menu_order*—Default is 0. The order it is displayed.
- *to_ping*—Whether to ping.
- *pinged*—Default is empty string.
- *post_password*—Default is empty string. The password to access the attachment.
- *guid*—Global unique ID for referencing the attachment.
- *post_content_filtered*—Post content filtered.
- *post_excerpt*—Post excerpt.

wp_update_post($postarr = array(), $wp_error = false)

Updates a post with provided post data.

- $postarr—A required array or object of post data. Arrays are expected to be escaped, objects are not.
- $wp_error—An optional Boolean that will allow for a WP_Error if returned false.

get_post($post = null, $output = OBJECT, $filter = *raw*)

Get post data from a provided post ID or a post object:

- $post—An optional integer or object of the post ID or post object you want to retrieve. The default is the current post you are on inside of the post loop, which is covered later in this chapter.

- $output—An optional string of the output format. The default value is OBJECT (WP_Post object) and the other values can be ARRAY_A (associative array) or AR RAY_N (numeric array).
- $filter—An optional string of how the context should be sanitized on output. The default value is raw, but other values can be edit, db, display, attribute, or js. Sanitization is covered in Chapter 8.

get_posts($args = null)

Returns a list of posts from matching criteria. This function uses the WP_Query class, which you will see examples of throughout the book: $args is an optional array of post arguments. The defaults are:

- *numberposts*—Default is 5. Total number of posts to retrieve. -1 is all.
- *offset*—Default is 0. Number of posts to pass over.
- *category*—What category to pull the posts from.
- *orderby*—Default is *post_date*. How to order the posts.
- *order*—Default is *DESC*. The order to retrieve the posts.
- *include*—A list of post IDs to include
- *exclude*—A list of post IDs to exclude
- *meta_key*—Any metadata key
- *meta_value*—Any metadata value. Must also use meta_key.
- *post_type*—Default is *post*. Can be *page*, or *attachment*, or the slug for any custom CPT. The string any will return posts from all post types.
- *post_parent*—The parent ID of the post.
- *post_status*—Default is *publish*. Post status to retrieve.

wp_delete_post($postid = 0, $force_delete = false)

This function will trash any post or permanently delete it if $force_delete is set to true:

- $postid—A required integer of the post ID you would like to trash or delete.
- $force_delete—An optional Boolean that if set to true will delete the post; if left blank, it will default to false and will move the post to a deleted status.

Example 2-4 demonstrates some of the basic functions for interacting with the wp_posts table.

Example 2-4. Working with the wp_posts table

```php
<?php
// insert post - set post status to draft
$args = array(
        'post_title'   => 'Building Web Apps with WordPress',
        'post_excerpt' => 'WordPress as an Application Framework',
        'post_content' => 'WordPress is the key to successful cost effective
        web solutions in most situations. Build almost anything on top of the
        WordPress platform. DO IT NOW!!!!!',
        'post_status'  => 'draft',
        'post_type'    => 'post',
        'post_author'  => 1,
        'menu_order'   => 0
);
$post_id = wp_insert_post( $args );
echo 'post ID: ' . $post_id . '<br>';

// update post - change post status to publish
$args = array(
        'ID'          => $post_id,
        'post_status' => 'publish'
);
wp_update_post( $args );

// get post - return post data as an object
$post = get_post( $post_id );
echo 'Object Title: ' . $post->post_title . '<br>';

// get post - return post data as an array
$post = get_post( $post_id, ARRAY_A );
echo 'Array Title: ' . $post['post_title'] . '<br>';

// delete post - skip the trash and permanently delete it
wp_delete_post( $post_id, true );

// get posts - return 100 posts
$posts = get_posts( array( 'numberposts' => '100') );
// loop all posts and display the ID & title
foreach ( $posts as $post ) {
        echo $post->ID . ': ' .$post->post_title . '<br>';
}

/*
The output from the above example should look something like this:
post ID: 589
Object Title: Building Web Apps with WordPress
Array Title: Building Web Apps with WordPress
"A list of post IDs and Titles from your install"
*/
?>
```

wp_postmeta

Sometimes you may want to store additional data along with a post. WordPress provides an easy way to do this without having to add additional fields to the posts table. You can store as much post metadata as you need to in the `wp_postmeta` table. Each record is associated to a post through the `post_id` field. When editing any post in the backend of WordPress, you can add/update/delete metadata or Custom Fields via the UI. Table 2-5 shows the database structure for the `wp_postmeta` table.

 Metadata keys that start with an underscore are hidden from the Custom Fields UI on the edit post page. This is useful to hide certain meta fields that you don't want end users editing directly.

Table 2-5. DB schema for `wp_postmeta` *table*

Column	Type	Collation	Null	Default	Extra
meta_id	bigint(20)		No	None	AUTO_INCREMENT
post_id	bigint(20)		No	0	
meta_key	varchar(255)	utf8_general_ci	Yes	NULL	
meta_value	longtext	utf8_general_ci	Yes	NULL	

Functions Found in /wp-includes/post.php

The following functions are found in */wp-includes/post.php*.

get_post_meta($post_id, $key = '', $single = false)

Get post metadata for a given post:

- $post_id—A required integer of the post ID, for which you would like to retrieve post meta.
- $key—Optional string of the meta key name for which you would like to retrieve post meta. The default is to return metadata for all of the meta keys for a particular post.
- $single—A Boolean of whether to return a single value or not. The default is `false`, and the value will be returned as an array.

There can be more than one meta key for the same post ID with different values. If you set `$single` to `true`, you will get the first key's value; if it is set to `false`, you will get an array of the values of each record with the same key.

update_post_meta($post_id, $meta_key, $meta_value, $prev_value = '')

This function will update post metadata but will also insert metadata if the passed-in key doesn't already exist:

- $post_id—A required integer of a post ID.

- $meta_key—A required string of the meta key name for the meta value you would like to store. If this meta key already exists, it will update the current row's meta value; if not, it will insert a new row.

- $meta_value—A required mixed value of an integer, string, array, or object. Arrays and objects will automatically be serialized.

- $prev_value—An optional mixed value of the current metadata value. If a match is found, it will replace the previous/current value with the new value you specified. If left blank, the new meta value will replace the first instance of the matching key. If you have five rows of metadata with the same key and you don't specify which row to update with this value, it will update the first row and remove the other four.

 This function relies on the update_metadata() function located in /wp-includes/meta.php. Check it out!

add_post_meta($post_id, $meta_key, $meta_value, $unique = false)

This function will insert brand-new post meta into the wp_postmeta table. We don't use this function so often anymore because we can just use the previous function we talked about, update_post_meta(), to insert new rows as well as update them. If you want to insure that a given meta key is only ever used once per post, you should use this function and set the $unique parameter to true:

- $user_id—A required integer of a post ID.

- $meta_key—A required string of the meta key name for the meta value you would like to store.

- $meta_value—A required mixed value of an integer, string, array, or an object.

- $unique—An optional Boolean that when set to true will make sure the meta key can only ever be added once for a given ID.

delete_post_meta($post_id, $meta_key, $meta_value = '')

Deletes post metadata for a provided post ID and matching key. You can also specify a matching meta value if you only want to delete that value and not other metadata rows with the same meta key:

- $post_id - A required integer of a post ID.
- $meta_key - A required string of the
- $meta_value - An optional mixed value of the meta value. If you have more than one record with the same meta key, you can specify which one to delete by matching this value. It defaults to nothing, which will delete all meta rows with a matching post_id and meta_key.

In Example 2-5 we will get the last post and add, update, and delete various post meta.

Example 2-5. Working with post metadata

```php
<?php
// get posts - return the latest post
$posts = get_posts( array( 'numberposts' => '1', 'orderby' =>
    'post_date', 'order' => 'DESC' ) );
foreach ( $posts as $post ) {
        $post_id = $post->ID;

        // update post meta - public metadata
        $content = 'You SHOULD see this custom field when editing your latest post.';
        update_post_meta( $post_id, 'bwawwp_displayed_field', $content );

        // update post meta - hidden metadata
        $content = str_replace( 'SHOULD', 'SHOULD NOT', $content );
        update_post_meta( $post_id, '_bwawwp_hidden_field', $content );

        // array of student logins
        $students[] = 'dalya';
        $students[] = 'ashleigh';
        $students[] = 'lola';
        $students[] = 'isaac';
        $students[] = 'marin';
        $students[] = 'brian';
        $students[] = 'nina';

        // add post meta - one key with array as value, array will be serialized
// automatically
        add_post_meta( $post_id, 'bwawwp_students', $students, true );

        // loop students and add post meta record for each student
        foreach ( $students as $student ) {
                add_post_meta( $post_id, 'bwawwp_student', $student );
        }
```

```
            // get post meta - get all meta keys
            $all_meta = get_post_meta( $post_id );
            echo '<pre>';
            print_r( $all_meta );
            echo '</pre>';

            // get post meta - get 1st instance of key
            $student = get_post_meta( $post_id, 'bwawwp_student', true );
            echo 'oldest student: ' . $student;

            // delete post meta
            delete_post_meta( $post_id, 'bwawwp_student' );
}

/*
The output from the above example should look something like this:
Array
(
    [_bwawwp_hidden_field] => Array
        (
        [0] => You SHOULD NOT see this custom field when editing your latest post.
        )

    [bwawwp_displayed_field] => Array
        (
            [0] => You SHOULD see this custom field when editing your latest post.
        )

    [bwawwp_students] => Array
        (
        [0] => a:7:{i:0;s:5:"dalya";i:1;s:8:"ashleigh";i:2;s:4:"lola";i:3;s:5:
        "isaac";i:4;s:5:"marin";i:5;s:5:"brian";i:6;s:4:"nina";}
        )

    [bwawwp_student] => Array
        (
            [0] => dalya
            [1] => ashleigh
            [2] => lola
            [3] => isaac
            [4] => marin
            [5] => brian
            [6] => nina
        )
)
oldest student: dalya
*/
?>
```

wp_comments

Comments can be left against any post. The `wp_comments` table stores individual comments for any post and default associated data. Table 2-6 shows the database structure for the `wp_comments` table.

Table 2-6. DB schema for `wp_comments` table

Column	Type	Collation	Null	Default	Extra
comment_ID	bigint(20)		No	None	AUTO_INCREMENT
comment_post_ID	bigint(20)		No	0	
comment_author	tinytext	utf8_general_ci	No		
comment_author_email	varchar(100)	utf8_general_ci	No		
comment_author_url	varchar(200)	utf8_general_ci	No		
comment_author_IP	varchar(100)	utf8_general_ci	No		
comment_date	datetime		No		0000-00-00 00:00:00
comment_date_gmt	datetime		No	0000-00-00 00:00:00	
comment_content	text	utf8_general_ci	No	None	
comment_karma	int(11)		No	0	
comment_approved	varchar(20)	utf8_general_ci	No	1	
comment_agent	varchar(20)	utf8_general_ci	No		
comment_type	varchar(20)	utf8_general_ci	No		
comment_parent	bigint(20)		No	0	
user_id	bigint(20)		No	0	

Functions Found in /wp-includes/comment.php

The following functions are found in */wp-includes/comment.php*.

get_comment($comment, $output = OBJECT)

Returns comment data from a comment ID or comment object. If the comment is empty, then the global comment variable will be used if set:

- $comment—An optional integer, string, or object of a comment ID or object.
- $output—An optional string that defines what format the output should be in. Possible values are OBJECT, ARRAY_A, and ARRAY_N.

get_comments($args = '')

This function retrieves a list of comments for specific posts or a single post. It calls the WP_Comment_Query class, which we will cover in the next chapter. $args are an optional array or string of arguments to query comments. The default arguments are:

- *author_email*—A string of a comment author's email address.
- *ID*—An integer of the ID of a comment.
- *karma*—An integer of a comment's karma, which can be used by plugins for rating.
- *number*—An integer of the number of comments to return. Default is all comments.
- *offset*—An integer of the number of comments to pass over. Default is 0.
- *orderby*—A string of the field to order the comment by. Allowed values are: comment_agent, comment_approved, comment_author, comment_author_email, comment_author_IP, comment_author_url, comment_content, comment_date, comment_date_gmt, comment_ID, comment_karma, comment_parent, comment_post_ID, comment_type, user_id.
- *order*—A string of how to order the selected order by argument. Defaults to DESC and also accepts ASC.
- *parent*—An integer of a comment's parent comment ID.
- *post_id*—An integer of the post ID a comment is attached to.
- *post_author*—An integer of the post author ID a comment is attached to.
- *post_name*—A string of the post name a comment is attached to.
- *post_parent*—An integer of the post parent ID a comment is attached to.
- *post_status*—A string of the post status a comment is attached to.
- *post_type*—A string of the post type a comment is attached to.
- *status*—A string of the status of a comment. Optional values are *hold*, *approve*, *spam*, or *trash*.
- *type*—A string of the type of a comment. Optional values are '', *pingback*, or *trackback*.
- *user_id*—An integer of the user ID of a comment.
- *search*—A string of search terms to search a comment on. Searches the comment_author, comment_author_email, comment_author_url, comment_author_IP, and comment_content fields.
- *count*—A Boolean that will make the query return a count or results. The default value is false.
- *meta_key*—The comment meta key of comment meta to search on.

- *meta_value*—The comment meta value of comment meta to search on; `meta_key` is required.

wp_insert_comment($commentdata)

Inserts a comment into the database:

- $commentdata—A required array of comment fields and values to be inserted. Available fields to be inserted are `comment_post_ID`, `comment_author`, `comment_au thor_email`, `comment_author_url`, `comment_author_IP`, `comment_date`, `com ment_date_gmt`, `comment_content`, `comment_karma`, `comment_approved`, `com ment_agent`, `comment_type`, `comment_parent`, and `user_id`.

wp_update_comment($commentarr)

Updates comment data and filters to make sure all required fields are valid before updating in the database:

- $commentarr - An optional array of arguments containing comment fields and values to be updated. These are the same field arguments just listed for the `wp_in sert_comment()` function.

wp_delete_comment($comment_id, $force_delete = false)

Deletes a comment. By default, it will trash the comment unless specified to permanently delete:

- $comment_id - A required integer of the comment ID to trash/delete.
- $force_delete - An optional Boolean that if set to `true` will permanently delete a comment. Example 2-6 demonstrates some of the basic functions for interacting with the `wp_comments` table.

Example 2-6 demonstrates managing comment data attached to a post.

Example 2-6. Working with the `wp_comments` table

```php
<?php
// insert post
$args = array(
 'post_title'   => '5 year anniversary on 9/10/16',
 'post_content' => 'Think of somthing cool to do and make a comment about it!',
 'post_status'  => 'publish'
);
$post_id = wp_insert_post( $args );
echo 'post ID: ' . $post_id . ' - ' . $args['post_title'] . '<br>';
```

```php
// make comments array
$comments[] = 'Take a trip to South Jersey';
$comments[] = 'Dinner at Taco Bell';
$comments[] = 'Make a baby';

//loop comments array
foreach ( $comments as $key => $comment ) {
        // insert comments
        $commentdata = array(
                'comment_post_ID' => $post_id,
                'comment_content' => $comments[$key],
        );
        $comment_ids[] = wp_insert_comment( $commentdata );
}
echo 'comments:<pre>';
print_r( $comments );
echo '</pre>';

// update comment
$commentarr['comment_ID'] = $comment_ids[0];
$commentarr['comment_content'] = 'Take a trip to Paris, France';
wp_update_comment( $commentarr );

// insert comment - sub comment from parent id
$commentdata = array(
        'comment_post_ID' => $post_id,
        'comment_parent' => $comment_ids[0],
        'comment_content' => 'That is a pretty good idea...',
);
wp_insert_comment( $commentdata );

// get comments - search taco bell
$comments = get_comments( 'search=Taco Bell&number=1' );
foreach ( $comments as $comment ) {
        // insert comment - sub comment of taco bell comment id
        $commentdata = array(
                'comment_post_ID' => $post_id,
                'comment_parent' => $comment->comment_ID,
                'comment_content' => 'Do you want to get smacked up?',
        );
        wp_insert_comment( $commentdata );
}

// get comment - count of comments for this post
$comment_count = get_comments( 'post_id= ' . $post_id . '&count=true' );
echo 'comment count: ' . $comment_count . '<br>';

// get comments - get all comments for this post
$comments = get_comments( 'post_id=' .$post_id );
foreach ( $comments as $comment ) {
        // update 1st comment
```

```
        if ( $comment_ids[0] == $comment->comment_ID ) {
         $commentarr = array(
          'comment_ID' => $comment->comment_ID,
          'comment_content' => $comment->comment_content . ' & make a baby!',
         );
                wp_update_comment( $commentarr );
                // delete all other comments
        }else {
                // delete comment
                wp_delete_comment( $comment->comment_ID, true );
        }
}

// get comment - new comment count
$comment_count = get_comments( 'post_id= ' . $post_id . '&count=true' );
echo 'new comment count: ' . $comment_count . '<br>';

// get comment - get best comment
$comment = get_comment( $comment_ids[0] );
echo 'best comment: ' . $comment->comment_content;

/*
The output from the above example should look something like this:
post ID: 91011 - 5 year anniversary on 9/10/16
comments:
Array
(
    [0] => Take a trip to South Jersey
    [1] => Dinner at Taco Bell
    [2] => Make a baby
)
comment count: 5
new comment count: 1
best comment: Take a trip to Paris, France & make a baby!
*/
?>
```

wp_commentsmeta

Just like the wp_usermeta and wp_postmeta table, this table stores any custom, additional data tied to a comment by the comment_id fields. Table 2-7 shows the database structure for the wp_commentsmeta table.

Table 2-7. DB schema for wp_commentsmeta table

Column	Type	Collation	Null	Default	Extra
meta_id	bigint(20)		No	None	AUTO_INCREMENT
comment_id	bigint(20)		No	0	
meta_key	varchar(255)	utf8_general_ci	Yes	NULL	
meta_value	longtext	utf8_general_ci	Yes	NULL	

Functions Found in /wp-includes/comment.php

The following functions are found in */wp-includes/comment.php*.

get_comment_meta($comment_id, $key = '', $single = false)

Get comment meta for a given comment ID:

- $comment_id—A required integer of the comment ID for which you would like to retrieve comment meta.
- $key—Optional string of the meta key name for which you would like to retrieve comment meta. The default is to return metadata for all of the meta keys for a particular post.
- $single—A Boolean of whether to return a single value or not. The default is false, and the value will be returned as an array.

add_comment_meta($comment_id, $meta_key, $meta_value, $unique = false)

Add comment meta for given comment ID:

- $comment_id—A required integer of a comment ID.
- $meta_key—A required string of the meta key name for the meta value you would like to store.
- $meta_value—A required mixed value of an integer, string, array, or object.
- $unique—An optional Boolean that when set to true will make sure the meta key can only ever be added once for a given ID.

update_comment_meta($comment_id, $meta_key, $meta_value, $prev_value = '')

- $comment_id—A required integer of a comment ID.
- $meta_key—A required string of the meta key name for the meta value you would like to store. If this meta key already exists, it will update the current row's meta value; if not, it will insert a new row.
- $meta_value—A required mixed value of an integer, string, array, or object. Arrays and objects will automatically be serialized.
- $prev_value—An optional mixed value of the current metadata value. If a match is found, it will replace the previous/current value with the new value you specified. If left blank, the new meta value will replace the first instance of the matching key. If you have five rows of metadata with the same key and you don't specify which row to update with this value, it will update the first row and remove the other four.

delete_comment_meta($comment_id, $meta_key, $meta_value = '')

Deletes comment metadata for a provided comment ID and matching key. You can also specify a matching meta value if you only want to delete that value and not other metadata rows with the same meta key:

- $comment_id—A required integer of a comment ID.
- $meta_key—A required string of the meta key name for the meta value you would like to delete.
- $meta_value—An optional mixed value of the meta value. If you have more than one record with the same meta key, you can specify which one to delete by matching this value. It defaults to nothing, which will delete all meta rows with a matching post_id and meta_key.

Example 2-7 demonstrates some of the basic functions for interacting with the wp_com mentsmeta table.

Example 2-7. Working with the wp_commentsmeta table

```php
<?php
// get comments - last comment ID
$comments = get_comments( 'number=1' );
foreach ( $comments as $comment ) {
        $comment_id = $comment->comment_ID;

        // add comment meta - meta for view date & IP address
        $viewed = array( date( "m.d.y" ), $_SERVER["REMOTE_ADDR"] );
        $comment_meta_id = add_comment_meta( $comment_id, 'bwawwp_view_date',
        $viewed, true );
        echo 'comment meta id: ' . $comment_meta_id;

        // update comment meta - change date format to format like
        // October 23, 2020, 12:00 am instead of 10.23.20
        $viewed = array( date( "F j, Y, g:i a" ), $_SERVER["REMOTE_ADDR"] );
        update_comment_meta( $comment_id, 'bwawwp_view_date', $viewed );

        // get comment meta - all keys
        $comment_meta = get_comment_meta( $comment_id );
        echo '<pre>';
        print_r( $comment_meta );
        echo '</pre>';

        // delete comment meta
        delete_comment_meta( $comment_id, 'bwawwp_view_date' );
}

/*
The output from the above example should look something like this:
comment meta id: 16
Array
```

```
(
    [bwawwp_view_date] => Array
        (
            [0] => a:2:{i:0;s:24:"August 11, 2013, 4:16 pm";i:1;s:9:"127.0.0.1";}
        )

)
*/
?>
```

wp_links

This table stores any links, URLs, or bookmarks you create. Since WordPress version 3.5, the links/blogroll manager UI has been hidden, so if you do a fresh install and don't see it, don't freak out. You can still use the links/blogroll manager if you choose by installing Andrew Nacin's link manager plugin (*http://bit.ly/link-manager*). If you are upgrading WordPress from a version prior to 3.5, you will still be able to access the UI. Why was this removed, you might ask? If Andrew pulled it out of core, you can bet he had a good reason for it. Once you read about custom post types in Chapter 5, you should be enlightened. Because this feature is on it's way out, we aren't going to go over some of the basic helper functions used to interact with this table. Table 2-8 shows the database structure for the wp_links table.

Table 2-8. DB schema for wp_links table

Column	Type	Collation	Null	Default	Extra
link_id	bigint(20)		No	None	AUTO_INCREMENT
link_url	varchar(255)	utf8_general_ci	No		
link_name	varchar(255)	utf8_general_ci	No		
link_image	varchar(255)	utf8_general_ci	No		
link_target	varchar(25)	utf8_general_ci	No		
link_description	varchar(255)	utf8_general_ci	No		
link_visible	varchar(20)	utf8_general_ci	No	Yes	
link_owner	bigint(20)		No	1	
link_rating	int(11)		No	0	
link_updated	datetime		No	0000-00-00 00:00:00	
link_rel	varchar(255)	utf8_general_ci	No		
link_notes	mediumtext	utf8_general_ci	No	None	
link_rss	varchar(255)	utf8_general_ci	No		

Bookmark functions can be found in */wp-includes/bookmark.php*.

wp_terms

The `wp_terms` table stores each category name or term name that you create. Each record is tied to its taxonomy in the `wp_term_taxonomy` table by the `term_id`. So you're familiar with post categories and tags? Well, each category or tag is stored in this table, and technically they are both taxonomies. Every term that is stored in the name column is a taxonomy term. We will be covering taxonomies in much more detail in Chapter 5, so if you don't fully grasp what a taxonomy is, you will soon. Table 2-9 shows the database structure for the `wp_terms` table.

Table 2-9. DB schema for wp_terms table

Column	Type	Collation	Null	Default	Extra
term_id	bigint(20)		No	None	AUTO_INCREMENT
name	varchar(200)		No		
slug	varchar(200)	utf8_general_ci	No		
term_group	bigint(10)		No	0	

Functions Found in /wp-includes/taxonomy.php

The following functions are found in */wp-includes/taxonomy.php*.

get_terms($taxonomies, $args = '')

Gets the terms of a specific taxonomy or an array of taxonomies:

- $taxonomies—A required string or array of a taxonomy or list of taxonomies.
- $args—An optional string or array of arguments. Available arguments are:

  - *orderby*—Default is name. Can be `name`, `count`, `term_group`, `slug`, or nothing, which will use `term_id`. Passing a custom value other than these will cause the terms to be ordered on that custom value.
  - *order*—ASC or DESC. The default is ASC.
  - *hide_empty*—The default value is `true`, which will only return terms that are attached to a post. If set to `false`, you can return all terms regardless, if they are being used by a post or not.

- *exclude*—An array or comma-separated or space-delimited string of term IDs to exclude from the query results. If include is being used, exclude will be ignored.

- *exclude_tree*—An array or comma-separated or space-delimited string of term IDs to exclude from the query results, including any child terms. If include is being used, *exclude_tree* will be ignored.

- *include*—An array or comma-separated or space-delimited string of term IDs to include in the query results.

- *number*—The number of terms for the query to return. The default is `all`.

- *offset*—The number by which to offset the terms query.

- *fields*—You can specify if you want to return term IDs or names. The default is `all`, which returns an array of term objects.

- *slug*—A string that will return any terms that have a matching slug.

- *hierarchical*—Includes all child terms if they are attached to posts. The default is `true`, so to not return terms hierarchically, set this to `false`.

- *search*—A string that will return any terms whose names match the value provided. The search is case-insensitive.

- *name_like*—A string that will return any terms whose names begin with the value provided. Like the search, this is case-insensitive.

- *pad_counts*—If set to `true`, the query results will include the count of each term's children.

- *get*—If set to `all`, returns terms regardless of ancestry or whether the terms are empty.

- *child_of*—When set to a term ID, the query results will contain all descendants of the provided term ID. The default is 0, which returns everything.

- *parent*—When set to a term ID, the query results will contain the direct children of the provided term ID. The default is an empty string.

- *cache_domain*—Enables a unique cache key to be produced when this query is stored in object cache.

get_term($term, $taxonomy, $output = OBJECT, $filter = *raw*)

Get all term data for any given term:

- $term—A required integer or object of the term to return.
- $taxonomy—A required string of the taxonomy of the term to return.

- $output—An optional string of the output format. The default value is OBJECT, and the other values can be ARRAY_A (associative array) or ARRAY_N (numeric array).
- $filter—An optional string of how the context should be sanitized on output. The default value is raw.

wp_insert_term($term, $taxonomy, $args = array())

Adds a new term to the database:

- $term—A required string of the term to add or update.
- $taxonomy—A required string of the taxonomy the term will be added to.
- $args—An optional array or string of term arguments to be inserted/updated. Available arguments are:
  - *alias_of*—An optional string of the slug that the term will be an alias of.
  - *description*—An optional string that describes the term.
  - *parent*—An optional integer of the parent term ID that this term will be a child of.
  - *slug*—An optional string of the slug of the term.

wp_update_term($term_id, $taxonomy, $args = array())

Updates an existing term in the database:

- $term_id—A required integer of the term ID of the term you want to update.
- $taxonomy—A required string of the taxonomy the term is associated with.
- $args—An optional array or string of term arguments to be updated. These are the same arguments used in wp_insert_term( ).

wp_delete_term($term, $taxonomy, $args = array())

Deletes a term from the database. If the term is a parent of other terms, then the children will be updated to that term's parent:

- $term—A required integer of the term ID of the term you want to delete.
- $taxonomy—A required string of the taxonomy the term is associated with.
- $args—An optional array to overwrite term field values.

wp_term_taxonomy

The `wp_term_taxonomy` table stores each taxonomy type you are using. WordPress has two taxonomy types built in, category and post_tag, but you can also register your own taxonomies. When a new term gets added in the `wp_terms` table, it is associated with its taxonomy in this table, along with that taxonomy term ID, description, parent, and count. Table 2-10 shows the structure for the `wp_term_taxonomy` table.

Table 2-10. DB schema for `wp_term_taxonomy` table

Column	Type	Collation	Null	Default	Extra
term_taxonomy_id	bigint(20)		No	None	AUTO_INCREMENT
term_id	bigint(20)		No	0	
taxonomy	varchar(32)	utf8_general_ci	No		
description	longtext	utf8_general_ci	No	None	
parent	bigint(20)		No	0	
count	bigint(20)		No	0	

/wp-includes/taxonomy.php

The following functions are found in */wp-includes/taxonomy.php*.

get_taxonomies($args = array(), $output = *names*, $operator = *and*)

This function returns a list of registered taxonomy objects or a list of taxonomy names:

- $args—An optional array of arguments to query what taxonomy objects get returned. There are a lot, and we will cover all of them in Chapter 5.

- $output—An optional string of either `names` or `objects`. The default is `names`, which will return a list of taxonomy names.

- $operator—An optional string of either `and` or `or`. The default is `and`, which means that all of the arguments passed in must match. If set to `or`, any of the arguments passed in can match.

get_taxonomy($taxonomy)

This function will first check that the parameter string given is a taxonomy object; and if it is, it will return it:

- $taxonomy—A required string of the name of the taxonomy object to return.

register_taxonomy($taxonomy, $object_type, $args = array())

This function creates or updates a taxonomy object. Registering custom taxonomies can really extend WordPress because you can categorize your posts anyway you see fit. We are going to go over registering taxonomies in much more detail in Chapter 5:

- $taxonomy - A required string of the name of the taxonomy.
- $object_type - A required array or string of the object types (post types like post and page) that this taxonomy will be tied to.
- $args - An optional array or string of arguments. There are a lot, and we will cover all of them in Chapter 5.

wp_term_relationships

The `wp_term_relationships` table relates a taxonomy term to a post. Every time you assign a category or tag to a post, it's being linked to that post in this table. Table 2-11 shows the structure for the `wp_term_relationships` table.

Table 2-11. DB schema for `wp_term_relationships` table

Column	Type	Collation	Null	Default	Extra
object_id	bigint(20)		No	0	
term_taxonomy_id	bigint(20)		No	0	
term_order	int(11)		No	0	

get_object_taxonomies($object, $output = *names*)

This function returns all taxonomies associated with a post type or post object:

- $object—A required array, string, or object of the name(s) of the post type(s) or post object(s).
- $output—An optional string of either names or objects. The default is names, which will return a list of taxonomy names.

wp_get_object_terms($object_ids, $taxonomies, $args = array())

This function returns terms associated with a supplied post object ID or IDs and a supplied taxonomy.

- $object_ids—A required string or array of object IDs for the object terms you would like to return. Passing in a post ID would return terms associated with that post ID.

- $taxonomies—A required string or array of the taxonomy names from which you want to return terms. Passing in the taxonomy `post_tag` would return terms of the `post_tag` taxonomy.
- $args—An optional array or string of arguments that change how the data is returned. The arguments that can be changed are:
  - *orderby*—Defaults to `name`; also accepts `count`, `slug`, `term_group`, `term_order`, and `none`.
  - *order*—Defaults to `ASC`; also accepts `DESC`.
  - *fields*—Defaults to `all`; also accepts `ids`, `names`, `slugs`, and `all_with_ob ject_id`. This argument will dictate what values will be returned.

wp_set_object_terms($object_id, $terms, $taxonomy, $append = false)

This function adds taxonomy terms to a provided object ID and taxonomy. It has the ability to overwrite all terms or to append new terms to existing terms. If a term passed into this function doesn't already exist, it will be created and then related to the provided object ID and taxonomy:

- $object_id—A required integer of the object ID (post ID) to relate your terms to.
- $terms—A required array, integer, or string of the terms you would like to add to an object (post).
- $taxonomy—A required array or string of the taxonomy or taxonomies you want to relate your terms to.
- $append—An optional Boolean that defaults to `false` that will replace any existing terms related to an object ID with the new terms you provided. If set to `true`, your new terms will be appended to the existing terms.

 Discussion is underway to remove the `wp_terms` table from Word-Press in a future release. The `name` and `slug` columns of `wp_terms` will be moved into the `wp_terms_taxonomy` table, and a MySQL view will be created called `wp_terms` that can be queried against, preserving backward compatibility for your custom queries.

Extending WordPress

If you are looking to write your own functionality or customize the data returned by WordPress, you might find the following core concepts in the next chapter very helpful. We will cover more of the various built-in functions and methods used to interact with WordPress data throughout the book. Chapter 3 covers the WordPress Plugin API, including some of the key features of WordPress that make extending it easy, powerful, and consistent!

Leveraging WordPress Plugins

Plugins are awesome! If you didn't know, now you know! Plugins can help you deploy a full-blown web application with little to no knowledge of actual code. Whether you are using a free plugin, premium plugin, or building your own, plugins can extend WordPress to give you the functionality your application requires.

As we mentioned earlier, the great advantage of open source software is that members of the community are invested in improving WordPress and often build plugins to achieve a desired feature. The definition of a plugin provided in the Wordpress codex is, "a program, or a set of one or more functions, written in the PHP scripting language, that adds a specific set of features or services to the WordPress weblog, which can be seamlessly integrated with the weblog using access points and methods provided by the WordPress Plugin Application Program Interface (API)." Plugins allow you to turn your site into anything you can think of, from a basic blog to an ecommerce site to a social network.

There are a couple of plugins that come standard with any new WordPress install: Hello Dolly and Akismet. If you didn't know, the Hello Dolly plugin adds a random lyric from the song "Hello Dolly" by Louis Armstrong to the top of your dashboard on each page load. It's not useful, but is a good way to see how to structure your own plugins. The Akismet plugin integrates with Akismet.com to auotmatically filter out spam comments from your blog. While Hello Dolly is useless outside of its educational value, Akismet is downright necessary on any site with commenting turned on. You always have the ability to deactivate these plugins or delete them altogether if you do not see any use for them on your site.

There are over 26,000 plugins available that can be accessed through the official Word-Press plugin repository (*http://wordpress.org/extend/plugins/*). Not all plugins can be found in the repository, so you can always do a search on the Internet for whatever functionality you are looking for. Many plugin creators have their work available for download through their personal or business sites and many of these are available for a fee. There are also premium plugins, which are plugins that you have to pay to use. Similar to mobile apps, there is sometimes a scaled-down version of the plugin available for free and then a more involved version available for a fee. Most premium plugins also offer developer licenses. This allows developers that may be working on building multiple sites to pay one price for the plugin files and then install them on multiple WordPress installs.

The GPLv2 License

No matter how you purchase or obtain a WordPress plugin, all WordPress plugins must use the GPLv2 code license, which states that if the source code is *distributed* (made available or sold online, etc.), then you can do anything you want to with the code as long as any derivative work retains the GPLv2 license. Some themes and plugins may use a split license, meaning the HTML, CSS, JavaScript, and images are distributed under a different license than the PHP files. Some themes and plugins do not mention the GPLv2 license or flat out deny it applies. There is a little bit of legal merit to their claims, but the authority figures in the WordPress.org community (namely Matt Mullenweg) state that all themes and plugins must be GPL compatible. Our stance is that if you want to do business in the WordPress community, you should follow their rules.

Overall, plugins are a great way to add enhanced functionality to your website without having to change any of the core WordPress files. If you are looking for a specific feature, you should first do a search to make sure that plugin does not already exist for that functionality. If not, you then have two options: you can choose to download and modify an existing plugin or build a new one from scratch.

Installing WordPress Plugins

To install a WordPress plugin, simply log in to the WordPress admin dashboard of your site, also know as the backend. Click on the Plugins section, as shown in Figure 3-1. You will then have the option to search the WordPress plugin repository or upload one if you have already downloaded a plugin from the repository or another source. Once you have completed your search and found a plugin you are interested in, click to install the plugin. Once the plugin is installed, you will then have the option to activate it. If you do not activate the plugin, it will remain deactivated in the "Plugins → Installed Plugins" page of your site. Also, please keep in mind that many plugins will need to be configured once activated, and you will usually see a message appear in the dashboard telling you to do so.

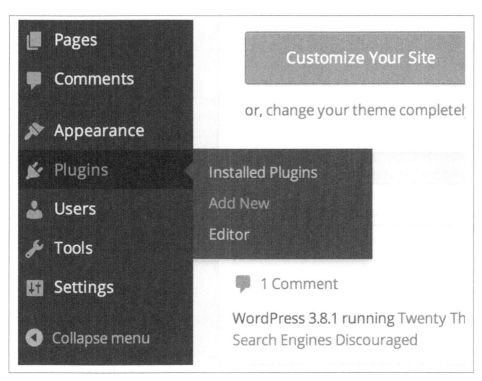

Figure 3-1. Add a new plugin

If you downloaded a plugin from a source other than the official Wordpress plugin repository, you should have a ZIP file of the plugin files. To upload the plugin to your site, you will need to click on Upload in the Plugins section of the dashboard and then choose that ZIP file from wherever you have it saved on your computer. You will be given the choice to activate the plugin if you wish to do so at that time.

Building Your Own Plugin

The true power of WordPress for app developers is that you can make your own custom plugin to extend WordPress anyway you see fit.

To create a plugin, first create a new folder in *wp-content/plugins* called *my-plugin* and make a PHP file in that folder called *my-plugin.php*. In *my-plugin.php*, write the following code, and feel free to replace any of the values:

```php
<?php
/*
* Plugin Name: My Plugin
* Plugin URI: http://webdevstudios.com/
* Description: This is my plugin description.
* Author: messenlehner, webdevstudios, strangerstudios
```

```
 * Version: 1.0.0
 * Author URI: http://bwawwp.com
 * License: GPLv2 or later
 */
?>
```

Save your *my-plugin.php* file. Congratulations, you are a WordPress plugin author! Even though your plugin doesn't do anything yet, you should be able to see it in */wp-admin/ plugins.php* and activate it. Go ahead and activate it.

Let's make your plugin actually do something. Let's add something to the footer of your WordPress install. Copy and save the following code after the plugin information:

```
<?php
function my_plugin_wp_footer() {
    echo 'I read Building Web Apps with WordPress
        and now I am a WordPress Genius!';
}
add_action( 'wp_footer', 'my_plugin_wp_footer' );
?>
```

If you go out to the frontend of your website (make sure you refresh), you should notice a new message in the footer. Now you are off to the races, and you can customize this basic plugin to do whatever you want. If you are already a PHP developer, start hacking away! If you are new to PHP and WordPress, a good way to kickstart your skills is to download and analyze the code in other plugins to see how they are doing what they do.

We will be going over more code that you can use in any of the plugins that you build throughout the book. This was just a very basic example to get you started.

File Structure for an App Plugin

When building a web app with WordPress, we recommend having one main app plugin to store the core functionality for your app. On the theme side (covered in Chapter 4), you will store the majority of your app's frontend code in the active theme.

Some plugins only do one or two things, and one *.php* file is all you need to get things done. Your main app plugin is probably going to be much more complicated, with asset files (CSS, images, and templates), included libraries, class files, and potentially thousands of lines of code you will want to organize into more than one file.

Here is our proposed file structure for an app's main plugin, using the SchoolPress plugin as an example. Not all of these folders and files may be necessary. We add them to a plugin as needed:

- */plugins/schoolpress/adminpages/*
- */plugins/schoolpress/classes/*

- */plugins/schoolpress/css/*
- */plugins/schoolpress/css/admin.css*
- */plugins/schoolpress/css/frontend.css*
- */plugins/schoolpress/js/*
- */plugins/schoolpress/images/*
- */plugins/schoolpress/includes/*
- */plugins/schoolpress/includes/lib/*
- */plugins/schoolpress/includes/functions.php*
- */plugins/schoolpress/pages/*
- */plugins/schoolpress/services/*
- */plugins/schoolpress/scheduled/*
- */plugins/schoolpress/schoolpress.php*

/adminpages/

Place the *.php* files for any dashboard page you add through your plugin in the */admin-pages/* directory. For example, here is how you would add a dashboard page and load it out of your */adminpages/* directory:

```php
<?php
// add a SchoolPress menu with reports page
function sp_admin_menu() {
    add_menu_page(
                'SchoolPress',
                'SchoolPress',
                'manage_options',
                'sp_reports',
                'sp_reports_page'
        );
}
add_action( 'admin_menu', 'sp_admin_menu' );

// function to load admin page
function sp_reports_page() {
        require_once dirname( __FILE__ ) . "/adminpages/reports.php";
}
?>
```

/classes/

Place any PHP class definitions in the */classes/* directory. In general, each file in this directory should include just one class definition. The class files should have names like *class.ClassName.php*, where ClassName is the name given to the class.

/css/

Place any CSS files used specifically for your plugin in the /css/ directory. Split your CSS into *admin.css* and *frontend.css* files depending on whether the CSS affects the Word-Press dashboard or something on the frontend.

Any CSS libraries needed, for example, to support an included JavaScript library, can also be placed in this folder.

Here is some code to enqueue the *admin.css* and *frontend.css* styles from the plugin's CSS folder:

```
---
<?php
function sp_load_styles() {
        if ( is_admin() ) {
                wp_enqueue_style(
                        'schoolpress-plugin-admin',
                        plugins_url( 'css/admin.css', __FILE__ ),
                        array(),
                        SCHOOLPRESS_VERSION,
                        'screen'
                );
        } else {
                wp_enqueue_style(
                        'schoolpress-plugin-frontend',
                        plugins_url( 'css/frontend.css', __FILE__ ),
                        array(),
                        SCHOOLPRESS_VERSION,
                        'screen'
                );
        }
}
add_action( 'init', 'sp_load_styles' );
?>
---
```

Any CSS that affects components of the WordPress dashboard should go into the *admin.css* file. Any CSS that affects the frontend of the site should go into *frontend.css*, but be careful when adding CSS rules to the *frontend.css* file. When adding frontend styles to your plugin files, ask yourself first if the CSS rules you are writing should go into the app's theme instead, since the majority of your frontend-style code should be handed by your theme.

The kind of CSS that would go into the plugin's CSS file are generally layout styles that would be appropriate no matter what theme was loaded. Imagine that your site had no theme or CSS loaded at all. What would be the bare minimum CSS needed to have the HTML generated by your plugin make sense? Expect the theme to build on and override that.

For example, your plugin's *frontend.css* should never include styles for coloring. However, a style saying an avatar is 64 px wide and floated left could be appropriate.

/js/

Place any JavaScript files needed by your plugin in this folder. Again, you can split things into an *admin.js* and *frontend.js* file depending on where the JS is needed.

Any third-party JavaScript libraries used may also be placed in this folder. Generally, they should be added to a subfolder of the */js/* directory.

Here is some code to load *admin.js* and *frontend.js* files from your plugin's */js/* directory:

```php
<?php
function sp_load_scripts() {
        if ( is_admin() ) {
                wp_enqueue_script(
                        'schoolpress-plugin-admin',
                        plugins_url( 'js/admin.js', __FILE__ ),
                        array( 'jquery' ),
                        SCHOOLPRESS_VERSION
                );
        } else {
                wp_enqueue_script(
                        'schoolpress-plugin-frontend',
                        plugins_url( 'js/frontend.js', __FILE__ ),
                        array( 'jquery' ),
                        SCHOOLPRESS_VERSION
                );
        }
}
add_action( 'init', 'sp_load_scripts' );
?>
```

Just like with stylesheets, it can be difficult to determine if some bit of JavaScript should be included in the plugin's JavaScript file or the theme's JavaScript file. In general, JS files that support the theme (e.g., slider effects and menu effects) should go in the theme, and JS files that support the plugin (e.g., AJAX code) should go in the plugin. In practice, however, you will find your plugin using JS defined in your theme and vice versa.

/images/

Place any images needed by your plugin in the */images/* directory.

/includes/

The */includes/* directory is a kind of catchall for any *.php* files your plugin needs. The only *.php* file in your plugin's root folder should be the main plugin file *school-*

press.php. All other *.php* files should go in one of the other folders; and if none are more appropriate, you either need to make another folder or place it in the */includes/* folder.

It is standard procedure to add a *functions.php* or *helpers.php* file to include any helper PHP code used by your plugin. This file should include any small scripts that don't have a central role in the logic or functionality of your plugin but are needed to support it. Examples include functions to trim text, generate random strings, or other framework-like functions that aren't already available through a core WordPress function.

/includes/lib/

Place any third-party libraries that you need for your app into the */includes/lib/* directory.

/pages/

Place any *.php* code related to frontend pages added by your plugin in the */pages/* directory. Frontend pages are typically added through shortcodes that you would embed into a standard WordPress page to show the content you want.

The following code snippet illustrates how to create a shortcode that can be placed on a WordPress page to generate a page from your plugin. The `preheader` here is a chunk of code to run before the `wp_head()` function loads, and thus before any HTML headers or code are sent to the browser. The shortcode function further down outputs HTML to the actual page at the place of the shortcode.

Place this code in */plugins/{your plugin folder}/pages/stub.php*, then include it (typically using the `require_once()` function) from your main plugin file. Then add the shortcode [`sp_stub`] to a page of your WordPress site.

```php
<?php
// preheader
function sp_stub_preheader() {
        if ( !is_admin() ) {
                global $post, $current_user;
                if ( !empty( $post->post_content ) && strpos
                  ( $post->post_content, "[sp_stub]" ) !== false ) {
                        /*
                                Put your preheader code here.
                        */
                }
        }
}
add_action( 'wp', 'sp_stub_preheader', 1 );

// shortcode [sp_stub]
function sp_stub_shortcode() {
        ob_start();
```

```
        ?>
        Place your HTML/etc code here.
        <?php
        $temp_content = ob_get_contents();
        ob_end_clean();
        return $temp_content;
    }
    add_shortcode( 'sp_stub', 'sp_stub_shortcode' );
    ?>
```

For the preheader code, we first check that the page is being loaded from outside the admin using !is_admin(); otherwise this code might run when editing the post in the dashboard. Then we look for the string [sp_stub] in the content of the $post global. This function is hooked to the wp hook, which runs after WordPress sets up the $post global for the current page, but before any headers or HTML is output.

The preheader code can be used to check permissions, process form submissions, or prep any code needed for the page. In an MVC model, this would be your model and/or controller code. Because this code is run before any headers are output, you can still safely redirect users to another page. For example, you can wp_redirect() them to the login or signup page if they don't have access to view the page.

In the shortcode function, we use ob_start(), ob_get_contents(), and ob_end_clean(), which are PHP functions used to buffer output to a variable. Using this code means that the code between the preceding ?> and <?php tags is placed into the $temp_content variable instead of output at the time of processing (which would have it echoed out above the <html> tag of your site). This isn't necessary; you could just define a $temp_content function and use PHP to add to that string. Using output buffering allows us to code in a more template-like way, mixing HTML and PHP, which is easier to read.

/services/

Place any .php code for AJAX calls in the /services/ directory.

/scheduled/

Place any .php code that is related to cron jobs or code that is meant to be run at scheduled intervals here.

/schoolpress.php

This is the main plugin file. For small plugins, this may be the only file needed. For large plugins, the main plugin file will only contain include statements, constant definitions, and some comments about which other files contain the code you might be looking for.

Add-Ons to Existing Plugins

Any plugin or piece of code that runs on WordPress and is distributed[1] is supposed to be open source and licensed under the GPL. You could take any plugin in the repository, change the name, and release it as a totally new plugin. Doing this could get you into a bar fight, so we suggest that you don't "fork" plugins like this unless you are also planning to improve on and maintain the new plugin.

What if you found a plugin that does 95% of what you need, but it needs a couple lines of code to get to 100%? Consider making an add-on for the plugin.

Most well-developed plugins will have their own hooks and filters, which can allow other developers to create an add-on plugin. Just as you would build a plugin to use hooks and filters in WordPress, you can build a plugin to use hooks and filters in other plugins. In some cases, you may need to hack the original plugin to do what you want, which is totally cool, but maybe you can suggest adding some hooks or filters where you need them to the original plugin author.

Use Cases and Examples

So what should we build with the free and premium plugins we just mentioned? Let's add a community around WordPress: SchoolPress.

Each teacher will be the administrator of her own group and can easily add students to it. Students can engage in the group activity, or the "Class Wall" as we will call it. With BuddyPress, students can add one another as friends, follow their friends or teachers, and private message their teachers if they have questions.

With BadgeOS and the BadgeOS Community add-on, we can allow teachers to create fun reward badges for their students to earn as they complete various homework assignments and projects that they can share with their friends on the social networks that they are already on.

We can use Gravity Forms to make a really easy way for students to submit their homework.

The WordPress Loop

The great and powerful WordPress Loop is what makes WordPress display its posts. Depending on what theme template file is being called on when navigating your website,

---

1. In the context of the GPL, distribution means selling your source code or offering it for download on a website like the WordPress.org plugin repository. Code that you personally install for someone does not need to inherit the GPL license.

WordPress queries the database and retrieves the posts that need to be returned to the end user and then loops through them.

Most correctly built WordPress themes usually have the following files that contain the WordPress loop:

- *index.php*
- *archive.php*
- *category.php*
- *tag.php*
- *single.php*
- *page.php*

If you open up any of these files, will contain code that may look something like this:

```php
<?php
if ( have_posts() ) {
        while ( have_posts() ) {
                the_post();
                // show each post title, excerpt/content , featured image and more
                the_title( '<h2>', '</h2>' );
                the_content();
        }
} else {
        // show a message like sorry no posts!
}
?>
```

The have_posts() function checks to see if there are any posts that need to be looped, and if so, the while loop is initiated. The the_post() function called first in each iteration of the loop sets up the post with all of its global variables so post-specific data can be displayed to the end user.

WordPress Global Variables

Global variables are variables that can be defined and then used anywhere after in the rest of your code. WordPress has a few built-in global variables that can really help you save a lot of time and resources when writing code.

If you wanted to see a full list of every global variable available to you, you can run the following code:

```php
<?php
echo '<pre>';
print_r( $GLOBALS );
echo '</pre>';
?>
```

To access a global variable in any custom code you are writing, use code like this:

```php
<?php
global $global_variable_name;
?>
```

Some global variables are only made available to you depending on where you are in WordPress. Below is a short list of some of the more popular global variables:

- $post—An object that contains all of the post data from the `wp_posts` table for the current post that you are on within the WordPress loop.
- $authordata—An object with all of the author data of the current post that you are on within the WordPress loop.

$wpdb

The `$wpdb` class is used to interact with the database directly. Once globalized, you can use `$wpdb` in custom functionality to select, update, insert, and delete database records. If you are new to WordPress and aren't familiar with all of the functions to push and pull from the database, `$wpdb` is going to be your best friend.

Queries using `$wpdb` are also useful when you need to manage custom tables required by your app or perform a complicated query (perhaps joining many tables) faster than the core WordPress functions would run on their own. Please don't assume that the built-in WordPress functions for querying the database are slow. Unless you know exactly what you are doing, you'll want to use the built-in functions for getting posts, users, and metadata. The WordPress core is smart about optimizing queries and caching the results from these calls, which will work well across all of the plugins you are running. However, in certain situations, you can shave a bit of time by rolling your own query. A few examples like this are covered in Chapter 16.

Using custom DB tables

In SchoolPress, we store the relationship of student submissions to assignments in a custom table. This keeps the core WordPress tables a bit cleaner[2] and allows us to easily query for things like "select all of Isaac's assignments."

To add our table to the database, we need to write up the SQL for the CREATE TABLE command and query it against the WordPress database. You can use either the `$wpdb->query()` method or the `dbDelta()` function in the WordPress core.

---

2. It would take a synced entry in both the `wp_usermeta` and `wp_postmeta` tables to provide the same lookup ability a single `wp_schoolpress_assignment_submissions` table offers.

There are a few things we need to do to keep track of our custom tables. We want to store a db_version for our app plugin so we know what version of the database schema we are working with in case it updates between versions. We can also check the version so we only run the setup SQL once for each version. Another common practice is to store your custom table name as a property of $wpdb to make querying it a bit easier later.

Example 3-1 shows a little bit of our database setup function for the SchoolPress app:

Example 3-1. Database setup for SchoolPress

```php
<?php
// setup the database for the SchoolPress app
function sp_setupDB() {
        global $wpdb;

        // shortcuts for SchoolPress DB tables
        $wpdb->schoolpress_assignment_submissions = $wpdb->prefix .
                'schoolpress_assignment_submissions';

        $db_version = get_option( 'sp_db_version', 0 );

        // create tables on new installs
        if ( empty( $db_version ) ) {
                global $wpdb;

                $sqlQuery = "
                CREATE TABLE '" . $wpdb->schoolpress_assignment_submissions . "' (
                  `assignment_id` bigint(11) unsigned NOT NULL,
                  `submission_id` bigint(11) unsigned NOT NULL,
                  UNIQUE KEY `assignment_submission` (`assignment_id`,`submission_id`),
                  UNIQUE KEY `submission_assignment` (`submission_id`,`assignment_id`)
                )
                ";

                require_once ABSPATH . 'wp-admin/includes/upgrade.php';
                dbDelta( $sqlQuery );

                $db_version = '1.0';
                update_option( 'sp_db_version', '1.0' );
        }
}
add_action( 'init', 'sp_dbSetup', 0 );
?>
```

The sp_dbSetup() function is run early in init (priority 0) so the table shortcuts are available to any other code you have running. You can't always assume a wp_ prefix, so the $wpdb->prefix property is used to get the database prefix for the WordPress install.

A DB version for the SchoolPress app is stored in the WordPress options table. We get the value out of options, and if it is empty, we run code to create our custom tables. The

CREATE TABLE SQL statement here is pretty standard. You should always try to run these commands directly on the MySQL database before pasting them into your plugin code to make sure they work.

We use the dbDelta() function to create the database table. This function will create a new table if it doesn't exist. Or if a table with the same name already exists, it will figure out the correct ALTER TABLE query to get the old table to match the new schema.

To use dbDelta(), you must be sure to include the *wp-admin/includes/upgrade.php* file since that file is only loaded when needed. Then pass dbDelta() the SQL for a CREATE TABLE query. Your SQL must be in a specific format a little more strict than the general MySQL format.

From the WordPress Codex on Creating Tables with Plugins (*http://bit.ly/create-table*):

1. You must put each field on its own line in your SQL statement.
2. You must have two spaces between the words PRIMARY KEY and the definition of your primary key.
3. You must use the keyword KEY rather than its synonym INDEX, and you must include at least one KEY.
4. You must not use any apostrophes or backticks around field names.

Running queries. Using dbDelta() is preferred when creating tables because it will automatically update older versions of your tables, but you can also run the CREATE TABLE query using $wpdb->query($sqlQuery);.

You can run any valid SQL statement using the $wpdb->query() method. The query() method sets a lot of properties on the $wpdb object that are useful for debugging or just keeping track of your queries:

- $wpdb->result will contain the raw result from your SQL query.
- $wpdb->num_queries is incremented each time a query is run.
- $wpdb->last_query will contain the last SQL query run.
- $wpdb->last_error will contain a string with the last SQL error generated if there was one.
- $wpdb->insert_id will contain the ID created from the last successful INSERT query.
- $wpdb->rows_affected is set to the number of affected rows.
- $wpdb->num_rows is set to the number of rows in a result for a SELECT query.

- `$wpdb->last_result` will contain an array of row objects generated through the `mysql_fetch_object()` PHP function.

The return value of the `$wpdb->query()` method is based on the top of query run and if the query was successful or not:

- `False` is returned if the query failed. You can test for this using code like `if($wpdb->query($query) === false) { wp_die("it failed!"); }`.
- The raw MySQL result is returned on CREATE, ALTER, TRUNCATE, and DROP queries.
- The number of rows affected is returned for INSERT, UPDATE, DELETE, and REPLACE queries.
- The number of rows returned is returned for SELECT queries.

Escaping in DB queries

It should be noted that values passed into the `query()` method are not escaped automatically. Therefore, you will always need to escape untrusted input when using the `query()` method directly.

There are two main ways of escaping values used in your SQL queries: you can wrap your variables in the `esc_sql()` function (see Example 3-2) or you can use the `$wpdb->prepare()` method to build your query.

Example 3-2. Using the esc_sql() function

```
global $wpdb;
$user_query = $_REQUEST['uq'];

$sqlQuery = "SELECT user_login FROM $wpdb->users WHERE
user_login LIKE '%" . esc_sql($user_query) . "%' OR
user_email LIKE '%" . esc_sql($user_query) . "%' OR
display_name LIKE '%" . esc_sql($user_query) . "%'
";
$user_logins = $wpdb->get_col($sqlQuery);

if(!empty($user_logins))
{
        echo "<ul>";
foreach($user_logins as $user_login)
        {
                echo "<li>$user_login</li>";
}
echo "</ul>";
}
```

Alternatively, you could create the query using the `prepare()` method, which functions similarly to the `sprintf()` and `printf()` functions in PHP. This method of the $wpdb class located in *wp-includes/wp-db.php* accepts two or more parameters:

- $query—A string of your custom SQL statement with placeholders for each dynamic value.
- $args—One or more additional parameters to be used to replace the placeholders in your SQL statement.

The following directives can be used in the SQL statement string:

- %d (integer)
- %f (float)
- %s (string)
- %% (literal percentage sign—no argument needed)

The directives %d, %f, and %s should be left unquoted in the SQL statement, and each placeholder used needs to have a corresponding argument passed in for it. Literals (%) as part of the query must be properly written as %%:

```
$sqlQuery = $wpdb->prepare("SELECT user_login FROM $wpdb->users WHERE
user_login LIKE %%%s%% OR
user_email LIKE %%%s%% OR
display_name LIKE %%%s%%", $user_query, $user_query, $user_query);
$user_logins = $wpdb->get_col($sqlQuery);
```

 If you use `$wpdb->prepare()` without including the `$args` parameter, you will get a PHP warning message: "Missing argument 2 for wpdb::prepare()". If your SQL doesn't use any placeholder values, you don't need to use `prepare()`.

Holy percent sign, Batman! The `%` is used in SQL as a wildcard in SELECT statements when using the LIKE keyword. So if you searched for `user_login LIKE %coleman%`, it would return users with user logins like "jcoleman" and "jasoncoleman" and "coleman1982." To keep these *literal* % signs in place with the `prepare()` method, we need to double them up to `%%`, which is translated into just one % in the final query.

The other % in there is used with `%s`, which is the placeholder where our `$user_query` parameter is going to be swapped in after being escaped.

You may have noticed we used the `$wpdb->get_col()` method in the previous code segment. WordPress offers many useful methods on the `$wpdb` object to SELECTs, INSERTs, and other common queries in MySQL.

SELECT queries with $wpdb

The WordPress $wpdb object has a few useful methods for selecting arrays, objects, rows, columns, or even single values out of the MySQL database using SQL queries.

`$wpdb→get_results($query, $output_type)` will run your query and return the `last_results` array, including all of the rows from your SQL query in the output type specified. By default, the result will be a "numerically indexed array of row objects." Here's the full list of output types from the WordPress Codex:

OBJECT
> Result will be output as a numerically indexed array of row objects.

OBJECT_K
> Result will be output as an associative array of row objects, using the first column's values as keys (duplicates will be discarded).

ARRAY_A
> Result will be output as an numerically indexed array of associative arrays, using column names as keys.

ARRAY_N
> Result will be output as a numerically indexed array of numerically indexed arrays.

The following code helps show how to use the array returned by `$wpdb->get_results()` when using the OBJECT output type:

```php
<?php
global $wpdb;
$sqlQuery = "SELECT * FROM $wpdb->posts
        WHERE post_type = 'assignment'
        AND post_status = 'publish' LIMIT 10";
$assignments = $wpdb->get_results( $sqlQuery );

// rows are stored in an array, use foreach to loop through them
foreach ( $assignments as $assignment ) {
// each item is an object with property names equal to the SQL column names?>
<h3><?php echo $assignment->post_title;?></h3>
<?php echo apply_filters( "the_content", $assignment->post_content );?>
<?php
}
?>
```

`$wpdb→get_col($query, $collumn_offset = 0)` will return an array of the values in the first column of the MySQL results. The `$collumn_offset` parameter can be used to grab other columns from the results (0 is the first, 1 is the second, and so on).

This function is most commonly used to grab IDs from a database table to be used in another function call or DB query:

```php
<?php
global $wpdb;
$sqlQuery = "SELECT ID FROM $wpdb->posts
        WHERE post_type = 'assignment'
        AND post_status = 'publish'
        LIMIT 10";
// getting IDs
$assignment_ids = $wpdb->get_col( $sqlQuery );

// result is an array, loop through them
foreach ( $assignment_ids as $assignment_id ) {
        // we have the id, we can use get_post to get more data
        $assignment = get_post( $assignment_id );
        ?>
        <h3><?php echo $assignment->post_title;?></h3>
        <?php echo apply_filters( "the_content", $assignment->post_content );?>
        <?php
}
?>
```

Note that we're putting that global $wpdb; line in most of our examples here to rein-force the point that you need to make sure that $wpdb is in scope before calling one of its methods. In practice, this line is usually at the top of the function or file you are working within.

$wpdb→get_row($query, $output_type, $row_offset) is used to get just one row from a result. Instead of getting an array of results, you will just get the first object (or array if the $output_type is specified) from the result set.

You can use the $row_offset parameter to grab a different row from the results (0 is the first, 1 is the second, and so on).

Insert, replace, and update. $wpdb→insert($table, $data, $format) can be used to insert data into the database. Rather than building your own INSERT query, you simply pass the table name and an associative array containing the row data and WordPress will build the query and escape it for you. The keys of your $data array must map to column names in the table. The values in the array are the values to insert into the table row:

```php
<?php
// processing new submissions for assignments
global $wpdb, $current_user;

// create submission
$assignment_id = intval( $_REQUEST['assignment_id'] );
$submission_id = wp_insert_post(
        array(
                'post_type'    => 'submission',
                'post_author'  => $current_user->ID,
```

```
                    'post_title'   => sanitize_title( $_REQUEST['title'] ),
                    'post_content' => sanitize_text_field( $_POST['submission'] )
            )
    );

    // connect the submission to the assignment
    $wpdb->insert(
        $wpdb->schoolpress_assignment_submissions,
        array( "assignment_id"=>$assignment_id, "submission_id"=>$submission_id ),
        array( '%d', '%d' )
    );

    /*
            This insert call will generate a SQL query like:
            INSERT INTO
            'wp_schoolpress_assignment_submissions'

            ('assignment_id','submission_id' VALUES (101,10)
    */
    ?>
```

In the previous code, we use `wp_insert_post()` to create the submission then use `$wpdb->insert()` to insert a row into our custom table connecting assignments with submissions.

We pass an array of formats to the third parameter to tell the method to format the data as integers when constructing the SQL query. The available formats are %s for strings, %d for integers, and %f for floats. If no format is specified, all data will be formatted as a string. In most cases, MySQL will properly cast your string into the format needed to store it in the actual table.

To relate two posts like this, we could also simply put the `assignment_id` into the `post_parent` column of the `wp_posts` table. This is adequate to create a parent/child relationship. However, if you want to do a many-to-many relationship (e.g., if you can post the same submission to multiple assignments), you need a separate table or some other way to connect a post to many other posts.

`$wpdb→replace($table, $data, $format)` is similar to the `$wpdb->insert()` method. The `$wpdb->replace()` method will literally generate the same exact SQL query as `$wpdb->insert()` but uses the MySQL REPLACE command instead of INSERT, which will override any row with the same keys as the `$data` passed in.

`$wpdb→update($table, $data, $where, $format = null, $where_format = null )` can be used to update rows in a database table. Rather than building your own UPDATE query, you simply pass the table and an associative array containing the updated columns and new data along with an associative array `$where` containing the fields to check against in the WHERE clause and WordPress will build the query and escape the UPDATE query for you.

The $where and $where_format parameters work the same as the $data and $format arrays, respectively.

The WHERE clause generated by the update() method will check that the columns are equal to the values passed and those checks are combined together by AND conditions.

The update() method is particularly useful in that you can update any number of fields in an table row using the same function. Here is some code that could be used to update orders in an ecommerce plugin:

```php
<?php
global $wpdb;
// just update the status
$wpdb->update(
        'ecommerce_orders',    //table name
        array( 'status' => 'paid' ), //data fields
        array( 'id' => $order_id )  //where fields
);

// update more data about the order
$wpdb->update(
        'ecommerce_orders',    //table name
        array( 'status' => 'pending',  //data fields
                'subtotal' => '100.00',
                'tax' => '6.00',
                'total' => '106.00'
        ),
        array( 'id' => $order_id )  //where fields
);
?>
```

- $wp_query—An object of the WP_Query class that can show you all of the post content returned by WordPress for any given page that you are on. We will talk more about the WP_Query class and its methods in the next chapter.

- $current_user—An object of all of the data associated with the currently logged-in user. Not only does this object return all of the data for the current user from the wp_users table, but it will also tell you the roles and capabilities of the current user:

```php
<?php
//welcome the logged-in user
global $current_user;
if ( !empty( $current_user->ID ) ) {
        echo 'Howdy, ' . $current_user->display_name;
}
?>
```

When writing your own code to run on WordPress, you can define and use your own global variables if it makes sense. Global variables can save you the hassle of rewriting code and recalling functions because once they are defined, you can use them over and over again.

Action Hooks

WordPress developers hook for a living! Hooks are great and they make adding functionality into WordPress plugins and themes simple and easy. Any place an action hook, or technically a do_action() function, exists in code running on WordPress, you can insert your own code by calling the add_action() function and passing in the action hook name and your custom function with the code you want to run:

- do_action($tag, $arg);
  - — $tag—The name of the action hook being executed.
  - — $arg—One or more additional arguments that will get passed through to the function called from the add_action() function referencing this do_action() function. Say what? Keep reading...

You can create your own hooks in a theme or plugin by adding your own do_action() functions. However, most of the time you will be using established hooks in the WordPress core or other plugins. For example, let's say we wanted to check if a user was logged in when WordPress first loads up but before any output is displayed to the browser. We can use the init hook:

```php
<?php
add_action( 'init', 'my_user_check' );

function my_user_check() {
        if ( is_user_logged_in() ) {
                // do something because a user is logged in
        }
}
?>
```

So what just happened? In the core of WordPress, there is an action hook, do_action(init), and we are calling a function called "my_user_check" from the add_action() function. At whatever point in time the code is being executed, when it gets to the init action hook, it will then run our custom my_user_check function to do whatever we want before continuing on.

Check out WordPress's reference page (*http://bit.ly/plugin-api*) for a list of the most used WordPress hooks.

Filters

Filters are kind of like action hooks in the sense that you can tap into them wherever they exist in WordPress. However, instead of inserting your own code where the hook or do_action() exists, you are filtering the returned value of existing functions that are using the apply_filters() function in WordPress core, plugins, and/or themes. In other words, by utilizing filters, you can hijack content before it is inserted into the database or before it is displayed to the browser as HTML:

- apply_filters($tag, $value, $var);
  - $tag—The name of the filter hook.
  - $value—The value that the filter can be applied on.
  - $var—Any additional variables, such as a string or an array, passed into the filter function.

If you search the core WordPress files for apply_filters you will find that the ap ply_filters() function is called all over the place, and like action hooks, the ap ply_filters() function can also be added to and called from any theme or plugin. Anywhere in code running on your WordPress site that you see the apply_filters() function being called, you can filter the value being returned by that function. For our example, we are going to filter the title of all posts before they are displayed to the browser. We can hook into any existing filters using the add_filter() function:

- add_filter($tag, $function, $priority, $accepted_args);
  - $tag—The name of the filter hook you want to filter. This should match the $tag parameter of the apply_filters() function call you want to filter the results for.
  - $function—The name of the custom function used to actually filter the results.
  - $priority—This number sets the priority in which your add_filter will run compared to other places in the code that might be referencing the same filter hook tag. By default, this value is 10.
  - $accepted_args—You can set the number of parameters that your custom function that handles the filtering can except. The default is 1, which is the $value parameter of the apply_filters function.

OK, so how would real code for this look? Let's start by adding a filter to alter the title of any post returned to the browser. We know of a filter hook for the_title that looks like this:

```
apply_filters( 'the_title', $title, $id );
```

$title is the title of the post and $id is the ID of the post:

```php
<?php
add_filter( 'the_title', 'my_filtered_title', 10, 2 );

function my_filtered_title( $value, $id ) {
        $value = '[' . $value . ']';
        return $value;
}
?>
```

The preceding code should wrap any post titles in brackets. If your post title was "hello world," it would now read "[hello world]." Note that we didn't use the $id in our custom function. If we wanted to, we could have only applied the brackets to specific post IDs.

 While add_action() is meant to be used with do_action() hooks and add_filter() is meant to be used with apply_filters() hooks, the functions work the same way and are interchangeable. For readability, it is still a good idea to use the proper function depending on whether you intend to return a filtered result or just perform some code at a specific time.

Free Plugins

Let's talk about some useful free plugins that can help extend your web application. There are plugins that exist for almost every purpose. In the event that you can't find the exact functionality you are looking for in an existing plugin, you could always modify an existing plugin (open source right) or create an entirely new one if you are up for the challenge.

All in One SEO Pack

This is a great plugin (*http://bit.ly/1-seo-pack*) to use if you are concerned about SEO (search engine optimization). This plugin was created by Semper Fi Web Design and once installed, it automatically optimizes your site for search engines. It also adds custom meta fields to each page and post that then allow you to add in custom titles as well as descriptions and keywords. There are pro or premium versions of the plugin that extend the functionality to allow for customization of search engine settings for each individual post or page as well as the option to set sitewide defaults in WordPress.

BadgeOS

This plugin (*http://bit.ly/badgeOS*) can transform any website into a platform for rewarding members achievements based on their activities. It allows the site admin to create different achievement types and award the members sharable badges once they complete all the requirements to earn that particular achievement or achievements. Badges are Mozilla OBI compatible and sharable via Credly.com.

Custom Post Type UI

This is a very powerful plugin (*http://bit.ly/custom-ui*) for building a web application. Custom Post Type UI allows you to create your own custom post types and taxonomies without touching any lines of code. We will be going over what custom post types and taxonomies are and how to register them in the next chapter, but you can use this plugin to get around writing your own code.

Posts 2 Posts

This is another very powerful plugin (*http://bit.ly/posts2posts*) for building a web application. This plugin allows you to create many-to-many relationships between posts, pages, and custom post types as well as many-to-many relationships between posts and users.

For an example, you could use P2P to make connections between custom post types for schools, teachers, and subjects. A school could have multiple teachers, and each teacher could be tied to one or more subjects.

P2P provides intuitive settings, feature-rich widgets, and an easy-to-use meta box attached to any post add/edit page for making new connections.

Most of the time, custom plugin developers should avoid creating additional database tables unless it absolutely makes sense. If we wanted to connect posts to other posts, we could store an array of post IDs in a custom field of another post, but this can become inefficient in a large scale application. P2P creates its own database tables for storing the relationships between posts more efficiently.

Table 3-1. DB schema for wp_p2p table

Column	Type	Collation	Null	Default	Extra
p2p_id	bigint(20)		No	None	AUTO_INCREMENT
p2p_from	bigint(20)		No	None	
p2p_to	bigint(20)		No	None	
p2p_type	varchar(44)	utf8_general_ci	No		

Table 3-2. DB schema for wp_p2pmeta table

Column	Type	Collation	Null	Default	Extra
meta_id	bigint(20)		No	None	AUTO_INCREMENT
p2p_id	bigint(20)		No	0	
meta_key	varchar(255)	utf8_general_ci	Yes	NULL	

Column	Type	Collation	Null	Default	Extra
meta_value	longtext	utf8_general_ci	Yes	NULL	

For more information on this plugin, make sure to check out the wiki on GitHub (*http://bit.ly/p2p-wiki*).

Members

Members (*http://bit.ly/members-wp*) extends the control that you have over user roles and capabilities in your site. It enables you to edit as well as create and delete user roles and capabilities. This plugin also allows you to set permissions for different user roles to determine which roles have the ability to add, edit, and/or delete various pieces of content. This is another must-have plugin for building an extensible web application because you can completely customize each user's experience by defining and managing the roles and capabilities he will have access to.

W3 Total Cache

Caching your content is a great idea for optimizing the performance of your website. You can save a lot of processing time by displaying cached pages to the end user instead of querying the database every time someone requests data. W3 Total Cache (*http://bit.ly/w3-cache*) has a lot of built-in features for managing what content gets cached and when the cache should be cleared.

Premium Plugins

Although there are a lot of great free plugins out there, there are also some premium plugins that are definitely worth the money. These plugins are usually available for purchase for one-time use, and some also offer developer licences that allow you to purchase the plugin for installation on multiple WordPress sites.

Gravity Forms

This plugin (*http://www.gravityforms.com/*) is an absolute must because it enables you to easily create custom contact forms for your site. It is extremely easy to create a form using the visual form editor, which allows you to drag and drop the fields you need into the form and reposition them as needed. Standard fields are included as well as the option to create your own custom fields. The forms are very flexible and can be set up as multiple page forms with progress bars. Conditional fields allow you to show or hide fields based on the user's selections in previous fields. Another great feature of this plugin is the ability for the forms, once completed, to be forwarded anywhere as chosen by the site admin in the form settings. All in all, this plugin is extremely useful and flexible for anyone needing to create a form on their site and easy to use for someone without coding knowledge.

Backup Buddy

The Backup Buddy plugin (*http://bit.ly/backup-b*) provides you with the opportunity to back up your entire WordPress install for safekeeping, restoring, or moving your site. Backups can be scheduled on a recurring basis, and the file can then be downloaded to your computer, emailed to you, or sent off to the storage location of your choice, such as Dropbox or an FTP server. This plugin also features a restore option that will easily restore your themes, widgets, and plugins. The plugin also allows you to easily move your site to a new server or domain right from the WordPress dashboard, which comes in handy if you work on a dev server and then move the sites over to a production environment upon launch.

WP All Import

This plugin (*http://www.wpallimport.com/*) comes in handy if you are looking to import data into WordPress from another source that is in either an XML or CSV file, which are two formats not routinely accepted by WordPress. There is also a pro or premium version of the plugin available for purchase that extends the functionality to allow you to import data into custom post types as well as custom fields. The pro version also allows you to import images from a URL and have them saved in the media library. Another helpful feature is the ability to set up recurring imports that will periodically check a file for changes or updates and then modify the corresponding post as needed.

Community Plugins

You can build a full-blown social network with WordPress and a few free plugins. Social networks are great to bring a niche community together. If you have an active social network, you will have lots of organic content being indexed by search engines. If you think you get a lot of comments and interaction on your existing WordPress website, try turning it into a social network to really get the conversions flowing.

BuddyPress

BuddyPress (*http://buddypress.org*) is social networking in a box. You can start up a social network with most of the same features as Facebook in a matter of minutes.

You can download BuddyPress from the plugin repository like you would any other plugin, or you can get it from the BuddyPress website. This plugin has come a long way since version 1.0 was released in April of 2009. It was originally built by Andy Peatling and only worked on WordPress MU (Multi User) at the time. Automattic saw the potential of a plugin that turns WordPress into a social networking application and started funding the project.

Since version 1.7, BuddyPress has been theme agnostic, meaning you can turn it on and it will work with any theme—well, most themes—if coded properly. Prior to version 1.7 (see Figure 3-2), you needed to use a BuddyPress theme in order to properly use the plugin. This was good for people wanting to build a social network from scratch because they could use the default theme that comes with BuddyPress, purchase a nice premium BuddyPress child theme, or plan to build their own BuddyPress child theme. It was kind of limiting to people that already had a WordPress website because they couldn't just turn on BuddyPress and have it work with their existing theme. In most cases, people with existing websites that wanted to turn on BuddyPress needed to do some customization, which is OK for someone who knows CSS, PHP, and how WordPress works. But noncoders would have to hire someone to turn their existing theme (which they may have already paid for) into a BuddyPress child or compatible theme. With newer version of BuddyPress, it just works!

Welcome to BuddyPress 1.9.2

BuddyPress
Version 1.9.2

It's a great time to use BuddyPress! 1.9.2 is our first version with a new component in over two years. Not only that, there are plenty of new features, enhancements, and bug fixes.

Check out the highlights:

Figure 3-2. Welcome to BuddyPress

People with existing websites can now turn on BuddyPress and any of its features and it should work in their existing theme. It is also very easy to override any of the existing styles to tailor the BuddyPress features more to your website. Special thanks to the more recent core contributors, John Jacoby, Boone Gorges, Paul Gibbs, and todo: real name RAY for making BuddyPress what it is today, a theme-independent plugin that turns WordPress into a social network.

Database tables

Unlike a lot of WordPress plugins, BuddyPress creates its own database tables in MySQL. If the original BuddyPress developers were to rewrite the plugin from scratch today, they would probably store activities and notifications as custom posts instead of using custom tables. However, custom post types weren't implemented when the original version of BuddyPress was released and it would take a lot of effort to change that architecture now. The custom tables that store groups and friend relationships between users are much easier to understand and faster to query against that if these kinds of things were stored as some combination of posts, user meta, and taxonomies.

For smaller distributed plugins, it makes sense to avoid custom tables whenever possible because it means there is less overhead for users of the plugin to worry about. However, for plugins specific to your app or plugins that include as much functionality as BuddyPress, custom tables can help to speed up or better organize your data. We've included the schema for each BuddyPress table here (Table 3-3 through Table 3-18) as an example of how you might go about structuring custom tables for your own apps and also to help you understand how BuddyPress data is stored in case you would like to query for that information directly.

Table 3-3. DB schema for wp_bp_activity table

Column	Type	Collation	Null	Default	Extra
id	bigint(20)		No	None	AUTO_INCREMENT
user_id	bigint(20)		No	None	
component	varchar(75)	utf8_general_ci	No	None	
type	varchar(75)	utf8_general_ci	No	None	
action	text	utf8_general_ci	No	None	
content	longtext	utf8_general_ci	No	None	
primary_link	varchar(255)	utf8_general_ci	No	None	
item_id	bigint(20)		No	None	
secondary_item_id	bigint(20)		Yes	NULL	
date_recorded	datetime		No	None	
hide_sitewide	tinyint(1)		Yes	0	
mptt_left	int(11)		No	0	
mptt_right	int(11)		No	0	
is_spam	tinyint(1)		No	0	

Table 3-4. DB schema for wp_bp_activity_meta table

Column	Type	Collation	Null	Default	Extra
id	bigint(20)		No	None	AUTO_INCREMENT
activity_id	bigint(20)		No	None	
meta_key	varchar(255)	utf8_general_ci	Yes	NULL	
meta_value	longtext	utf8_general_ci	Yes	NULL	

Table 3-5. DB schema for wp_bp_friends table

Column	Type	Collation	Null	Default	Extra
id	bigint(20)		No	None	AUTO_INCREMENT
initiator_user_id	bigint(20)		No	None	
friend_user_id	bigint(20)		No	None	
is_confirmed	tinyint(1)		Yes	0	
is_limited	tinyint(1)		Yes	0	
date_created	datetime		No	None	

Table 3-6. DB schema for wp_bp_groups table

Column	Type	Collation	Null	Default	Extra
id	bigint(20)		No	None	AUTO_INCREMENT
creator_id	bigint(20)		No	None	
name	varchar(100)	utf8_general_ci	No	None	
slug	varchar(200)	utf8_general_ci	No	None	
description	longtext	utf8_general_ci	No	None	
status	varchar(100)	utf8_general_ci	No	Public	
enable_forum	tinyint(1)		No	1	
date_created	datetime		No	None	

Table 3-7. DB schema for wp_bp_groups_groupmeta table

Column	Type	Collation	Null	Default	Extra
id	bigint(20)		No	None	AUTO_INCREMENT
group_id	bigint(20)		No	None	
meta_key	varchar(255)	utf8_general_ci	Yes	NULL	
meta_value	longtext	utf8_general_ci	Yes	NULL	

Table 3-8. DB schema for wp_bp_groups_members table

Column	Type	Collation	Null	Default	Extra
id	bigint(20)		No	None	AUTO_INCREMENT

Column	Type	Collation	Null	Default	Extra
group_id	bigint(20)		No	None	
user_id	bigint(20)		No	None	
inviter_id	bigint(20)		No	None	
is_admin	tinyint(1)		No	0	
is_mod	tinyint(1)		No	0	
user_title	varchar(100)	utf8_general_ci	No	None	
date_modified	datetime		No	None	
comments	longtext	utf8_general_ci	No	None	
is_confirmed	tinyint(1)		No	0	
is_banned	tinyint(1)		No	0	
invite_sent	tinyint(1)		No	0	

Table 3-9. DB schema for wp_bp_messages_messages table

Column	Type	Collation	Null	Default	Extra
id	bigint(20)		No	None	AUTO_INCREMENT
thread_id	bigint(20)		No	None	
sender_id	bigint(20)		No	None	
subject	varchar(200)	utf8_general_ci	No	None	
message	longtext	utf8_general_ci	No	None	
date_sent	datetime		No	None	

Table 3-10. DB schema for wp_bp_messages_notices table

Column	Type	Collation	Null	Default	Extra
id	bigint(20)		No	None	AUTO_INCREMENT
subject	varchar(200)	utf8_general_ci	No	None	
message	longtext	utf8_general_ci	No	None	
date_sent	datetime		No	None	
is_active	tinyint(1)		No	0	

Table 3-11. DB schema for wp_bp_messages_recipients table

Column	Type	Collation	Null	Default	Extra
id	bigint(20)		No	None	AUTO_INCREMENT
user_id	bigint(20)		No	None	
thread_id	bigint(20)		No	None	
unread_count	int(10)		No	0	
sender_only	tinyint(1)		No	0	

Column	Type	Collation	Null	Default	Extra
is_deleted	tinyint(1)		No	0	

Table 3-12. DB schema for wp_bp_notifications table

Column	Type	Collation	Null	Default	Extra
id	bigint(20)		No	None	AUTO_INCREMENT
user_id	bigint(20)		No	None	
item_id	bigint(20)		No	None	
secondary_item_id	bigint(20)		Yes	NULL	
component_name	varchar(75)	utf8_general_ci	No	None	
component_action	varchar(75)	utf8_general_ci	No	None	
date_notified	datetime		No	None	
is_new	tinyint(1)		No	0	

Table 3-13. DB schema for wp_bp_user_blogs table

Column	Type	Collation	Null	Default	Extra
id	bigint(20)		No	None	AUTO_INCREMENT
user_id	bigint(20)		No	None	
blog_id	bigint(20)		No	None	

Table 3-14. DB schema for wp_bp_user_blogs_blogmeta table

Column	Type	Collation	Null	Default	Extra
id	bigint(20)		No	None	AUTO_INCREMENT
blog_id	bigint(20)		No	None	
meta_key	varchar(255)	utf8_general_ci	Yes	NULL	
meta_value	longtext	utf8_general_ci	Yes	NULL	

Table 3-15. DB schema for wp_bp_xprofile_data table

Column	Type	Collation	Null	Default	Extra
id	bigint(20)		No	None	AUTO_INCREMENT
field_id	bigint(20)		No	None	
user_id	bigint(20)		No	None	
value	longtext	utf8_general_ci	No	None	
last_updated	datetime		No	None	

Table 3-16. DB schema for wp_bp_xprofile_fields table

Column	Type	Collation	Null	Default	Extra
id	bigint(20)		No	None	AUTO_INCREMENT

Column	Type	Collation	Null	Default	Extra
group_id	bigint(20)		No	None	
parent_id	bigint(20)		No	None	
type	varchar(150)	utf8_general_ci	No	None	
name	varchar(150)	utf8_general_ci	No	None	
description	longtext	utf8_general_ci	No	None	
is_required	tinyint(1)		No	0	
is_default_option	tinyint(1)		No	0	
field_order	bigint(20)		No	0	
option_order	bigint(20)		No	0	
order_by	varchar(15)	utf8_general_ci	No		
can_delete	tinyint(1)		No	1	

Table 3-17. DB schema for wp_bp_xprofile_groups table

Column	Type	Collation	Null	Default	Extra
id	bigint(20)		No	None	AUTO_INCREMENT
name	varchar(150)	utf8_general_ci	No	None	
description	mediumtext	utf8_general_ci	No	None	
group_order	bigint(20)		No	0	
can_delete	tinyint(1)		No	None	

Table 3-18. DB schema for wp_bp_xprofile_meta table

Column	Type	Collation	Null	Default	Extra
id	bigint(20)		No	None	AUTO_INCREMENT
object_id	bigint(20)		No	None	
object_type	varchar(150)	utf8_general_ci	No	None	
meta_key	varchar(255)	utf8_general_ci	Yes	NULL	
meta_value	longtext	utf8_general_ci	Yes	NULL	

Components

After activating BuddyPress, head on over to the Components panel in Settings → BuddyPress or */wp-admin/options-general.php?page=bp-components* to set up what components you would like to use. See Figure 3-3 for an illustration of the panel.

You will see the following components:

Extended Profiles
> Just like any typical social network, BuddyPress has member profiles. A member can join and have complete control of her own profile. Out of the box, all members

are listed in a members directory; once you click on a member, you will be taken to her profile page.

Account Settings

Members can update their email address, change their password, and even manage the email notifications they will receive when other members interact with them.

Friend Connections

Members can add each other as friends. When one member requests to be friends with another, the other member will receive a friend request. Think Facebook friends.

Private Messaging

Members can send private messages to each other and view all of their messages in one place, like an inbox for your social network. Members can reply, mark as read, delete, and perform other actions with messages you might expect with any large social network.

Activity Streams

Members can post activity updates to their profiles and groups, leave comments on other members' or groups' activity, and favorite any activity post. Sounds kind of like Facebook, right? BuddyPress has an @mention feature that is kind of like when someone mentions you on Twitter. @mentions are automatically linked to the mentioned member's profile page, and if that member doesn't have his notifications turned off, he will receive an email about it. Activity also comes standard with RSS feeds.

User Groups

A very powerful component of BuddyPress, groups can be created organically (or not) by network members. Each group is listed on a Groups listing page, and clicking on that group's avatar brings you to that group's profile page. The group profile is set up very similar to the member profile page, but with group-specific subpages like group activity, members, admin settings, and invite friends. Groups can be public, private, or hidden and members can be promoted to group admins or group moderators.

Site Tracking

Any new posts and comments on your site will create BuddyPress activity posts. If you are running BuddyPress on a WordPress multisite network, any posts and comments created on any site in your network will also create BuddyPress activity posts.

All of these core BuddyPress components can be extended with BuddyPress plugins. It can be a little confusing if you are new to all of this, but you can install additional plugins specific to BuddyPress or build your own. There are approximately 485 WordPress plugins that extend or integrate with BuddyPress in one way or another.

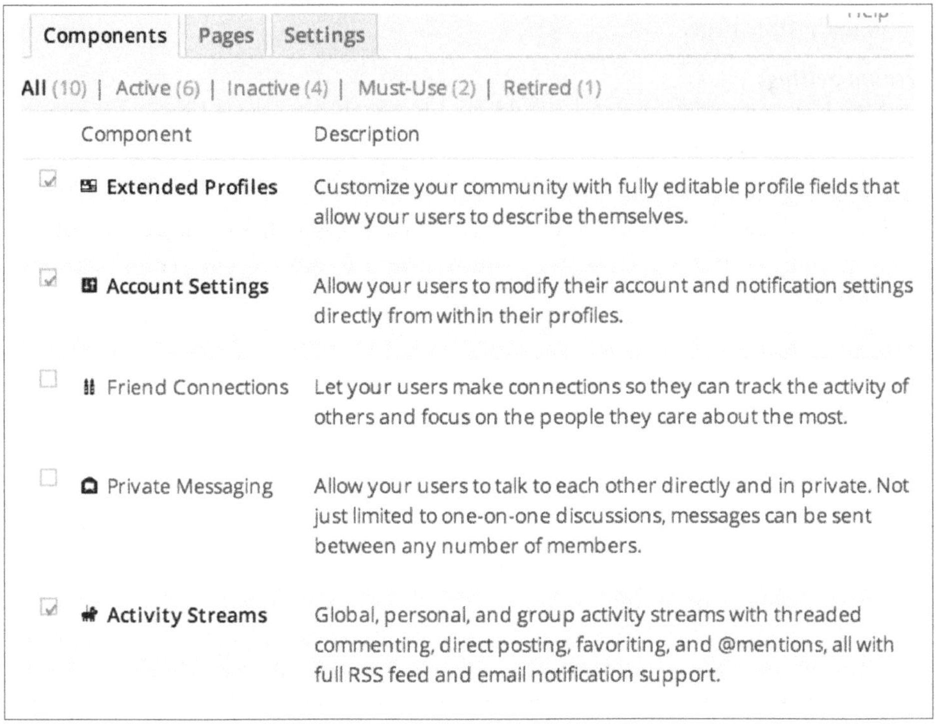

Figure 3-3. BuddyPress components

Pages

Once you have decided which core components you want to use, go to the Pages tab at Settings → BuddyPress → Pages (shown in Figure 3-4). BuddyPress maps the components it is using to new or existing pages. By default, BuddyPress will try to make a new page for each component. If you wanted to call members "Students" instead of "Members," you could create a regular WordPress page called "Students" and map the members component to this new page. The same goes for other BuddyPress components. You will notice two pages that need to be created for member registration, Register and Activate. You will need to map both of these to pages if you wish to have open registration on your social network.

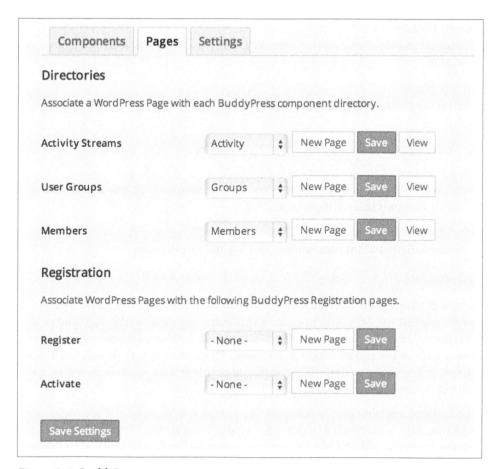

Figure 3-4. BuddyPress pages

To allow open registration, you will also have to make sure that anyone can register; check the "Anyone can register" checkbox under Settings → General.

Settings

In the Settings panel (Settings → BuddyPress → Settings) or */wp-admin/admin.php?page=bp-settings*, you can configure some additional BuddyPress settings:

Toolbar

By default, BuddyPress shows the WordPress admin bar with a Login and Register link for non-logged-in users. If you would like to turn this off, you can do so here.

Account Deletion
  You can decide if you want to allow registered users to be able to delete their accounts.

Avatar Uploads
  Allow registered members to upload avatars.

Profile Syncing
  Enable BuddyPress to WordPress profile syncing.

Group Creation
  Allow your registered members to create their own groups. Site admins can still create groups if this setting is turned off.

Blog & Forum Comments
  Allow activity stream commenting on blog and forum posts.

Profile fields

Located at Users → Profile Fields or */wp-admin/users.php?page=bp-profile-setup*, this BuddyPress feature allows you to create any number of profile field groups and profile fields for your members. You can collect data such as location, date of birth, likes, dislikes, favorite color, and/or whatever you want. This feature is very flexible in allowing you to organize your profile fields into different profile groups, all of which will be made available on any member's frontend profile page.

When adding any new profile field, you are provided with a slick UI for deciding to make your new field required or not, what type of form element it should be, what the default visibility is, and whether you want your members to be able to decide if they can change the visibility for the field. This form is shown in Figure 3-5.

 By default, all of the profile fields in the "Base" profile group will show up on the registration page.

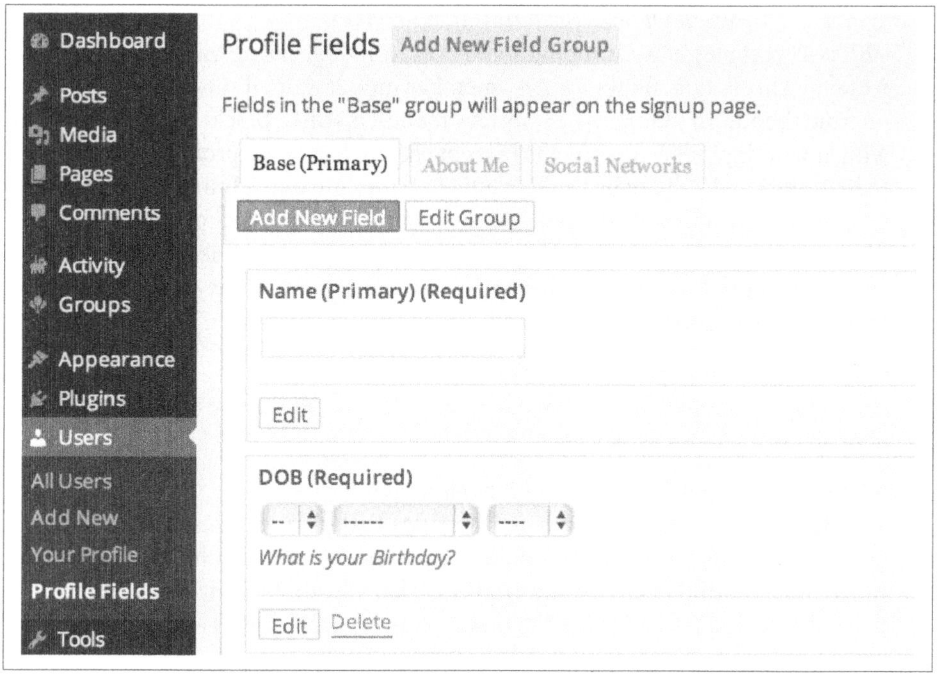

Figure 3-5. BuddyPress profile fields

BuddyPress plugins

As you can see, BuddyPress is a very intuitive and easy-to-use plugin. We talked briefly about installing additional BuddyPress specific plugins. Below is a quick list of some cool BuddyPress plugins so you can get an idea of how BuddyPress can be extended:

BuddyPress Toolbar (http://bit.ly/bp-toolbar)
> Adds a BuddyPress menu to the existing WordPress admin menu. This is a great plugin for administering your BuddyPress web application.

BuddyPress FollowMe (http://bit.ly/bp-follow)
> Allows your members to follow each other. This is kind of like the built-in friending functionality but more like a Twitter or Instagram approach where a member can follow other members that they are interested in. Each member will be able to see in her profile all of the activity of the other members she's following.

BuddyPress Media (http://bit.ly/bp-rtmedia)
> This plugin allows your members to upload photos, music, and videos to their activity posts. It also allows for your members to organize all of their photos into photo albums on their profile page. There is mobile device support that includes automatic audio and video conversion.

BuddyPress Registration Options (http://bit.ly/bp-regis)

This is a great plugin for stopping spam bots from registering on your BuddyPress website! This plugin allows for new member moderation, if moderation is turned on from the admin settings page; any new members will be blocked from interacting with any BuddyPress components (except editing their own profile and uploading their avatar) and will not be listed in any directory until an administrator approves or denies their account. If moderation is turned on, admins can create custom display messages and email alert messages for approved or denied accounts. When an admin approves or denies, custom emails get sent out to new members telling them they were approved or denied.

BuddyMobile (http://bit.ly/buddymobile)

This plugin automatically provides a slick UI for BuddyPress when browsing your site from a mobile device.

BadgeOS Community Add-on (http://bit.ly/badgeos)

The BadgeOS Community Add-on integrates BadgeOS features into BuddyPress and bbPress. Site members complete achievements and earn badges based on a range of community activity and triggers. This add-on to BadgeOS also includes the ability to display badges and achievements on user profiles and activity feeds.

bbPress (http://bbpress.org/)

Got forums? bbPress can fulfill all of your forum needs. Unlike BuddyPress, bbPress utilizes custom post types, so it does not create its own tables in the database like it used to in prior versions.

Using bbPress can require a bit of theme work if your theme isn't already styled to support bbPress, but it is by far the easiest way to add forum functionality to a WordPress site.

## CHAPTER 4

Themes

WordPress themes drive the frontend of your web app. In Chapter 1, we presented the analogy that WordPress themes are like views in a traditional MVC framework. The analogy isn't perfect by any means, but themes and views are similar in that they both control the way your app will look and are where your designers will spend most of their time.

NThe WordPress community has put together a Theme Developer Handbook (*http://bit.ly/theme-handb*) that is the definitive source for learning how to build themes for WordPress in a standards-based way. All theme developers should use that resource. This chapter will cover areas of theme development especially important to app developers.

Themes Versus Plugins

At some level, all source files in your themes and plugins are just *.php* files loaded at different times by WordPress. In theory, your entire app code could reside in one theme or one plugin. In practice, you'll want to reserve your theme for code related to the frontend (views) of your website and use plugins for your app's backend (models and controllers).

Where you decide to put some code will depend on whether you are primarily building a full app or an individual plugin or theme.

When Developing Apps

If you are building a full web app, basically one install of WordPress, you will have full access to the site and what themes and plugins are installed. Your code could go anywhere. Even so, you should follow *some* thought process when deciding if a particular feature should be coded as a module of your app's plugin or theme or as a separate plugin.

The main benefactor of your good planning at this step will be your developers (maybe just you). Properly organizing your code is going to make it easier for you to maintain your app and develop it further.

When building apps, we try to use the following guidelines:

- One main plugin to store the core app code, and one theme to manage the frontend code.
- Any modular functionality that could be useful on other projects or potentially replaced by another plugin should be coded as a separate plugin.
- Never hack the core![1]

So what is core app code and what is frontend code? Again our pseudo-MVC framework looks like this:

Plugins = Models
All of your code-defining data structures, business logic, and AJAX services should go into the core plugin. Things like definitions for custom post types and taxonomies, form processing, and class wrappers for the Post and User classes should go in your core plugin.

Themes = Views
All of your templating code and frontend logic should go in your theme. The frame of your website, header, footer, menu, and sidebars should be coded in your theme. Simple logic like if(is_user_logged_in()) { //show menu } else { //show login } should go into your theme.

One thing to consider when deciding where to code features is your development team. If your team consists of one person, you're going to know what decision you make. If you have a separate designer and programmer, you should be more inclined to put things the designer is going to be concerned with in the theme and things the programmer is going to be concerned with in the core plugin. Even if you have to wiggle a little bit, having things clearly separated like that will make it easier for your developers to find what they are looking for.

When Developing Plugins

If you are building a plugin to be used on other websites or modular features that can be used across projects, it makes sense to keep your code within one plugin. In these cases, you can store template files inside your plugin to handle the UI components. It

---

1. If you find that you *must* hack the core to get something to work, first reconsider if you really need to hack the core. If you do need to change a core WordPress file, add hooks instead and submit those hooks as a patch to the next version of WordPress.

is common practice to allow these files to be overwritten by the active WordPress theme, which will be covered later in this chapter.

When Developing Themes

Similarly, if you are developing a theme to be distributed that relies on custom post types or another customization that would typically be coded in a plugin, it might make sense to include that inside your theme instead. If your users must activate a plugin before your theme works at all, you might as well move the plugin code into your theme. If your theme makes large underlying changes to WordPress, consider putting that plugin-like code into a parent theme and putting your design-related code into a child theme. That way if your users want to change their site's design without losing the other functionality provided by a theme, they can do so more easily.

On the other hand, if code you are about to add to your theme is not crucial to the theme working or there are other plugins that could be used as alternatives for your code, you should move that code into a plugin and distribute your theme as a bundle including the themes and recommended plugins. As an example, many premium themes add SEO-related fields to the edit post page to manage page titles, meta description, and meta keywords. This makes sense, since these SEO-related fields represent a kind of view that is seen by Google and other web crawlers. However, there are a few really popular plugins that do this same functionality, and it's hard to argue that your theme wouldn't work without the SEO functionality installed. We would recommend theme developers put their SEO functionality into plugins or otherwise make it easy to disable so other plugins can be used.

In the end, the decision of where to put what code and how to package things should be based on your users, both end users and developers who will be using your themes and plugins. Part of the beauty of WordPress is that it is flexible in terms of the ways you can go about customizing it. There are no strict rules. Consider everything you read about this topic (including from us) as guidelines. If moving some code from a plugin file to a theme file will make it easier to work with, do it.

The Template Hierarchy

When a user visits your site and navigates to a page, WordPress uses a system called the *Template Hierarchy* to figure out which file in the active theme should be used to render the page. For example, if the user browses to a single post page, WordPress will look for *single-post.php*. If that's not found, it will look for *single.php*. If that's not found it will look for *index.php*.

The *index.php* file is the fallback for all page loads and along with *style.css* is the only required file for your theme. More typically, you will have a list of files like:

- *404.php*
- *author.php*
- *archive.php*
- *attachment.php*
- *category.php*
- *comments.php*
- *date.php*
- *footer.php*
- *front-page.php*
- *functions.php*
- *header.php*
- *home.php*
- *image.php*
- *index.php*
- *page.php*
- *search.php*
- *sidebar.php*
- *single.php*
- *single-(post-type).php*
- *style.css*
- *tag.php*
- *taxonomy.php*

Some files in this list are loaded when you call a specific `get` function. For example, `get_header()` loads *header.php*, `get_footer()` loads *footer.php*, and `get_sidebar()` loads *sidebar.php*. Passing a `name` parameter to these functions will add it to the filename loaded; so, for example, `get_header('alternate');` will load *header-alternate.php* from the theme folder.

The function `comments_template()` will load *comments.php* unless you pass a different filename as the first parameter.

The function `get_search_form()` will look for the file *searchform.php* in your theme folder or output the default WordPress search form if no file is found.

WordPress has good documentation for the Template Hierarchy (*http://bit.ly/temp-hier*), which lays out all the various files WordPress will look for in a theme folder when they are loaded. You can also take a look at the Twenty Twelve Theme (*http://bit.ly/2012-theme*) or some other well-coded theme to see what filenames are going to be detected by WordPress. Read the comments in those themes to see when each page is loaded.

When developing apps with custom post types, it's common to want to use a different template when viewing your post types on the frontend. You can override the single post and archive view for your post types by adding files with the names *single-(post_type).php* and *archive-(post_type).php*, where *(post_type)* is set to the value used when the post type was registered.

Page Templates

One of the easiest ways to get arbitrary PHP code running on a WordPress website is to build a page template into your theme and then use that template on one of your pages.

Some common templates found in WordPress themes include contact forms and landing page forms.

Sample Page Template

Example 4-1 is a pared-down version of a contact form template that you can drop into your theme's folder.

Example 4-1. Sample page template

```php
<?php
/*
Template Name: Page - Contact Form
*/

//get values possibly submitted by form
$email = sanitize_email( $_POST['email'] );
$cname = sanitize_text_field( $_POST['cname'] );
$phone = sanitize_text_field( $_POST['phone'] );
$message = sanitize_text_field( $_POST['message'] );
$sendemail = !empty( $_POST['sendemail'] );

// form submitted?
if ( !empty( $sendemail )
    && !empty( $cname )
        && !empty( $email )
        && empty( $lname ) ) {

        $mailto = get_bloginfo( 'admin_email' );
        $mailsubj = "Contact Form Submission from " . get_bloginfo( 'name' );
        $mailhead = "From: " . $cname . " <" . $email . ">\n";
```

```php
        $mailbody = "Name: " . $cname . "\n\n";
        $mailbody .= "Email: $email\n\n";
        $mailbody .= "Phone: $phone\n\n";
        $mailbody .= "Message:\n" . $message;

        // send email to us
        wp_mail( $mailto, $mailsubj, $mailbody, $mailhead );

        // set message for this page and clear vars
        $msg = "Your message has been sent.";

        $email = "";
        $cname = "";
        $phone = "";
        $message = "";
}
elseif ( !empty( $sendemail ) && !is_email( $email ) )
        $msg = "Please enter a valid email address.";
elseif ( !empty( $lname ) )
        $msg = "Are you a spammer?";
elseif ( !empty( $sendemail ) && empty( $cname ) )
        $msg = "Please enter your name.";
elseif ( !empty( $sendemail ) && !empty( $cname ) && empty( $email ) )
        $msg = "Please enter your email address.";

// get the header
get_header();
?>
<div id="wrapper">
 <div id="content">
 <?php if ( have_posts() ) : while ( have_posts() ) : the_post(); ?>
  <h1><?php the_title(); ?></h1>
  <?php if ( !empty( $msg ) ) { ?>
   <div class="message"><?php echo $msg?></div>
  <?php } ?>
  <form class="general" action="<?php the_permalink(); ?>" method="post">
   <div class="form-row">
        <label for="cname">Name</label>
        <input type="text" name="cname" value="<?php echo esc_attr($cname);?>"/>
        <small class="red">* Required</small>
   </div>
   <div class="hidden">
        <label for="lname">Last Name</label>
        <input type="text" name="lname" value="<?php echo esc_attr($lname);?>"/>
        <small class="red">LEAVE THIS FIELD BLANK</small>
   </div>
   <div class="form-row">
        <label for="email">Email</label>
        <input type="text" name="email" value="<?php echo esc_attr($email);?>"/>
        <small class="red">* Required</small>
   </div>
   <div class="form-row">
```

```
        <label for="phone">Phone</label>
        <input type="text" name="phone" value="<?php echo esc_attr($phone);?>"/>
    </div>
    <div class="form-row">
        <label for="message">Question or Comment</label>
        <textarea class="textarea" id="message" name="message" rows="4" cols="55">
            <?php echo esc_textarea( $message )?>
        </textarea>
    </div>

    <div class="form-row">
        <label for="sendemail"> </label>
        <input type="submit" id="sendemail" name="sendemail" value="Submit"/>
    </div>
  </form>
 <?php endwhile; endif; ?>
 </div>
</div>
<?php
// get the footer
get_footer();
?>
```

WordPress will scan all *.php* files in your active theme's folder and subfolders (and the parent theme's folder and subfolders) for templates. Any file with a comment including the phrase `Template Name:` in it will be made available as a template.

The template is loaded after the WordPress `init` and `wp` actions have already fired. The theme header and the `wp_head` action will not load until you call `get_header()` in your template. So you can use the top of your template file to process form input and potentially redirect before any headers are sent to the page.

Your template file will need to include the same HTML markup as your theme's *page.php* or single post template. In the preceding example, I include a wrapper div and content div around the content of the contact form.

The preceding code has a few other notable features. It uses the `sanitize_text_field()` and `sanitize_email()` functions to clean up values submitted by the form. Similarly, it uses the `esc_attr()` and `esc_textarea()` functions to prevent cross-site scripting attacks. These functions are covered more in Chapter 8.

The preceding contact form also incorporates a "honey pot." A field called "lname" would be hidden using CSS. So normal users would not see this field and thus leave it blank when submitting the form. Bots looking to take advantage of your contact form to send you spam will see the lname field and will put some value into it. The code processing the form checks to make sure that the lname field is blank before sending out the email. Like a honey pot drawing bees to it, the hidden lname field draws spammers into it so you don't end up sending email on their behalf.

Using Hooks to Copy Templates

If you'd rather not change multiple template files when you update the ID or class names of your wrapper divs, you can create a template that uses the `the_content` filter or another action specific to your theme to place content into the main content area of your page. Then you can load another template file, like the core *page.php* template, which will include calls to load your site's frame and default layout. Example 4-2 shows how to create a page template that loads the *page.php* template and adds additional content below it on certain pages.

Example 4-2. Hooking template

```php
<?php
/*
    Template Name: Hooking Template Example
*/

//what's the main post_id for this page?
global $post, $main_post_id;
$main_post_id = $post->ID;

//use the default page template
require_once(dirname(__FILE__) . "/page.php");

//now add content using a function called during the the_content hook
function template_content($content)
{
    global $post, $main_post_id;

    //we don't want to filter posts that aren't the main post
    if($post->ID != $main_post_id)
        return $content;

    //capture output
    ob_start();
    ?>
    <p>This content will show up under the page content.</p>
    <?php
    $temp_content = ob_get_contents();
    ob_end_clean();

    //append and return template content
    return $content . $temp_content;
}
add_action("the_content", "template_content");
```

In the previous example, we do a little trick to store the main post ID in a global variable. Typically the global $post will be the main post of the page you have navigated to. However, other loops on your page will temporarily set the global $post to whatever post they are dealing with at the time. For example, if your template uses a WordPress menu, that is really a loop through posts of type "menu." Many sidebars and footer sections will loop through other sets of posts.

So at any given moment (like when trying to filter the the_content hook) you can't be sure which post is set in the global $post. At the start of the template file, we know we are not in a loop, and the global $post will be the same as the page you are currently viewing. So we can copy the ID into another global variable to remember. Later on in the template_content function, we check if the $post we are filtering has the same ID as the main post. If not, we just return the content. If we are filtering the main post, we add our template section to the end of it.

You can also insert your own hook into your *page.php* and other core templates to do something similar. Just add something like do_action('my_template_hook'); at the point in your page template where you'd like to add in extra content.

When to Use a Theme Template

In Chapter 3, we covered a way to use shortcodes to create pages for your plugins. The shortcodes are useful because they allow you to add CMS-managed content above and below the shortcode in the post content field and keep your code organized within your plugin.

So if you are distributing a plugin and need that page template to go along with it, you should use the shortcode method to generate your page.

Similarly, if you are distributing a theme by itself, any templates needed for the theme will need to be included within the theme folder. You could include code for shortcode-based templates within your theme, but templates are a more standard way of templating a page.

And finally, if your template needs to alter the HTML of your default page layouts, you will want to use a template file inside of your theme. Example 4-2 piggybacks on the *page.php* template to avoid having to rewrite the wrapping HTML. But if the whole point of the template is to rewrite the wrapping HTML (e.g., with a landing page template where you want to hide the default header, footer, and menu), then you definitely need to use a template.

Theme-Related WP Functions

Next we'll discuss get_template_part($slug,$name = null); the get_tem plate_part() function can be used to load other *.php* files (template parts) into a file in your theme.

According to the Codex, $slug refers to "the slug name for the generic template," and $name refers to "the name of the specialized template." In reality, both parameters are simply concatenated with a dash to form the filename looked for: *slug-name.php*.

The Twenty Twelve theme uses get_template_part() to load a specific post format "content" part into the WordPress loop:

```
<?php /* Start the Loop */ ?>
<?php while ( have_posts() ) : the_post(); ?>
        <?php get_template_part( 'content', get_post_format() ); ?>
<?php endwhile; ?>
```

If your template part is in a subfolder of your theme, add the folder name to the front of the slug:

```
get_template_part('templates/content', 'page');
```

The get_template_part() function uses the locate_template() function of WordPress to find the template part specified, which then loads the file using the load_template() function. locate_template() first searches within the child theme. If no matching file is found in the child theme, the parent theme is searched.

Besides searching both the child and parent themes for a file, the other benefit to using get_template_part() over a standard PHP include or require call is that a set of WordPress global variables are set up before the file is included. Here is the source for the load_template() function from WordPress 3.6, showing the global variables that are set. Notice that the query_vars array is also extracted into the local scope:

```
<?php
function load_template( $_template_file, $require_once = true ) {
        global $posts, $post, $wp_did_header, $wp_query, $wp_rewrite;
        global $wpdb, $wp_version, $wp, $id, $comment, $user_ID;

        if ( is_array( $wp_query->query_vars ) )
                extract( $wp_query->query_vars, EXTR_SKIP );

        if ( $require_once )
                require_once( $_template_file );
        else
                require( $_template_file );
}
?>
```

Using locate_template in Your Plugins

A common design pattern used in plugins is to include templates in your plugin folder and allow users to override those templates by adding their own versions to the active theme. For example, in SchoolPress, teachers can invite students to their class. The invite form is stored in a template within the plugin:

```
//schoolpress/templates/invite-students.php
?>
<p>Enter</p>
<form action="" method="post">
        <label for="email">Email:</label>
<input type="text" id="email" name="email" value="" />
        <input type="submit" name="invite" value="Invite Student" />
</form>
```

SchoolPress is envisioned as a software as a service application, but we also plan to release a plugin version for others to use on their own sites. Users of the plugin may want to override the default template without editing the core plugin since any edits to the core plugin, would be overwritten when the plugin was upgraded.

To enable users of our plugin to override the invite template, we'll use code like the following when including the template file:

```
//schoolpress/shortcodes/invite-students.php
function sp_invite_students_shortcode($atts, $content=null, $code="")
{
        //start output buffering
ob_start();

        //look for an invite-students template part in the active theme
        $template = locate_template("schoolpress/templates/invite-students.php");

        //if not found, use the default
        if(empty($template))
                $template = dirname(__FILE__) .
            "/../templates/invite-students.php";

        //load the template
        load_template($template);

        //get content from buffer and output it
        $temp_content = ob_get_contents();
        ob_end_clean();
        return $temp_content;
}
add_shortcode("invite-students", "sp_invite_students_shortcode");
```

The preceding code uses our shortcode template from Chapter 3. But instead of embedding the HTML directly into the shortcode function, we load it from a template file. We first use `locate_template()` to search for the template in the active child and parent themes. Then if no file is found, we set `$template` to the path of the default template bundled with the plugin. The template is loaded using `load_template()`.

Style.css

The *style.css* file of your theme must contain a comment used by WordPress to track the theme's version and other information to show in the WordPress dashboard. Here is the comment from the top of *style.css* in the Twenty Thirteen theme:

```
/*
Theme Name: Twenty Thirteen
Theme URI: http://wordpress.org/themes/twentythirteen
Author: the WordPress team
Author URI: http://wordpress.org/
Description: The 2013 theme for WordPress takes us back to the blog,
featuring a full range of post formats, each displayed beautifully in their
own unique way. Design details abound, starting with a gorgeous color scheme and
matching header images, optional display fonts for beautiful typography, and a
wide layout that looks great on large screens yet remains device-agnostic
and is readable on any device.
Version: 0.1
License: GNU General Public License v2 or later
License URI: http://www.gnu.org/licenses/gpl-2.0.html
Tags: black, brown, orange, tan, white, yellow, light, one-column, two-columns,
right-sidebar, flexible-width, custom-header, custom-menu, editor-style,
featured-images, microformats, post-formats, rtl-language-support,
sticky-post, translation-ready
Text Domain: twentythirteen


This theme, like WordPress, is licensed under the GPL.
Use it to make something cool, have fun, and share what you've learned
with others.
*/
```

The *style.css* file of the active theme (and parent theme if applicable) is automatically enqueued by WordPress.

Versioning Your Theme's CSS Files

It's good practice to set a version for your CSS files when loading them through wp_en queue_style(). This way, if you update your CSS, you can update the version as well and avoid having your site's users see a seemingly broken site using a version of the stylesheet cached by the browser.

When WordPress enqueues your theme's *style.css* file for you, it uses the overall WordPress version when loading the stylesheet. The line output in your site's head tag will look like this:

```
<link rel='stylesheet'
        id='twentytwelve-style-css'
        href='.../wp-content/themes/twentytwelve/style.css?ver=3.5.2'
        type='text/css'
        media='all' />
```

Updates to the stylesheet, your app's version number, or even the version number set in the *style.css* comment won't update the version added to the stylesheet when enqueued. It will always match the WordPress version number.

One solution is to remove all CSS from your *style.css* file into other CSS files in your theme and load *those* CSS files through wp_enqueue_style() calls in the theme's *functions.php* file. It would look like this for *style.css*:

```
/*
    Theme Name: SchoolPress
    Version: 1.0

    That's it! All CSS can be found in the "css" folder of the theme.
*/
```

and like this for *functions.php*:

```php
<?php
define( 'SCHOOLPRESS_VERSION', '1.0' );
function sp_enqueue_theme_styles() {
        if ( !is_admin() ) {
                wp_enqueue_style( 'schoolpress-theme',
                        get_stylesheet_directory_uri() . '/css/main.css',
                        NULL,
                        SCHOOLPRESS_VERSION
                );
        }
}
add_action( 'init', 'sp_enqueue_theme_styles' );
?>
```

A constant like SCHOOLPRESS_VERSION would typically be defined in our main plugin file, but it's included here for clarity. The preceding code will load our new */css/ main.css file* with the main app version appended so new versions of the app won't conflict with browser-cached stylesheets.

There is another way to change the version of the main *style.css* file without moving it to another file entirely. We use the wp_default_styles filter. This filter passes an object containing the default values used when a stylesheet is enqueued. One of those values is the default_version, which can be changed like so:

```
define('SCHOOLPRESS_VERSION', '1.0');
function sp_wp_default_styles($styles)
{
    //use release version for stylesheets
        $styles->default_version = SCHOOLPRESS_VERSION;
}
add_action("wp_default_styles", "sp_wp_default_styles");
```

Now our main stylesheet will be loaded using the SchoolPress app version instead of the main WordPress version. We can keep our CSS in *style.css* if we want to, though it's often a good idea to move at least some parts of the CSS into separate files in a "css" folder of your theme:

```
<link rel='stylesheet'
      id='twentytwelve-style-css'
      href='.../wp-content/themes/twentytwelve/style.css?ver=1.0'
      type='text/css'
      media='all' />
```

Functions.php

The *functions.php* file of your active theme (and parent theme if applicable) is loaded every time WordPress loads. For this reason, the *functions.php* file is a popular place to add little hacks and other random bits of code. On a typical WordPress site, the *functions.php* file can quickly become a mess.

However, we're developing a well-planned WordPress app, and *our function.php* files don't have to be a mess. Just like we break up the core functions of our main app plugin into smaller includes, you should do the same with your theme's *functions.php*. You could add files similar to the following to your theme's folder:

- */includes/functions.php*—Where you really place helper functions.
- */includes/settings.php*—For code related to theme settings and options.
- */includes/sidebars.php*—To define sidebars/widget areas.

Additionally, make sure that code you are adding to your theme's *functions.php* is related to the frontend display of your site. Code that applies to the WordPress dashboard, backend processing for your app, or your entire app in general should most likely be added somewhere within the main app plugin.

Themes and Custom Post Types

Custom post types are just posts, so by default, your CPTs will be rendered using the *single.php* template or *index.php* if no *single.php* template were available.

Custom post types, including specifying templates for them, are covered in more detail in Chapter 5.

Popular Theme Frameworks

There are a lot of theme frameworks, both WordPress-specific frameworks and general-purpose HTML/CSS frameworks, that you can use when building apps with Word-Press. Whether you intend to use the theme framework to build a quick proof of concept or to use it as a core component of your custom-built theme, using a theme framework can save you a lot of time.

We'll briefly cover some popular theme frameworks and dive deeper into how to use two of the most popular theme frameworks used in WordPress app development.

But first, what does a theme framework provide?

WP Theme Frameworks

WordPress theme frameworks are themes that are meant to be used as parent themes or starter themes to jumpstart your frontend development. Theme frameworks will typically include basic styles and layouts for blog posts, archives, pages, sidebars, and menus. Some are heavier or lighter weight than others. Some include CSS classes, shortcodes, and other handy bits of code to help you create new layouts and add UI elements to your pages. All frameworks are likely to save you a lot of time.

There are two reasons to choose one theme framework over another. You either choose a child theme that visually looks very close to your vision for your app or you choose a framework that is coded in a way that feels right when working with it.

_s (Underscores)

_s (pronounced "underscores") is a starter theme published by Automattic that has all the common components you need in a WordPress theme. Unlike most other frameworks, _s is not meant to be used as a parent theme. It's meant to be used as a starting point for your own parent theme. All of the themes developed by Automattic for Word-Press.com are based on the _s theme.

To use _s, you should download the code and change the directory name and all references to _s with the name of your theme. There are good instructions for doing this in the project's readme file (*http://bit.ly/s-readme*) or, even better, a tool to do it for you automatically on the underscores website (*http://www.underscores.me*).

The stylesheet in _s is very minimal with no real styling, just a bit of code for layout and some common readability and usability settings.

_s is best for designers who are able to and want to build their own theme from scratch. It's basically code you would have to write somehow for your theme yourself. The _s code is not abstracted as heavily as some of the other theme frameworks, and so using the framework should be easier to pick up for designers more familiar with HTML and CSS than PHP.

StartBox

StartBox is a theme framework written by Brian Richards and maintained by Brian Messenlehner's company WebDevStudios that is focused on providing "valid markup and dynamically generated classes and IDs throughout the entire layout"[2] that makes it easier to control the look and feel of the theme through CSS. Or stated another way, customizing a StartBox theme will require less tweaking of the underlying HTML markup than needed when customizing other themes.

StartBox is meant to be used as a parent theme. You can write your own child theme that inherits it or you can use one of the child themes provided by StartBox. As stated before, the theme dynamically generates useful CSS classes on elements in the theme to help you style certain sections and pages. The theme also provides many shortcodes, widgets, hooks, and filters that can be used to build out your pages and customize the default functionality of the parent theme.

StartBox is best for designer-developers and really our choice for starting themes based on its balance of framework support on the design and coding side of theme development.

Genesis

Genesis is a theme framework developed by StudioPress and used in over 40 child themes published by StudioPress and in many more themes published by third-party designers.

Like StartBox, the Genesis theme is meant to be used as a parent theme. StudioPress has child themes that are appropriate across a number of business and website types. Or you can create your own child theme that inherits from Genesis.

The Genesis framework abstracts the underlying HTML and CSS more than the other frameworks listed here. We find this makes it a little harder to work with when doing larger customizations. However, Genesis would be a good choice if you find one of their child themes is 80% of the way toward the look you want or if you find their framework easier to work with than other options.

Non-WP Theme Frameworks

In addition to WordPress theme frameworks, there are also application UI frameworks that provide markup, stylesheets, and images for common UI patterns and elements. Some popular UI frameworks include Twitter Bootstrap (*http://getbootstrap.com/*), Zurb's Foundation (*http://foundation.zurb.com/*), and Gumby (*http://gumbyframe work.com*).

Incorporating a UI framework into your theme can be as easy as copying a few files into the theme folder and enqueueing the stylesheets and JavaScript, and will give you easy

---

2. This quote is taken from the StartBox about page (*http://wpstartbox.com/about/*).

access to styled UI elements like buttons, tabs, pagination, breadcrumbs, labels, alerts, and progress bars.

Below we'll cover how to add Bootstrap assets into a StartBox child theme, but the same process should work for other combinations of WordPress themes and UI frameworks.

Creating a Child Theme for StartBox

To create your theme, you'll need to follow these steps:

1. Create a new folder in your *wp-content/themes* folder, for example, *startbox-child*.

2. Create a *style.css* file in the *startbox-child* folder.

3. Paste the following into your *style.css* file:

```
/*
THEME NAME: StartBox Child
THEME URI: http://bwawwp.com/wp-content/themes/startbox-child/
DESCRIPTION: StartBox Child Theme
VERSION: 0.1
AUTHOR: Jason Coleman
AUTHOR Uri: http://bwawwp.com
TAGS: startbox, child, tag
TEMPLATE: startbox
*/
@import url("../startbox/style.css");
```

   The key field in the comment is the TEMPLATE field, which needs to match the folder of the parent theme, in this case *startbox*. The only required file for a child theme is *style.css*. So at this point, you've created a child theme.

   You can either copy all of the CSS from the parent theme's *style.css* into the child theme's *style.css* and edit what you want to or you can use @import_url like we do above to import the rules from the parent theme's stylesheet and add more rules below to override the parent theme's styles.

   In order to enqueue the bootstrap files, you will also need a *functions.php* file.

4. Create an empty *functions.php* file in the *startbox-child* folder for now.

Including Bootstrap in Your App's Theme

In general, importing Bootstrap into the StartBox theme is kind of silly compared to finding a theme based on Bootstrap or just copying in the CSS rules you need. However, importing frameworks and libraries into your theme is something you might run into. The following will give you an idea of how to go about importing other libraries and frameworks into your theme.

Download the Bootstrap ZIP file (*http://getbootstrap.com*) into your *startbox-child* folder. After unzipping it, you will have a *dist* folder containing the CSS and JS files for bootstrap. You can rename this folder to *bootstrap* and delete the Bootstrap ZIP file. Your child theme folder should look like this now:

- *startbox-child*
  — *bootstrap*
     — *css*
     — *js*
  — *functions.php*
  — *style.css*

Now we will enqueue the Bootstrap CSS and JS by adding this code into the *functions.php* file inside your child theme:

```php
<?php
function startbox_child_init() {
        wp_enqueue_style(
                'bootstrap',
                get_stylesheet_directory_uri() .
        '/bootstrap/css/bootstrap.min.css',
                'style',
                '3.0'
        );
        wp_enqueue_script(
                'bootstrap',
                get_stylesheet_directory_uri() .
        '/bootstrap/js/bootstrap.min.js',
                'jquery',
                '3.0'
        );
}
add_action( 'init', 'startbox_child_init' );
?>
```

Note that we set the dependencies for the Bootstrap CSS to `style`, which will make sure that the Bootstrap stylesheet loads after the StartBox stylesheet. We also set the Bootstrap JS to depend on `jquery` and set the version of both files to `3.0` to match the version of Bootstrap used.

At this point you could use any of your favorite Bootstrap styles or JavaScript in your WordPress theme. Many of the Bootstrap styles for columns and layout aren't being used in the StartBox markup (StartBox has its own layout system), and so they won't be applicable to your theme. But the styles for form elements and buttons would be useful for app developers.

Menus

Menus are an important part of most apps, and apps often have special needs for their menus that other websites don't have.

Some apps have multiple menus. Many mobile apps have a main navigational menu at the top and a toolbar-like menu along the bottom.

Some apps have dynamic menus. Many apps have different menus or menu items for logged-in users than for logged-out users. Menu items can be based on a user's membership level or admin capabilities.

Before we get into how to build more complicated menus and navigational elements with WordPress, lets cover the standard way to add a menu to your theme.

Nav Menus

Since WordPress version 3.0, there has been a standard method for adding navigation menus to themes. This involved registering the menu in the theme's code, designating where in the theme the menu is going to appear, and then managing the menu through the WordPress dashboard.

The main benefit to using the built-in menu functionality in WordPress is that end users can control the content of their menus using the GUI in the dashboard. Even if you are a developer with full control over your app, it is still a good idea to use the built-in menus in WordPress since you may have stakeholders who would want to manage menus or you may want to distribute you theme to others in the future. The WordPress navigation menus are also very easy to reposition and can take advantage of other code using menu-related hooks or CSS styles.

To register a new navigational menu, use the `register_nav_menu($location, $de scription)` function. The `$location` parameter is a unique slug used to identify the menu. The `$description` parameter is a longer title for the menu shown in the drop-down in my menu tool in the dashboard:

```
register_nav_menu("main", "Main Menu");
```

You can also register many menus at once using the `register_nav_menus()` (with an s) variant. This function accepts an array of locations where the keys are the `$loca tion` slugs and the values are the `$description` titles:

```
register_nav_menus(array(
        "main" => "Main Menu",
        "logged-in" => "Logged-In Menu"
));
```

To place a navigational menu into your theme, use the `wp_nav_menu()` function:

```
wp_nav_menu( array('theme_location' => 'main' ));
```

The theme_location parameter should be set to the $location set with regis
ter_nav_menu(). The wp_nav_menu() function can take many other parameters to
change the behavior and markup of the menu. The WordPress Codex page on Navigation Menus (*http://bit.ly/nav-codex*) is a good resource on the various parameters to the
wp_nav_menu() function and other ways to customize menus. We cover some of our
favorite recipes in the following sections.

Dynamic Menus

There are two main methods to make your WordPress menus dynamic so that different
menu items show up on different pages or different circumstances. The first is to set up
two menus and load a different menu in different cases. Here is a code example from
the Codex showing how to show a different menu to logged-in users and logged-out
users:

```
if ( is_user_logged_in() ) {
    wp_nav_menu( array( 'theme_location' => 'logged-in-menu' ) );
} else {
    wp_nav_menu( array( 'theme_location' => 'logged-out-menu' ) );
}
```

The other way to make your menu dynamic is to use the nav_menu_css_class filter to
add extra CSS classes to specific menu items. Then you can use CSS to hide/show certain
menu items based on their CSS class.

Say you want to remove a login link from a menu when you are on the login[3] page. You
could use code like this:

```
function remove_login_link($classes, $item)
{
        f(is_page('login') && $item->title == "Login")
                $classes[] = "hide";    //hide this item

        return $classes;
}
add_filter("nav_menu_css_class", "sp_nav_menu_css_class", 10, 2);
```

Another way to customize the markup of your menus is to use a Custom Walker class.
Custom Walker classes are covered in Chapter 7.

---

3. You could check $_SERVER['PHP_SELF'] to see if you are on the *wp-login.php* page. In this example, we
   assume our login is on a WordPress page with the slug "login."

Responsive Design

We could write a whole book about responsive design. Luckily for us, many people already have, including Clarissa Peterson, who wrote *Learning Responsive Web Design* (O'Reilly). The general concept behind responsive design is somehow detecting properties of the client device and adjusting your apps layout, design, and functionality to work best for that device. We will cover a few different techniques for doing this here.

Device and Display Detection in CSS

The main method of device detection in CSS is *media queries*. Media queries are used in stylesheets or added as a property of the `<link>` tag used to embed a stylesheet to limit the scope of the CSS rules inside of the stylesheet to a particular media type or cases where a particular media feature is available.

Mozilla has a good document (*http://mzl.la/css-mq*) explaining media queries and listing the various properties and operators you can use to construct a media query.

A common use of media queries is to hide certain elements and adjust font and element sizes when someone is printing. Here is how you would specify that media query in a `<link>` tag, inside of a stylesheet, and through a `wp_enqueue_style` call:

```
<link rel="stylesheet" media="print" href="example.css" />

<style>
@media print
{
        .hide-from-print {display: none;}
        .show-when-printing {display: auto;}
}
</style>

<?php
        wp_enqueue_style('example', 'example.css', NULL, '1.0', 'print');
?>
```

A more typical example in the responsive design world is to check for a `min-width` and/ or `max-width` in the media query to adjust styles as the screen gets smaller or larger. The following is an example from the Bootstrap responsive stylesheet that adjusts CSS rules for screens between 768 and 979 pixels, which is the width of a typical browser window on a modern monitor. Sizes above 979 pixels could be considered extra wide:

```
@media (min-width: 768px) and (max-width: 979px) {
  .hidden-desktop {
    display: inherit !important;
  }
  .visible-desktop {
    display: none !important ;
  }
```

```
.visible-tablet {
  display: inherit !important;
}
.hidden-tablet {
  display: none !important;
}
}
```

Another common task handled with media queries is to change styles, and specifically swap images, when a browser has a Retina[4] screen.

Here is a mix of media queries used in some of the WordPress dashboard CSS to detect a high-resolution display. The queries test against pixel ratio and DPI. Values vary from display to display, but most standard definition displays will have a 1:1 pixel ratio and 96 DPI. A Retina display has a pixel ratio of 2:1 and DPI of 196 or higher, but we can test for minimal values somewhere between standard definition and Retina-level definition to catch other high-resolution displays:

```
@media(-o-min-device-pixel-ratio: 5/4),          /* Opera */
      (-webkit-min-device-pixel-ratio: 1.25),    /* Webkit */
      (min-resolution: 120dpi) {                  /* Others */
          /* add your high res CSS here */
      }
```

Media queries are powerful and can be used to make UIs that are very flexible. Browsers and CSS standards are constantly evolving. It's important to stay on top of things so the latest phones, tablets, and monitors will show your app the way you intend.

Which properties to look out for and how to adjust your stylesheet to accommodate them is outside the scope of this book, but hopefully you get the idea and understand how to incorporate media queries into your WordPress themes.

Device and Feature Detection in JavaScript

Your app's JavaScript can also benefit from device and feature detection. jQuery offers methods to detect the window and screen sizes and other information about the browser. Many HTML5 features that may or may not be available in a certain browser can be tested before being put to use.

Detecting the screen and window size with JavaScript and jQuery

JavaScript makes the width and height of the screen available in the `screen.width` and `screen.height` properties. You can also use `screen.availWidth` and `screen.avail Height` to get the available width and height, which accounts for pixels taken up by toolbars and sidebar panels in the browser window.

---

4. Retina is a brand name that Apple for their high-resolution displays. However, the term "Retina" is often used in code comments and documentation to refer to any high-resolution display.

If you are already using jQuery, you can use the `width()` method on any element on your page to get its width, but you can also use it on the `$(document)` and `$(window)` objects to get the width of the document and window, respectively. You can also use the `height()` property on the document and window objects and any element on your page.

The values for `$(window).width()` and `$(window).height()` should be the same as `screen.availWidth` and `screen.availHeight`, namely the available size of the browser viewport minus any toolbars or sidebar panels, or more accurately how much room you have for displaying HTML.

The width and height of the `$(document)` will return the total scrollable width and height of your rendered web page.

When using the width and height in your JavaScript code, you will often want to update things if the window size changes. This can happen if someone resizes a browser window on their desktop, rotates a phone from portrait to landscape, or any number of things that could change the width or height of the window. jQuery offers an easy way to detect these changes so you can update your layout accordingly:

```
//bind an event to run when the window is resized
jQuery(window).resize(function() {
width = jQuery(window).width();
height = jQuery(window).height();
//update your layout, etc
});
```

You can bind a resize event to any element, not just the full window. Elements on your page might grow and contract as a user interacts with your page, possibly adding elements through AJAX forms or dragging resizable elements on the screen, or otherwise moving things around.

Feature detection in JavaScript

When building a modern app UI using HTML5 features, you will sometimes want to detect if a certain HTML5 feature is unavailable so you can provide an alternative or fallback. Mark Pilgrim's *Dive into HTML5* (*http://diveintohtml5.info*) has a good list of general methods for detecting HTML5 features:

1. Check if a certain property exists on a global object (such as window or navigator).
2. Create an element, then check if a certain property exists on that element.
3. Create an element, check if a certain method exists on that element, then call the method and check the value it returns.
4. Create an element, set a property to a certain value, then check if the property has retained its value.

If you only need to do one such detection, some of the examples on the Dive into HTML5 website will give you an idea of how to roll your own bit of detection. If you need to do a lot of feature detection, a library like Modernizr.js (*http://modernizr.com*) will help.

To use Modernizr.js, grab the version of the script you need from the website (Modernizr offers a tool on its site that will ask you which parts of the script you need and then generate a minimized *.js* file containing only those bits) and place it in your theme or plugin folder and enqueue it:

```php
<?php
function sp_wp_footer_modernizr() {
        wp_enqueue_script(
                'modernizr',
                get_stylesheet_directory_uri() . '/js/modernizr.min.js'
        );?>
        <script>
                //change search inputs to text if unsupported
                if(!Modernizr.inputtypes.search)
                        jQuery('input[type=search]').attr('type', 'text');
        </script>
        <?php
}
add_action( 'wp_footer', 'sp_wp_footer_modernizr' );
?>
```

The Modernizr documentation (*http://bit.ly/modern-doc*) contains a list of features detectable with Modernizr.js.

jQuery also provides a similar set of checks limited to things that jQuery needs to check itself through the `jQuery.support` object. If a check you are trying to do is done by jQuery already, you can avoid the overhead of Modernizr.js by using the jQuery check. A list of features flags set by `jQuery.support` can be found on the jQuery website (*http://bit.ly/jquery-doc*):

```javascript
jQuery(document).ready(function() {
        //only load AJAX code if AJAX is available
        if(jQuery.support.ajax)
        {
                //AJAX code goes here
        }
});
```

Device Detection in PHP

Device detection in PHP is based on the `$_SERVER['HTTP_USER_AGENT']` global created by PHP. This value is set by the browser itself and so is definitely not standardized, often misleading, and potentially spoofed by web crawlers and other bots. It's best to avoid PHP-based browser detection if you can by making your code as standards based as possible and using the CSS and JavaScript methods described for feature detection.

If you want a general idea of the kind of browser accessing your app, the user agent string is the best we have.

Here is a simple test script echoing the user agent string and an example of what one will look like:

```php
<?php
echo $_SERVER['HTTP_USER_AGENT'];

/*
        Outputs something like:
        Mozilla/5.0 (Macintosh; Intel Mac OS X 10_8_4)
        AppleWebKit/537.36 (KHTML, like Gecko) Chrome/28.0.1500.95 Safari/537.36
*/
?>
```

This user agent string includes some useful information, but perhaps too much. There are no fewer than five different browser names in that string. So which browser is it? Mozilla, KHTML, Gecko, Chrome, or Safari? In this case, I was running Chrome on a MacBook Air running OS X.

Did I already mention that there is no standard for the user agent string browsers will send? Historically, browsers include the names of older browsers to basically say, "I can do everything this browser does, too."

A funny summary of the history of various user agent strings can be found at WebAIM (*http://bit.ly/webaim-history*), including this bit explaining the pedigree of the Chrome browser.

> And then Google built Chrome, and Chrome used Webkit, and it was like Safari, and wanted pages built for Safari, and so pretended to be Safari. And thus Chrome used WebKit, and pretended to be Safari, and WebKit pretended to be KHTML, and KHTML pretended to be Gecko, and all browsers pretended to be Mozilla, and Chrome called itself Mozilla/5.0 (Windows; U; Windows NT 5.1; en-US) AppleWebKit/525.13 (KHTML, like Gecko) Chrome/0.2.149.27 Safari/525.13, and the user agent string was a complete mess, and near useless, and everyone pretended to be everyone else, and confusion abounded.
>
> — Aaron Anderson

Browser detection in WordPress core

Luckily, WordPress has done a bit of the work behind parsing the user agent string and exposes some global variables and a couple of methods that cover the most common browser detection–related questions.

The following globals are set by WordPress in *wp-includes/vars.php*:

- $is_lynx
- $is_gecko

- $is_winIE
- $is_macIE
- $is_opera
- $is_NS4
- $is_safari
- $is_chrome
- $is_iphone
- $is_IE

And for detecting certain servers, we have the following:

- $is_apache
- $is_IIS
- $is_iis7

Finally, you can use the wp_is_mobile() function, which checks for the word "mobile" in the user agent string as well as a few common mobile browsers.

Here is a quick example showing how you might use these globals to load different scripts and CSS:

```php
<?php
function sp_init_browser_hacks() {
        global $is_IE;
        if ( $is_IE ) {
                //check version and load CSS
                $user_agent = strtolower( $_SERVER['HTTP_USER_AGENT'] );
                if ( strpos( 'msie 6.', $user_agent ) !== false &&
                        strpos( 'opera', $user_agent ) === false ) {
                        wp_enqueue_style(
                                'ie6-hacks',
                                get_stylesheet_directory_uri() . '/css/ie6.css'
                        );
                }
        }

        if ( wp_is_mobile() ) {
                //load our mobile CSS and JS
                wp_enqueue_style(
                        'sp-mobile',
                        get_stylesheet_directory_uri() . '/css/mobile.css'
                );
                wp_enqueue_script(
                        'sp-mobile',
                        get_stylesheet_directory_uri() . '/js/mobile.js'
                );
```

```
        }
}
add_action( 'init', 'sp_init_browser_hacks' );
?>
```

Browser detection with PHP's get_browser()

PHP actually has a great function for browser detection built in: get_browser(). Here
is a simple example calling get_browser() and displaying some typical results:

```
<?php
$browser = get_browser();
print_r($browser);

/*
        Would produce output like:

        stdClass Object (
[browser_name_regex] => §^mozilla/5\.0 \(.*intel mac os x.*\)
applewebkit/.* \(khtml, like gecko\).*chrome/28\..*safari/.*$§
[browser_name_pattern] => Mozilla/5.0 (*Intel Mac OS X*)
AppleWebKit/* (KHTML, like Gecko)*Chrome/28.*Safari/*
[parent] => Chrome 28.0
[platform] => MacOSX
[win32] =>
[comment] => Chrome 28.0
[browser] => Chrome
[version] => 28.0
[majorver] => 28
[minorver] => 0
[frames] => 1
[iframes] => 1
[tables] => 1
[cookies] => 1
[javascript] => 1
[javaapplets] => 1
[cssversion] => 3
[platform_version] => unknown
[alpha] =>
[beta] =>
[win16] =>
[win64] =>
[backgroundsounds] =>
[vbscript] =>
[activexcontrols] =>
[ismobiledevice] =>
[issyndicationreader] =>
[crawler] =>
[aolversion] => 0
)
*/
```

This is pretty amazing stuff! So why is this function last in the section on detecting a browser with PHP? The answer is that the `get_browser()` function is unavailable or out of date on most servers. To get the function to give you useful information, or in most cases work at all, you need to download an up-to-date *browscap.ini* file and configure PHP to find it. If you are distributing your app, you'll want to use a different method to detect browser capabilities. However, if you are running your own app on your own servers, `get_browser()` is fair game.

An up-to-date *browscap.ini* file can be found at the Browser Capabilities Project website (*http://bit.ly/browsercap*). Make sure you get one of the files formatted for PHP. We recommend the *lite_php_browscap.ini* file, which is half the size but contains info on the most popular browsers.

Once you have the *.ini* file on your server, you'll need to update your *php.ini* file to point to it. Your *php.ini* file probably has a line for browscap commented out. Uncomment it and make sure it's pointing to the location of the *.ini* file you downloaded. It should look something like this:

```
[browscap]
browscap = /etc/lite_php_browscap.ini
```

Now restart your web server (apache, Nginx, etc.) and `get_browser()` should be working.

Final Note on Browser Detection

We spent a lot of space here on browser detection, but in practice it should be used as a last resort. When a certain browser is giving you pain with a piece of design or functionality, it is tempting to try to detect it and code around it. However, if it's possible to find another workaround that gets a similar result without singling out specific browsers, it's usually better to go with that solution.

For one, as we've seen here, the user agent string has no standards, and your code to parse it may have to be updated regularly to account for new browsers and browser versions.

Second, in some cases, a browser-specific issue is a symptom of a bigger problem in your code. There may be a way to simplify your design or functionality to work better across multiple browsers, devices, and screen sizes.

The goal with responsive design and programming is to build something that will be flexible enough to account for all of the various browsers and clients accessing your app, whether you know about them or not.

Versioning CSS and JS Files

When you call `wp_enqueue_script()` or `wp_enqueue_style()`, you can pass a version number. This version number is tacked on to the end of the filename and prevents the browser or web client from using a cached version of the script or stylesheet when the version is updated. For example, here is the `wp_enqueue_style()` call from our preceding Bootstrap example and the HTML generated by it:

```php
<?php
// load our stylesheet
wp_enqueue_style(
        'bootstrap',
        get_stylesheet_directory_uri() . '/bootstrap/css/bootstrap.min.css',
        'style',
        '3.0'
);

// and this shows up in the head section of the site (note the 3.0)
/*
<link rel='stylesheet'
id='bootstrap-css'
href='/wp-content/themes/startbox-child/bootstrap/css/bootstrap.min.css?ver=3.0'
type='text/css'
media='all' />
*/
```

A good idea is to define a constant to store the version of your plugin, theme, or app and use that as the version parameter to your enqueue calls. That way you only have to update your version in one place if you've done a lot of work.

There is, however, one stylesheet that you won't be able to version this way and that is the *style.css* found in your theme or child theme. This stylesheet is automatically enqueued by WordPress, and the version attached to it is the version of WordPress you are running.

You don't want to update the WordPress version every time you update your theme, but you do want to update the version of *style.css* if you change that file. There are two ways to get around this issue:

1. You can empty out your *style.css* and load all of your stylesheets through `wp_en queue_stylesheet` calls. This way you can specify your own version.

2. You can use the `wp_default_styles` action to change the default version used when enqueueing a stylesheet without a set version. The `$styles` object is passed by reference to this action, and so you only need to edit the object itself and don't need to (and really shouldn't) return the `$styles` object like you would in a typical filter:

```php
function sp_wp_default_styles($styles)
{
```

```
            //use our app version constant
            $styles->default_version = SCHOOLPRESS_VERSION;
}
add_action("wp_default_styles", "sp_wp_default_styles");
```

## CHAPTER 5

Custom Post Types, Post Metadata, and Taxonomies

Custom post types (CPTs) are what really make WordPress a content management system. With CPTs, you can quickly build out custom functionality and store data in a consistent way.

Default Post Types and Custom Post Types

With a default installation of WordPress, you have several post types already being used. The post types you may be most familiar with are pages and posts, but there are a few more. These post type values are all stored in the database `wp_posts` table, and they all use the `post_type` field to separate them.

Page

WordPress pages are what you use for your static content pages like home, about, contact info, bio, or any custom page you want. Pages can be indefinitely nested under each other in any hierarchical structure. Pages can also be sorted by `menu_order` value.

Post

Your posts are your blog or news or whatever you want to call your constant barrage of content to be indexed by search engines on the Internet. You can categorize your posts, tag them with keywords, set publish dates, and more. In general, posts are shown in some kind of list view in reverse chronological order on the frontend of your website.

Attachment

Any time you upload an image or file to a post, it stores the file not only on the server but also as a post in the wp_posts table with a post_type attachment.

Revisions

WordPress has your back and saves your posts as revisions every time you or anyone edits a post. This feature is on by default and can be used to revert your content back to what it was if something got messed up along the way.

Sometimes the wp_posts table gets flooded with post revisions if your application is set up to make a lot of post_content changes, so you may want to limit the amount of revisions stored in the wp_posts table. To do this, put the following code in your *wp-config.php* file: define('WP_POST_REVISIONS', 5); The number 5 is the number of revision posts to store for a given post. A value of 0 will turn off post revisions. A value of true or -1 will store an infinite number of revisions (it can take a lot of disk space to store infinity something).

Nav Menu Item

Every time you build a custom menu using the WordPress core menu builder (wp-admin → appearance → menus) you are storing posts with information for your menus.

Defining and Registering Custom Post Types

Just like the default WordPress post types, you can create your own CPTs to manage any data you need, depending on what you are building. Every CPT is really just a post used differently. You could register a custom post type for a dinner menu at a restaurant, for cars for an auto dealer, for people to track patient information and documents at a doctors office, or for pretty much anything you can think of. No, really any type of content you can think of can be stored as a post with attached files, custom metadata, and custom taxonomies.

In our SchoolPress example, we are going to be building a CPT for managing homework assignments on a teacher's website. Our teacher wants to make a post of some kind where he can add assignments and their students can get to them on the class website. He also wants to be able to upload supporting documents and have commenting available in case any of his students has questions. A CPT sounds in order, doesn't it?

We can store this information the same way posts are dealt with and display them to the end user in the theme using the same wp_query loop we would with posts.

register_post_type($post_type, $args);

You can register a CPT with the function `register_post_type()`, and in most cases, you are going to register your CPT in your theme's *functions.php* file or in a custom plugin file. This function expects two parameters: the name of the post type you are creating and an array of arguments:

- $post_type—The name of your custom post type; in our example, our custom post type name is "homework." This string must be no longer than 20 characters and can't have capital letters, spaces, or any special characters except a hyphen or an underscore.
- $args—This is an array of many different arguments that will dictate how your custom post type will be set up. The following is a list of all of the available arguments and what they are used for.

label

The display name of your post type. In our example, we use "Homework."

labels

An optional array of labels to use for describing your post type throughout the user interface:

- *name*—The plural display name of your post type. This will override the label argument.
- *singular_name*—The singular name for any particular post. This defaults to the name if not specified.
- *add_new*—Defaults to the string "Add New."
- *add_new_item*—Defaults to "Add New Post."
- *edit_item*—Defaults to "Edit Post."
- *new_item*—Defaults to "New Post."
- *view_item*—Defaults to "View Post."
- *search_items*—Defaults to "Search Posts."
- *not_found*—Defaults to "No Posts Found."
- *not_found_in_trash*—Defaults to "No posts found in Trash."
- *parent_item_colon*—Defaults to "Parent Page:" and is only used on hierarchical post types.
- *all_items*—Defaults to "All Posts."

menu_name

The menu name for the post type, usually the same as `label` or `labels->name`.

description

An optional string that describes your post type.

publicly_queryable

An optional Boolean that specifies if queries on your post type can be run on the frontend or theme of your application. By default, `publicly_queryable` is turned on.

exclude_from_search

An optional Boolean that specifies if your post type posts can be queried and displayed in the default WordPress search results. This is off by default so that your posts will be searchable.

capability_type

An optional string or array. If not specifically defined, `capability_type` will default to `post`. You can pass in a string of an existing post type, and the new post type you are registering will inherit that post type's capabilities. You can also define your own capability type, which will set default capabilities for your custom post type for reading, publishing, editing, and deleting. You can also pass in an array if you want to use different singular and plural words for your capabilities. For example, you can just pass in the string "homework" since the singular and plural forms for "homework" are the same, but you would pass in an array like `array( 'submission', 'submissions' )` when the forms are different.

capabilities

An optional array of the capabilities of the post type you are registering. You can use this instead of `capability_type` if you want more granular control over the capabilities you are assigning to your new custom post type.

There are two types of capabilities: meta and primitive. Meta capabilities are tied to specific posts, whereas primitive capabilities are more general purpose. In practice, this means that when checking if a user has a meta capability, you must pass in a `$post_id` parameter:

```
//meta capabilities are related to specific posts
if(current_user_can("edit_post", $post_id))
{
    //the current user can edit the post with ID = $post_id
}
```

Unlike meta capabilities, primitive capabilities aren't checked against a specific post:

```
//primitive capabilities aren't related to specific posts
if(current_user_can("edit_posts"))
{
   //the current user can edit posts in general
}
```

The capabilities that can be assigned to your custom post type are:

- *edit_post*—A meta capability for a user to edit a particular post.
- *read_post*—A meta capability for a user to read a particular post.
- *delete_post*—A meta capability for a user to delete a particular post.
- *edit_posts*—A primitive capability for a user to be able to create and edit posts.
- *edit_others_posts*—A primitive capability for a user to be able to edit others' posts.
- *publish_posts*—A primitive capability for a user to be able to publish posts.
- *read_private_posts*—A primitive capability for a user to be able to read private posts.
- *read*—A primitive capability for a user to be able to read posts.
- *delete_posts*—A primitive capability for a user to be able to delete posts.
- *delete_private_posts*—A primitive capability for a user to be able to delete private posts.
- *delete_published_posts*—A primitive capability for a user to be able to delete posts.
- *delete_others_posts*—A primitive capability for a user to be able to delete other peoples posts.
- *edit_private_posts*—A primitive capability for a user to be able to edit private posts.
- *edit_published_posts*—A primitive capability for a user to be able to publish posts.

map_meta_cap

Whether to use the internal default meta capability handling (capabilities and roles are covered in Chapter 6). Defaults to false. You can always define your own capabilities using capabilities; but if you don't, setting map_meta_cap to true will make the following primitive capabilities be used by default or in addition to using capability_type:

- *read*
- *delete_posts*
- *delete_private_posts*
- *delete_published_posts*
- *delete_others_posts*

- *edit_private_posts*
- *edit_published_posts*

hierarchical

An optional Boolean that specifies if a post can be hierarchical and have a parent post or not. WordPress pages are set up like this so you can nest pages under other pages. The hierarchical argument is turned off by default.

public

An optional Boolean that specifies if a post type is supposed to be used publicly or not in the backend or frontend of WordPress. By default, this argument is `false`; so without including this argument and setting it to `true`, you wouldn't be able to use this `post_type` in your theme. If you set `public` to `true`, it will automatically set `exclude_from_search`, `publicly_queryable` and `show_ui_nav_menus` to `true` unless otherwise specified.

Most CPTs will be public so they are shown on the frontend or available to manage through the WordPress dashboard. Other CPTs (like the default Revisions CPT) are updated behind the scenes based on other interactions with your app and would have `public` set to `false`.

rewrite

An optional Boolean or array used to create a custom permalink structure for a post type. By default, this is set to `true`, and the permalink structure for a custom post is `/post_type/post_title/`. If set to `false`, no custom permalink would be created. You can completely customize the permalink structure of a post by passing in an array with the following arguments:

slug
> Defaults to the `post_type` but can be any string you want. Remember not to use the same slug in more than one post type because they have to be unique.

with_front
> Whether or not to prepend the "front base" to the front of the CPT permalink. If set to `true`, the slug of the "front page" set on the Settings → Reading page of the dashboard will be added to the permalink for posts of this post type.

feeds
> Boolean that specifies if a post type can have an RSS feed. The default value of this argument is set to the value of the `has_archive` argument. If `feeds` is set to `false`, no feeds will be available.

---

pages

> Boolean that turns on pagination for a post type. If `true`, archive pages for this post type will support pagination.

ep_mask

> EP or endpoints can be very useful. With this argument you assign an endpoint mask for a post type. For instance, we could set up an endpoint for a post type of homework called "pop-quiz." The permalink would look like `/homework/post-title/pop-quiz/`. In MVC terminology, a CPT is similar to a module, and endpoints can be thought of as different views for that module. Endpoints and other rewrite functions are covered in Chapter 7.

has_archive

An optional Boolean or string that specifies if a post type can have an archive page or not. By default this argument is set to `false`, so you will want to set it to `true` if you would like to use it in your theme. The *archive-{post_type}.php* file in your theme will be used to render the archive page. If that file is not available, the *archive.php* or *index.php* file will be used instead.

query_var

An optional Boolean or string that sets the `query_var` key for the post type. This is the name of your post type in the database and used when writing queries to work with this post type. The default value for this argument is set to the value of `post_type` argument. In most cases you wouldn't need your `query_var` and your `post_type` to be different, but you can imagine a long post type name like directory_entry that you would want to use a shorter slug like "dir" for.

supports

An optional Boolean or array that specifies what meta box features will be made available on the new post or edit post page. By default, an array with the arguments of `title` and `editor` are passed in. The following is a list of all of the available arguments:

- title
- editor
- comments
- revisions
- trackbacks
- author
- excerpt

- page-attributes
- thumbnail
- custom-fields
- post-formats

If you plan to use one of these features with your CPT, make sure it is included in the `supports` array.

register_meta_box_cb

An optional string that allows you to provide a custom callback function for integrating your own custom meta boxes.

permalink_epmask

An optional string for specifying which endpoint types you would like to associate with a custom post type. The default rewrite endpoint bitmask is EP_PERMALINK. For more information on endpoints, see Chapter 7.

taxonomies

An optional array that specifies any built-in (categories and tags) or custom registered taxonomies you would like to associate with a post type. By default, no taxonomies are referenced. For more information on taxonomies, please see "Creating Custom Taxonomies" on page 137.

show_ui

An optional Boolean that specifies if the basic post UI will be made available for a post type in the backend. The default value is set to the value of the `public` argument. If `show_ui` is `false`, you will have no way of populating your posts from the backend admin area.

 It's a good idea to set `show_ui` to `true`, even for CPTs that won't generally be added or edited through the admin dashboard. For example, the bbPress plugin adds Topics and Replies as CPTs that are added and edited through the forum UI on the frontend. However, `show_ui` is set to `true`, providing another interface for admins to search, view, and manage topics and replies from.

menu_position

An optional integer used to set the menu order of a post type menu item in the backend, left-side navigation.

The WordPress Codex provides a nice list of common menu position values (*http://bit.ly/reg-post-type*) to help you figure out where to place the menu item for your CPT:

- 5—below Posts
- 10—below Media
- 15—below Links
- 20—below Pages
- 25—below comments
- 60—below first separator
- 65—below Plugins
- 70—below Users
- 75—below Tools
- 80—below Settings
- 100—below second separator

menu_icon

An optional string of a URL to a custom icon that can be used to represent a post type.

can_export

An optional Boolean that specifies if a post type can be exported via the WordPress exporter in Tools → Export. This argument is set to `true` by default, allowing the admin to export.

show_in_nav_menus

An optional Boolean that specifies if posts from a post type can be added to a custom navigation menu in Apperance → Menus. The default value of this argument is set to the value of the public argument.

show_in_menu

An optional Boolean or string that specifies whether to show the post type in the backend admin menu and possibly where to show it. If set to `true`, the post type is displayed as its own item on the menu. If set to `false`, no menu item for the post type is shown. You can also pass in a string of the name of any other menu item. Doing this will place the post type in the submenu of the passed-in menu item. The default value of this argument is set to the value of the `show_ui` argument.

show_in_admin_bar

An optional Boolean that specifies if a post type is available in the WordPress admin bar. The default value of this argument is set to the value of the `show_in_menu` argument.

delete_with_user

An optional Boolean that specifies whether to delete all of the posts for a post type created by any given user. If set to `true`, posts the user created will be moved to the trash when the user is deleted. If set to `false`, posts will not be moved to the trash when the user is deleted. By default, posts are moved to the trash if the argument `post_type_supports` has `author` within it. If not, posts are not moved to the trash.

_builtin

You shouldn't ever need to use this argument. Default WordPress post types use this to differentiate themselves from custom post types.

_edit_link

The URL of the edit link on the post. This is also for internal use, and you shouldn't need to use it. If you'd like to change the page linked to when clicking to edit a post, use the `get_edit_post_link` filter, which passes the default edit link along with the ID of the post.

Example 5-1 illustrates registering new *homework* and *submissions* custom post types using `register_post_type()`. You can find the code for the `register_post_type()` function in *wp-includes/post.php*. Notice that in our example we are only using a few of the many available arguments.

Example 5-1. Registering a custom post type

```php
<?php
// custom function to register a "homework" post type
function schoolpress_register_post_type_homework() {
    register_post_type( 'homework',
        array(
            'labels' => array(
                        'name' => __( 'Homework' ),
                            'singular_name' => __( 'Homework' )
                    ),
                'public' => true,
                'has_archive' => true,
                )
        );
}
// call our custom function with the init hook
add_action( 'init', 'schoolpress_register_post_type_homework' );

// custom function to register a "submissions" post type
```

```
function schoolpress_register_post_type_submission() {
    register_post_type( 'submissions',
        array(
            'labels' => array(
                            'name' => __( 'Submissions' ),
                            'singular_name' => __( 'Submission' )
                    ),
                'public' => true,
                'has_archive' => true,
                )
        );
}
// call our custom function with the init hook
add_action( 'init', 'schoolpress_register_post_type_submission' );
?>
```

If you dropped the preceding code in your active theme's *functions.php* file or an active plugin, you should notice two new menu items on the WordPress admin called "Homework" and "Submissions" under the "Comments" menu item.

 If you get tired of writing your own functions to register the various custom post types that you want to use, you can use this cool plugin called Custom Post Types UI (*http://bit.ly/posttype-ui*).

What Is a Taxonomy and How Should I Use It?

We briefly touched on taxonomies in Chapter 2, but what exactly is a taxonomy? Taxonomies group posts by terms. Think post categories and post tags; these are just built-in taxonomies attached to the default "post" post type. You can define as many custom taxonomies or categories as you want and span them across multiple post types. For example, we can create a custom taxonomy called "Subject" that has all school-related subjects as its terms and is tied to our "Homework" custom post type.

Taxonomies Versus Post Meta

One question you will tackle often when you want to attach bits of data to posts is whether to use a taxonomy or a post meta field (or both). Generally, terms that group different posts together should be coded as taxonomies, while data that is specific to each individual post should be coded as post meta fields.

Post meta fields are good for data that is specific to individual posts and not used to group posts together. In SchoolPress, it makes sense to code things like required assignment length (e.g., 500 words) as a meta field. In practice, there are only going to be a few different lengths used, but we won't ever need to "get all assignments that require 500 words." So a post meta field is adequate for this information.

Taxonomies are good for data that is used to group posts together. In SchoolPress, it makes sense to code things like an assignment's subject (e.g., math or English) as a taxonomy. Unlike assignment length, we will want to run queries like "get all Math assignments." This is easily done through a taxonomy query. More importantly, queries like this will run faster on taxonomy data than they do on meta fields.

Why are taxonomy queries generally faster? Meta fields are stored in the `wp_postmeta`. If we were storing an assignment's due date as a post meta field, it would look like this:

meta_id	post_id	meta_key	meta_value
1	1	due_date	2014-09-07
2	2	due_date	2014-09-14

The `meta_id`, `post_id`, and `meta_key` columns are indexed, but the `meta_value` column is not. This means that queries like "get the due date for this assignment" will run quickly, but queries like "get all assignments due on 2014-09-07" will run slower, especially if you have a large site with lots of data piled into the `wp_postmeta` table. The reason the `meta_value` key is the lone column in `wp_postmeta` without an index is that adding an index here would greatly increase both the storage required for this table and also the insert times. In practice, a site is going to have many different meta values, whereas there will be a smaller set of post IDs and meta keys to build indexes for.

If you stored assignment due dates in a custom taxonomy, the "get all assignments due on this date" query will run much faster. Each specific due date would be a term in the `wp_terms` table with a corresponding entry in the `wp_terms_taxonomy` table. The `wp_terms_relationships` table that attaches terms to posts has both the `object_id` (posts are objects here) and `term_taxonomy_id` fields indexed. So "get all posts with this term_taxonomy_id" is a speedy query.

If you just want to show the due date on the assignment page, you should store it in the post meta fields. If you want to offer a report of all assignments due on a certain date, you should consider adding a taxonomy to track due dates.

On the other hand, due to the nature of due dates (you potentially have 365 new terms each year), using a taxonomy for them might be overkill. You would end up with a lot of useless terms in your database keeping track of which assignments were due two years ago.

Also, in this specific case, the speed increases might be negligible because the due date report is for a subset of assignments within a specific class group. In practice, we won't be querying for assignments by due date across the entire `wp_postmeta` table. We'll filter the query to only run on assignment posts for a specific class. While there may be millions and millions of rows in the `wp_postmeta` table for a SchoolPress site at scale (hundreds of schools, thousands of teachers and classes), there are only going be a few assignments for a specific class or group of classes one student is in.

Another consideration when choosing between meta fields and taxonomies is how that data is going to be managed by users.

If a field is only going to be used in the backend code, and you don't have query speed issues, storing it in post meta is as simple as one call to `update_post_meta()`.

If you'd like admins to be able to create new terms, write descriptions for them, build hierarchies, and use dropdowns or checkboxes to assign them to posts, well then I've just described exactly what you get for free when you register a taxonomy. When using post meta fields, you need to build your own UI into a meta box.

Finally, I did mention earlier that there are times when you want to use both a meta field *and* a taxonomy to track one piece of data. An example of this in the context of the SchoolPress app could be tracking a textbook and chapter for an assignment. Imagine you want a report for a student with all of her assignments organized by textbook and ordered by chapter within those books.

Because you want to allow teachers to manage textbooks as terms in the admin, and you will want to do queries like "get all assignments for this textbook," it makes sense to store textbooks in a custom taxonomy.

On the other hand, chapters can be stored in post meta fields. Chapters are common across books and assignments, but it doesn't make sense to query for "all chapter 1 assignments" across many different textbooks. Since we'll be able to pre-filter to get all assignments by textbook or by student, we can use a chapter meta field, or possibly a textbook_chapter meta field with data like "PrinciplesOfMath.Ch1" to order the assignments for the report.

Phew… now that we've figured out when we'll want to use taxonomies, let's find out how to create them.

Creating Custom Taxonomies

You can register your own taxonomies with the function `register_taxonomy()`, which is found in *wp-includes/taxonomy.php*.

register_taxonomy($taxonomy, $object_type, $args)

The `register_taxonomy()` function accepts the following three parameters:

- $taxonomy—A required string of the name of your taxonomy. In our example, our taxonomy name is "subject."

- $object_type—A required array or string of the custom post type(s) you are attaching this taxonomy to. In our example, we are using a string and attaching the subject taxonomy to the homework post type. We could set it to more that one post type by passing in an array of post type names.

- $args—This is an optional array of many different arguments that dictate how your custom taxonomy will be set up. Notice that in our example we are only using a few of the many available arguments that could be passed into the `register_taxonomy()` function. Below is a list of all of the available arguments:

label

Optional string of the display name of your taxonomy.

labels

Optional array of labels to use for describing your taxonomy throughout the user interface:

name
  The plural display name of your taxonomy. This will override the label argument.

singular_name
  The name for one object of this taxonomy. Defaults to "Category."

search_items
  Defaults to "Search Categories".

popular_items
  This string isn't used on hierarchical taxonomies. Defaults to "Popular Tags."

all_items
  Defaults to "All Categories".

parent_item
  This string is only used on hierarchical taxonomies. Defaults to "Parent Category."

parent_item_colon
  The same as the parent_item argument but with a colon at the end.

edit_item
  Defaults to "Edit Category."

view_item
  Defaults to "View Category."

update_item
  Defaults to "Update Category."

add_new_item
> Defaults to "Add New Category."

new_item_name
> Defaults to "New Category Name."

separate_items_with_commas
> This string is used on nonhierarchical taxonomies. Defaults to "Separate tags with commas."

add_or_remove_items
> This string is used on nonhierarchical taxonomies. Defaults to "Add or remove tags."

choose_from_most_used
> This string is used on nonhierarchical taxonomies. Defaults to "Choose from the most used tags."

hierarchical

Optional Boolean that specifies if a taxonomy is hierarchical or that a taxonomy term may have parent terms or subterms. This is just like the default categories taxonomy. Nonhierarchical taxonomies are like the default tags taxonomy. The default value for this argument is set to `false`.

update_count_callback

Optional string that works like a hook. It's called when the count of the associated post type is updated.

rewrite

Optional Boolean or array that is used to customize the permalink structure of a taxonomy. The default rewrite value is set to the taxonomy slug.

query_var

Optional Boolean or string that can be used to customize the query var, `?$query_var=$term`. By default, the taxonomy name is used as the query var.

public

Optional Boolean that specifies if the taxonomy should be publicly queryable on the frontend. The default is set to `true`.

show_ui

Optional Boolean that specifies if the taxonomy will have a backend admin UI, similar to the categories or tags interface. The default value of this argument is set to the value of the `public` argument.

show_in_nav_menus

Optional Boolean that specifies if a taxonomy will be available in navigation menus. The default value of this argument is set to the value of the `public` argument.

show_tagcloud

Optional Boolean that specifies if the taxonomy can be included in the Tag Cloud Widget. The default value of this argument is set to the value of the `show_ui` argument.

show_admin_column

Optional Boolean that specifies if a new column will be created for your taxonomy on the post type it is attached to on the post type's edit/list page in the backend. This is `false` by default.

capabilities

Optional array of capabilities for this taxonomy with a default of none. You can pass in the following arguments and/or any custom-created capabilities:

- manage_terms
- edit_terms
- delete_terms
- assign_terms

In our homework post type example, we are going to make a taxonomy called "Subject" so we can create a term for each subject like math, science, language arts, and social studies:

```php
<?php
// custom function to register the "subject" taxonomy
function schoolpress_register_taxonomy_subject() {
    register_taxonomy(
        'subject',
        'homework',
        array(
            'label' => __( 'Subjects' ),
            'rewrite' => array( 'slug' => 'subject' ),
            'hierarchical' => true
        )
    );
```

```
}
// call our custom function with the init hook
add_action( 'init', 'schoolpress_register_taxonomy_subject' );
?>
```

Notice in the preceding code the subject taxonomy is set up like categories on a post because it's hierarchical argument is set to true. You can create as many subjects as you would like and nest them under each other.

Under Homework → Subjects in the backend, you can add your terms the same way you would add new categories to a post.

register_taxonomy_for_object_type($taxonomy, $object_type)

What if you wanted to use a default taxonomy on a custom post type? Say you want to use the same tags taxonomy attached to the posts post type on our homework post type. You can use the register_taxonomy_for_object_type() function to attach any taxonomies to any post types. The register_taxonomy_for_object_type() function is also located in *wp-includes/taxonomy.php*.

The register_taxonomy_for_object_type() function accepts two parameters:

- $taxonomy—Required string of the name of the taxonomy.
- $object_type—Required string of the name of the post type to which you want to attach your taxonomy.

In this example, we are attaching the default tags taxonomy to our custom homework post type:

```
<?php
function schoolpress_register_taxonomy_for_object_type_homework(){
        register_taxonomy_for_object_type( 'post_tag', 'homework' );
}
add_action( 'init', 'schoolpress_register_taxonomy_for_object_type_homework' );
?>
```

If you run the example, you should notice that the "tags" taxonomy is now available under the Homework menu item. The Custom Post Types UI plugin (*http://bit.ly/posttype-ui*) also has a UI for creating and managing custom taxonomies.

Using Custom Post Types and Taxonomies in Your Themes and Plugins

Most of the time when building a web application with WordPress, you will want to display your custom post type posts in the frontend within your theme.

The Theme Archive and Single Template Files

Most WordPress themes will have an *archive.php* file that renders your posts on a archive/listing page and a *single.php* file that is responsible for rendering information about a single post. You can create dedicated archive and single files for your registered CPTs very easily.

Make a copy of *archive.php* and name it *archive-homework.php*. You should now automatically have a listing archive page of all of your homework assignment posts in the same format of your regular posts archive page (at *domain.com/homework/*).

This same method can be applied to the *single.php* file. Make a copy if it and call it *single-homework.php*. You should now have a single page for each of your homework assignments (at *domain.com/homework/science-worksheet/*). Now you can change the markup of the CPT archive or single file to display your data differently from how your blog posts are displayed.

 In order to use a custom archive file, you must set the `has_archive` argument when registering your custom post type to `true`. The `has_archive` argument is part of the `register_post_type()` function.

Good Old WP_Query and get_posts()

In some instances, creating an archive and single *.php* file for your custom post type may not be enough for the custom functionality you require. What if you wanted to loop through all of the posts for a specific post type in a sidebar widget or in a shortcode on a page? With `WP_Query` or `get_posts()`, you can set the `post_type` parameter to query and loop through your CPT posts the same way you would with regular posts.

In Example 5-2, we will build a homework submission form below any content provided for the single post of the homework post type.

Example 5-2. Homework submission form

```php
<?php
function schoolpress_the_content_homework_submission($content){

    global $post;

    // Don't do this for any other post type than homework
    // and if a user is not logged in
    $current_user = wp_get_current_user();
    if ( ! is_single() || $post->post_type != 'homework' || ! $current_user )
                return $content;

        // check if the current user has already made a submission to this
```

```
// homework assignment
    $submissions = get_posts( array(
            'post_author'    => $current_user->ID,
            'posts_per_page' => '1',
            'post_type'      => 'submissions',
            'meta_key'       => '_submission_homework_id',
            'meta_value'     => $post->ID
    ) );
    foreach ( $submissions as $submission ) {
            $submission_id = $submission->ID;
    }

    // Process the form submission if the user hasn't already
    if ( !$submission_id &&
                isset( $_POST['submit-homework-submission'] ) &&
                isset( $_POST['homework-submission'] ) ) {

            $submission = $_POST['homework-submission'];
            $post_title = $post->post_title;
            $post_title .= ' - Submission by ' . $current_user->display_name;
            // Insert the current users submission as a post into our
    // submissions CPT.
            $args = array(
                    'post_title'   => $post_title,
                    'post_content' => $submission,
                    'post_type'    => 'submissions',
                    'post_status'  => 'publish',
                    'post_author'  => $current_user->ID
            );
            $submission_id = wp_insert_post( $args );
            // add post meta to tie this submission post to the
    // homework post
            add_post_meta( $submission_id, '_submission_homework_id',
    $post->ID );
            // create a custom message
            $message = __(
                    'Your homework has been submitted and is
        awaiting review.',
                    'schoolpress'
            );
            $message = '<div class="homework-submission-message">' . $message .
    '</div>';
            // drop message before the filtered $content variable
            $content = $message . $content;
    }

    // Add a link to the user's submission if a submssion was already made
    if( $submission_id ) {

            $message = sprintf( __(
                    'Click %s here %s to view your submission to this homework
        assignment.',
```

```
                                          'schoolpress' ),
                                          '<a href="' . get_permalink( $submission_id ) . '">',
                                          '</a>' );
                    $message = '<div class="homework-submission-link">' . $message .
        '</div>';
                    $content .= $message;

            // Add a basic submission form after the $content variable being filtered.
            } else {

                ob_start();
                ?>
                <h3><?php _e( 'Submit your Homework below!', 'schoolpress' );?></h3>
                <form method="post">
                <?php
                wp_editor( '', 'homework-submission', array( 'media_buttons' => false ) );
                ?>
                <input type="submit" name="submit-homework-submission" value="Submit" />
                </form>
                <?php
                $form = ob_get_contents();
                ob_end_clean();
                $content .= $form;
            }

            return $content;

    }
    // add a filter on 'the_content' so we can run our custom code to deal with
    // homework submissions
    add_filter( 'the_content', 'schoolpress_the_content_homework_submission', 999 );
    ?>
```

You probably noticed the following functions that we haven't discussed yet:

- ob_start()—This PHP function is used to turn output buffering on. While output buffering is active, no output is sent to the browser; instead the output is stored in an internal buffer.

- wp_editor()—This WordPress function outputs the same WYSIWYG editor that you get while adding or editing a post. You can call this function anywhere you would like to stick an editor. We thought the homework submission form would be a perfect place. We will cover all of the parameters of this function later in Chapter 7.

- ob_get_contents()—We set a variable called $form to this PHP function. This makes all content between calling the ob_start() function and this function into a variable called $form.

- `ob_end_clean()`—This PHP function clears the output buffer and turns off output buffering.

We used these functions in the previous sequence because the `wp_editor()` function does not currently have an argument to return the editor as a variable and outputs it to the browser when it's called. If we didn't use these functions, we wouldn't be able to put our editor after the `$content` variable passed into the `the_content` filter.

In the following code, we are going to make sure that only administrators have access to all homework submissions and that all other users only have access to homework submissions that they made:

```php
<?php
function schoolpress_submissions_template_redirect(){
    global $post, $user_ID;

    // only run this function for the submissions post type
    if ( $post->post_type != 'submissions' )
        return;

    // check if post_author is the current user_ID
    if ( $post->post_author == $user_ID )
        $no_redirect = true;

    // check if current user is an administrator
    if ( current_user_can( 'manage_options' ) )
        $no_redirect = true;

    // if $no_redirect is false redirect to the home page
    if ( ! $no_redirect ) {
        wp_redirect( home_url() );
        exit();
    }
}
// use the template_redirect hook to call a function that decides if the
// current user can access the current homework submission
add_action( 'template_redirect', 'schoolpress_submissions_template_redirect' );
?>
```

Metadata with CPTs

You can utilize the same post meta functions we went over in detail in Chapter 2 with any CPT you create. Getting, adding, updating, and deleting post metadata is consistent across all posts types.

If you registered a CPT and added custom-fields in the supports argument, then by default, when adding a new post or editing a post of that post type, you will see a meta box called "Custom Fields." You may already be familiar with the Custom Fields meta box; it's a very basic form used to maintain metadata attached to a post. What if you require a more slick UI for adding metadata on the backend? Well, building a custom meta box would be the solution for you.

add_meta_box($id, $title, $callback, $screen, $context, $priority, $callback_args)

- $id—A required string of a unique identifier for the meta box you are creating.
- $title—A required string of the title or visible name of the meta box you are creating.
- $callback—A required string of a function name that gets called to output the HTML inside of the meta box you are creating.
- $screen—An optional string or object of post types and/or screen names (*dashboard*, *links*) that your meta box will show up on.
- $context—An optional string of the context within the page where your meta box should show (*normal*, *advanced*, *side*). The default is advanced.
- $priority—An optional string of the priority within the context where the boxes should show (*high*, *low*).
- $callback_args—An optional array of arguments that will be passed in the callback function you referenced with the $callback parameter. Your callback function will automatically receive the $post object and any other arguments you set here.

In Example 5-3, we are going to build a custom meta box for all posts of our homework post type. This meta box will contain a checkbox for if a homework submission is required and a date selector for the due date of the homework assignment.

Example 5-3. Custom meta box

```php
<?php
// function for adding a custom meta box
function schoolpress_homework_add_meta_boxes(){

    add_meta_box(
        'homework_meta',
        'Additonal Homework Info',
        'schoolpress_homework_meta_box',
        'homework',
        'side'
    );

}
// use the add_meta_boxes hook to call a custom function to add a new meta box
add_action( 'add_meta_boxes', 'schoolpress_homework_add_meta_boxes' );

// this is the callback function called from add_meta_box
function schoolpress_homework_meta_box( $post ){
    // doing this so the url will fit in the book ;)
```

```php
    $jquery_url = 'http://ajax.googleapis.com/ajax/libs/';
    $jquery_url.= 'jqueryui/1.8.2/themes/smoothness/jquery-ui.css';

    // enqueue jquery date picker
    wp_enqueue_script( 'jquery-ui-datepicker' );
    wp_enqueue_style( 'jquery-style', $jquery_url );

    // set meta data if already exists
    $is_required = get_post_meta( $post->ID,
        '_schoolpress_homework_is_required', 1 );

    $due_date = get_post_meta( $post->ID,
        '_schoolpress_homework_due_date', 1 );
    // output meta data fields
    ?>
    <p>
    <input type="checkbox"
    name="is_required" value="1" <?php checked( $is_required, '1' ); ?>>
    This assignment is required.
    </p>
    <p>
    Due Date:
    <input type="text"
    name="due_date" id="due_date" value="<?php echo $due_date;?>">
    </p>
    <?php // attach jquery date picker to our due_date field?>
    <script>
    jQuery(document).ready(function() {
        jQuery('#due_date').datepicker({
            dateFormat : 'mm/dd/yy'
        });
    });
    </script>
    <?php
}

// function for saving custom meta data to the database
function schoolpress_homework_save_post( $post_id ){

  // don't save anything if WP is auto saving
  if ( defined( 'DOING_AUTOSAVE' ) && DOING_AUTOSAVE )
     return $post_id;

  // check if correct post type and that the user has correct permissions
  if ( 'homework' == $_POST['post_type'] ) {

    if ( ! current_user_can( 'edit_page', $post_id ) )
       return $post_id;

  } else {

    if ( ! current_user_can( 'edit_post', $post_id ) )
```

```php
        return $post_id;
    }

    // update homework meta data
    update_post_meta( $post_id,
        '_schoolpress_homework_is_required',
        $_POST['is_required']
    );
    update_post_meta( $post_id,
        '_schoolpress_homework_due_date',
        $_POST['due_date']
    );

}
// call a custom function to handle saving our meta data
add_action( 'save_post', 'schoolpress_homework_save_post' );
?>
```

If you are a good developer, you are probably thinking to yourself: Where are the nonces? How come these $_POST values aren't sanitized? If you aren't thinking this, you should be because security is very important! If you don't know what we are talking about right now, that's OK because we will be covering these best practices in more detail in Chapter 8. We deliberately left out this additional code in our example to try to keep it short and sweet, but know that when you are writing custom code, you should always use nonces and sanitize your data.

 When creating meta boxes and custom meta fields, we recommend utilizing Custom Metaboxes and Fields for WordPress (*http://bit.ly/ metaboxes-fields*), or CMB for short. You can easily include CMB in your theme or any custom plugin to give you a fast and easy way to create custom meta boxes and the meta fields inside them.

Custom Wrapper Classes for CPTs

CPTs are just posts. So you can use a call like get_post($post_id) to get an object of the WP_Post class to work with. For complex CPTs, it helps to create a wrapper class so you can interact with your CPT in a more object-oriented way.

The basic idea is to create a custom-defined PHP class that includes as a property a post object generated from the ID of the CPT post. In addition to storing that post object, the wrapper class also houses methods for all of the functionality related to that CPT.

Example 5-4 shows the outline of a wrapper class for our Homework CPT.

Example 5-4. Homework CPT wrapper class

```php
<?php
/*
```

```
    Class Wrapper for Homework CPT
    /wp-content/plugins/schoolpress/classes/class.homework.php
*/
class Homework {
    //constructor can take a $post_id
    function __construct( $post_id = NULL ) {
        if ( !empty( $post_id ) )
            $this->getPost( $post_id );
    }

    //get the associated post and prepopulate some properties
    function getPost( $post_id ) {
        //get post
        $this->post = get_post( $post_id );

        //set some properties for easy access
        if ( !empty( $this->post ) ) {
        $this->id = $this->post->ID;
        $this->post_id = $this->post->ID;
        $this->title = $this->post->post_title;
        $this->teacher_id = $this->post->post_author;
        $this->content = $this->post->post_content;
        $this->required = $this->post->_schoolpress_homework_is_required;
        $this->due_date = $this->post->due_date;
        }

        //return post id if found or false if not
        if ( !empty( $this->id ) )
            return $this->id;
        else
            return false;
    }
}
?>
```

The constructor of this class can take a `$post_id` as a parameter and will pass that to
the `getPost()` method, which attaches a `$post` object to the class instance and also
prepopulates a few properties for easy access. Example 5-5 shows how to instantiate an
object for a specific Homework assignment and print out the contents.

Example 5-5. Get and print a specific homework assignment

```
$assignment_id = 1;
$assignment = new Homework($assignment_id);
echo '<pre>';
print_r($assignment);
echo '</pre>';
//Outputs:
/*
Homework Object
(
    [post] => WP_Post Object
```

```
(
    [ID] => 1
    [post_author] => 1
    [post_date] => 2013-03-28 14:53:56
    [post_date_gmt] => 2013-03-28 14:53:56
    [post_content] => This is the assignment...
    [post_title] => Assignment #1
    [post_excerpt] =>
    [post_status] => publish
    [comment_status] => open
    [ping_status] => open
    [post_password] =>
    [post_name] => assignment-1
    [to_ping] =>
    [pinged] =>
    [post_modified] => 2013-03-28 14:53:56
    [post_modified_gmt] => 2013-03-28 14:53:56
    [post_content_filtered] =>
    [post_parent] => 0
    [guid] => http://schoolpress.me/?p=1
    [menu_order] => 0
    [post_type] => homework
    [post_mime_type] =>
    [comment_count] => 3
    [filter] => raw
    [format_content] =>
)

[id] => 1
[post_id] => 1
[title] => Assignment 1
[teacher_id] => 1
[content] => This is the assignment...
[required] => 1
[due_date] => 2013-11-05
)
*/
```

Extending WP_Post Versus Wrapping It

Another option here would be to extend the WP_Post class, but this is not possible right now since the WP_Post class is defined as final, meaning it is a class that can't be extended. The core team has said they are doing this to keep people from building plugins that rely on extending the WP_Post object since WP_Post is due for an overhaul in future versions of WordPress. We think they're being big fuddy duddies.[1]

In Chapter 6, we'll extend the WP_User class (which isn't defined as final). But the best we can do with WP_Post is to create a wrapper class for it.

---

1. But seriously, the core team is really smart and makes a good point.

Why Use Wrapper Classes?

Building a wrapper class for your CPT is a good idea for a few reasons:

- You can put all of your code to register the CPT in one place.
- You can put all of your code to register related taxonomies in one place.
- You can build all of your CPT-related functionality as methods on the wrapper class.
- Your code will read better.

Keep Your CPTs and Taxonomies Together

Put all of your code to register the CPT and taxonomies in one place. Instead of having one block of code to register a CPT and define the taxonomies and a separate class wrapper to handle working with the CPT, you can simply place your CPT and taxonomy definitions into the class wrapper itself:

```
/*
        Class Wrapper for Homework CPT with Init Function
        /wp-content/plugins/schoolpress/classes/class.homework.php
*/
class Homework
{
        //constructor can take a $post_id
        function __construct($post_id = NULL)
        {
                if(!empty($post_id))
                        $this->getPost($post_id);
        }

        //get the associated post and prepopulate some properties
        function getPost($post_id)
        {
                /* snipped */
        }

        //register CPT and Taxonomies on init
        function init()
        {
                //homework CPT
                register_post_type(
                        'homework',
                        array(
                                'labels' => array(
                                        'name' => __( 'Homework' ),
                                        'singular_name' => __( 'Homework' )
                                ),
                                'public' => true,
                                'has_archive' => true,
```

```
                )
        );

        //subject taxonomy
        register_taxonomy(
                'subject',
                'homework',
                array(
                        'label' => __( 'Subjects' ),
                        'rewrite' => array( 'slug' => 'subject' ),
                        'hierarchical' => true
                )
        );
    }
}

//run the Homework init on init
add_action('init', array('Homework', 'init'));
```

The code is snipped[2] but shows how you would add an init() method to your class that is hooked into the init action. The init() method then runs all the code required to define the CPT. You could also define other hooks and filters here, with the callbacks linked to other methods in the Homework class.

There are other ways to organize things, but we find that having all of your CPT-related code in one place helps a lot.

Keep It in the Wrapper Class

Build all of your CPT-related functionality as methods on the wrapper class. When we registered our "Homework" CPT, a page was added to the dashboard allowing us to "Edit Homework." Teachers can create homework like any other post, with a title and body content. Teachers can publish the homework when it's ready to be pushed out to students. All of this post-related functionality is available for free when you create a CPT.

On the other hand, there is a lot of functionality around many CPTs, including our Homework CPT, that needs to be coded up. With a wrapper class in place, this functionality can be added as methods of our Homework class.

For example, one thing we want to do with our homework posts is gather up all the submissions for a particular assignment. Once we have submissions gathered, we can render them in a list or process them in some way. Example 5-6 shows a couple of methods we can add to our Homework class to gather related submissions and to calculate a flat scale grading curve.

---

2. The full version can be found on the BWAwWP site.

Example 5-6. Adding methods to the Homework class

```php
<?php
class Homework
{
        /* Snipped constructor and other methods from earlier examples */

        /*
                Get related submissions.
                Set $force to true to force the method to get children again.
        */
        function getSubmissions($force = false)
        {
                //need a post ID to do this
                if(empty($this->id))
                        return array();

                //did we get them already?
                if(!empty($this->submissions) && !$force)
                        return $this->submissions;

                //okay get submissions
                $this->submissions = get_children(array(
                        'post_parent' => $this->id,
                        'post_type' => 'submissions',
                        'post_status' => 'published'
                ));

                //make sure submissions is an array at least
                if(empty($this->submissions))
                        $this->submissions = array();

                return $this->submissions;
        }

        /*
                Calculate a grade curve
        */
        function doFlatCurve($maxscore = 100)
        {
                $this->getSubmissions();

                //figure out the highest score
                $highscore = 0;
                foreach($this->submissions as $submission)
                {
                        $highscore = max($submission->score, $highscore);
                }

                //figure out the curve
                $curve = $maxscore - $highscore;

                //fix lower scores
```

```
                foreach($this->submissions as $submission)
                {
                        update_post_meta(
                                $submission->ID,
                                "score",
                                min( $maxscore, $submission->score + $curve )
                        );
                }
        }
}
?>
```

Wrapper Classes Read Better

In addition to organizing your code to make things easier to find, working with wrapper classes also makes your code easier to read and understand. With fully wrapped Homework and Submission CPTs and special user classes (covered in Chapter 6), code like the following is possible:

```php
<?php
//static function of Student class to check if the current user is a student
if ( Student::is_student() ) {
    //student defaults to current user
    $student = new Student();

    //let's figure out when their next assignment is due
    $assignment = $student->getNextAssignment();

    //display info and links
    if ( !empty( $assignment ) ) {
    ?>
    <p>Your next assignment
    <a href="<?php echo get_permalink( $assignment->id );?>">
    <?php echo $assignment->title;?></a>
    for the
    <a href="<?php echo get_permalink( $assignment->class_id );?>">
    <?php echo $assignment->class->title;?></a>
    class is due on <?php echo $assignment->getDueDate();?>.</p>
    <?php
    }
}
?>
```

The code would be much more complicated if all of the get_post() calls and loops through arrays of child posts were out in the open. Using an object-oriented approach makes this code more approachable to other developers working with your code.

## CHAPTER 6

Users, Roles, and Capabilities

Back in Chapter 1, we established logins as a crucial component of any web app. One of the great things about using WordPress for your apps is that you get fully featured user management out of the box.

The base WordPress app includes:

- Secure logins with passwords that are salted and hashed
- User records with an email address, username, display name, avatar, and bio
- Admin views to browse, search, add, edit, and delete users
- User roles to separate administrators from editors, authors, contributors, and subscribers
- Pages for users to login, register, and reset passwords

By using various WordPress functions and APIs, we can:

- Add and manage user meta or profile fields for each user.
- Define custom roles and capabilities for finer control over which users have access to what.

Managing users in WordPress is a fairly straightforward affair. The User tab in the dashboard makes it easy to browse, search, add, edit, and delete users. It's easy to manage users via code as well.

This chapter will cover:

- How to access user data in your code
- How to add custom fields to users
- How to customize the user profiles and reports in the dashboard

- How to add, update, and delete users
- How to define custom roles and capabilities
- How to extend the WordPress User class to create your own user-focused classes

Getting User Data

In this section, we'll go over how to instantiate a WordPress user object in code and how to get basic user information, like login and email address, and user metadata out of that object.

The workhorse for managing WordPress users in code is the WP_User class. Just like anything else in WordPress and PHP, there are a few different ways to get a WP_User object to work with. Here are some of the most popular methods:

```
// get the WP_User object WordPress creates for the currently logged-in user
global $current_user;

// get the currently logged-in user with the wp_get_current_user() function
$user = wp_get_current_user();

// set some variables
$user_id = 1;
$username = 'jason';
$email = 'jason@strangerstudios.com';

// get a user by ID
$user = wp_getuserdata( $user_id );

// get a user by another field
$user1 = wp_get_user_by( 'login', $username );
$user2 = wp_get_user_by( 'email', $email );

// use the WP_User constructor directly
$user = new WP_User( $user_id );

//use the WP_User constructor with a username
$user = new WP_User( $username );
```

Once you have a WP_User object, you can get any piece of user data you want:

```
// get the currently logged-in user
$user = wp_get_current_user();

// echo the user's display_name
echo $user->display_name;

// use user's email address to send an email
wp_mail( $user->user_email, 'Email Subject', 'Email Body' );
```

```
// get any user meta value
echo 'Department: ' . $user->department;
```

Data stored in the wp_users table (user_login, user_nicename, user_email, user_url, user_registered, user_status, and display_name) can be accessed using the arrow operator, for example, $user->display_name.

Any value in the wp_usermeta table can also be accessed by using the arrow operator, for example, $user->meta_key, or by using the get_user_meta() function. These two lines of code produce the same result:

```php
<?php
$full_name = trim( $user->first_name . ' ' . $user->last_name );
$full_name = trim( get_user_meta( $user->ID, 'first_name' ) .
    ' ' . get_user_meta( $user->ID, 'last_name' ) );
?>
```

It's useful to understand the trick WordPress is using to allow you to access user meta on demand as if each meta field was a property of the WP_User class. The WP_User class is using overloaded properties or the __get() "magic method."[1]

With magic methods, any property of the WP_User object that you try to get that isn't an actual property of the object will be passed to the _get() method of the class. Here is a simplified[2] version of the _get() method used in the WP_User class:

```
function __get( $key ) {
if ( isset( $this->data->$key ) ) {
        $value = $this->data->$key;
        } else {
                $value = get_user_meta( $this->ID, $key, true );
        }

        return $value;
}
```

Let's analyze this. The method first checks if a value exists in the $data property of the WP_User object. If so, that value is used. If not, the method uses the get_user_meta() function to see if any meta value exists using the key passed in.

Because we're loading meta values on demand this way, there is less memory overhead when instantiating a new WP_User object. On the other hand, because meta values aren't available until you specifically ask for them, you can't dump all metadata on a user using code like print_r($user) or print_r($user->data).

---

1. Any class method starting with two underscores is considered a magic method in PHP because they are magically kicked off during certain events.

2. For clarity, we took out parts of the method that were for reverse compatibility and filtering in certain circumstances. The preceding code contains the spirit of the method.

To loop through all the metadata for a user, use the `get_user_meta()` function with no `$key` parameter passed in:

```
// dump all metadata for a user
$user_meta = get_user_meta( $user_id );
foreach( $user_meta as $key => $value )
    echo $key . ': ' . $value . '<br />';
```

Knowing how WordPress uses the `__get()` function is interesting, but also important so you avoid a couple of the limitations of the `__get()` magic method.

The `__get()` and `__set()` methods are not called when assignments are chained together. For example, the code `$year = $user->graduation_year = '2012'` would produce inconsistent results.

Similarly `__get()` is not called when coded within an `empty()` or `isset()` function call. So `if(empty($user->graduation_year))` will also be false, even if there exists some user meta with the key `graduation_year`.

The solution to these two issues is to get a little more verbose with your code:

```
// Split assignments into multiple lines when using magic methods.
$user->graduation_year = '2012';
$year = '2012';

//To test if a meta value is empty, set a local variable first.
$year = $user->graduation_year;
if ( empty( $year ) )
    $year = '2012';
```

Add, Update, and Delete Users

We touched on some basic functions for adding, updating, and deleting users in Chapter 2, but since working with user data is such an important part of any web application, we will do a brief overview with some additional examples and different use case scenarios here.

Occasionally, you will need to add users through code instead of using the WordPress dashboard. In our SchoolPress app, we might want to allow teachers to enter a list of email addresses and generate a user for each email entered.

Or maybe you want to customize the registration process. The built-in WordPress registration form is difficult to customize. It's often easier to build your own form and use WordPress functions to add the user yourself on the backend.[3]

---

3. This is how the Paid Memberships Pro plugin registers users from the checkout page.

As you should already know, the function for adding a user to WordPress is `wp_in sert_user()`, which takes an array of user data and inserts it into the `wp_users` and `wp_usermeta` tables:

```
// insert user from values we've gathered
$user_id = wp_insert_user( array(
        'user_login' => $username,
        'user_pass' => $password,
        'user_email' => $email,
        'first_name' => $firstname,
        'last_name' => $lastname
    )
);

// check if username or email has already been used
if ( is_wp_error( $user_id ) ){
    echo $return->get_error_message();
} else {
    // continue on with whatever you want to do with the new $user_id
}
```

The following code will automatically log someone in after adding that person's user. The `wp_signon()` function authenticates the user and sets up the secure cookies to log the user in:

```
// okay, log them in to WP
$creds = array();
$creds['user_login'] = $username;
$creds['user_password'] = $password;
$creds['remember'] = true;
$user = wp_signon( $creds, false );
```

Updating users is as easy as adding them with the `wp_update_user()` function. You pass in an array of user data and metadata. As long as there is an ID key in the array with a valid user ID as the value, WordPress will set any specified user values:

```
// this will update a user's email and leave other values alone
$userdata = array( 'ID' => 1, 'user_email' => 'jason@strangerstudios.com' );
wp_update_user( $userdata );

// this function is also perfect for updating multiple user meta fields at once
wp_update_user( array(
    'ID' => 1,
    'company' => 'Stranger Studios',
    'title' => 'CEO',
    'personality' => 'crescent fresh'
));
```

A user's user_login cannot be updated through wp_update_user. Also, if a user's user_pass is updated, the user will be logged out. You can use the preceding auto-login code above to log the user back in using the new password.

You can also update one user meta value at a time using the up date_user_meta($user_id, $meta_key, $meta_value, $prev_value) function.

The following code segments illustrate some more features:

```
// arrays will get serialized
$children = array( 'Isaac', 'Marin');
update_user_meta( $user_id, 'children', $children );

// you can also store array by storing multiple values with the same key
update_user_meta( $user_id, 'children', 'Isaac' );
update_user_meta( $user_id, 'children', 'Marin' );

// when storing multiple values, specify the $prev_value parameter
// to select which one changes
update_user_meta( $user_id, 'children', 'Isaac Ford', 'Isaac' );
update_user_meta( $user_id, 'children', 'Marin Josephine', 'Marin' );

//delete all user meta by key
delete_user_meta( $user_id, 'children' );

//delete just one row when there are multiple values for one key
delete_user_meta( $user_id, 'children', 'Isaac Ford' );
```

Note that in the code, I show two different ways to store arrays in user meta. This is similar to storing options via update_option() or post meta via up date_post_meta(). The first method (one serialized value per key) keeps row count down on the wp_usermeta table, which can make queries by meta_key faster. The second method (multiple values per key) allows you to query by meta_value. For example, storing child names as separate user meta entries lets you do queries like this:

```
<?php
// get the IDs of all users with children named Isaac
$parents_of_isaac = $wpdb->get_col( "SELECT user_id
        FROM $wpdb->usermeta
        WHERE meta_key = 'children'
        AND meta_value = 'Isaac'" );
?>
```

While it's possible to query the wp_usermeta and wp_postmeta tables by meta_value, be careful about query times. The meta_value column is not indexed, and so queries against large datasets may be slow. Many-to-one relationships like this can also be stored in custom taxonomies, which can show better performance.

Deleting a user, while dangerous, is incredibly easy to do in code:

```
//this file contains wp_delete_user and is not always loaded, so let's make sure
require_once( ABSPATH . '/wp-admin/includes/user.php' );

//delete the user
wp_delete_user( $user_id );

//or delete a user and reassign their posts to user with ID #1
wp_delete_user( $user_id, 1 );
```

For network site setups, you will need to use the wpmu_delete_user() function to delete the user from the entire network. Otherwise wp_delete_user() just deletes the user from the current blog. You can use the is_multisite() function to detect which function should be used:

```
// I want to make sure we really delete the user.
if ( is_multisite() )
    wp_delete_user( $user_id );
else
    wpmu_delete_user( $user_id );
```

Hooks and Filters

Perhaps more common than adding and updating user data yourself are scenarios where you want to do some other bit code when new users are added or deleted. For example, you may want to create and link a new CPT post to a user when she registers. Or maybe you want to clean up connections and data stored in custom tables when a user is deleted. This can be done through some user-related hooks and filters.

The hook to run code after a user is registered is user_register. The hook passes in the user ID of the newly created user:

```
//create a new "course" CPT when a teacher registers
function sp_user_register( $user_id ){
    // check if the new user is a teacher (see chapter 15 for details)
    if ( pmpro_hasMembershipLevel( 'teacher', $user_id ) ) {
        // add a new "course" CPT with this user as author
        wp_insert_post( array(
            'post_title' => 'My First Course',
            'post_content' => 'This is a sample course...',
            'post_author' => $user_id,
            'post_status' => 'draft',
            'post_type' => 'course'

        ) );
    }
}
add_action( 'user_register', 'sp_user_register' );
```

The hook to run code just *before* deleting a user is `delete_user`. A similar hook `de leted_user` (note the past tense) runs just *after* a user has been deleted.

These hooks are mostly interchangeable, but there are a couple things to note:

- If you hook on `delete_user` early enough, you might be able to abort the user delete.

- If you hook on `deleted_user`, some user data and connections may already be gone and unavailable:

```php
<?php
// send an email when a user is being deleted
function sp_delete_user( $user_id ){
    $user = get_userdata( $user_id );
    wp_mail( $user->user_email,
        "You've been deleted.",
        'Your account at SchoolPress has been deleted.'
    );
}
// want to be able to get user_email so hook in early
add_action( 'delete_user', 'sp_delete_user' );
?>
```

What Are Roles and Capabilities?

Roles and capabilities are how WordPress controls what users have access to view and do on your site. Each user may have one role, and each role will have one or many capabilities. Each capability will determine if a user can or can't view a certain type of content or perform a certain action.

There are five default roles in every WordPress install: Admin, Editor, Author, Contributor, and Subscriber. If you are running a network site, you'll have a sixth role, Super Admin, which has admin access to all sites on the network.

A full list of capabilities and how they map to the default WordPress roles can be found on the WordPress Codex Roles and Capabilities page (*http://bit.ly/roles-caps*).

In a little bit, we'll go over how to create new roles outside of the WordPress defaults. However, for most apps it makes sense to stick to the default roles: have your app administrators use the Admin role and have all of your users/customers use the Subscriber role.

If your app users will be creating content, consider making them Authors (can create and publish posts) or Contributors (can create, but not publish posts). If your app has moderators, consider making them Editors.

Using the default roles is a good idea because certain plugins will expect your users to have one of these roles. If your admins are really users with an office manager role, you may have a bit of extra work to get a third-party plugin to work with those users. The opposite is sometimes true as well. You might have to hide functionality made available to your users based on the roles they have, especially if you are using roles outside of Admin (access to everything) and Subscribers (can just view stuff).

Checking a User's Role and Capabilities

Sometimes you'll need to check if a user is able to do something before you let her do it. You do this with the `current_user_can()` function. This function takes one parameter, which is a string value for the `$capability` to check. The following code illustrates the usage of this function:

```
if ( current_user_can( 'manage_options' ) ) {
    // has the manage options capability, typically an admin
}

if ( current_user_can( 'edit_user', $user_id ) ) {
    // can edit the user with ID = $user_id.
    // typically either the user himself or an admin
}

if ( current_user_can( 'edit_post', $post_id ) ) {
    // can edit the post with ID = $post_id.
    // typically the author of the post or an admin or editor
}

if ( current_user_can( 'subscriber' ) ) {
    // one way to check if the current user is a subscriber
}
```

You can also use the function `user_can()` to check if someone other than the current user has a capability. Pass in the `$user_id` of the user you want to check, the capability, and any other arguments needed:

```
/*
    Output comments for the current post,
    highlighting anyone who has capabilities to edit it.
*/
global $post;   // current post we are looking at

$comments = get_comments( 'post_id=' . $post->ID );
foreach( $comments as $comment ){
    // default CSS classes for all comments
    $classes = 'comment';

    // add can-edit CSS class to authors
    if ( user_can( $comment->user_id, 'edit_post', $post->ID ) )
        $classes .= ' can-edit';
?>
<div id="comment-<?php echo $comment->comment_ID;?>"
```

```
        class="<?php echo $classes;?>">
        Comment by <?php echo $comment->comment_author;?>:
        <?php echo wpautop( $comment->comment_content );?>
    </div>
    <?php
    }
```

While it is possible to check for a user's role using `current_user_can()`, it is better practice to test a user's capabilities instead of her role. This will allow your code to continue to work even if users are given different roles or roles are assigned different capabilities. For example, checking for `manage_options` will work how you intend whether the user is an Admin or a custom role with the `manage_options` capability added.

Testing a user's role should be limited to cases where you really need to know her role instead of her capability. If you find yourself checking for someone's role before performing certain actions, you should take it as a hint that you need to add a new capability.

The following is a function to upgrade any Subscriber whose ID is passed in to the Author role. To be extra sure, we check the roles array of the user object instead of using the `user_can()` function. We use the `set_role()` method of the user class to set the new role:

```
function upgradeSubscriberToAuthor( $user_id ) {
    $user = new WP_User( $user_id );
    if ( in_array( 'subscriber', $user->roles ) )
            $user->set_role( 'author' );
}
```

Creating Custom Roles and Capabilities

As we said earlier, it's a good idea to stick with the default WordPress roles if possible. However, if you have different classes of users and need to restrict what they are doing in new ways, adding custom roles and capabilities is the way to do it.

In our SchoolPress app, teachers are just Authors and students are just Subscribers. However, we do need a custom role for office managers who can manage users but cannot edit content, themes, options, plugins, or the general WordPress settings. We can setup the Office Manager role like so:

```
function sp_roles_and_caps() {
    // Office Manager Role
    remove_role('office');        // in case we updated the caps below
    add_role( 'office', 'Office Manager', array(
        'read' => true,
        'create_users' => true,
        'delete_users' => true,
        'edit_users' => true,
        'list_users' => true,
        'promote_users' => true,
```

```
            'remove_users' => true,
                'office_report' => true // new cap for our custom report
        ));
    }
    // run this function on plugin activation
    register_activation_hook( __FILE__, 'sp_roles_and_caps' );
```

When the `add_role()` function is run, it updates the `wp_user_roles` option in the `wp_options` table, where WordPress looks to get information on roles and capabilities. So you only want to run this function once upon activation instead of every time at runtime. That's why we register this function using `register_activation_hook()`.

We also run `remove_role('office')` at the start there, which is useful if you want to delete a role completely, but is also useful to clear out the "office" role before adding it again in case you edited the capabilities or other settings for the role. Without the `remove_role()` line, the `add_role()` line will not run since the role already exists.

The `add_role()` function takes three parameters: a role name, a display name, and an array of capabilities. Use the reference in the Codex to find the names of the default capabilities or look them up in the */wp-admin/includes/schema.php* file of your Word-Press install.

Adding new capabilities is as simple as including a new capability name in the `add_role()` call or using the `add_cap()` method on an existing role. Here is an example showing how to get an instance of the role class and add a capability to it:

```
// give admins our office_report cap to let them view that report
$role = get_role( 'administrator' );
$role->add_cap( 'office_report' );
```

Again, this code only needs to run once, which will save it in the database. Put code like this inside of a function registered via `register_activation_hook()` just like the last example.

You can also use the `remove_cap()` method of the role class, which is useful if you want to remove some functionality from the default roles. For example, the following code will remove the `edit_pages` capabilities from Editors so they can edit any blog post, but no pages (post of type "page"):

```
// don't let editors edit pages
$role = get_role( 'editor' );
$role->remove_cap( 'edit_pages' );
```

You can do some powerful things by adding and editing roles and capabilities. Defining what users have access to view and do is an important part of building an app. Different roles can be built for different membership levels or upgrades associated with your product. Chapter 15 introduces the Paid Memberships Pro plugin, which adds "membership levels" as a separate classification for your users, which can sometimes be used in place of custom roles, but more often is used in conjunction with them. For more details on how membership levels and roles can work together, see Chapter 15.

Extending the WP_User Class

Similar to how we wrapped the WP_Post class in Chapter 5 to create a more specific class for our custom post types, we can extend the WP_User class to create useful classes that will help us organize our code related to different types of users.

For example, in our SchoolPress app, we have two main user types: Teachers and Students.[4] Both Teachers and Students are just WordPress users at their core, but each type of user will also have functionality unique to them. We can encapsulate that unique functionality by writing Teacher and Student classes that extend the WP_User class.

Wouldn't it be great if we could write code like this?

```php
<?php
// Student is a class that extends WP_User
$student = new Student();
foreach( $student->getAssignments() as $assignment ) {
        // assignment here is an instance of a class that extends WP_Post
    $assignment->print();
}
?>
```

And here is how that code would look in a less object-oriented way:

```php
$student = wp_get_current_user(); // return WP_User object for current user
foreach( sp_getAssignmentsByUser( $student->ID ) as $assignment ) {
    sp_printAssignment( $assignment->ID );
}
```

Both blocks of code are functionally equivalent, but the first example is easier to read and work with. Perhaps more importantly, having all of your student-related functions coded as methods on the Student class will help keep things organized.

Here are the initialization and getAssignments() method for the Student class:

```php
<?php
class Student extends WP_User {
    // no constructor so WP_User's constructor is used

    // method to get assignments for this Student
    function getAssignments() {
        // get assignments via get_posts if we haven't yet
        if ( ! isset( $this->data->assignments ) )
            $this->data->assignments = get_posts( array(
```

---

4. When talking about teachers and students as people, we will leave them lowercase. When talking about our Teacher and Student user types and objects, we will capitalize them

```
                'post_type' => 'assignment',// assignments
                'numberposts' => -1,          // all posts
                'author' => $this->ID          // user ID for this Student
        ));

        return $this->data->assignments;
    }

    // magic method to detect $student->assignments
    function __get( $key ) {
        if ( $key == 'assignments' )
        {
            return $this->getAssignments();
        }
        else
        {
            // fallback to default WP_User magic method
            return parent::__get( $key );
        }
    }
}
}
?>
```

Above we define the Student class to extend the WP_User class by just adding extends WP_User to the class definition.

We don't write our own constructor function because we want to use the same one as the WP_User class. Namely, we want to be able to write $student = new Student($user_ID); to get a Student/User by ID.

The getAssignments() method uses the get_posts() function to get all posts of type "assignment" that are authored by the user associated with this Student. We store the array of assignment posts in the $data property, which is defined in the WP_User class and stores all of the base user data and metadata. This allows us to use code like $student->assignments to get the assignments later.

Normally if $student->assignments is a defined property of $student, the value of that property will be returned. But if there is no "assignments" property, PHP will send "assignments" as the $key parameter to your __get method. Here we check that $key == "assignments" and then return the value of the getAssignments() method defined later. If $key is something other than "assignments" we pass it to the __get() method of the parent WP_User class, which checks for the value in the $data property of the class instance or failing that sends the key to the get_user_meta() function.

At first blush, all this does is allow you to type $student->assignments instead of $student->getAssignments(), which I suppose is true. However, coding things this way allows us to cache the assignments in the $data property of the object so we don't have to query for it again if it's accessed more than once. It will also make your code more consistent with other WordPress code: If you want the student's email, it's `$student->user_email`; if you want student's first_name, it's `$student->first_name`; if you want the student's assignments, it's `$student->assignments`. The person using the code doesn't have to know that one of them is stored in the `wp_users` table, one is stored in `wp_usermeta`, and one is the result of a post query.

Adding Registration and Profile Fields

It's very common to need to add additional profile fields for users in your app. In the previous section, we discussed how to use the `wp_update_user()` and `up date_user_meta()` functions to manage those values. In this section, we'll go over how to add editable fields for our user meta to the registration and profile pages.

In our SchoolPress app, we need to capture some data about our users. For students, we want to capture their graduation year, major, minor, and advisor's name. For teachers, we want to capture their department and office location. For both types of users, we want to capture their gender, age, and phone number.

There are a few different plugins out there that will help you do this more quickly. For example, if you install the PMPro Register Helper plugin,[5] you can use the the code in Example 6-1 to add these fields to the registration and profile pages.

Example 6-1. Registering additional fields for users

```php
<?php
function ps_registration_fields(){
    // store fields in an array
    $fields = array();

    // fields for all users
    $fields[] = new PMProRH_Field(
        'gender',
        'select',
        array(
            'options' => array(
                '' => 'Choose One',
                'male' => 'Male',
                'female' => 'Female'
            ),
            'profile' => true,
            'required' => true
        )
    );
    $fields[] = new PMProRH_Field(
        'age',
```

---

5. PMPro Register Helper (*http://bit.ly/pmp-reg*) was built to work with Paid Memberships Pro, but it will work without it as well.

```
        'text',
        array(
            'size' => 10,
            'profile' => true,
            'required' => true
        )
);
$fields[] = new PMProRH_Field(
        'phone',
        'text',
        array(
            'size' => 20,
            'label' => 'Phone Number',
            'profile' => true,
            'required' => true
        )
);

// fields for teachers
$fields[] = new PMProRH_Field(
        'department',
        'text',
        array(
            'size' => 40,
            'profile' => true,
            'required' => true
        )
);
$fields[] = new PMProRH_Field(
        'office',
        'text',
        array(
            'size' => 40,
            'profile' => true,
            'required' => true
        )
);

// fields for students
$fields[] = new PMProRH_Field(
        'graduation_year',
        'text',
        array(
            'label' => 'Expected Graduation year',
            'size' => 10,
            'profile' => true,
            'required' => true
        )
);
$fields[] = new PMProRH_Field(
        'major',
        'text',
```

```
        array( 'size' => 40, 'profile' => true, 'required' => true )
    );
    $fields[] = new PMProRH_Field(
        'minor',
        'text',
        array( 'size' => 40, 'profile' => true )
    );

    // add fields to the registration page
    foreach( $fields as $field )
        pmprorh_add_registration_field( 'after_password', $field );
}
add_action( 'init', 'ps_registration_fields' );
?>
```

Full instructions on how to use PMPro Register Helper and the syntax for defining fields can be found in the plugin's readme file. Instead of covering that here, let's go through adding one field to the register and profile pages by hand using the same hooks and filters PMPro Register Helper uses.

1. Add our field to the registration page:

```
<?php
function sp_register_form(){
    // get the age value passed into the form
    if ( ! empty( $_REQUEST['age'] ) )
        $age = intval( $_REQUEST['age'] );
    else
        $age = '';

    // show input
    $age = esc_attr( $age );?>
    <p>
    <label for="age">Age<br />
    <input type="text" name="age" id="age" class="input"
        value="<?php echo $age ?>" />
    </label>
    </p>
    <?php
}
add_action( 'register_form', 'sp_register_form');
?>
```

 We check if (! empty($_REQUEST['age'])) to avoid a PHP warning when users first visit the registration page and there isn't any form data in $_REQUEST yet.

2. Update our user's age after registering:

```php
function sp_register_user( $user_id ){
    // get the age value passed into the form
    $age = intval( $_REQUEST['age'] );

    // update user meta
    update_user_meta( $user_id, 'age', $age );
}
add_action( 'register_user', 'sp_register_user' );
```

3. Add the age field to the user profile page. We need to hook into both show_user_pro
   file and edit_user_profile to show our custom field both when users are viewing
   their own profile and when admins are editing other users' profiles:

```php
<?php
function sp_user_profile( $user ){
    // show input
    $age = esc_attr( $user->age );?>
    <table class="form-table">
    <tbody>
    <tr>
            <th><label for="age">Age</label></th>
            <td>
            <input type="text" name="age" id="age" class="input"
        value="<?php echo $age; ?>"/>
            </td>
        </tr>
    </tbody>
    </table>
    <?php
}
//user's own profile
add_action( 'show_user_profile', 'sp_user_profile' );
//admins editing user profiles
add_action( 'edit_user_profile', 'sp_user_profile' );
?>
```

Note how the default WordPress registration page HTML uses <p> tags to separate
fields, while the default profile HTML in the dashboard uses table rows.

4. Update our field when updating a profile:

```php
<?php
function sp_profile_update( $user_id ){
    //make sure the current user can edit this user
    if ( ! current_user_can( 'edit_user', $user_id ) )
        return false;

    // check if value has been posted
    if ( isset( $_POST['age'] ) ){
        // update user meta
        update_user_meta( $user_id, 'age', intval( $_POST['age'] ) );
    }
}
```

```
// user's own profile
add_action( 'personal_options_update', 'sp_profile_update' );
// admins editing
add_action( 'edit_user_profile_update', 'sp_profile_update' );
?>
```

Again, we're hooking into two separate hooks. One for when users are viewing their own profile, and one for when admins are editing other users' profiles.

So that's how you add a field to the registration and profile pages. Just iterate through that for each field you want to add (or piggyback on plugins like PMPro Register Helper to do it for you), and you're good to go.

Customizing the Users Table in the Dashboard

With all of this extra metadata for our users, it is sometimes necessary to extend the basic users list table in the WordPress dashboard.

You can create your own admin page, with custom queries, and a report that mimics the style of the dashboard list tables (that's what we did for the "Members List" in Paid Memberships Pro). Or you can use hooks and filters provided by WordPress to add columns and filters to the standard user list, which is what we will cover here.

To do this, we use the `manage_users_columns` and `manage_users_custom_column` filters. Let's add our age field to the user's list:

```
// add our column to the table
function sp_manage_users_columns( $columns ){
    $columns['age'] = 'Age';
    return $columns;
}
add_filter( 'manage_users_columns', 'sp_manage_users_columns' );

// tell WordPress how to populate the column
function sp_manage_users_custom_column( $value, $column_name, $user_id ){
    $user = get_userdata( $user_id );
    if ( $column_name == 'age' )
        $value = $user->age;

    return $value;
}
add_filter( 'manage_users_custom_column',
    'sp_manage_users_custom_column', 10, 3);
```

The `manage_users_columns` filter passes in an array containing all of the default Word-Press columns (and any added by other plugins). You can add columns, remove them (using `unset( $columns['column_name' ])`), and reorder them. The keys in the `$col umns` array are unique strings to identify them. The values in the `$columns` array are the headings for each column.

The `manage_users_custom_column` filter is applied to each column in the `man age_users_columns` array that isn't a default WordPress column (i.e., any custom column you add). In the `sp_manage_users_custom_column()` callback, you can do any calculations needed to get the values for each custom column. Typically the function contains a large if/then/else block or a switch statement checking the value of `$col umn_name` and returning the correct value for each column.

If you use the preceding code, you will get an Age column added to your users page, but by default you won't be able to click on it to sort the users list by age like you can with some of the default users list columns. Here's the code for that:

```php
<?php
// make the column sortable
function sp_manage_users_sortable_columns( $columns ){
    $columns['age'] = 'Age';
        return $columns;
}
add_filter( 'manage_users_sortable_columns',
    'sp_manage_users_sortable_columns' );

// update user_query if sorting by Age
function sp_pre_user_query( $user_query ){
    global $wpdb, $current_screen;

    // make sure we are viewing the users list in the dashboard
    if ( $current_screen->id != 'users' )
        return;

    // order by age
    if ( $user_query->query_vars['orderby'] == 'Age' ){
        $user_search->query_from .= " INNER JOIN $wpdb->usermeta m1
            ON $wpdb->users u1
            AND (u1.ID = m1.user_id)
            AND (m1.meta_key = 'age')";
        $user_search->query_orderby = " ORDER BY m1.meta_value
            " . $user_query->query_vars['order'];
    }
}
add_action( 'pre_user_query', 'sp_pre_user_query' );
?>
```

Above we define Age as a sortable column with the `manage_users_sortable_columns` filter. We use the `pre_user_query` filter to detect the &sortby=Age parameter on the users list page and update the `$user_query` object to join on the wp_usermeta table and order by age. Notice how we use the `$current_screen` global, which is set in the admin, to make sure we are on the users list page before editing the query.

Plugins

Now that you've seen how to customize various aspects of the WordPress user management system, let's go over a few user-related plugins that will make your life building web apps a little easier.

Theme My Login

Your members don't have to know that your site is built on WordPress. Part of that is using a login form that is integrated seamlessly with your site design rather than the default WordPress login. The Theme My Login (*http://bit.ly/theme-login*) plugin does this perfectly. Traffic to *wp-login.php* is redirected to a login page that looks like the rest of your site instead of the WordPress backend.

Theme My Login also has useful modules for theming user profiles, hiding the dashboard from non-admins, and controlling where users are redirected on login and logout.

Hide Admin Bar from Non-Admins

This plugin (*http://bit.ly/hide-bar*) does exactly what the title states. Only administrators will see the WordPress admin bar when browsing the frontend of your site. The plugin is just a few lines of code and can be edited to your needs, for example, to let editors and authors view the admin bar.

Paid Memberships Pro

Paid Memberships Pro (*http://bit.ly/paid-pro*) is brought to you by Stanger Studios and allows you to monetize the content on your site by creating a membership community. This is ideal for any business or blogger looking to lock down some or all of the content or collect fees for services provided. This plugin easily integrates with payment gateways such as Stripe, Paypal, and Authorize.net. Settings for recurring or one-time payments are included. Paid Memberships Pro allows for the creation of different membership levels within your site.

PMPro Register Helper

The Register Helper plugin (*http://bit.ly/pmp-reg-help*) was initially programmed to work with Paid Memberships Pro, but can be used without it as well. This plugin simplifies the process of adding extra fields to the registration and profile fields. Instead of a set of three hooks and functions for each field, fields can be added in a couple lines of code like:

```php
<?php
$text = new PMProRH_Field(
        'company',
```

```
            'text',
            array(
                    'size' => 40,
                    'class' => 'company',
                    'profile' => true,
                    'required' => true
            )
    );
    pmprorh_add_registration_field( 'after_billing_fields', $text );
    ?>
```

The Register Helper plugin also has shortcodes to insert signup forms into your pages
and sidebars and modules to act as starting points for your own registration, profile,
and members directory pages.

Members

The Members plugin (*http://bit.ly/members-wp*) extends the control that you have over
user roles and capabilities in your site. It enables you to edit as well as create and delete
user roles and capabilities. This plugin also allows you to set permissions for different
user roles to determine which roles have the ability to add, edit, and/or delete various
pieces of content.

You could always write your own code to add roles and capabilities, but Members adds
a nice GUI on top of that functionality that is often useful.

## CHAPTER 7

Other WordPress APIs, Objects, and Helper Functions

In this chapter, we cover several WordPress APIs, objects, and helper functions that aren't otherwise covered in the rest of the book but are still important pieces of a WordPress developer's arsenal.

Shortcode API

Shortcodes are specially formatted pieces of text that can be used to insert dynamic output into your posts, pages, widgets, and other static content areas.

Shortcodes come in three main flavors.

1. A single shortcode like [myshortcode].

2. Shortcodes with attributes like [myshortcode id="1" type="text"].

3. Enclosing shortcodes like [myshortcode id="1"] ... some content here ... [/myshortcode].

In Chapter 3, we shared an example of how to use shortcodes to add arbitrary content into a WordPress post or page. In that example, like flavor number one, we simply swapped out the shortcode for our content. You can also add attributes to the shortcode to affect the callback function processing it or wrap some content in an opening and closing shortcode pair to filter some particular content.

The basics of creating shortcodes is to define the callback function for your shortcode using the add_shortcode() function. Any attributes are added to an array that is passed to the callback as the first $atts parameter. Any enclosed content is passed to the callback as the second $content parameter.

The following code creates a shortcode called msg and makes use of attributes and enclosed content:

```php
<?php
/*
  shortcode callback for [msg] shortcode
  Example: [msg type="error"]This is an error message.[/msg]
  Output:
  <div class="message message-error">
      <p>This is an error message.</p>
  </div>
*/
function sp_msg_shortcode($atts, $content)
{
  //default attributes
  extract( shortcode_atts( array(
        'type' => 'information',
      ), $atts ) );
  $content = do_shortcode($content);    //allow nested shortcodes
  $r = '<div class="message message-' .
    $type . '"><p>' . $content . '</p></div>';
  return $r;
}
add_shortcode('msg', 'sp_msg_shortcode');
?>
```

Notice that the content you want displayed is returned from the callback function rather than echoed to the output buffer. This is because the shortcode filter is typically run before any content has been pushed to the screen. If there were any echo calls inside this function, the output would show up at the top of the page instead of inline where you want it.

Shortcode Attributes

The other important piece demonstrated in the preceding code is how the default attributes are set. The shortcode_atts() function takes three parameters: $pairs, $atts, and $shortcode.

$pairs is an array of default attributes, where each key is the attribute name and each value is the attribute value.

$atts is a similar array of attributes, usually passed in straight from the $atts parameter passed to the shortcode callback function. The shortcode_atts() function merges the default and passed attributes into one array.

The $shortcode parameter is optional. If set to match the shortcode name, it will trigger a filter shortcode_atts_{shortcode} that can be used by other plugins/etc. to override the default attributes.

The results of shortcode_atts() are then passed to the PHP function extract(), which creates a variable in the local scope for every key in the attributes array.

In this way, the variable $type in our example is available to the rest of the function and either contains the default value of message or whatever value was set in the shortcode itself.

Nested Shortcodes

Finally, we pass the inner $content through the do_shortcode() function to enable nested shortcodes. If you had a [help_link] shortcode that generated a link to your documentation depending on what section of a site you were on or the type of user logged in, you might might want to use that shortcode within the [msg] shortcode:

```
[msg type="error"]
        An error has occured. Use the following link for help: [help_link].
[/msg]
```

As long as the callback function for the [msg] shortcode passes its results through do_shortcode(), the inner [help_link] shortcode will be filtered as intended.

While nested shortcodes of different types will work, nesting the same shortcode within itself will break. The regex parser that pulls the shortcodes out of content is engineered for speed. The parser only needs to scan through the content once. Handling nested shortcodes of the same type would require multiple passes through the content, which would slow the algorithm down. The solution to this is to either (1) avoid nesting the same shortcode within itself, (2) use differently named shortcodes that link to the same callback function, or (3) write a custom regex parser for your shortcode and parse the shortcodes out yourself.

The do_shortcode() function can also be used to apply shortcodes to custom fields, content pulled from custom tables, or other content that is not already being run through the the_content filter. In most cases outside of shortcode callback functions themselves, it will be more appropriate to use apply_filters('the_content', $content), which will apply all filters on the the_content hook including the shortcode filter:

```php
<?php
global $post;
$sidebar_content = $post->sidebar_content;
?>
<div class="post">
  <?php the_content(); ?>
</div>
<div class="sidebar">
  <?php
```

```
    //echo do_shortcode($sidebar_content);
    echo apply_filters('the_content', $sidebar_content);
  ?>
</div>
```

Removing Shortcodes

Like actions and filters, you can remove registered shortcodes to keep them from being applied to a certain post or on content you are passing directly to do_shortcode() or through the the_content filter. The remove_shortcode() function takes the shortcode name as its only parameter and will unregister the specified shortcode. re move_all_shortcodes() will unregister all shortcodes.

 When calling remove_shortcode(), make sure that the calls comes late enough in the execution of WordPress for the shortcode you want removed to have already been added. For example, if a plugin adds the shortcode during the init action on priority 10, you will want to put your call to remove_shortcode() during the init action on priority 11 or higher or through another hook that fires after init.

The array of registered shortcodes is stored in a global variable $shortcode_tags. It can be useful to make copies of this variable or edit it directly. For example, if you want to exclude certain shortcodes from a specific piece of content, you can make a backup copy of all shortcodes, remove the offending shortcodes, apply shortcodes, then restore the original list of shortcodes:

```
//make a copy of the original shortcodes
global $shortcode_tags;
$original_shortcode_tags = $shortcode_tags;

//remove the [msg] shortcode
unset($shortcode_tags['msg']);

//do shortcodes and echo
$content = do_shortcode($content);
echo $content;

//restore the original shortcodes
$shortcode_tags = $original_shortcode_tags;
```

Other Useful Shortcode-Related Functions

shortcode_exists($tag)
> Checks if the shortcode $tag has been registered.

has_shortcode($content, $tag)
> Checks if the shortcode $tag appears within the $content variable.

`shortcode_parse_atts($text)`

> Pulls attributes out of a shortcode. This is done for you when parsing a shortcode, but can be called directly if you want to pull attributes out of other text like HTML tags or other templates.

`strip_shortcodes($text)`

> Strips all shortcodes out of the `$text` variable and replace them with empty text instead of calling the callback function.

Other details about the Shortcode API can be found in the WordPress Codex (*http:// bit.ly/shortc-api*).

Widgets API

Widgets allow you to place contained pieces of code and content in various widget areas throughout your WordPress site. The most typical use cases are to add widgets to a sidebar or footer area. You could always hardcode these sections on a website, but using widgets allows your nondevelopers to drag and drop widgets from one area to another or to tweak their settings through the widgets page in the admin dashboard. WordPress comes with many built-in widgets, including the basic text widget shown in Figure 7-1.

Figure 7-1. Text widget settings

Plenty of plugins also include widgets for showing various content. We won't go into the use and styling of widgets here, since their use is covered well in the WordPress Codex page on widgets (*http://bit.ly/widgets-codex*), but we will cover how to add widgets and widget areas to your plugins and themes.

 The UI of the widgets page in the admin dashboard is going through an overhaul for WordPress version 3.8; however the functions and API calls to add new widgets through code should not be affected much, if at all.

Before You Add Your Own Widget

Before you go about developing a new widget, it's worth spending some time to see if an existing widget will work for you. If you get creative, you can sometimes avoid building a new widget.

Search the repository for plugins that may already have the widget you need. If so, double-check the code there and see if it will work.

Text widgets can be used to add arbitrary text into a widget space. You can also embed JavaScript code this way or add a shortcode to the text area and use a shortcode to output the functionality you want (you may have created the shortcode already for other use) instead of creating a new widget.

If your widget is displaying a list of links, it might make sense to build a menu of those links and use the Custom Menu widget that is built into WordPress. Other widgets that display recent posts from a category will often work with CPTs and custom taxonomies either out of the box or with a little bit of effort.

If you do need to add a brand-new widget, the following section will cover the steps required.

Adding Widgets

To add a new widget to WordPress, you must create a new PHP class for the widget that extends the WP_Widget class of WordPress. The WP_Widget class can be found in *wp-includes/widgets.php* and is a good read. The comments in the code explain how the class works and which methods you must override to build your own widget class. There are four main methods that you must override, shown clearly in the following code by the sample widget class from the WordPress Codex page for the Widgets API (*http://codex.wordpress.org/Widgets_API*):

```
/*
  Taken from the Widgets API Codex Page at:
  http://codex.wordpress.org/Widgets_API
*/
```

```
class My_Widget extends WP_Widget {

        public function __construct() {
                // widget actual processes
        }

        public function widget( $args, $instance ) {
                // outputs the content of the widget
        }

        public function form( $instance ) {
                // outputs the options form on admin
        }

        public function update( $new_instance, $old_instance ) {
                // processes widget options to be saved
        }
}
add_action( 'widgets_init', function(){
    register_widget( 'My_Widget' );
});
```

The add_action() call passes an anonymous function as the second parameter, which
is only supported in PHP versions 5.3 and higher. Technically, WordPress only requires
PHP version 5.2.4 or higher. The alternative is to use the create_function() function
of PHP, which is slower and potentially less secure than using an anonymous function. However, if you plan to release your code to a wide audience, you might want to
use the alternative method shown in the following code:

```
/*
  Taken from the Widgets API Codex Page at:
  http://codex.wordpress.org/Widgets_API
*/
add_action('widgets_init',
    create_function('', 'return register_widget("My_Widget");')
);
```

Pulling this all together, Example 7-1 presents a new widget for the SchoolPress site.
This widget will show either a globally defined note set in the widget settings or a note
specific to the current BuddyPress group set by the group admins.

Example 7-1. SchoolPress note widget

```
<?php
/*
  Widget to show the current class note.
  Teachers (Group Admins) can change note for each group.
  Shows the global note set in the widget settings if non-empty.
*/
class SchoolPress_Note_Widget extends WP_Widget
{
  public function __construct() {
```

```php
    parent::__construct(
      'schoolpress_note',
        'SchoolPress Note',
        array( 'description' => 'Note to Show on Group Pages' );
}

public function widget( $args, $instance ) {
      global $current_user;

      //saving a note edit?
      if ( !empty( $_POST['schoolpress_note_text'] )
            && !empty( $_POST['class_id'] ) ) {
        //make sure this is an admin
        if(groups_is_user_admin($current_user->ID,intval($_POST['class_id']))){
              //should escape the text and possibly use a nonce
              update_option(
                    'schoolpress_note_' . intval( $_POST['class_id'] ),
                    $_POST['schoolpress_note_text']
              );
        }
      }

      //look for a global note
      $note = $instance['note'];

      //get class id for this group
      $class_id = bp_get_current_group_id();

      //look for a class note
      if ( empty( $note ) && !empty( $class_id ) ) {
            $note = get_option( "schoolpress_note_" . $class_id );
      }

      //display note
      if ( !empty( $note ) ) {
            ?>
            <div id="schoolpress_note">
                  <?php echo wpautop( $note );?>
            </div>
            <?php

            //show edit for group admins
            if ( groups_is_user_admin( $current_user->ID, $class_id ) ) {
            ?>
            <a id="schoolpress_note_edit_trigger">Edit</a>
            <div id="schoolpress_note_edit" style="display: none;">
            <form action="" method="post">
            <input type="hidden"
                  name="class_id"
                  value="<?php echo intval($class_id);?>" />
            <textarea name="schoolpress_note_text" cols="30" rows="5">
            <?php echo esc_textarea(get_option('schoolpress_note_'.$class_id))
```

```php
                ;?>
                </textarea>
                <input type="submit" value="Save" />
                <a id="schoolpress_note_edit_cancel" href="javascript:void(0);">
                        Cancel
                </a>
                </form>
                </div>
                <script>
                jQuery(document).ready(function() {
                        jQuery('#schoolpress_note_edit_trigger').click(function(){
                                jQuery('#schoolpress_note').hide();
                                jQuery('#schoolpress_note_edit').show();
                        });
                        jQuery('#schoolpress_note_edit_cancel').click(function(){
                                jQuery('#schoolpress_note').show();
                                jQuery('#schoolpress_note_edit').hide();
                        });
                });
                </script>
                <?php
                }
        }
}

    public function form( $instance ) {
        if ( isset( $instance['note'] ) )
                $note = $instance['note'];
        else
                $note = "";
        ?>
        <p>
                <label for="<?php echo $this->get_field_id( 'note' ); ?>">
                        <?php _e( 'Note:' ); ?>
                </label>
                <textarea id="<?php echo $this->get_field_id( 'note' ); ?>"
                        name="<?php echo $this->get_field_name( 'note' ); ?>">
                        <?php echo esc_textarea( $note );?>
                </textarea>
        </p>
        <?php
    }

    public function update( $new_instance, $old_instance ) {
        $instance = array();
        $instance['note'] = $new_instance['note'];

        return $instance;
    }
}
add_action( 'widgets_init', function() {
                register_widget( 'SchoolPress_Note_Widget' );
```

```
    } );
?>
```

Defining a Widget Area

In order to add widget areas or sidebar to your theme, you need to do two things. First, you need to register the widget area with WordPress. Then you need to add code to your theme at the point where you want your widget area to appear.

Registering a widget area is fairly straightforward using the `register_sidebar()` function, which takes an array of arguments as its only parameter. The available arguments are as follows, taken from the WordPress Codex page on the `register_sidebar()` function (*http://bit.ly/reg-sidebar*):

name
> Sidebar name (defaults to `\Sidebar#`, where # is the ID of the sidebar)

id
> Sidebar ID—must be all in lowercase, with no spaces (default is a numeric auto-incremented ID)

description
> Text description of what/where the sidebar is. Shown on widget management screen since 2.9 (default: empty)

class
> CSS class name to assign to the widget HTML (default: empty)

before_widget
> HTML to place before every widget (default: `<li id="%1$s" class="widget %2$s">`); uses sprintf for variable substitution

after_widget
> HTML to place after every widget (default: `</li>\n`)

before_title
> HTML to place before every title (default: `<h2 class="widgettitle">`)

after_title
> HTML to place after every title (default: `</h2>\n`)

To register a bare-bones sidebar for the assignment pages of our SchoolPress theme, we would add the following code to our theme's *functions.php* or *includes/sidebars.php* file:

```
register_sidebar(array(
  'name' => 'Assignment Pages Sidebar',
  'id' => 'schoolpress_assignment_pages',
  'description' => 'Sidebar used on assignment pages.',
  'before_widget' => '',
```

```
    'after_widget' => '',
    'before_title' => '',
    'after_title' => ''
));
```

The values for before/after_widget and before/after_title would be set based on
how our theme styles widgets and titles. Some expect <li> elements; others use <div>
elements. But if all of the styling is handled by our widget's code, we can just set everything to empty strings. Next we need to actually embed the widget area into our
theme. This is done using the dynamic_sidebar() function, which takes the ID of a
registered sidebar as its only parameter:

```
if(!dynamic_sidebar('schoolpress_student_status'))
{
  //fallback code in case my_widget_area sidebar was not found
}
```

The code will load the schoolpress_student_status sidebar if found. If it is not found,
dynamic_sidebar() will return false and the code inside of the curly braces there will
be executed instead. This can be used to show default content in a sidebar area if the
sidebar area doesn't have any widgets inside of it or doesn't exist at all.

Historically, WordPress themes were developed with a sidebar area, and themes would
hardcode certain features into them. Widgets were first introduced primarily to replace
these static sidebars with dynamic sidebars that could be controlled through the Widgets
page of the dashboard. This is why the term *sidebar* is used to define widget areas, even
though widgets are used in places other than just sidebars.

If you need to know whether a sidebar is registered and in use (has widgets) without
actually embedding the widgets, you can use the is_active_sidebar() function. Just
pass in the ID of the sidebar, and the function will return true if the sidebar is registered
or false if it is not. The Twenty Thirteen theme uses this function to check that a sidebar
has widgets before rendering the wrapping HTML for the sidebar:

```
<?php
//from twenty-thirteen/sidebar.php
if ( is_active_sidebar( 'sidebar-2' ) ) : ?>
        <div id="tertiary" class="sidebar-container" role="complementary">
                <div class="sidebar-inner">
                        <div class="widget-area">
                                <?php dynamic_sidebar( 'sidebar-2' ); ?>
                        </div><!-- .widget-area -->
                </div><!-- .sidebar-inner -->
        </div><!-- #tertiary -->
<?php endif; ?>
```

Embedding a Widget Outside of a Dynamic Sidebar

The normal process to add widgets to your pages is described in the previous section, where you define a dynamic sidebar and then add your widget to the sidebar through the Widgets page in the admin dashboard.

Alternatively, if you know exactly which widget you want to include somewhere and don't want the placement of the widget left up to the admins controlling the Widgets settings in the dashboard, you can embed a widget using the `the_widget($widget, $instance, $args)` function:

- $widget—The PHP class name for your widget

- $instance—An array containing the settings for your widget

- $args—An array containing the arguments normally passed to `register_side bar()`

Besides hardcoding the placement of the widget, using the `the_widget()` function also allows you to set the settings of the widget programmatically. In the following code, we embed the StudentPress Note widget directly into a theme page. We set the instance array to include an empty string for the `$note` value, ensuring that the group note is shown if available:

```
//show note widget, overriding global note
the_widget('SchoolPress_Note_Widget',  //classname
           array('note'=>''),          //instance vars
           array(                      //widget vars
               'before_widget' => '',
               'after_widget' => '',
               'before_title' => '',
               'after_title' => ''
           )
);
```

Dashboard Widgets API

Dashboard widgets are the boxes that show up on the homepage of your WordPress admin dashboard (see Figure 7-2).

By default, WordPress includes a few different dashboard widgets. By adding and removing widgets from the dashboard using the Dashboard Widgets API, you can make your WordPress app more useful by placing the information and tools most required by your app right there on the dashboard homepage. It's a nice touch that should be done by all WordPress apps with users who will be accessing the WordPress admin.

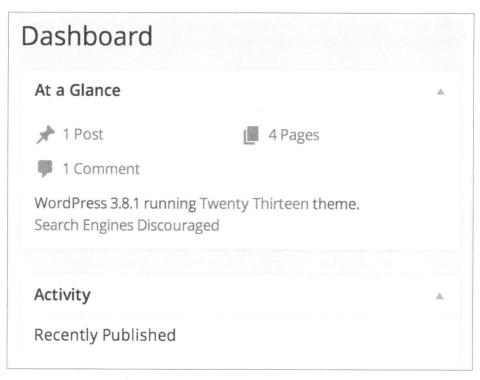

Figure 7-2. Dashboard widgets

Removing Dashboard Widgets

The dashboard widgets are really just meta boxes assigned to the dashboard page of the admin. The WordPress Codex page on the Dashboard Widgets API has a list of the default widgets shown on the WordPress dashboard:

```
// From the Dashboard Widgets API Codex Page
// Main column:
$wp_meta_boxes['dashboard']['normal']['high']['dashboard_browser_nag']
$wp_meta_boxes['dashboard']['normal']['core']['dashboard_right_now']
$wp_meta_boxes['dashboard']['normal']['core']['dashboard_recent_comments']
$wp_meta_boxes['dashboard']['normal']['core']['dashboard_incoming_links']
$wp_meta_boxes['dashboard']['normal']['core']['dashboard_plugins']

// Side Column:
$wp_meta_boxes['dashboard']['side']['core']['dashboard_quick_press']
$wp_meta_boxes['dashboard']['side']['core']['dashboard_recent_drafts']
$wp_meta_boxes['dashboard']['side']['core']['dashboard_primary']
$wp_meta_boxes['dashboard']['side']['core']['dashboard_secondary']
```

To remove widgets from the dashboard, you can use the `remove_meta_box($id, $page, $context)` function:

- $id—The ID defined when the meta box was added. This is set as the id attribute of the <div> element created for the meta box.

- $page—The name of the admin page the meta box was added to. Use dashboard to remove dashboard meta boxes.

- $context—Either normal, advanced, or side, depending on where the meta box was added.

To remove all of the default widgets, you can hook into wp_dashboard_setup and make a call to remove_meta_box() for each widget you'd like to remove:

```
// Remove all default WordPress dashboard widgets
function sp_remove_dashboard_widgets()
{
        remove_meta_box('dashboard_browser_nag', 'dashboard', 'normal');
        remove_meta_box('dashboard_right_now', 'dashboard', 'normal');
        remove_meta_box('dashboard_recent_comments', 'dashboard', 'normal');
        remove_meta_box('dashboard_incoming_links', 'dashboard', 'normal');
        remove_meta_box('dashboard_plugins', 'dashboard', 'normal');

        remove_meta_box('dashboard_quick_press', 'dashboard', 'side');
        remove_meta_box('dashboard_recent_drafts', 'dashboard', 'side');
        remove_meta_box('dashboard_primary', 'dashboard', 'side');
        remove_meta_box('dashboard_secondary', 'dashboard', 'side');
}
add_action('wp_dashboard_setup', 'sp_remove_dashboard_widgets');
```

There are a different set of widgets added to the multisite network dashboard, and a different hook must be used to remove the network dashboard widgets. The following code hooks on wp_network_dashboard_setup and removes the meta boxes added to the "dashboard-network" $page:

```
//Remove network dashboard widgets
function sp_remove_network_dashboard_widgets()
{
  remove_meta_box('network_dashboard_right_now', 'dashboard-network', 'normal');
  remove_meta_box('dashboard_plugins', 'dashboard-network', 'normal');
  remove_meta_box('dashboard_primary', 'dashboard-network', 'side');
  remove_meta_box('dashboard_secondary', 'dashboard-network', 'side');
}
add_action('wp_network_dashboard_setup', 'sp_remove_network_dashboard_widgets');
```

You could use similar code to remove default meta boxes from other dashboard pages, like the edit page and edit post pages. The $page value to use when removing meta boxes there are page and post, respectively.

Adding Your Own Dashboard Widget

The `wp_add_dashboard_widget()` function is a wrapper to `add_meta_box()` that will add a widget to your admin dashboard page. The `wp_add_dashboard_widget()` function takes four parameters:

- $widget_id—An ID for your widgets that is added as a CSS class name to the wrapper for the widget and also used as the array key for the dashboard widgets array.
- $widget_name—Name of the widget displayed in the widget heading.
- $callback—Callback function that renders the widget.
- $control_callback—Optional. Defaults to `NULL`. Callback function to handle the display and processing of a configuration page for the widget.

Example 7-2 adds a dashboard widget to show the status of current assignments (Figure 7-3). The code includes the call to `wp_add_dashboard_widget()` to register the dashboard widget and also includes the callback function to display that actual widget and another callback function to handle the configuration view (Figure 7-4) of that widget.

Example 7-2. Assignments dashboard widget

```php
<?php
/*
    Add dashboard widgets
*/
function sp_add_dashboard_widgets() {
    wp_add_dashboard_widget(
            'schoolpress_assignments',
            'Assignments',
            'sp_assignments_dashboard_widget',
            'sp_assignments_dashboard_widget_configuration'
    );
}
add_action( 'wp_dashboard_setup', 'sp_add_dashboard_widgets' );

/*
    Assignments dashboard widget
*/
//widget
function sp_assignments_dashboard_widget() {
    $options = get_option( "assignments_dashboard_widget_options", array() );

    if ( !empty( $options['course_id'] ) ) {
        $group = groups_get_group( array(
                'group_id'=>$options['course_id']
                ) );
    }
```

```php
        if ( !empty( $group ) ) {
                echo "Showing assignments for class " .
                        $group->name . ".<br />...";
                /*
                        get assignments for this group and list their status
                */
        }
        else {
                echo "Showing all assignments.<br />...";
                /*
                        get all assignments and list their status
                */
        }
}
//configuration
function sp_assignments_dashboard_widget_configuration() {
        //get old settings or default to empty array
        $options = get_option( "assignments_dashboard_widget_options", array() );

        //saving options?
        if ( isset( $_POST['assignments_dashboard_options_save'] ) ) {
                //get course_id
                $options['course_id'] = intval(
                        $_POST['assignments_dashboard_course_id']
                        );

                //save it
                update_option( "assignments_dashboard_widget_options", $options );
        }

        //show options form
        $groups = groups_get_groups( array( 'orderby'=>'name', 'order'=>'ASC' ) );
        ?>
        <p>Choose a class/group to show assignments from.</p>
        <div class="feature_post_class_wrap">
                <label>Class</label>
                <select name="assignments_dashboard_course_id">
                <option value="" <?php selected( $options['course_id'], "" );?>>
                        All Classes
                </option>
                <?php
                $groups = groups_get_groups( array( 'orderby'=>'name',
                                                'order'=>'ASC' ) );

                if ( !empty( $groups ) && !empty( $groups['groups'] ) ) {
                        foreach ( $groups['groups'] as $group ) {
                        ?>
                        <option value="<?php echo intval( $group->id );?>"
                        <?php selected( $options['course_id'], $group->id );?>>
                        <?php echo $group->name;?>
                        </option>
                        <?php
```

```
                }
            }
            ?>
            </select>
        </div>
        <input type="hidden" name="assignments_dashboard_options_save" value="1" />
        <?php
    }
    ?>
```

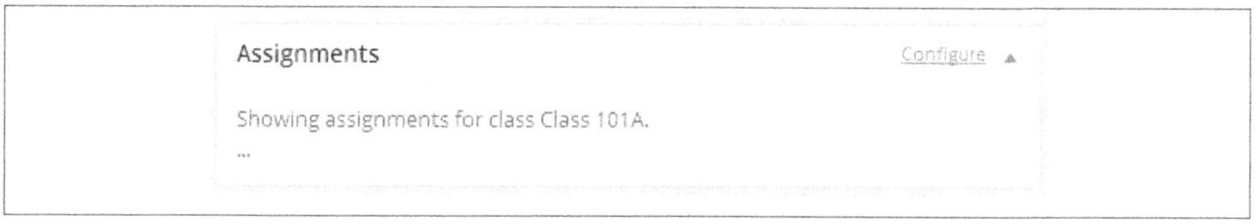

Figure 7-3. Our assignments widget

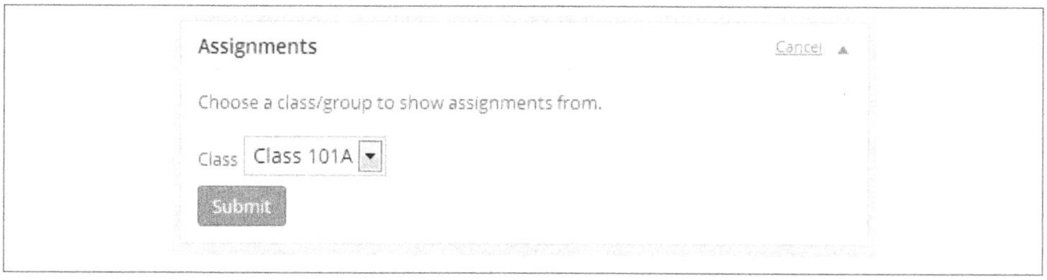

Figure 7-4. The configuration view of our assignments widget

Note that we hook into `wp_dashboard_setup` for the function that adds our widget. If we wanted our widget to show up on the network dashboard, we would need to use the `wp_network_dashboard_setup` hook.

The `sp_assignments_dashboard_widget()` function draws the actual widget shown on the dashboard page. This is where we would add our code to loop through assignments and show stats on what percentage of assignments have been turned in.

The `sp_assignments_dashboard_widget_configuration()` function draws the configuration form and also includes code to process the form submission and update the option we use to store the configuration.

Settings API

WordPress offers an API that can be used to generate options and settings forms for your plugins in the admin dashboard.

The Settings API is very thoroughly documented in the WordPress Codex (*http://bit.ly/settings-api*). There is also a great tutorial by Tom Mcfarlin at Tutsplus called The Complete Guide to the WordPress Settings API (*http://bit.ly/guide-wp*). These resources cover the details of adding menu pages and settings within them for use in your plugins and themes. Below are some tips specific to app developers.

Do You Really Need a Settings Page?

Before spending the time to create a settings page and adding to the technical debt of your app, consider using a global variable to store an array of the options used by your plugin or app:

```
global $schoolpress_settings;
$schoolpress_settings = array(
  'info_email' => 'info@schoolpress.me',
  'info_email_name' => 'SchoolPress'
);
```

For apps that won't be managed by nondevelopers and/or won't be distributed, using a global of settings may be enough. Just store a global variable like the one in the preceding code at the top of your plugin file or inside of a *includes/settings.php* file. Why build the UI if you aren't going to use it?

Even if your plugin or theme will eventually be distributed, we like to start with a global variable like this anyway. The settings that you think you need in the beginning may not be the ones you need at the end of your project. Settings may be added or removed throughout development. Settings you think need a dropdown may need a free text field instead. The Settings API makes it easy to add settings and update them later, but it is still much easier to change one element in a global array than it is to add or modify a handful of function calls and definitions.

If most of the statements below apply to you, consider using a global variable for your settings instead of building a settings UI:

- This plugin is not going to be distributed outside my team.
- The only people changing these settings are developers.
- These settings do not need to be different across our different environments.
- These settings are likely to change before release.

Could You Use a Hook or Filter Instead?

Another alternative to adding a setting to your plugin through the Settings API is to use a hook or filter instead. If a setting you are imagining would only be used by a minority of your users, consider adding a hook or filter to facilitate the setting.

For example, someone using our WP-Doc plugin may request the ability to restrict .*doc* generation to admins only or a specific subset of WordPress roles. We could add a settings page with a list of roles with checkboxes to enable or disable .*doc* downloads for that role. Maybe it should just be one checkbox to enable downloads for all roles or just admins. Maybe it should be a free text field to enter a capability name to check for before allowing the download.

A filter might be a better way to do this. We can add a capability check before the .*doc* is served and use a filter to let developers override the default array of capabilities checked. This code should be added to the `wpdoc_template_redirect()` function of the WP-Doc plugin, before the .*doc* page is rendered:

```
//don't require any caps by default, but allow developers to add checks
$caps = apply_filters('wpdoc_caps', array());

if(!empty($caps))
{
  //guilty until proven innocent
  $hascap = false;

  //must be logged in to have any caps at all
  if(is_user_logged_in())
  {
    //make sure the current user has one of the caps
    foreach($caps as $cap)
    {
      if(current_user_can($cap))
      {
        $hascap = true;
        break;  //stop checking
      }
    }
  }

  if(!$hascap)
  {
    //don't show them the file
    header('HTTP/1.1 503 Service Unavailable', true, 503);
    echo "HTTP/1.1 503 Service Unavailable";
    exit;
  }
}
```

You could then override the `wpdoc_caps` array by adding actions like these:

```
//require any user account
add_filter('wpdoc_caps', function($caps) { return array('read'); });

//require admin account
add_filter('wpdoc_caps', function($caps) { return array('manage_options'); });
```

```
//authors only or users with a custom capability (doc)
add_filter('wpdoc_caps', function($caps) { return array('edit_post', 'doc'); });
```

 The preceding example uses anonymous functions, also known as closures, so the add_filter() call can be written on one line without using a separate callback function. This syntax requires PHP version 5.3 or higher.

To recap, the more the following statements are true, the more it makes sense to use a hook or filter instead of a settings UI:

- Only a small number of people will want to change this setting.
- The people changing this setting are likely to be developers.
- The people changing this setting are likely to have custom needs.
- This setting would require a large number of individual settings or more complicated UI.

Use Standards When Adding Settings

If and when you do need to add settings to your plugin or theme, be sure to use the tutorials listed earlier in this chapter to make sure you are using the Settings API correctly to add your settings.

Using the Settings API takes a little bit of up-front work, but does let you add and edit settings more easily later on. Also, since you are doing things the WordPress way, other developers will understand how your code works and will be able to hook into it. If a developer wants to make an add-on for your plugin, she will be able to hook into your existing menus and settings sections to add additional settings for her plugins.

Using the Settings API will also ensure that your settings look similar to the other settings through a user's WordPress dashboard. You don't want developers to have to learn a new UI just to use your plugin.

Ignore Standards When Adding Settings

While you typically want to use the Settings API and the WordPress standards when adding settings for your plugin, sometimes it make sense to ignore those standards.

The main case here is if you have a large number of settings that deserve a very custom UI. If you only have one or two settings, users won't be spending a lot of time inside the settings screens. They will just want to change those two settings as fast as possible.

However, if your plugin requires dozens of settings, possibly across multiple tabs or screens, possibly related to one another, it makes sense to treat the settings for your app as an app itself. You should devote some attention to make sure that the UI and UX for your settings screen is as optimized as possible.

The WordPress Settings API is pretty flexible in terms of how things are displayed. You can control how each section is rendered and how each individual setting field is rendered. But in the end, it really is focused on one or more tabs with sections with fields on them. For applications with a large number of settings that interact with one another, you may want to use a different organization for your settings.

Don't be scared to ignore the standards here. Add a menu to the dashboard, have the callback function for it include a set of organized .php files to generate the settings form and process it, and follow these tips if possible:

- Add your menu sections and items per the standards, even if your settings pages themselves use a custom layout.
- Remember to sanitize your inputs and use nonces when appropriate.
- Use hooks and filters to whenever possible, if you'd like to allow others to extend your settings.
- Use the same HTML elements and CSS classes whenever possible so the general style stays consistent with the rest of WordPress now and through future updates.

Due to the complexity of ecommerce software, it makes sense that ecommerce plugins often have complicated settings screens. Here are two examples of plugins doing custom settings pages well:

- Paid Memberships Pro (*http://bit.ly/paid-pro*) (whose code is posted on GitHub (*http://bit.ly/pmp-github*))
- WooCommerce (*http://bit.ly/wcomm-plugin*) (whose code is posted on GitHub (*http://bit.ly/wc-github*))

Rewrite API

Apache comes with a handy module called mod_rewrite that allows you to route incoming URLs to different URLs or file locations using rules that are typically added to an *.htaccess* file in your site root folder. Other Web servers have similar URL rewriting systems; here are the standard rules for WordPress:

```
# BEGIN WordPress
<IfModule mod_rewrite.c>
RewriteEngine On
RewriteBase /
```

```
RewriteRule ^index\.php$ - [L]
RewriteCond %{REQUEST_FILENAME} !-f
RewriteCond %{REQUEST_FILENAME} !-d
RewriteRule . /index.php [L]
</IfModule>
# END WordPress
```

David Walsh does an excellent line-by-line explanation of the WordPress .htaccess file on his blog (*http://bit.ly/dw-htaccess*) if you'd like to understand more about Apache's mod_rewrite module and how the WordPress rules work. Generally, these rules reroute all incoming traffic to *any* nondirectory or nonfile URL to the *index.php* file of your WordPress install.

WordPress then parses the actual URL to figure out which post, page, or other content to show. For example, under most permalink settings, the URL */about/* will route to the page or post with the slug "about."

For the most part, you can let WordPress do its thing and handle permalink redirects on its own. However, if you need to add your own rules to handle certain URLs in particular ways, that can be done through the Rewrite API.

Adding Rewrite Rules

The basic function to add a rewrite rule is add_rewrite_rule($rule, $rewrite, $position):

- $rule—A regular expression to match against the URL, just like you would use in an Apache rewrite rule.
- $rewrite—The URL to rewrite to if the rule is matched. Matched groups from the rule regular expressions are contained in an array called $matches.
- $position—Specifies whether to place the rules above the default WordPress rules (top) or below them (bottom).

Say we want to pass a subject line to our contact form through the URL. We could have URLs like */contact/special-offer/*, which would load the contact page and prepopulate the subject to "special-offer." We could add a rewrite rule like this:

```
add_rewrite_rule(
        '/contact/([^/]+)/?',
        'index.php?name=contact&subject=' . $matches[1],
        'top'
    );
add_rewrite_rule(
flush_rewrite_rules();
```

With this rule added to the rewrite rules, a visit to */contact/special-offer/* would redirect to the */contact/* page and populate the global $wp_query->query_vars['subject'] with the value "special-offer," or whatever text was added after *contact/*. Your contact form could use this value to prepopulate the subject value of the email sent.

Flushing Rewrite Rules

WordPress caches the rewrite rules. So when you add a rule like this, you need to flush the rewrite rules so they take effect. Flushing the rewrite rules can take some time, so it's important that you don't do it on every page load. To keep the rewrite rules in order, every plugin that affects the rewrite rules should do these three things:

1. Add the rule during plugin activation and immediately flush the rewrite rules using the flush_rewrite_rules() function.

2. Add the rule during the init hook in case the rules are flushed manually through the Permalinks Settings page of the dashboard or by another plugin.

3. Add a call to flush_rewrite_rules() during deactivation so the rule is removed on deactivation.

The following code shows how our contact subject rule should be added according to the three previous steps:

```
//Add rule and flush on activation.
function sp_activation()
{
        add_rewrite_rule(
          '/contact/([^/]+)/?',
          'index.php?name=contact&subject=' . $matches[1],
          'top'
        );
        flush_rewrite_rules();
}
register_activation_hook(__FILE__, 'sp_activation');

/*
  Add rule on init in case another plugin flushes,
  but don't flush cause it's expensive
*/
function sp_init()
{
        add_rewrite_rule(
          '/contact/([^/]+)/?',
          'index.php?name=contact&subject=' . $matches[1],
          'top'
        );
}
add_action('init', 'sp_init');

//Flush rewrite rules on deactivation to remove our rule.
function sp_deactivation()
```

```
{
        flush_rewrite_rules();
}
register_deactivation_hook(__FILE__, 'sp_deactivation');
```

Other Rewrite Functions

WordPress offers some other functions to insert special kinds of rewrite rules. These include:

add_rewrite_tag() *(http://bit.ly/rewrite-api)*
: Another way to add custom querystring variables.

add_feed() *(http://bit.ly/rewrite-add)*
: Add a new kind of feed to function like the RSS and ATOM feeds.

add_rewrite_endpoint *(http://bit.ly/rewrite-end)*
: Add querystring variables to the end of a URL.

The Codex pages for each function explains things well. Some functions will make more sense for certain uses versus others. Example 7-3 shows how to use the add_re write_endpoint() function to detect when */doc/* is added to the end of a URL and to force the download of a *.doc* file. This code makes use of the fact that any HTML document with a *.doc* extension will be read by Microsoft Word as a *.doc* file.

The add_rewrite_endpoint() function takes two parameters:

- $name*—Name of the endpoint, for example, 'doc'.

- $places*—Specifies which pages to add the endpoint rule to. Uses the EP_* constants defined in *wp-includes/rewrite.php*.

Example 7-3. The WP DOC plugin

```php
<?php
/*
Plugin Name: WP DOC
Plugin URI: http://bwawwp.com/wp-docx/
Description: Add /doc/ to the end of a page or post to download a .docx version.
Version: .1
Author: Stranger Studios
*/

/*
        Register Rewrite Endpoint
*/
//Add /doc/ endpoint on activation.
function wpdoc_activation()
{
        add_rewrite_endpoint('doc', EP_PERMALINK | EP_PAGES);
        flush_rewrite_rules();
```

```php
}
register_activation_hook(__FILE__, 'wpdoc_activation');

//and init in case another plugin flushes, but don't flush cause it's expensive
function wpdoc_init()
{
        add_rewrite_endpoint('doc', EP_PERMALINK | EP_PAGES);
}
add_action('init', 'wpdoc_init');

//flush rewrite rules on deactivation to remove our endpoint
function wpdoc_deactivation()
{
        flush_rewrite_rules();
}
register_deactivation_hook(__FILE__, 'wpdoc_deactivation');

/*
        Detect /doc/ use and return a .doc file.
*/
function wpdoc_template_redirect()
{
        global $wp_query;
        if(isset($wp_query->query_vars['doc']))
        {
                global $post;

                //double check this is a post
                if(empty($post->ID))
                        return;

                //headers for MS Word
                header("Content-type: application/vnd.ms-word");
                header('Content-Disposition: attachment;Filename='.
            $post->post_name.'.doc');

                //html
                ?>
                <html>
                <body>
                <h1><?php echo $post->post_title; ?></h1>
                <?php
                        echo apply_filters('the_content', $post->post_content);
                ?>
                </body>
                </html>
                <?php

                exit;
        }
}
```

```
add_action('template_redirect', 'wpdoc_template_redirect');
?>
```

Note in the preceding example that we follow the three steps we used in the `add_re write_rule()` example to define our rule on activation and init and flush all rules on activation and deactivation.

We used `EP_PERMALINK | EP_PAGES` when defining our endpoint, which will add the endpoint to single post pages and page pages.[1] The full list of endpoint mask constants is shown below:

```
EP_NONE
EP_PERMALINK
EP_ATTACHMENT
EP_DATE
EP_YEAR
EP_MONTH
EP_DAY
EP_ROOT
EP_COMMENTS
EP_SEARCH
EP_CATEGORIES
EP_TAGS
EP_AUTHORS
EP_PAGES
EP_ALL
```

For more information on the Rewrite API, both the Codex page on the Rewrite API (*http://bit.ly/rewrite-codex*) and the Codex page on the WP_Rewrite class (*http://bit.ly/ class-ref-wp*) are good sources of information. There is a lot more that can be done with the WP_Rewrite class that we didn't get into here.

WP-Cron

A cron job is a script that is run on a server at set intervals. The WP-Cron functions in WordPress extend that functionality to your WordPress site. Cron jobs, sometimes called events, can be set up to run every few minutes, every few hours, every day, or on specific days of the week or month. Some typical uses of cron jobs include queueing up digest emails, syncing data with third-party APIs, and preprocessing CPU-intensive computations used in reports and comparative analysis.

There are three basic parts to adding a cron job to your app:

1. Schedule the cron event. This will fire a specific hook/action at the defined interval.

2. Hook a function to that action.

---

1. Posts with `post_type` page.

---

3. Place the code you actually want to run within the callback function.

This code can be added to a custom plugin file to schedule some cron jobs:[2]

```
//schedule crons on plugin activation
function sp_activation()
{
        //do_action('sp_daily_cron'); will fire daily
        wp_schedule_event(time(), 'daily', 'sp_daily_cron');
}
register_activation_hook(__FILE__, 'sp_activation');

//clear our crons on plugin deactivation
function sp_deactivation()
{
        wp_clear_scheduled_hook('sp_daily_cron');
}
register_deactivation_hook(__FILE__, 'sp_deactivation');

//function to run daily
function sp_daily_cron()
{
        //do this daily
}
add_action("sp_daily_cron", "sp_daily_cron");
```

The function wp_schedule_event($timestamp, $recurrence, $hook, $args) has the following attributes:

- $timestamp—Timestamp for first time to run the hook. You can typically set it to time().

- $recurrence—How often the event should run. You can pass hourly, daily, or twicedaily, or use the cron_schedules hook to add other intervals.

- $hook—The name of the action to fire on each recurrence.

- $args—Any arguments you'd like to pass along to the hook fired can be added to the end of the wp_schedule_event() call.

We like to give our cron events generic names based on the interval. This way, if we wanted to run another function daily, we could just add add_action('sp_daily_cron', 'new_function_name'); to our codebase.

---

2. If you move this code into a subdirectory of your plugin, you will need to update the register_activa tion_hook() and register_deactivation_hook() calls to point to the main plugin file.

Adding Custom Intervals

By default, the `wp_schedule_event()` function will only accept intervals of hourly, daily, or twicedaily. To add other intervals, you need to use the `cron_schedules` hook:

```
//add a monthly interval to use in cron jobs
function sp_cron_schedules($schedules)
{
        $schedules['monthly'] = array(
                'interval' => 60*60*24*30, //really 30 days
                'display' => 'Once a Month'
        );
}
add_filter( 'cron_schedules', 'sp_cron_schedules' );
```

Unlike Unix-based cron jobs, WP-Cron doesn't support intervals based on day of the week. To do this, you can use a daily cron job and have the function called check the day of the week:

```
//run on Mondays
function sp_monday_cron()
{
        //get day of the week, 0-6, starting with Sunday
        $weekday = date("w");

        //is it Monday?
        if($weekday == "1")
        {
                //execute this code on Mondays
        }
}
add_action("sp_daily_cron", "sp_monday_cron");
```

You could write similar code to check for a specific day of the month (`date("j")`) or even specific months (`date("m")`)

Scheduling Single Events

The preceding examples show how to execute code at some interval. You may also have times when you want to fire an event once at some point in the future. For example, you may want to schedule email delivery of new blog posts one hour after they are posted. This will give authors one hour to fix any issues with the blog posts before it gets pushed around the world. The `wp_schedule_single_event()` function can be used in these cases where we want schedule an event to fire just once.

Kicking Off Cron Jobs from the Server

In all of the previous examples, we assumed that events scheduled with `wp_sched` `ule_event()` would actually run when they are scheduled. That's almost true.

On Unix systems, the cron service runs every minute (generally) to check if there is a script to run. In WordPress, that check is done on every page load. So if no one loads your website in a given day, or only pages from a static cache are loaded, your cron jobs may not fire off that day. They will fire off with the next page load.

This setup is fine for casual WordPress sites, but our apps need reliability. Luckily, it is easy to disable the internal cron timer and set one up on your web server to fire when you need it to.

To disable the WordPress cron timer, simply add the following to your *wp-config.php* file:

```
define('DISABLE_WP_CRON', true);
```

This constant just enables or disables the *check* for events that are ready to fire. You still add and manage events as we did up above. We just need to manually hit the *wp-cron.php* file in our WordPress install often enough to fire our scripts when needed.

If all you have are daily scripts, you can add a cron job like this via the `crontab -e` command:

```
0 0 * * * wget -O - -q -t 1 http://yoursite.com/wp-cron.php?doing_wp_cron=1
```

Information on how to use cron can be found at its Wikipedia entry (*http://bit.ly/cron wiki*). Information on how to use `wget` can be found at the `wget` manual (*http://bit.ly/ gnu-manual*).

The `0 0 * * *` part of the preceding entry tells cron to execute this script at 0 minutes on the 0th hour (midnight) every day of the week.

The `wget -O - -q -t 1 http://yoursite.com/wp-cron.php?doing_wp_cron=1` part uses the `wget` command to load up the *wp-cron.php* page in your WordPress install. The `-O -` tells `wget` to send output to devnull, and the `-q` enables quiet mode. This will keep cron from adding files to your server or emailing you the outputs of each cron run. The `-t 1` tells cron to try once. This will keep `wget` from hitting your server multiple times if the first try fails. If the call to *wp-cron.php* is failing, the rest of your website is probably failing too; hopefully you've already been notified.

Be sure to change `yoursite.com` to your actual site URL. And finally, the `?do ing_wp_cron=1` on the end of the URL is needed since *wp-cron.php* will check for that `$_GET` parameter before running.

Make sure that the URL to *wp-cron.php* is excluded from any caching mechanisms you may have installed on your site.

This one cron job will fire every day, and any daily cron jobs you scheduled inside of WordPress will fire daily. If you need your crons to run more often, you can change the cron entry to run every hour or every few minutes. Note that a call to *wp-cron.php* is basically a hit to your website. A check every minute is effectively the same as an additional 1,440 users hitting your site. So schedule your cron jobs conservatively.

Using Server Crons Only

If you aren't distributing your code or don't mind telling your users that they have to set up server-side cron jobs, you don't need to schedule your cron events in WordPress at all. You can just schedule a server-side cron job that calls a special URL to kick off your callback function. This is especially useful if you need to have more control over what times of day your crons run or otherwise just feel more comfortable managing your cron jobs in Unix instead of WordPress.

 The information on scheduling server-side cron jobs in this section can be used to replace WP-Cron for recurring events. Single events set using `wp_schedule_single_event()` will need to be handled using WP-Cron still or some other mechanism.

If we were running our Monday cron job from earlier, we would update the code in WordPress:

```
//run on Mondays
function sp_monday_cron()
{
        //check that cron param was passed in
        if(empty($_REQUEST['sp_cron_monday']))
                return false;

        //execute this code on Mondays
}
add_action("init", "sp_monday_cron");
```

And your cron job entry would look like this:

```
0 0 * * 1 wget -O - -q -t 1 http://yoursite.com/?sp_cron_monday=1
```

Again, make sure that the URL to `?sp_cron_monday=1` is excluded from any caching mechanisms you may have installed on your site.

WP Mail

The `wp_mail()` function is a replacement for PHP's built-in `mail()` function. It looks like this:

```
wp_mail($to, $subject, $message, $headers, $attachments)
```

and its attributes are:

- $to—A single email address, comma-separated list of email addresses, or array of email addresses the email will be sent to (using the "To:" field).
- $subject—The subject of the email.
- $message—The body of the email. By default, the email is sent as a plain-text message and should not include HTML. However, if you change the content type (see the following example), you should include HTML in your message.
- $headers—Optional array of mail headers to send with the message. This can be used to add CCs, BCCs, and other advanced mail headers.
- $attachments—A single filename or array of filenames to be attached to the outgoing email.

There are two major improvements `wp_mail()` makes over `mail()`.

1. The `wp_mail()` function is hookable. The `wp_mail` filter will pass an array of all of the parameters passed into the `wp_mail()` function for you to filter. You can also filter the sending address using the `wp_mail_from` and `wp_mail_from_name` filters.

2. The `wp_mail()` function can be passed a single filename or array of filenames in the `$attachments` parameters, which will be attached to the outgoing email. Attaching files to emails is very complicated, but `wp_mail()` makes it easy by wrapping around the PHPMailer class, which itself wraps around the default PHP `mail()` function.

Sending Nicer Emails with WordPress

By default, emails sent through the `wp_mail()` function are sent from the admin email address set on the General Settings page of the admin dashboard, with "WordPress" used as the name. This is not ideal. You can change these values using the wp_mail_from and wp_mail_from_name filters.

Also by default, emails are sent using plain text. You can use the wp_mail_con tent_type filter to send your emails using HTML.

Finally, it is nice to add a styled header and footer to all of your outgoing emails. This can be done by filtering the email message using the wp_email filter.

The following code combines these techniques to pretty up the emails being sent by your WordPress app:

```
//Update from email and name
function sp_wp_mail_from($from_email)
{
  return 'info@schoolpress.me';
}
function sp_wp_mail_from_name($from_name)
{
  return 'SchoolPress';
}
add_filter('wp_mail_from', 'sp_wp_mail_from');
add_filter('wp_mail_from_name', 'sp_wp_mail_from_name');

//send HTML emails instead of plain text
function sp_wp_mail_content_type( $content_type )
{
  if( $content_type == 'text/plain')
  {
    $content_type = 'text/html';
  }
  return $content_type;
}
add_filter('wp_mail_content_type', 'sp_wp_mail_content_type');

//add a header and footer from files in the active theme
function sp_wp_mail_header_footer($email)
{
  //get header
  $headerfile = get_stylesheet_directory() . "email_header.html";
  if(file_exists($headerfile))
    $header = file_get_contents($headerfile);
  else
    $header = "";

  //get footer
  $footerfile = get_stylesheet_directory() . "email_footer.html";
  if(file_exists($footerfile))
    $footer = file_get_contents($footerfile);
  else
    $footer = "";
```

```
    //update message
    $email['message'] = $header . $email['message'] . $footer;

    return $email;
}
add_filter('wp_mail', 'sp_wp_mail_header_footer');
```

Sending emails from your server can present interesting network problems. Running a local SMTP server for sending emails can be time-consuming on top of the work of running a web server. Deliverability of your emails can be affected by spam filters that haven't whitelisted your apps IP range. The Configure SMTP (*http://bit.ly/config-smtp*) plugin can be used to send your outgoing email through an external SMTP server like a Google Apps account. Services like Mandril and Sendgrid, each with their own WordPress plugin, also offer ways to send email from their trusted servers with additional tracking of open and bounce rates.

File Header API

The comment block at the top of the main theme and plugin files are often referred to as headers. The File Header API consists of three functions, get_plugin_data(), wp_get_theme(), and get_file_data(), which allow you to parse these comment blocks.

As a reminder, here is what a plugin's file header may look like:

```
/*
Plugin Name: Paid Memberships Pro
Plugin URI: http://www.paidmembershipspro.com
Description: Plugin to Handle Memberships
Version: 1.7.3.2
Author: Stranger Studios
Author URI: http://www.strangerstudios.com
*/
```

You can pull this data into an array by calling the get_plugin_data() function:

get_plugin_data($plugin_file, $markup = true, $translate = true)

Its attributes are:

- $plugin_file—The absolute path to the main plugin file where the header will be parsed.

- $markup—A flag, which if set to true, will apply HTML markup to some of the header values. For example, the plugin URI will be turned into a link.

- $translate—A flag, which if set to true, will translate the header values using the current locale and text domain.

The following code loops through the plugins directory and will show data for *most* of the plugins there. It actually takes quite a bit of logic to find all plugins in all formats. For that you can use the `get_plugins()` function, which will return an array of all plugins or take a look at the code for that function found in *wp-admin/includes/plugin.php*. More information on `get_plugins()` can be found in the WordPress Codex (*http://bit.ly/funct-ref*):

```
//must include this file
require_once(ABSPATH . "wp-admin/includes/plugin.php");

//remember current directory
$cwd = getcwd();

//switch to themes directory
$plugins_dir = ABSPATH . "wp-content/plugins";
chdir($plugins_dir);

echo "<pre>";

//loop through theme directories and print theme info
foreach(glob("*", GLOB_ONLYDIR) as $dir)
{
        $plugin = get_plugin_data($plugins_dir .
        "/" . $dir . "/" . $dir . ".php", false, false);
        print_r($plugin);
}

echo "</pre>";

//switch back to current directory just in case
chdir($cwd);
```

Similarly, you can use `wp_get_theme()` to get information out of a theme's file header:

`wp_get_theme($stylesheet, $theme_root)`

Its attributes are:

- $stylesheet—The name of the directory for the theme. If not set, this parameter will be the current theme's directory.
- $theme_root—The absolute path to the theme's root folder. If not set, the value returned by `get_raw_theme_root()` is used.

The following code loops through the themes directory and will show data for *most* of the themes there. It actually takes quite a bit of logic to find all themes. For that you can use the `wp_get_themes()` function, which will return an array of all `WP_Theme` objects or take a look at the code for that function found in *wp-includes/theme.php*. More information on `wp_get_themes()` can be found in the WordPress Codex (*http://bit.ly/wp-get-theme*):

```
//remember current directory
$cwd = getcwd();

//switch to themes directory
$themes_dir = dirname(get_template_directory());
chdir($themes_dir);

echo "<pre>";

//loop through theme directories and print theme info
foreach(glob("*", GLOB_ONLYDIR) as $dir)
{
        $theme = wp_get_theme($dir);
        print_r($theme);
}

echo "</pre>";

//switch back to current directory just in case
chdir($cwd);
```

Adding File Headers to Your Own Files

Both the `get_plugin_info()` and `wp_get_theme()` functions make use of the `get_file_data()` function. You can access the `get_file_data()` function directly to pull file headers out any file. This can help you to create your own drop-ins or sub-plugins (often referred to as modules or add-ons) for your plugins.

`get_file_data($file, $default_headers, $context = "")` has the following attributes:

- $file—The full path and filename of the file to pull data from.

- $default_headers—An array of the header fields to look for. The keys of the array should be the header names, and the values of the array should be regex expressions for parsing the label that comes before the ":" in the comment. You can usually just enter the header name as the regex as well.

- $context—A label to differentiate between different kinds of headers. This parameter determines which `extra_{context}_headers` filter is applied to the default headers passed in:

    ```
    //set headers for our files
    $default_headers = array(
            "Title" => "Title",
            "Slug" => "Slug",
            "Version" => "Version"
    );

    //remember current directory
    ```

```
$cwd = getcwd();

//change to reports directory
$reports_dir = dirname(__FILE__) . "/reports";
chdir($reports_dir);

echo "<pre>";

//loop through .php files in reports directory
foreach (glob("*.php") as $filename)
{
        $data = get_file_data($filename, $default_headers, "report");
        print_r($data);
}

echo "</pre>";

//change back to the current directory in case someone expects the default
chdir($cwd);
```

Adding New Headers to Plugins and Themes

Example 7-4 adds an `Allow Updates` header to plugins. If this header is found and the value is `no` or `false`, then that plugin will not be flagged to update.

Example 7-4. The Stop Plugin Updates plugin

```
<?php
/*
Plugin Name: Stop Plugin Updates
Plugin URI: http://bwawwp.com/plugins/stop-plugin-updates/
Description: "Allow Updates: No" i a plugin's header keeps it from updating.
Version: .1
Author: Stranger Studios
Author URI: http://www.strangerstudios.com
*/

//add AllowUpdates header to plugin
function spu_extra_plugin_headers( $headers ) {
    $headers['AllowUpdates'] = "Allow Updates";
        return $headers;
}
add_filter( "extra_plugin_headers", "spu_extra_plugin_headers" );

/*
        loop through plugins
        check if updates are disallowed and if so remove it from list
*/
function spu_pre_set_site_transient_update_plugins( $update_plugins ) {
  //see if there are any plugins needing updates
  if ( !empty( $update_plugins ) && !empty( $update_plugins->response ) ) {
    //loop through plugins
```

```php
    $new_plugins = array();
    foreach ( $update_plugins->response as $pluginpath => $plugin ) {
        //check if the plugin is allowed or not
        $plugin_data = ABSPATH . '/wp-content/plugins/' . $pluginpath;
        $plugin_data = get_plugin_data( $plugin_data );
        if ( strtolower( $plugin_data['Allow Updates'] ) == "no" ||
          strtolower( $plugin_data['Allow Updates'] ) == "false" ) {
          //change checked version and don't add to the new response
          $update_plugins->checked[$pluginpath] = $plugin_data['Version'];
        }
        else {
                //not blocked. add plugin to new response
                $new_plugins[$pluginpath] = $plugin;
        }
    }
    $update_plugins->response = $new_plugins;
  }

return $update_plugins;
}
add_action(
        'pre_set_site_transient_update_plugins',
        'spu_pre_set_site_transient_update_plugins'
);
?>
```

## CHAPTER 8

Secure WordPress

Hackers beware! This chapter is packed full of tips and advice on how to make WordPress sites more secure and hopefully prevent them from falling prey to any malicious intent.

Why It's Important

No matter what size website you are running, security is something that you do not want to overlook. Any size site can fall victim to hackers or malware. Being knowledgeable and proactive about WordPress security will help you be less vulnerable and hopefully avoid any attacks.

One of the most popular types of attacks is called a brute-force attack in which a bot or script of code tries to gain access to your site by guessing the correct username and password combination. It may not sound that dangerous, but keep in mind that these bots are huge networks of computers making hundreds or even thousands of guesses every second! Even if these bots don't gain access to your WordPress admin, they will often take your site down anyway through the sheer amount of resources it takes your server to respond to the malicious requests. This is called a denial of service (or DoS) attack, and can be caused by a targeted attack or by automated spammers and brute-force hacks.

A standard WordPress install comes with some built-in security features that we will discuss in this chapter along with other tips that you can easily follow to make your site more secure. There are also some plugins we will highlight that can help with other issues such as spam.

Some very bad things that can happen to you if you decide to not read the rest of this chapter. Here are some pretty frequent scenarios:

- You pull up your website and notice that it's not there anymore. Downtime is bad! Hopefully you have a backup and can restore it quickly.
- You notice that you start showing up in search results for Viagra and other male enhancement drugs. This can be bad for business if your website is not specifically selling these drugs.
- Your application is sending out emails to all of your members with links to download a computer virus. Nobody wants that.
- Your application is hacked and access to personal information of your members is exposed like their names, addresses, phone numbers, and email addresses.
- Your website is hacked and is used to infect other websites with malware. This is the quickest way to get blacklisted.

Security Basics

These are the simplest but most important security tips to consider. Pay attention here because it could save you a lot of time, money, and upset visitors/members.

Update Frequently

The first and most important security tip is to always make sure you upgrade to the most recent version of WordPress as soon as a new version becomes available and also always update any plugins/themes that you have installed on your site. Many of the updates that are pushed out involve security updates; therefore, it is always important to upgrade your software in order to stay up to date and safe.

Don't Use the Username "admin"

Another important item to take care of is making sure not to use "admin" as one of your user accounts. Many bots will automatically try to login to your site with the username "admin." Knowing that most people don't change this account is half the battle; all they really need to focus on is guessing the password. When installing WordPress, the default username will be "admin" unless you specifically change it, and you SHOULD specifically change it! If you are already using WordPress and are using the username "admin," you should create a new user account with an administrator role, login with that new user, and delete the default admin account. *Make sure to change any posts or pages created by your admin account to this new account.*

Use a Strong Password

Choosing a secure password is also very important, especially for your administrator accounts. Don't use one word or one name. Jumble your password up and make it not connected to you personally.

Make sure your password is a combination of upper- and lowercase letters as well as numbers and special characters. A good password should also be at least 10 characters long; the more characters you use, the stronger your password will be. If you are having trouble coming up with one yourself, just mash on your keyboard a bit or use a service like Random.org (*http://www.random.org/passwords/*). Make sure you memorize it or copy it somewhere and secure it properly. WordPress will tell you if you are using a strong password; please take this into consideration.

Examples of Bad Passwords

- password
- password123
- pa55w0rd
- 123456789
- qwerty
- batman
- mustang
- letmein

Using any variation of password or single words, numbers, or names is a bad idea:

- usmarine (I was in the Marines)
- brianmessenlehner (my first and last name)
- brian&robin91011 (my name, my wife's name, and our anniversary)
- Dalya-Brian (my daughter's name and my son's name)
- ThaiShortiMaxx (my pets)
- IAMAWESOME! (everybody knows this, so it could be easy to guess)

Anybody that knows anything about me and my family could potentially guess passwords like these.

Examples of Good Passwords

- U$s(#8H27@!
- !lik32EaTF1$h&CHIp5
- #Uk@nN0tBr3akTh1s$h1t!!!
- *[0mG-LoL-R0Fl-T0T3$CraY]!*

It can be a pain in the neck and take an extra second or two entering in a good password but it's well worth it if it can prevent your website/application from getting hacked.

Hardening Your WordPress Install

Let's go over a few techniques for making it harder for your application to hacked.

Don't Allow Admins to Edit Plugins or Themes

By default, WordPress allows administrators to edit the source code of any plugin or theme directly in the web browser. You should disable this functionality so just in case a hacker is able to login to one of your admin accounts, he can't add any malicious code via the admin user interface for editing code. To disable this functionality, add this code to your *wp-config.php* file:

```php
<?php
define( 'DISALLOW_FILE_EDIT', true );
?>
```

Change Default Database Tables Prefix

The standard WordPress install uses `wp_` as a prefix for all tables in the database. By simply changing this prefix to something else, you will make your site a lot less vulnerable to hackers who attempt SQL injections and assume that you are using the generic `wp_` prefix. On a brand new WordPress install, you will have the option to use any table prefix you want; you should change the default `wp_` prefix to something custom.

If you would like to do this on a WordPress site that is already up and running, you can follow these steps:

1. Make a database backup just in case you mess this up!
2. Open *wp-config.php* and change

   `$table_prefix = 'wp_';`

   to

```
$table_prefix = 'anyprefix_';
```

3. Update the existing table names in your database to include your new prefix with the following SQL commands using phpMyAdmin or any SQL client such as MySQL Workbench:

```
rename table wp_commentmeta to anyprefix_commentmeta;
rename table wp_comments to anyprefix_comments;
rename table wp_links to anyprefix_links;
rename table wp_options to anyprefix_options;
rename table wp_postmeta to anyprefix_postmeta;
rename table wp_posts to anyprefix_posts;
rename table wp_terms to anyprefix_terms;
rename table wp_term_relationships to anyprefix_term_relationships;
rename table wp_term_taxonomy to anyprefix_term_taxonomy;
rename table wp_usermeta to anyprefix_usermeta;
rename table wp_users to anyprefix_users;
```

 You will have to run a similar rename SQL query for any custom tables added by your app or plugins you are using.

Using SQL commands or a SQL client update any instance of wp_ in the prefix_options and anyprefix_usermeta tables and change any values like wp_ to prefix_:

```
update anyprefix_options set option_name = replace(
option_name,'wp_','anyprefix_');
update anyprefix_usermeta set meta_key = replace(
meta_key,'wp_','anyprefix_');
```

Test out your site and make sure everything is working as it should.

If you don't feel comfortable manually making these changes, there are some plugins that can change your table prefix for you:

- Change Table Prefix (*http://bit.ly/change-tp*)
- Change DB Prefix (*http://bit.ly/change-db*)

Move wp-config.php

The WordPress *wp-config.php* file stores valuable information like your database location, username, and password and your WordPress authentication keys. Since these values are stored in PHP variables and they are not displayed to the browser, it is not likely that anybody could gain access to this data, but it could happen. You can move *wp-config.php* to one level above your WordPress install, which in most cases should be a nonpublic directory. WordPress will automatically look one level up for *wp-config.php* if it doesn't find it in your root directory. For example, move */username/public_html/wp-config.php* to */username/wp-config.php*.

You can also store *wp-config.php* as any filename in any directory location. To do this, make a copy of *wp-config.php*, name the copy whatever you want, and move it to any directory above your root install of WordPress. In your original *wp-config.php* file, remove all of the code and add an include to the relative path and filename of the copy you made. For example, copy */username/public_html/wp-config.php* to */username/someotherfolder/stuff.php*. Change the code in *wp-config.php* to `include('/username/someotherfolder/stuff.php');`

Hide Login Error Messages

Normally when trying to login in to your site, WordPress will display a message if you have put in the wrong username or password. Unfortunately this lets hackers know exactly what they are doing wrong or right when attempting to access your site.

Luckily there is a simple fix for this, which is to add a line of code into your theme *functions.php* file or in a custom plugin which will hide or alter those messages:

```php
<?php
add_filter( 'login_errors',
create_function(
 '$a', '"Invalid username or
password.";'
) );
?>
```

Hide Your WordPress Version

A lot of bots will scour the Internet in search of WordPress sites to target specifically by the version of WordPress they are running. They are looking for sites with known vulnerabilities they can exploit. By default, WordPress displays the following code within the <head></head> of every page:

```
<meta name="generator" content="WordPress 3.8.1" />
```

You can easily hide the version of WordPress you are using by implementing the following code:

```php
<?php
add_filter( 'the_generator', '__return_null' );
?>
```

Don't Allow Logins via wp-login.php

Some bots are smarter than others. We just talked about hiding your WordPress version from some bots, but sometimes just knowing that you are using WordPress is all a bot may be looking for, and this is pretty easy if it sends a POST request to *wp-login.php*. Once a bot realizes *wp-login.php* exists, it can then begin to try to login to your site.

We like to redirect *wp-login.php* to the homepage, which prevents bots from specifically trying to login via *wp-login.php*. Follow these steps to make an alternative login page and hide the default *wp-login.php* login page:

1. Add the following rewrite rule to your *.htaccess* file:

   ```
   RewriteRule ^new-login$ wp-login.php
   ```

   Note that new-login will be the URL you can use to actually log in to *wp-admin*; you can change this to whatever you want.

2. In your theme *functions.php* file or in a custom plugin, add this code:

   ```php
   <?php
   function schoolpress_wp_login_filter( $url, $path, $orig_scheme ) {
       $old = array( "/(wp-login\.php)/" );
       $new = array( "new-login" );
           return preg_replace( $old, $new, $url, 1 );
   }
   add_filter( 'site_url', 'schoolpress_wp_login_filter', 10, 3 );

   function schoolpress_wp_login_redirect() {
           if ( strpos( $_SERVER["REQUEST_URI"], 'new-login' ) === false ) {
                   wp_redirect( site_url() );
                   exit();
           }
   }
   add_action( 'login_init', 'schoolpress_wp_login_redirect' );
   ?>
   ```

If you don't want to write any custom code, you can use the following plugins to achieve similar results:

- iThemes security (*http://bit.ly/ithemes-sec*)
- WP Admin (*http://bit.ly/lockdown-wp*)

Add Custom .htaccess Rules for Locking Down wp-admin

If you are the only user that needs to log in to the backend of your application, or if you only have a handful of backend users, you can restrict access to the backend by certain IP addresses. Create a new *.htaccess* file in the *wp-admin* directory of your WordPress install and add the following code, replacing `127.0.0.1` with your actual external IP address. Go to *http://ipchicken.com/* if you are not sure of your external IP address:

```
order deny,allow
allow from 127.0.0.1 #(repeat this line for multiple IP addresses)
deny from all
```

If you suspect that certain IP addresses hitting your application are bots or malicious users, you can block them by their IP addresses with the following code:

```
order allow,deny
deny from 127.0.0.1 #(repeat this line for multiple IP addresses)
allow from all
```

If people really want to get around their banned IP address, they will use a proxy server.

If you think your IP address of you or your backend users may change often or you have way too many backend users to manage all of their IP addresses, you can add a separate username and password to access the *wp-admin* directory. This adds a nice second layer of authentication because all of your backend users will be required to enter an htaccess username and password and their standard WordPress username and password:

```
AuthType Basic
AuthName "restricted area"
AuthUserFile /path/to/protected/dir/.htpasswd
require valid-user
```

Notice the `AuthUserFile` line; you will need to create a *.htpasswd* file somewhere in a directory above or outside of your WordPress install. In this file, you will need to add a username and password. The password can't just be plain text; use a tool like htaccess password generator (*http://bit.ly/htaccess-pw*) to create an encrypted password.

So the username/password for:

`letmein/Pr3tTyPL3a$3!`

after encryption should be:

`letmein:E5Dj7cUaQVcN.`

Add the entire encrypted string `letmein:E5Dj7cUaQVcN.` to your *.htpasswd* file; and when users try to go to */wp-admin*, they will be prompted for a username and password. Make sure to let your backend users know what this username and password is and tell them not to share it with anybody.

Backup Everything!

It is important to make regularly scheduled backups of your site's content (your database) as well as the *wp-content* folder. This makes it much easier to restore your site in the event that it does fall victim to a hacker. We recommend scheduling a backup at the very least once a week; but depending upon how much new content you are adding, you may feel that you need to increase or decrease the frequency. Of course a daily backup is always the best choice.

Scan Scan Scan!

Scanning or monitoring your application is essential to know if you have been attacked. If your application ever gets hacked, it is important to know right away so you can immediately address the issue.

Be proactive about protecting your web application against malware. There are several services that will scan your web applications for you so you can take a more hands-off approach. We recommend using Sucuri (*http://sucuri.net/*). Not only will Sucuri find malware and alert you if your application has been infected, but it will also clean it up for you. Tony Perez, the COO of Sucuri, is also a former US Marine and a martial arts master, so why wouldn't you want Sucuri to have your back? Sucuri also has a great security plugin (*http://bit.ly/sucuri-plugin*) for WordPress.

Useful Security Plugins

Below are some very useful and powerful WordPress plugins that will help you increase security for your application and also help you to recover quickly if you to fall victim to a malicious attack.

Spam-Blocking Plugins

Akismet

This plugin is used to block comment spam from getting through to your site. It was developed by Automattic, also the creators of WordPress, and therefore comes standard with any new WordPress install. Although the plugin will be installed on your site, you will need to activate it by registering for an API key at Akismit.com (*https://akismet.com/*). An API key is free if your site is for personal use; however, there is a small charge for business websites. The way Akismet works is each time a comment is posted to your site, Akismet will run it through a series of tests to ensure it is a real comment, and if it is identified as spam, it is automatically moved to the spam folder in your dashboard. This saves you tons of time from having to sort through all of your comments and determine which ones are spam or legitimate comments.

Bad Behavior

This plugin (*http://bit.ly/bad-behavior*) works to block link spam from your site and functions best when run in conjunction with another spam service. It works to not only look at the content of the spam, but also looks at the method through which the spam is being delivered by the spammer and the software being used, and blocks that as well.

Backup Plugins

Backups are very helpful to have in the event that your site is compromised. Here are a few popular backup plugins.

Backup Buddy

This plugin (*http://bit.ly/backup-b*) works to make backups of all of the content on your WordPress site for safekeeping, restoring, or moving your site. Backups can be scheduled on a recurring basis and the file can then be downloaded to your computer, emailed to you, or sent off to the storage location of your choice such as Dropbox or an FTP server. This plugin also features a restore option that will easily restore your themes, widgets, and plugins. Backup Buddy also allows you to easily move your site to a new server or domain right from the WordPress dashboard, which comes in handy if you work on a dev server and then move the sites over to a production environment upon launch.

VaultPress

VaultPress (*http://vaultpress.com/*) is another plugin created by the team at Automattic and offers users the opportunity to have all of their site content backed up in real time on cloud servers. Once installed, this plugin will automatically detect any changes to the content on your site as well as site settings and then update the backup copy with those changes. The plugin also features a one-click database restore in the event that your site ever becomes compromised. This is a premium plugin, meaning there is a fee for service, and different levels are offered. The premium version of the plugin also includes a daily security scan of your site to detect any issues as well as fixes for those issues.

Scanner Plugins

WP Security Scan

This is a free plugin (*http://bit.ly/acunetix-wp*) that will perform a scan of your site and detect any areas of vulnerability in your site's security. It will then suggest fixes for any of the issues it finds. One of the important security issues this plugin helps with is changing your database table prefix, which can be tricky if you are not that familiar with the standard WordPress database structure. It also helps you to hide which version of WordPress you are using, which is information that hackers look for to use against you when attacking your site. This plugin was developed by WebsiteDefender.com, which also offers a service to monitor your website for potential security threats, including malware and hacker activity (*http://bit.ly/acunetix-sec*).

Exploit Scanner

This plugin (*http://bit.ly/exploit-scan*) will scan through all the files on your site and then alert you if it comes across anything that looks like it could be a potential threat.

BBQ

Block Bad Queries (*http://bit.ly/bbq-wp*) works as a type of firewall for your site by scanning all incoming traffic and then blocking all kinds of different malicious requests.

Antivirus-Once

Once this plugin (*http://bit.ly/antivirus-wp*) is installed and activated, it will run a daily scan on your theme template files and database tables and alert you of any potential problems with email notifications. It will also add a message into the WordPress admin bar to alert you of any viruses.

Login and Password-Protection Plugins

Limit Login Attempts

This is a great plugin (*http://bit.ly/limit-login*) to fight against brute-force attacks like someone running an automated script that will try to login to WordPress using random combinations of words. By default, WordPress will allow an unlimited amount of login attempts. This plugin limits the number of login attempts. If someone tries *x* times to log in and fails each time, she will be blocked from attempting to log in again for a set amount of time.

Ask Apache Password Protect

This plugin (*http://bit.ly/ask-apache*) is different from other WordPress security plugins in that it works at the network level to prevent attacks rather than at the site level. You choose a unique username and password that then protect your login page and entire *wp-admin* folder. This plugin does require the use of an Apache web server and web host support for *.htaccess* files.

Writing Secure Code

You want to make sure any custom code you write is secure and isn't hackable. If you take notice and apply the following methods, you should be in pretty good shape against attacks.

Check User Capabilities

Each of your users has unique standard or custom roles and capabilities. If you are writing some code that provides custom functionality for your application's administrators, then make sure to give administrators and only administrators access to it. There are a few built-in WordPress functions for telling you if a user has certain roles or capabilities. All of these functions are located in *wp-includes/capabilities.php* and return a boolean of whether the user has the passed-in role name or capability. You can pass in any default or custom-made roles or capabilities.

user_can($user, $capability)

Whether a particular user has a particular role or capability.

- $user—A required integer of a user ID or an object of the user.
- $capability—A required string of the capability or role name.

current_user_can($capability)

Whether the current user has a particular role or capability.

- $capability—A required string of the capability or role name.

current_user_can_for_blog($blog_id, $capability)

Whether the current user has a particular role or capability for a particular site on a multisite network.

- $user—A required integer of a blog ID.
- $capability—A required string of the capability or role name.

In the following code, we don't want to let ordinary users into the backend of our application. We want them to only interact with the custom UI we created within the theme on the frontend so we will redirect anybody that is not an administrator and may wander to */wp-admin* back to the frontend:

```php
<?php
function schoolpress_admin_check() {
        global $user_ID;
        if ( !user_can( $user_ID, 'administrator' ) )
                wp_redirect( site_url() );
}
add_action( 'admin_init', 'schoolpress_admin_check' );
?>
```

For a complete reference of standard default WordPress roles and capabilities, see Chapter 6 or the WordPress codex (*http://bit.ly/roles-caps*).

Custom SQL Statements

Sometimes the built-in WordPress functions that interact with the database may not be enough for your needs, and depending on what you are building, you may want to write custom SQL statements. When writing your own SQL statements, you need to make sure they are written in a way that will not allow for any potential SQL injections. First of all, always use the $wpdb object and make sure to escape and prepare all custom SQL statements.

As we talked about in Chapter 3, the $wpdb object can be used to access any standard or custom tables in your WordPress database and provides easy-to-use methods for doing so. One very important thing to remember is that when writing custom queries with any dynamic values being passed in, you need to use the esc_sql() function or the prepare() method to sanitize and escape those dynamic values. By sanitizing and escaping dynamic values, you are making sure those values are not made up of invalid characters and are not any malicious SQL code that can hijack your query (SQL injections).

The esc_sql() and $wpdb->prepare() functions are covered in detail in Chapter 3.

Data Validation, Sanitization, and Escaping

DO NOT TRUST YOUR USERS! Again, DO NOT TRUST YOUR USERS! Don't be that web application, website, or blog that spreads malware.

Validate, sanitize, and escape every piece of data going into and coming out of your database. You want to make sure that the data your users are submitting to your database is in the format it should be in; the database doesn't care what the data is as long as the data being submitted is of the same datatype.

For example, let's say you have a custom form used to collect user data with a textbox for date of birth. You plan on storing the DOB as user meta in the meta_value column of the wp_usermeta table. The meta_value column has a datatype of longtext, meaning the value can be super duper long[1] and the database isn't going to care what value you store there. It's up to you as the developer to make sure the data being stored as DOB is a date and nothing else.

---

1. In technical terms, "super duper long" is equal to about 4 GB of data.

So what exactly is the difference between validation, sanitization, and escaping?

- *Validating* is the process of making sure the data received from the end user is in the correct format you expect it to be in. You want to validate data before saving it into the database.

- *Sanitizing* is the process of cleaning data received from the end user before saving it to the database.

- *Escaping* is the process of cleaning data you may already have before displaying it to the end user.

Now you know!

You want to validate and sanitize data before putting it into your database. When pulling data out of your database, you want to sanitize it just to be safe in case somehow you are storing unsanitized data.

PHP has validation and sanitization functions, but WordPress has a bunch of helper functions built-in; and this is a book about WordPress, so let's talk about some of those functions.

 Most validation and sanitization helper functions are located in *wp-includes/formatting*.

esc_url($url, $protocols = null, $_context = *display*)

Checks and cleans a URL by checking if it has the proper protocol, stripping invalid characters and encoding special characters. Use this if displaying a URL to an end user:

- $url—A required string of the URL that needs to be cleaned.

- $protocols—An optional array of whitelisted protocols. Defaults to `array( http, https, ftp, ftps, mailto, news, irc, gopher, nntp, feed, telnet, mms, rtsp, svn )` if not specifically set.

- $context—An optional string of how the URL is being used. Defaults to `display`, which sends the URL through `wp_kses_normalize_entities()` and replaces &amp with & and ' with '.

esc_url_raw($url, $protocols = null)

This function calls the `esc_url()` function but passes db as the value for the `$_con text` parameter. Do not use this function for displaying URLs to the end user; only use it in database queries.

esc_html($text)

Escape HTML blocks in any content. This function is a nice little wrapper for the `_wp_specialchars()` function which, basically converts a number of special characters into their HTML entities:

- $text—A required string of the text you want to escape HTML tags on.

esc_js($text)

Escapes strings in inline JavaScript. Escaped strings need to be wrapped in single quotes for this to work:

- $text—A required string of the text you want to escape single quotes, HTML special characters (" < > &), and fix line endings on.

esc_attr($text)

Escapes HTML attributes and encodes such characters as <, >, &,", and '. This is important to use when including values in form input elements such as ID, name, alt, title, and value:

- $text—A required string of the text you want to escape HTML attributes on.

esc_textarea($text)

Escaping for `textarea` values. Encodes text for use inside a `<textarea>` element:

- $text—A required string of the text you want to escape HTML on.

sanitize_option($option, $value)

This function can be used to sanitize the value of any predefined WordPress option. Depending on what option is being used, the value will be sanitized via various functions:

- $option—A required string of the name of the option.

- $value—A required string of the unsanitized option value you wish to sanitize.

sanitize_text_field($str)

Sanitizes any string input by a user or pulled from the database. Checks for invalid UTF-8; converts single < characters to entity; strips all tags; removes line breaks, tabs, and extra white space; and strips octets:

- $str—The required string you want to sanitize.

sanitize_user($username, $strict = false)

This function cleans a username of any illegal characters:

- $username—A required string of the username to be sanitized.
- $strict—An optional boolean that if set to true will limit the username to specific characters.

sanitize_title($title, $fallback_title = ")

Sanitizes a title stripping out any HTML or PHP tags, or returns a fallback title for a provided string:

- $title—A required string of the title to be sanitized.
- $fallback_title—An optional string to use if the title is empty.

sanitize_email($email)

Sanitizes an email address by stripping out any characters not allowed in an email address:

- $email—The email address to be sanitized.

sanitize_file_name($filename)

Sanitizes a filename, replacing whitespace with dashes. Removes special characters that are illegal in filenames on certain operating systems and special characters requiring special escaping to manipulate at the command line. Replaces spaces and consecutive dashes with a single dash. Trims period, dash, and underscore from beginning and end of filename:

- $filename—Required string of the file name to be sanitized.

wp_kses($string, $allowed_html, $allowed_protocols = array ())

This function makes sure that only the allowed HTML element names, attribute names, and attribute values plus only sane HTML entities will occur in the string you provide. You have to remove any slashes from PHP's magic quotes before you call this function:

- $string—A required string that you want filtered through kses.
- $allowed_html—A required array of allowed HTML elements.
- $allowed_protocols—An optional array of allowed protocols in any URLs in the string being filtered. The default allowed protocols are http, https, ftp, mailto, news, irc, gopher, nntp, feed, telnet, mms, rtsp, and svn. This covers all common link protocols, except for javascript, which should not be allowed for untrusted users.

The following code validates and sanitizes an email address:

```php
<?php
// let's pretend that a user added an email address "brian @ webdevstudios.com"
$user_email = 'brian @ webdevstudios.com';

// we can check if this is a valid email
$user_email = is_email( $user_email );

// we know it's not because it's set to nothing from is_email()
if ( ! $user_email )
        echo 'invalid email<br>';

// let's try again with sanitizing the email
$user_email = 'brian @ webdevstudios.com';

// use sanitize_email() to try to fix any invalid email
$user_email = sanitize_email( $user_email );

$user_email = is_email( $user_email );

if ( ! $user_email )
        echo 'invalid email<br>';
else
        echo 'valid email: ' . $user_email;
?>
```

Nonces

Nonce stands for "number used once," and using nonces is critical to protecting your application from CSRF (cross-site request forgery) attacks.

Normally your server-side scripts for form processing are processing forms from your own site. People visit your site, log in, and submit a form to perform some action on your site. However, if your server-side code were simply looking for $_POST values to determine what to do, those values could be submitted from *any* form, even forms on other websites.

The first line of defense is to check that a user is really logged in and has the capabilities to do the requested action. However, this isn't enough to stop CSRF attacks because you might be logged in on your WordPress site (e.g., in a background tab) while some malicious code on another site/tab kicks off the form request with the correct $_POST variable to send a spammy message to your friends or initiate account deletion or something else you don't want to do.

What's needed is a way to make sure that the request comes from the WordPress site and not another site. This is what a nonce does. The basic outline of using a nonce is as follows:

1. Generate a nonce string every time a page is loaded.
2. Add the nonce string as a hidden element on the form.
3. When processing a submitted form, generate the nonce the same way and check that it matches the one submitted from the form.

Because the nonce is generated using a combination of the secret salt keys in your *wp-config.php* and the server time, it is very hard for attackers to guess the nonce string for their own forms.

Nonces are useful for nonform links and AJAX calls as well. The process is basically the same:

1. Generate a nonce string every time a page is loaded.
2. Add the nonce string as a parameter to the URL.
3. When processing the request, generate the nonce the same way and check that it matches the one submitted through the URL.

Whether protecting your forms, links, or AJAX requests, WordPress has a few helper functions to make this process very easy to implement.

wp_create_nonce($action = -1)

This function creates a random token that can only be used once and is located in *wp-includes/pluggable.php*:

$action—An optional string or int that describes what action is being taken for the nonce created. You should always set an action to be more secure:

```php
<?php
function schoolpress_footer_create_nonce(){
        $nonce = wp_create_nonce('random_nonce_action');
        $url = add_query_arg( array( 'sp_nonce' => $nonce ) );
        echo '<p><a href="' . $url . '">Verify this Nonce</a></p>';
}
add_action( 'wp_footer', 'schoolpress_footer_create_nonce' );
?>
```

wp_verify_nonce($nonce, $action = -1)

This function is used to verify that the correct nonce was used within the allocated time limit. If the correct nonce is passed into this function and everything checks out OK, then the function will return a value that evaluates to true.[2] If not, it will return false. This function is located in *wp-includes/pluggable.php*:

- $nonce—A required string of the nonce value being used to verify.

- $action—An optional string or int that should be descriptive to what is taking place and should match the action from when the nonce was created.

```php
<?php
function schoolpress_init_verify_nonce(){
  if ( isset( $_GET['sp_nonce'] )
    && wp_verify_nonce( $_GET['sp_nonce'], 'random_nonce_action' ) ) {
    echo 'You have a valid nonce!';
    } else {
    echo 'You have an invalid nonce!';
        }
}
add_action( 'init', 'schoolpress_init_verify_nonce' );
?>
```

---

2. The wp_verify_nonce() function will return 1 if the nonce is under 12 hours old. If the nonce is between 12 and 24 hours old, it will return 2. If it is older than 24 hours old, it will return false. This way you can test if the result evaluates to true or if you wanted to check for a slightly fresher nonce, you could check if it is equal to 1 exactly.

check_admin_referer($action = -1, $query_arg = _wpnonce)

This function calls the wp_verify_nonce function, so it verifies nonces but also checks to see that the referrer or the page that got you to the current page you are on is from the same website. This function is located in *wp-includes/pluggable.php*:

- $action—An optional string, but you should specify a nonce action to be verified.
- $query_arg—An optional string of the query argument that has the nonce as its value.

```php
<?php
// checking the same nonce "sp_nonce" that was created earlier
function schoolpress_init_check_admin_referer(){
        if ( isset( $_GET['sp_nonce'] )
                && check_admin_referer( 'random_nonce_action', 'sp_nonce' ) ) {
                echo '<p>You have a valid nonce!</p>';
        } else {
                echo '<p>You have an invalid nonce!</p>';
        }
}
add_action( 'init', 'schoolpress_init_check_admin_referer' );
?>
```

wp_nonce_url($actionurl, $action = -1)

This function also utilizes the wp_create_nonce() function and adds a nonce to any URL. If you create any actions based off of a query string, you should always tie a nonce to your URL with this function:

- $actionurl—A required string of the URL to add a nonce action to.
- $action—An optional string for the action name. You should always set this.

This function is located in *wp-includes/functions.php*:

```php
<?php
// simple url with querystring example
function schoolpress_footer_nonce_url(){
        $url = wp_nonce_url(
                add_query_arg( array( 'action' => 'get_users' ) ),
                'get_users_nonce'
        );
        echo '<p><a href="' . $url . '">Get Users</a></p>';
}
add_action( 'wp_footer', 'schoolpress_footer_nonce_url' );

// querystring action
function schoolpress_footer_nonce_url_action(){
        // check if querystring action is get_users and for the nonce
        if ( isset( $_GET['action'] )
                && 'get_users' == $_GET['action']
```

```
                        && check_admin_referer( 'get_users_nonce' ) ) {
                        echo 'Your action: ' . $_GET['action'];
                        // or get your users and display them here...
                }
        }
        add_action( 'init', 'schoolpress_footer_nonce_url_action' );
        ?>
```

wp_nonce_field($action = -1, $name = "_wpnonce", $referer = true , $echo = true)

This function retrieves or displays a hidden nonce field in a form. It has the `wp_cre`
`ate_nonce()` function baked into it, so you should always use this nice helper function
when dealing with forms.

The nonce field is used to validate that the contents of the form came from the location
on the current site and not somewhere else. The nonce does not offer absolute protection, but should protect against most cases. It is very important to use a nonce field in
forms.

The `$action` and `$name` parameters are optional, but if you want to have better security,
it is strongly suggested to set those two parameters. It is easier to just call the function
without any parameters, because validation of the nonce doesn't require any parameters,
but since crackers know what the default is, it won't be difficult for them to find a way
around your nonce and cause damage.

The input name will be whatever `$name` value you gave. The input value will be the nonce
creation value. This function is located in *wp-includes/functions.php*:

- $action—An optional string for the action name. You should always set this.

- $name—An optional string for the nonce name. You should always set this.

- $referer—An optional boolean of whether to set the referer field for validation. The
  default value is `true`.

- $echo—An optional boolean of whether to display or return a hidden form field.
  The default value is `true`.

```
<?php
// simple submission form example
function schoolpress_footer_form(){
        ?>
        <form method="post">
                <?php // create our nonce
                wp_nonce_field( 'email_list_form', 'email_list_form_nonce' );
                ?>
                <h3>Join our email list</h3>
                Email Address: <input type="text" name="email_address">
                <input type="submit" name="submit_email" value="Submit">
        </form>
```

```php
        <?php
    }
    add_action( 'wp_footer', 'schoolpress_footer_form' );

    // form action
    function schoolpress_footer_form_action(){
        if ( isset( $_POST['submit_email'] )
            && isset( $_POST['email_address'] )
            && check_admin_referer( 'email_list_form',
            'email_list_form_nonce' ) ) {
            echo 'You submitted: ' . $_POST['email_address'];
            // or process your form here...
        }
    }
    add_action( 'init', 'schoolpress_footer_form_action' );
    ?>
```

check_ajax_referer($action = -1, $query_arg = false, $die = true)

When using AJAX, you should still be using nonces. This function allows you to do a nonce and referer check while processing an AJAX request. This function is located in *wp-includes/pluggable.php*:

- $action—An optional string of the nonce action being referenced.

- $query_arg—An optional string of where to look for nonce in $_REQUEST.

- $die—An optional boolean of whether you want to AJAX script to die if an invalid nonce is found.

Throughout the book, you may have noticed code snippets that didn't use nonces or sanitize data. We did this to try to keep the code examples short and sweet, but you should *always* use nonces and sanitize your data. Any custom form submission or URL with custom query strings should utilize nonces, and every time you write $_POST['any thing'] or $_GET['anything'], they should be wrapped in a sanitization or escaping function.

## CHAPTER 9

JavaScript, jQuery, and AJAX

JavaScript is a major component of any modern web app. jQuery is a popular JavaScript library that makes doing many things with JavaScript a lot easier. One of the things that is easier to do with jQuery is AJAX calls. This chapter will not teach you how to code in JavaScript or jQuery. This chapter will, however, teach you how to properly integrate your JavaScript code into your WordPress app.

 The term "JavaScript," when used in this chapter and throughout the book, refers to core JavaScript or any code written in JavaScript that runs in the client browser, including jQuery and AJAX calls done in jQuery.

What Is AJAX?

The term AJAX stands for "Asynchronous JavaScript and XML" and is a way to use JavaScript to query the server after a page has already loaded. Historically, XML data would be returned and then processed by the browser using more JavaScript. These days, we more typically send back JSON-encoded data or straight up HTML to be incorporated into the app. In this chapter, we will cover executing an AJAX call via the jQuery `ajax()` method and also through the new Heartbeat API for WordPress.

What Is JSON?

JSON stands for "JavaScript Object Notation" and is a machine and human-readable format for transmitting data. It is especially useful when working with JavaScript, since a properly encoded JSON statement will be evaluated by JavaScript with no extra processing. To work with JSON in PHP, we will use the `json_encode` and `json_decode` functions that have been part of PHP core since version 5.2.

WordPress only requires PHP version 4.3, which doesn't include the `json_encode` and `json_decode` functions. WordPress has its own versions of these functions that are used if the native PHP functions are not available. Even so, it's a good idea to run the latest version of PHP supported by your hosting environment.

jQuery and WordPress

WordPress comes installed with the latest version of jQuery, which is used in the admin dashboard for various UI and AJAX-related scripting. Because jQuery is already on your server, including it in the frontend of your WordPress app is a breeze.

The jQuery JS file is located at *wp-includes/lib/js/jquery.js*. Typically you would add a link like this to the `<head>` tag of your website to load jQuery:

```
<script lang="JavaScript" src="/wp-includes/lib/js/jquery.js" />
```

This will work if added to your theme's *header.php* or through the `wp_head` hook; however, the proper way to include a JavaScript file in your WordPress site is to use the `wp_enqueue_script()` function. You can add the line `wp_enqueue_script('jquery');` to an init function called by the inside of your main plugin file, like so:

```
function sp_enqueue_scripts()
{
    wp_enqueue_script('jquery');
}
add_action('init', 'sp_enqueue_scripts');
```

The first parameter of the `wp_enqueue_script()` function is a label for the JavaScript file to enqueue. WordPress already knows what `jquery` is and where it's located, so that is the only parameter you need to enqueue it.

Enqueuing Other JavaScript Libraries

To enqueue other JavaScript libraries that WordPress doesn't already know about, pass the full list of parameters. Your main app plugin may include code like this to load jQuery and any number of required JavaScript libraries. Also, instead of building your function on the `init` hook, you should use the `wp_enqueue_scripts` and `admin_enqueue_scripts` hooks. The `wp_enqueue_scripts` hook fires on the frontend just before enqueuing scripts, while the `admin_enqueue_scripts` hook fires in the dashboard just before enqueuing scripts:

```
<?php
//frontend JS
function sp_wp_enqueue_scripts() {
    wp_enqueue_script( 'jquery' );
        wp_enqueue_script(
```

```
                'schoolpress-plugin-frontend',
                plugins_url( 'js/frontend.js', __FILE__ ),
                array( 'jquery' ),
                '1.0'
        );
}
add_action( "wp_enqueue_scripts", "sp_wp_enqueue_scripts" );

//admin JS
function sp_admin_enqueue_scripts() {
        wp_enqueue_script(
                'schoolpress-plugin-admin',
                plugins_url( 'js/admin.js', __FILE__ ),
                array( 'jquery' ),
                '1.0'
        );
}
add_action( 'admin_enqueue_scripts', 'sp_admin_enqueue_scripts' );
?>
```

Using `wp_enqueue_scripts` and `admin_enqueue_scripts` lets you load different JS files on the frontend and backend of your site. You could add other checks in here to make sure that jQuery is only loaded on certain pages, which could improve load times on those pages that don't need jQuery loaded. Common methods include checking attributes of the global `$post` or checking `$_REQUEST` values used in the admin like `$_REQUEST['page']` or `$_REQUEST['post_type']`.

Remember, the first parameter of the `wp_enqueue_script()` function is a reference label. The second parameter of the *wp_enqueue_script()* function tells WordPress where the script is located. The `plugins_url()` function is used to figure out the URL relative to the current file `__FILE__`. This works when this code is included in the main plugin file. You would pass `dirname(__FILE__)` as the parameter to this call if the file you are editing is in a subdirectory of the plugin.

The third parameter of the `wp_enqueue_script()` function allows you to state dependencies for your script. By passing `array('jquery')` for our *frontend.js* and *admin.js* scripts, we make sure that jQuery is loaded first.

Where to Put Your Custom JavaScript

Once again we will run into situations where we need to decide where to put a certain bit of code. Should it go into the theme code or the plugin code? Here are the general rules we use when deciding where a particular bit of JavaScript code will go:

1. If the code will be only used once and is generally specific to the page it is used on, it is coded directly into that page within a <script> tag.

2. If the JavaScript is used more than once (a function or module) and is related to theme functionality or UI, it is placed in a JS file within the theme (e.g., */themes/schoolpress/js/schoolpress.js*).

3. If the JavaScript is used more than once on admin screens of your app, it is placed in an *admin.js* file inside of your plugin (e.g., */plugins/schoolpress/js/admin.js*).

4. If the JavaScript is used more than once on the frontend of your app, but not part of the theme UI, it is placed in a *frontend.js* file inside of your plugin (e.g., */plugins/schoolpress/js/frontend.js*).

5. If splitting some JS code into its own file, to be loaded on specific pages, will result in a needed increase in performance, than that code will be placed in a separate JS file.[1]

These rules are specific to how we like to develop and are only a suggestion. Some developers will cringe particularly hard at the thought of adding JavaScript code inside of script tags instead of placing all JavaScript inside of *.js* files. If you like coding this way or perhaps have a dedicated JavaScript programmer on your team, by all means put all of your JavaScript code inside of *.js* files.

The important thing is that *you* understand how your JavaScript files and code are organized so that working on your site is intuitive.

AJAX Calls with WordPress and jQuery

AJAX calls in WordPress will require two components: the JavaScript code on the frontend to kick off the AJAX request and the PHP code in the backend to process the request and return HTML or JSON-encoded data.

Say you want to adjust your signup page to automatically check if the username entered has been used already. You could warn the person signing up before he hits the submit button and allow him to change the username he picked, saving a bit of grief.

The first thing we need to do is add a quick JavaScript to the head of our pages to define our `ajaxurl`. This is the URL that all AJAX queries will run through. It looks like this:

```
<script type="text/JavaScript">
var ajaxurl = '/wp-admin/admin-ajax.php';
</script>
```

In the WordPress dashboard, this script will be embedded by default. But for frontend AJAX, we'll need to embed it ourselves. Here's the code to define the `ajaxurl` variable for frontend AJAX:

---

1. Standalone JavaScript files can be cached or served through a content delivery network (CND). JavaScript embedded in dynamic PHP files cannot be cached as easily.

```
function my_wp_head_ajax_url()
{
?>
<script type="text/JavaScript">
var ajaxurl = '<?php echo admin_url("admin-ajax.php");?>';
</script>
<?php
}
add_action('wp_head', 'my_wp_head_ajax_url');
```

Now the variable ajaxurl is available to the rest of the JavaScript on our frontend pages and can be used in our AJAX calls. Here is the JavaScript code to add to the bottom of the registration page to perform the username check:

```
<?php
//our JS for the page
function my_wp_footer_registration_JavaScript()
{
    //make sure we're on the registration page
    if(empty($_REQUEST['action']) || $_REQUEST['action'] != 'register')
        return;
?>
<script>
    //wait til DOM is loaded
    jQuery(document).ready(function() {
        //var to keep track of our timeout
        var timer_checkUsername;

        //detect when the user_login field is changed
        jQuery('#user_login').bind.('keyup change', function() {
            //use a timer so check is triggered 1 second after they stop typing
            timer_checkUsername = setTimeout(function(){checkUsername();}, 1000);
        });
    });

    function checkUsername()
    {
        //make sure we have a username
        var username = jQuery('#user_login').val();
        if(!username)
            return;

        //check the username
        jQuery.ajax({
        url: ajaxurl,type:'GET',timeout:5000,
                dataType: 'html',
                data: "action=check_username&username="+username,
                error: function(xml){
                        //timeout, but no need to scare the user
                },
                success: function(response){
                //hide any flag we may have already shown
```

```
            jQuery('#username_check').remove();

            //show if the username is good (1) or taken (0)
            if(response == 1)
                jQuery('#user_login').after(
                    '<span id="username_check" class="okay">Okay</span>'
                );
            else
                jQuery('#user_login').after(
                    '<span id="username_check" class="taken">Taken</span>'
                );
        }
        });
    }
</script>
<?php
}
add_action('wp_footer', 'my_wp_footer_registration_JavaScript');
?>
```

The preceding code is hooked into wp_footer so the JavaScript will be added to the end of the HTML output. We first check that $_REQUEST['action'] == "register" to make sure we're on the default WP registration page.

If you're using a plugin like Paid Memberships Pro that has its own registration page, you'll want to use a check like if(!is_page("membership-checkout")) to check which page you are on. You'll also need to make sure that the #user_login check in your JavaScript code is updated to use the ID used for the username field on the registration page.

In the code, we use jQuery(document).ready() to detect that the DOM is loaded and then use jQuery('#user_login').bind('keyup change', ...) to detect when a user has either typed inside the field or otherwise changed it. When this happens, we use setTimeout() to queue up a username check in one second. If the user types again before the timer runs, it is reset to wait one second again. The effect is that one second after the user stops typing or changing the field, the checkUsername() function is kicked off.

In the checkUsername() function, we have the jQuery.ajax() call. Before we do that though, we check the value from the username field to see if it's empty or not.

In the jQuery.ajax() call, we set the URL to ajaxurl, which should have been set via wp_head earlier.

We set the type of call to GET. You can also use the POST method. The DELETE and PUT methods are also available, but may not be supported by all browsers. Use the same logic you would when deciding which type to use on a <form> you are submitting to decide which method to use in an AJAX call. If you are "getting" data like we are in this example, GET makes sense. If you are submitting data to be saved, you can use the POST method.

We set a timeout of 5,000 (or 5 seconds) here. After this time, the request will be cancelled and the defined error action will be kicked off. You should set the timeout value based on the reasonable amount of time it might take your server to process this particular request. If you set it too low, you will prematurely cancel requests. If you set it too high, people will be waiting really long for requests that may have hung up on the server side.

We set the datatype to `html` here. This tells jQuery to take the output and place it into a string. A datatype of `json` will evaluate the output and place it into a JavaScript object variable. There are a few other datatypes including `xml`, `jsonp`, `script`, and `text`. The jQuery documentation addresses when you would use these and how jQuery processes each datatype.

We set the data to `"action=check_username&username="+username`, which will pass our defined action and the username as parameters to the *wp-admin-ajax.php* script and our service-side code.

Then we set a handler in case of errors and in case of success. In case of error, you could alert the user, but since this isn't a critical function, we just go about our business. In case of success, we remove the old `#username_check` element and append an "OK" or "Taken" message after the username field.

 jQuery hosts the full API documentation for the `jQuery.ajax()` on its website (*http://bit.ly/ajax-jq*).

Now let's see the backend code. Here is the code you would put into *functions.php*, your custom plugin, or a *.php* in your plugin's */services/* directory to listen for the AJAX request and send back a 1 or 0 if a username if available or not:

```php
<?php
//detect AJAX request for check_username
function wp_ajax_check_username() {
    global $wpdb;
        $username = $_REQUEST['username'];

        $taken = $wpdb->get_var( "
                SELECT user_login
                FROM $wpdb->users
                WHERE user_login = '" . $wpdb->escape( $username ) . "' LIMIT 1"
                );

        if ( $taken )
                echo "0";    //taken
```

```
        else
                echo "1";    //available
    }
    add_action( 'wp_ajax_check_username', 'wp_ajax_check_username' );
    add_action( 'wp_ajax_nopriv_check_username', 'wp_ajax_check_username' );
    ?>
```

- `wp_ajax_{action}`—Runs for logged-in users
- `wp_ajax_nopriv_{action}`—Runs for nonusers

On the registration page, users are by definition not logged in, so we need to use the `wp_ajax_nopriv_` hook. But we may also want to use this check on the add new user screen in the admin, so we'll hook into `wp_ajax_` as well to handle that case.

If you have an AJAX service that will only be used by users, just use the `wp_ajax_` hook. If you need your service available for users and nonusers, you'll need to use both hooks.

Also, notice how the `action` parameter we're looking for ("check_username") is added to the hook in the action definition. This hook will only fire if `$_REQUEST['action'] == "check_username"`.

Managing Multiple AJAX Requests

When working with AJAX requests, it's important to keep track of them. If not, you can put undue stress on your server and the client's browser, leading to a lockup of their session or the entire site.

For example, in the preceding code, we wait one second after the username field is updated before kicking off the AJAX request to check if the username is available. But once the request goes out, the user might keep on typing, kicking off another AJAX request. If your server isn't able to get back within one second, those requests might start to build up on each other.

Now, our username checker might not have too much potential to get out of hand, but it's possible in a lot of situations. A simple example would be one where an AJAX request is kicked off when a user clicks a button. If the user clicks the button 20 times, that could be 20 hits on your server. So keep track of them.

Generally, you want to do one of two things when managing your AJAX requests:

1. Keep a user from submitting a request if another request of the same type is still processing.
2. Cancel any existing request of the same type if a new request is submitted.

Which option you use depends on what the AJAX request is doing. Generally if you are "getting" data, you'll want to cancel earlier requests and submit the fresher one. If you are "posting" data, you'll want to ignore the new request until the old one is completed.

Depending on your app and the request at hand, there will be many ways to disable or cancel requests. Since the "complete" callback in jQuery's ajax method is called whether the request is successful or errors out, you can use it to re-enable a button or other element that's being used to kick off a specific AJAX request:

```
//Option #1: Disabling a button while an AJAX request is processing
jQuery('#button').click(function() {
    //disable the button
    jQuery(this).attr('disabled', 'disabled');

    //do the ajax request
    jQuery.ajax({
        url: ajaxurl,type:'GET',timeout:5000,
        dataType: 'html',
        error: function(xml){
                //error stuff
        },
        success: function(response){
            //success stuff
        }
        complete: function() {
            //enable the button again
            jQuery('#button').removeAttr('disabled');
        }
    });
});
```

Similarly, here is some code that will cancel an old request when a new one comes in:

```
//Option #2: Cancel an older request when a new one comes in
var ajax_request;
jQuery('#button').click(function() {
    //cancel any existing requests
    if(typeof ajax_request !== 'undefined')
        ajax_request.abort();

    //do the ajax request
    ajax_request = jQuery.ajax({
        url: ajaxurl,type:'GET',timeout:5000,
        dataType: 'html',
        error: function(xml){
                //error stuff
        },
        success: function(response){
            //success stuff
        }
    });
});
```

Heartbeat API

Earlier in this chapter, we built an AJAX call that was triggered by a form field being updated. Sometimes you will want certain updates to happen on their own periodically as your web app is running. For example, you may want to check for new comments on a discussion forum and automatically pull in fresh comments as they are posted. With JavaScript, this is typically done by polling the backend every few seconds using an AJAX call kicked off by the `setInterval` function. Alternatively, you can use the WordPress Heartbeat API.

The Heartbeat API is new to WordPress 3.6 and can be used to facilitate quasi-realtime updates in your app. Every 15 seconds (or less if you change the settings), your app will send a heartbeat request from the client to the server and back. During this round trip, you can do things like autosave app states or load fresh content. In WordPress 3.6, the Heartbeat API is being used for autosaving posts, locking posts, and giving login expiration warnings. In this section, we'll cover how you can use the Heartbeat API for your app.

Like anything else, the Heartbeat API can seem complicated, but at its heart, it's simply a bunch of data passed back and forth from the client to the server through periodic AJAX calls. Using hooks, you can tap into the data being sent or received to get the information you need to and from the server.

Here is a minimal example demonstrating the Heartbeat API. The only thing this code does is send a message `marco` to the server. If the server sees that message, it sends `polo` back to the client. Both messages are logged to the JavaScript console, so every 15 seconds, you should see the following in your console:

```
Client: marco
Server: polo
```

Using the Heartbeat API can be broken down into three sections: initialization, client-side JavaScript, and server-side PHP:

Initialization

```
//enqueue heartbeat.js and our JavaScript
function hbdemo_init()
{
    /*
        //Add your conditionals here so this runs on the pages you want, e.g.
                if(is_admin())
                        return;                     //don't run this in the admin
        */

    //enqueue the Heartbeat API
    wp_enqueue_script('heartbeat');
```

```
    //load our JavaScript in the footer
    add_action("wp_footer", "hbdemo_wp_footer");
}
add_action('init', 'hbdemo_init');
```

This first function enqueues the *heartbeat.js* file and sets up an action to put our Java-
Script code in the the footer via the wp_footer hook. If you only wanted this heartbeat
code to run on certain pages (very likely), you would put your checks here.

Client-side JavaScript

```
<?php
//our JavaScript to send/process from the client side
function hbdemo_wp_footer()
{
?>
<script>
  jQuery(document).ready(function() {
        //hook into heartbeat-send: client will send the message
        //'marco' in the 'client' var inside the data array
        jQuery(document).on('heartbeat-send', function(e, data) {
                console.log('Client: marco');

                //need some data to kick off AJAX call
                data['client'] = 'marco';
        });

        //hook into heartbeat-tick: client looks for a 'server'
        //var in the data array and logs it to console
        jQuery(document).on('heartbeat-tick', function(e, data) {
                if(data['server'])
                        console.log('Server: ' + data['server']);
        });

        //hook into heartbeat-error to log errors
        jQuery(document).on('heartbeat-error',
                function(e, jqXHR, textStatus, error) {
                        console.log('BEGIN ERROR');
                        console.log(textStatus);
                        console.log(error);
                        console.log('END ERROR');
                });
  });
</script>
<?php
}
?>
```

This second function dumps our JavaScript into the footer. In the JavaScript code, we
use jQuery(document).ready() to run our code after the DOM has loaded. Then we
hook into three JavaScript events triggered by the Heartbeat API:

1. The `heartbeat-send` event is fired right before the heartbeat sends data back to the server. To send your data, add a value to the "data" array passed through the event.

2. The `heartbeat-tick` event is fired when the server replies. To see what data the server has sent, look for it in the "data" array that is passed through the event.

3. The `heartbeat-error` event is fired if there is an error in the `jQuery.ajax()` call used to send the data to the server. You can include code here for debugging or degrade nicely if AJAX doesn't seem to be working in your production environment.

Server-side PHP

```php
//processing the message on the server
function hbdemo_heartbeat_received($response, $data)
{
    if($data['client'] == 'marco')
                $response['server'] = 'polo';

        return $response;
}
add_filter('heartbeat_received', 'hbdemo_heartbeat_received', 10, 2);
```

This third PHP function in the previous example runs on the `heartbeat_received` hook and processes the data from the client. We can add data to go back to the client by updating the `response` variable.

Now let's try a more realistic example. SchoolPress has a section of the assignments page showing how many assignments have been submitted and how many are left. Let's use the Heartbeat API to update this number if new assignments have been posted.

In our template, the assignment count will be displayed something like this:

```php
?>
<div>
    Submitted:
    <span id="assignment_count">
        <?php echo count($assignment->submissions);?>
    </span>
    /
    <?php echo count($course->students);?>
</div>
<?php
```

Initialization

```php
function sp_init_assignments_heartbeat()
{
    //Ignore if we're not on an assignment page.
        if(strpos($_SERVER['REQUEST_URI'], "/assignment/") === false)
                return;
```

```php
    //enqueue the Heartbeat API
    wp_enqueue_script('heartbeat');

    //load our JavaScript in the footer
    add_action("wp_footer", "sp_wp_footer_assignments_heartbeat");
}
add_action('init', 'sp_init_assignments_heartbeat');
```

Things are pretty similar to our minimal example so far. We're just making sure we don't run this code on nonassignment pages by checking for *assignment/* in the URI:

Client-side JavaScript

```php
<?php
function sp_wp_footer_assignments_heartbeat()
{
    global $post;    //post for current assignment
?>
<script>
jQuery(document).ready(function() {
  //heartbeat-send
  jQuery(document).on('heartbeat-send', function(e, data) {
        //make sure we have an array for SchoolPress data
  if(!data['schoolpress'])
    data['schoolpress'] = new Array();

    //send to server the post_id of this assignment and current count
    data['schoolpress']['assignment_post_id'] = '<?php echo $post->ID;?>';
    data['schoolpress']['assignment_count'] = jQuery('#assignment-count').val();
  });

  //heartbeat-tick
  jQuery(document).on('heartbeat-tick', function(e, data) {
        //update assignment count
  if(data['schoolpress']['assignment_count'])
        jQuery('#assignment-count').val(data['schoolpress']['assignment_count']);
  });
});
</script>
<?php
}
?>
```

Notice that we're storing our data in a schoolpress array within the data array. We'll store all Heartbeat-related data in this array as a kind of namespacing to make sure our variable names don't conflict with any other plugins that might be using the Heartbeat API.

Each time the heartbeat sends data to the server, we send along the assignment's post ID and the current count value.

It's important that you send *something* to the server through the heartbeat. If there is no data to send, the heartbeat won't bother hitting the server at all.

Server-side PHP

```
//processing the message on the server
function sp_heartbeat_received_assignment_count($response, $data)
{
    //check for assignment post id
        if(!empty($data['schoolpress']['assignment_post_id']))
        {
                $assignment = new Assignment(
                    $data['schoolpress']['assignment_post_id']
                    );
                $response['schoolpress']['assignment_count'] = count(
                    $assignment->submissions
                    );
        }

        return $response;
}
add_filter('heartbeat_received',
        'sp_heartbeat_received_assignment_count', 10, 2);
```

Here we check for the `assignment_post_id` value passed from the client. If found, we load up the assignment and return the count of submissions as `assignment_count`, which our frontend JavaScript will be looking for.

This code could be updated to detect changes in the assignment count (by comparing the number sent from the client to the number found server side) and in those cases pass back a message notifying the teacher to refresh to view the new submissions. Or we could send some data about the new submissions themselves and push them into the list on the page.

Finally, if you want to speed up or slow down the heartbeat, you can override the settings using the following code:

```
function sp_heartbeat_settings($settings = array())
{
    $settings['interval'] = 20;  //20 seconds vs. 15 second default
    return $settings;
}
add_filter('heartbeat_settings', 'sp_heartbeat_settings');
```

Note that at the time of this writing, the API will only let you use a value between 15 and 60 seconds. Anything faster or slower will be set to 15 or 60 seconds, respectively. This limitation is actually a good idea for the Heartbeat API, since at any given time, multiple plugins and processes may be using that same heartbeat. If you need a certain poll to occur faster than once every 15 seconds, you should probably set it up as a separate AJAX call using your own `setInterval` or `setTimeout` calls in JavaScript.

You can think of the Heartbeat API as a more casual way of doing polling between the client and server. If you need something more hardcore (and polling your server every second is pretty hardcore), then you should roll your own heartbeat-like system.

WordPress Limitations with Asynchronous Processing

Most WordPress applications execute PHP scripts through an Apache or Nginx server. When optimized, you can serve a lot of small, simultaneous connections on these setups, which is perfect for asynchronous JavaScript applications. However, the servers themselves, and perhaps more importantly, the general overhead of loading WordPress on server-side calls, means that a WordPress service running on Apache or Nginx will never be as fast as a smaller JavaScript service running on something like *node.js*, which was built specifically to handle asynchronous JavaScript calls.

That said, you can still get a lot done with WordPress and the architecture behind it. Our suggestion is always to build it the obvious way first and selectively pull out parts of your application for scaling later when performance becomes an issue.

Does your app have a user base consisting solely of the 30 people inside your company? Then you are probably going to be fine using WordPress for your realtime JavaScript coding.

Do you plan to have thousands of users, with dozens of simultaneous connections? You'll need some beefy hardware, but you'll also probably be fine keeping everything in WordPress.

Do you plan to have millions of users, with tens of thousands of simultaneous connections? If so, you need some top-notch engineers, so hopefully you have the money for them. In any case, you'll either be pushing WordPress to its limits or using other platforms to serve your realtime interactions.

These kinds of scaling questions are covered further in Chapter 16.

Backbone.js

When people say that you can't build apps with WordPress, we point out that WordPress itself is an application built on the WordPress framework. That WordPress application is currently about 86% PHP and 14% JavaScript. Some people in the WordPress community expect that ratio to get closer to 50/50 over the next few years.

Why the big move to JavaScript? On the frontend side of things, rendering a website with JavaScript can be much lighter than rendering it with PHP. As you navigate around the typical website, loading all of the HTML DOM is pretty wasteful. The header, footer, menu, and other pieces of the site may not change at all. With JavaScript, you can simply load the new part of the website, change the class on the items in your menu, and voila: new page. This is a much more app-like experience and perfect for using web apps over mobile networks where bandwidth is more scarce.

 Using AJAX to update pages instead of loading new pages is sometimes referred to as building a single page application, or SPA.

One thing limiting a move to JavaScript is that all of our handy functions and data structures are native to PHP. As more development is done on the JavaScript side of the WordPress platform, there is a greater need for some kind of framework to help organize the JavaScript development.

Backbone.js is a framework for JavaScript consisting of models, views, and collections of models. This setup is very similar to the MVC frameworks used for server-side PHP development. In traditional MVC frameworks, the C stands for "controller." With Backbone.js, the controlling of an app is handled within the views and honestly outside of the JavaScript framework itself.

Backbone.js has already been used extensively in the Media Library and Theme Customizer updated and added in recent versions of WordPress. The JavaScript developers working on the WordPress core will likely transition more of the platform code to use Backbone.js as they build out new features and rework old ones. For this reason, it is becoming more common to see developers building their themes and apps using Backbone.js as well.

The best practices for Backbone.js development, let alone Backbone+WordPress development, are still being worked out. In general, if you are simply adding some dynamic AJAX-based UI to an existing PHP-based page, the more traditional AJAX technique laid out here will be faster and easier to implement and maintain. However, if a fairly large portion of your app will live inside of JavaScript, a Backbone.js implementation will help you organize things and will make things easier for you. Backbone.js is not the kind of tool to use piecemeal. It works best when you go all in with it.

If you are using Backbone.js to render the frontend of your app, the main intersection point with WordPress will be when your collections and models are saved to the database through the backend.

Imagine an interface on the SchoolPress site for adding student groups to an assignment. There may be an input box for naming the group and a button labeled Add Group to add the group. Using the traditional AJAX technique outlined in this chapter, the turn of events would look like this:

1. User enters a new group name.
2. User clicks the Add Group button.
3. The group name is sent to the server via AJAX.
4. The server (WordPress) processes the name, adds the new group, and returns some data.
5. The client uses JavaScript to parse the response and update the list of groups on the frontend.

With a Backbone.js app, you mirror the list of groups more thoroughly in the model and collection you would set up in JavaScript. You could use a similar workflow as the typical AJAX app, but a more appropriate workflow for a Backbone.js app would be:

1. User enters a new group name.
2. User clicks the Add Group button.
3. The group name is used to create a new instance of the group model and added to the group collection in Backbone.js.
4. The collection will be coded to update the server (WordPress) through AJAX whenever the collection changes.
5. A representation of the current collection of groups is sent to the server.
6. WordPress updates the internal representation of the collection in the database to match what was sent.

So instead of first updating things in the backend and the backend telling the frontend what to look like, with Backbone.js things are first updated on the frontend, and the frontend tells the backend how to save the data.

An example of some SchoolPress functionality coded both with the traditional AJAX technique and then using Backbone.js can be found at *http://bwawwp.com/backbonejs-example/*.

Here are some resources to learn more about Backbone.js and how to use it with Word-Press:

- Official Backbone.js site (*http://backbonejs.org/*)
- "Backbone.js and WordPress Resources" (*http://bit.ly/bb-wp-knight*) by Peter R. Knight

## CHAPTER 10

XML-RPC

WordPress is awesome, and you can build a lot of really cool applications just with it, but what if your application needs to communicate with other applications or other WordPress installations?

XML-RPC is a remote procedure call (RPC) protocol that uses XML to encode its calls and HTTP as a transport mechanism. WordPress uses an XML-RPC interface to easily allow developers to access and post data from other applications, including other Word-Press sites.

We've compiled a list of some of the available methods of the wp_xmlrpc_server class along with the arguments that can be used and what values each function returns.

If you would like to follow along with the code examples for some of the following methods, set up the following function in a custom plugin or in your theme's *functions.php file*. Also, be careful because some of the examples update and delete data:

```php
<?php
add_action( 'init', 'wds_include_IXR' );
function wds_include_IXR() {
    // You need to include this file in order to use the IXR class.
    require_once ABSPATH . 'wp-includes/class-IXR.php';
    global $xmlrpc_url, $xmlrpc_user, $xmlrpc_pass;
    // Another WordPress site you want to push and pull data from
    $xmlrpc_url = 'http://anotherwordpresssite.com/xmlrpc.php';
    $xmlrpc_user = 'admin'; // Hope you're not using "admin" ;)
    $xmlrpc_pass = 'password'; // Really hope you're not using "password" ;)
}
?>
```

wp.getUsersBlogs

Calls the function wp_getUsersBlogs($args) and requires an array:

- $username—A string of the username used to log in to the given WordPress URL.
- $password—A string of the password used to log in to the given WordPress URL.

This function returns an array:

- isAdmin
- URL
- blogid
- blogName
- xmlrpc—URL of XML-RPC endpoint

```php
<?php
function bwawwp_xmlrpc_getUsersBlogs() {
    global $xmlrpc_url, $xmlrpc_user, $xmlrpc_pass;
    $rpc = new IXR_CLIENT( $xmlrpc_url );
    // returns all blogs in a multisite network
    $rpc->query( 'wp.getUsersBlogs', $xmlrpc_user, $xmlrpc_pass );
    echo '<h1>Blogs</h1>';
    echo '<pre>';
    print_r( $rpc->getResponse() );
    echo '</pre>';
    exit();
}
add_action( 'init', 'bwawwp_xmlrpc_getUsersBlogs', 999 );
?>
```

wp.getPosts

Calls the function wp_getPosts($args) and requires an array:

- $blog_id
- $username
- $password
- $filter—An optional array of fields you would like to query posts by. The array can contain keys for post_type, post_status, number, offset, orderby, and/or order.
- $fields—An optional array of the post fields and their values you would like to return.

This function returns an array of posts with the post fields you specified in the $fields parameter:

```php
<?php
function bwawwp_xmlrpc_getPosts() {
    global $xmlrpc_url, $xmlrpc_user, $xmlrpc_pass;
```

```
$rpc = new IXR_CLIENT( $xmlrpc_url );

// returns all posts of post post_type
$rpc->query( 'wp.getPosts', 0, $xmlrpc_user, $xmlrpc_pass );
echo '<h1>posts</h1>';
echo '<pre>';
print_r( $rpc->getResponse() );
echo '</pre>';

// returns all posts of page post_type (or any specific post type)
$filter = array( 'post_type' => 'page' );
$rpc->query( 'wp.getPosts', 0, $xmlrpc_user, $xmlrpc_pass, $filter );
echo '<h1>pages</h1>';
echo '<pre>';
print_r( $rpc->getResponse() );
echo '</pre>';

// returns 5 published page titles in abc order
$filter = array(
    'post_type' => 'page',
    'status' => 'publish',
    'number' => '5',
    'orderby' => 'title',
    'order'   => 'ASC'
);
$fields = array( 'post_title' );
$rpc->query('wp.getPosts', 0, $xmlrpc_user, $xmlrpc_pass, $filter, $fields);
echo '<h1>5 published page titles</h1>';
echo '<pre>';
print_r( $rpc->getResponse() );
echo '</pre>';

exit();
}
add_action( 'init', 'bwawwp_xmlrpc_getPosts', 999 );
?>
```

wp.getPost

Calls the function wp_getPost($args) and requires an array:

- $blog_id
- $username
- $password
- $post_id—A required integer of the post ID of the post you want to get.
- $fields—An optional array of the post fields and values you would like to return.

This function returns an array of fields based on the $fields parameter. You can use any of the following fields:

- post_id
- post_title
- post_date
- post_date_gmt
- post_modified
- post_modified_gmt
- post_status
- post_type
- post_name
- post_author
- post_password
- post_excerpt
- post_content
- link
- comment_status
- ping_status
- sticky
- custom_fields
- terms
- categories
- tags
- enclosure

```php
<?php
function bwawwp_xmlrpc_getPost() {
    global $xmlrpc_url, $xmlrpc_user, $xmlrpc_pass;
    $rpc = new IXR_CLIENT( $xmlrpc_url );
    $method = 'wp.getPost';
    // return last post to get a post ID
    $filter = array('number' => '1', 'orderby' => 'date', 'order' => 'DESC');
    $fields = array('post_id');
    $rpc->query('wp.getPosts', 0, $xmlrpc_user, $xmlrpc_pass, $filter,
      $fields);
    $response = $rpc->getResponse();
    $post_id = $response[0]['post_id'];
```

```
            // return all data on last $post_id
            $rpc->query( 'wp.getPost', 0, $xmlrpc_user, $xmlrpc_pass, $post_id );
            echo '<h1>Post ID: '.$post_id.'</h1>';
            echo '<pre>';
            print_r( $rpc->getResponse() );
            echo '</pre>';
            exit();
        }
        add_action( 'init', 'bwawwp_xmlrpc_getPost', 999 );
        ?>
```

wp.newPost

Calls the function wp_newPost($args) and requires an array:

- $blog_id—An integer of the blog ID to add the post to.
- $username
- $password
- $content—An array of post data for creating a new post. This array can contain any of the fields the function wp_insert_post() supports.

This function returns a string of the post_id:

```
<?php
function bwawwp_xmlrpc_newPost() {
    global $xmlrpc_url, $xmlrpc_user, $xmlrpc_pass;
    $rpc = new IXR_CLIENT( $xmlrpc_url );
    // create an array with post data
    $content = array(
        'post_title' => 'New Post with XML-RPC'
    );
    $rpc->query( 'wp.newPost', 0, $xmlrpc_user, $xmlrpc_pass, $content );
    $post_id = $rpc->getResponse();
    echo '<h1>New Post ID: '. $post_id .'</h1>';
    exit();
}
add_action( 'init', 'bwawwp_xmlrpc_newPost', 999 );
?>
```

wp.editPost

Calls the function wp_editPost($args) and requires an array:

- $blog_id
- $username
- $password

- $post_id —A required integer of the post ID you want to update.
- $content—An array of post data for updating an existing post. Only fields in the array will be updated.

This function returns true on success:

```php
<?php
function bwawwp_xmlrpc_editPost() {
    global $xmlrpc_url, $xmlrpc_user, $xmlrpc_pass;
    $rpc = new IXR_CLIENT( $xmlrpc_url );
    // return last post to get a post ID
    $filter = array('number' => '1', 'orderby' => 'date', 'order' => 'DESC');
    $fields = array('post_id');
    $rpc->query('wp.getPosts', 0, $xmlrpc_user, $xmlrpc_pass, $filter, $fields);
    $response = $rpc->getResponse();
    $post_id = $response[0]['post_id'];
    // create an array with new post data
    $content = array(
        'post_title' => 'Updated Post with XML-RPC',
        'post_status' => 'publish'
    );
    $rpc->query('wp.editPost', 0, $xmlrpc_user, $xmlrpc_pass, $post_id,
        $content);
    echo '<h1>Updated Post ID: '. $post_id .'</h1>';
    exit();
}
add_action( 'init', 'bwawwp_xmlrpc_editPost', 999 );
?>
```

wp.deletePost

Calls the function wp_deletePost($args) and requires an array:

- $blog_id
- $username
- $password
- $post_id

This function returns true on success:

```php
<?php
function bwawwp_xmlrpc_deletePost() {
    global $xmlrpc_url, $xmlrpc_user, $xmlrpc_pass;
    $rpc = new IXR_CLIENT( $xmlrpc_url );
    // return last post to get a post ID
    $filter = array('number' => '1', 'orderby' => 'date', 'order' => 'DESC');
    $fields = array('post_id');
    $rpc->query('wp.getPosts', 0, $xmlrpc_user, $xmlrpc_pass, $filter, $fields);
```

```php
    $response = $rpc->getResponse();
    $post_id = $response[0]['post_id'];
    // delete post by $post_id
    $rpc->query( 'wp.deletePost', 0, $xmlrpc_user, $xmlrpc_pass, $post_id );
    echo '<h1>Deleted Post ID: '. $post_id .'</h1>';
    exit();
}
add_action( 'init', 'bwawwp_xmlrpc_deletePost', 999 );
?>
```

wp.getTerms

Calls the function wp_getTerms($args) and requires an array:

- $blog_id
- $username
- $password
- $taxonomy—A required string of the taxonomy of the terms you want to retrieve.
- $filter—An optional array of parameters used to alter the query used to retrieve the terms. The array can contain number, offset, orderby, order, hide_empty, and/or search.

This function returns an array of terms and their fields:

```php
<?php
function bwawwp_xmlrpc_getTerms() {
    global $xmlrpc_url, $xmlrpc_user, $xmlrpc_pass;
    $rpc = new IXR_CLIENT( $xmlrpc_url );
    $rpc->query( 'wp.getTerms', 0, $xmlrpc_user, $xmlrpc_pass, 'category' );
    echo '<h1>Category Terms</h1>';
    echo '<pre>';
    print_r( $rpc->getResponse() );
    echo '</pre>';
    exit();
}
add_action( 'init', 'bwawwp_xmlrpc_getTerms', 999 );
?>
```

wp.getTerm

Calls the function wp_getTerm($args) and requires an array:

- $blog_id
- $username
- $password

- $taxonomy_name—A required string of the taxonomy of the term you want to retrieve.
- $term_id—A required string of the term ID of the term you want to retrieve.

This function returns an array of term fields:

- `term_id`
- `name`
- `slug`
- `term_group`
- `term_taxonomy_id`
- `taxonomy`
- `description`
- `parent`
- `count`

```php
<?php
function bwawwp_xmlrpc_getTerm() {
    global $xmlrpc_url, $xmlrpc_user, $xmlrpc_pass;
    $rpc = new IXR_CLIENT( $xmlrpc_url );
    $rpc->query( 'wp.getTerm', 0, $xmlrpc_user, $xmlrpc_pass, 'category', 1 );
    echo '<h1>Term ID 1</h1>';
    echo '<pre>';
    print_r( $rpc->getResponse() );
    echo '</pre>';
    exit();
}
add_action( 'init', 'bwawwp_xmlrpc_getTerm', 999 );
?>
```

wp.newTerm

Calls the function `wp_newTerm($args)` and requires an array:

- $blog_id
- $username
- $password
- $content—An array of term data for adding a new term. The array can contain keys for `name`, `taxonomy`, `parent`, `description`, and `slug`.

This function returns a string of the `term_id`.

wp.editTerm

Calls the function `wp_editTerm($args)` and requires an array:

- $blog_id
- $username
- $password
- $term_id—A required string of the term ID of the term you want to update.
- $content—An array of term data you would like to update. The array can contain keys for `name`, `taxonomy`, `parent`, `description`, and `slug`.

This function returns a string of the `term_id`.

wp.deleteTerm

Calls the function `wp_deleteTerm($args)` and requires an array:

- $blog_id
- $username
- $password
- $taxonomy_name—A required string of the taxonomy of the term you want to delete.
- $term_id—A required string of the term ID of the term you want to delete.

This function returns `true` on success and an error message if it fails.

wp.getTaxonomies

Calls the function `wp_getTaxonomies($args)` and requires an array:

- $blog_id
- $username
- $password

This function returns an array of taxonomies and their settings:

```php
<?php
function bwawwp_xmlrpc_getTaxonomies() {
    global $xmlrpc_url, $xmlrpc_user, $xmlrpc_pass;
    $rpc = new IXR_CLIENT( $xmlrpc_url );
    $rpc->query( 'wp.getTaxonomies', 0, $xmlrpc_user, $xmlrpc_pass );
    echo '<h1>Taxonomies</h1>';
```

```
        echo '<pre>';
        print_r( $rpc->getResponse() );
        echo '</pre>';
        exit();
    }
    add_action( 'init', 'bwawwp_xmlrpc_getTaxonomies', 999 );
    ?>
```

wp.getTaxonomy

Calls the function wp_getTaxonomy($args) and requires an array:

- $blog_id
- $username
- $password
- $taxonomy—A required string of the taxonomy you want to retrieve.

This function returns an array of taxonomy settings.

wp.getUsers

Calls the function wp_getUsers($args) and requires an array:

- $blog_id
- $username
- $password
- $filter—An optional array of fields you would like to query users by. The array can contain keys for number (default: 50), offset (default: 0), role, who, orderby, and/or order.
- $fields—An optional array of the user fields and values you would like to return. You can use any of the following fields:
  — user_id
  — username
  — first_name
  — last_name
  — registered
  — bio
  — email
  — nickname

— nicename

— url

— display_name

— roles

This function returns an array of users with the user fields you specified in the $fields parameter:

```php
<?php
function bwawwp_xmlrpc_getUsers() {
    global $xmlrpc_url, $xmlrpc_user, $xmlrpc_pass;
    $rpc = new IXR_CLIENT( $xmlrpc_url );
    $rpc->query( 'wp.getUsers', 0, $xmlrpc_user, $xmlrpc_pass );
    echo '<h1>Users</h1>';
    echo '<pre>';
    print_r( $rpc->getResponse() );
    echo '</pre>';
    $filter = array( 'role' => 'administrator' );
    $fields = array( 'username', 'email' );
    $rpc->query('wp.getUsers', 0, $xmlrpc_user, $xmlrpc_pass, $filter, $fields);
    echo '<h1>Filtered Users</h1>';
    echo '<pre>';
    print_r( $rpc->getResponse() );
    echo '</pre>';
    exit();
}
add_action( 'init', 'bwawwp_xmlrpc_getUsers', 999 );
?>
```

wp.getUser

Calls the function wp_getUser($args) and requires an array:

- $blog_id
- $username
- $password
- $user_id—A required integer of a user ID of the user you would like to retrieve.
- $fields—An optional array of user fields you would like to return. You can use the same fields as in the wp_getUsers() function.

This function returns an array of fields based on the $fields parameter.

wp.getProfile

Calls the function wp_getProfile($args) and requires an array:

- $blog_id
- $username
- $password
- $fields—An optional array of user fields you would like to return.

This function returns an array of user fields for the logged-in user from the `$fields` parameter. You can use the same fields as in the `wp_getUser()` function.

wp.editProfile

Calls the function `wp_editProfile($args)` and requires an array:

- $blog_id
- $username
- $password
- $content—An array of user data for updating the current user. The array can contain keys for `first_name`, `last_name`, `website`, `display_name`, `nickname`, `nicename`, and `bio`.

This function returns `true` on success.

wp.getCommentCount

Calls the function `wp_getCommentCount($args)` and requires an array:

- $blog_id
- $username
- $password
- $post_id

This function returns an array of the following comment counts:

- approved
- awaiting_moderation
- spam
- total_comments

wp.getPageTemplates

Calls the function wp_getPageTemplates($args) and requires an array:

- $blog_id
- $username
- $password

This function returns an array of page templates.

wp.getOptions

Calls the function wp_getOptions($args) and requires an array:

- $blog_id
- $username
- $password
- $options—An optional array of options to return values for. If no options are passed in, then all options will be returned.

This function returns an array of options:

```php
<?php
function bwawwp_xmlrpc_getOptions() {
    global $xmlrpc_url, $xmlrpc_user, $xmlrpc_pass;
    $rpc = new IXR_CLIENT( $xmlrpc_url );
    $rpc->query( 'wp.getOptions', 0, $xmlrpc_user, $xmlrpc_pass );
    echo '<h1>All Options</h1>';
    echo '<pre>';
    print_r( $rpc->getResponse() );
    echo '</pre>';
    $options = array( 'blog_url', 'template' );
    $rpc->query( 'wp.getOptions', 0, $xmlrpc_user, $xmlrpc_pass, $options );
    echo '<h1>Filter 2 Options</h1>';
    echo '<pre>';
    print_r( $rpc->getResponse() );
    echo '</pre>';
    exit();
}
add_action( 'init', 'bwawwp_xmlrpc_getOptions', 999 );
?>
```

wp.setOptions

Calls the function wp_setOptions($args) and requires an array:

- $blog_id
- $username
- $password
- $options—A required key and value array of options to update.

This function returns an array of updated options:

```php
<?php
function bwawwp_xmlrpc_setOptions() {
    global $xmlrpc_url, $xmlrpc_user, $xmlrpc_pass;
    $rpc = new IXR_CLIENT( $xmlrpc_url );
    $options = array(
        'blog_title' => 'Site Title via XML-RPC',
        'blog_tagline' => 'Just another WordPress site via XML-RPC'
    );
    $rpc->query( 'wp.setOptions', 0, $xmlrpc_user, $xmlrpc_pass, $options );
    echo '<h1>Set Options</h1>';
    echo '<pre>';
    print_r( $rpc->getResponse() );
    echo '</pre>';
    exit();
}
add_action( 'init', 'bwawwp_xmlrpc_setOptions', 999 );
?>
```

wp.getComment

Calls the function wp_getComment($args) and requires an array:

- $blog_id
- $username
- $password
- $comment_id—A required integer of the comment ID of the comment you would like to retrieve.

This function returns an array of comment data:

- date_created_gmt
- user_id
- comment_id
- parent
- status
- content

- link
- post_id
- post_title
- author
- author_url
- author_email
- author_ip
- type

wp.getComments

Calls the function wp_getComments($args) and requires an array:

- $blog_id
- $username
- $password
- $filter—An optional array of filterable comment values. The array can contain keys for status, post_id, offset, and/or number (default: 10).

This function returns an array of comments with the same individual comment data that gets returned with the wp_getComment() function:

```php
<?php
function bwawwp_xmlrpc_getComments() {
    global $xmlrpc_url, $xmlrpc_user, $xmlrpc_pass;
    $rpc = new IXR_CLIENT( $xmlrpc_url );
    $filter = array( 'status' => 'approve', 'number' => '20' );
    $rpc->query( 'wp.getComments', 0, $xmlrpc_user, $xmlrpc_pass, $filter );
    echo '<h1>Approved Comments</h1>';
    echo '<pre>';
    print_r( $rpc->getResponse() );
    echo '</pre>';
    exit();
}
add_action( 'init', 'bwawwp_xmlrpc_getComments', 999 );
?>
```

wp.deleteComment

Calls the function wp_deleteComment($args) and requires an array:

- $blog_id

- $username
- $password
- $comment_id—A required integer of the comment ID of the comment you would like to delete.

This function returns `true` on success.

wp.editComment

Calls the function `wp_editComment($args)` and requires an array:

- $blog_id
- $username
- $password
- $comment_id—A required integer of the comment ID of the comment you would like to update.
- $content—A required array of comment keys and values. The array can contain keys for `author`, `author_url`, `author_email`, `content`, `date_created_gmt`, and/or `status`.

This function returns `true` on success.

wp.newComment

Calls the function `wp_newComment($args)` and requires an array:

- $blog_id
- $username
- $password
- $post_id—A required integer of the post ID of the post to which you would like to add a new comment.
- $content—A required array of comment keys and values. The array can contain keys for `author`, `author_url`, `author_email`, `content`, `date_created_gmt`, and/or `status`.

This function returns the new comment ID.

wp.getMediaLibrary

Calls the function `wp_getMediaLibrary($args)` and requires an array:

- $blog_id
- $username
- $password
- $filter—An optional array of filterable attachment values. The array can contain keys for `parent_id`, `mime_type`, `offset`, and/or `number`.

This function returns an array of attachments with the same individual attachment data that gets returned with the `getMediaItem()` function:

```php
<?php
function bwawwp_xmlrpc_getMediaLibrary() {
    global $xmlrpc_url, $xmlrpc_user, $xmlrpc_pass;
    $rpc = new IXR_CLIENT($xmlrpc_url);
    $filter = array('number' => '20');
    $rpc->query('wp.getMediaLibrary', 0, $xmlrpc_user, $xmlrpc_pass, $filter);
    echo '<h1>Media Library</h1>';
    echo '<pre>';
    print_r( $rpc->getResponse() );
    echo '</pre>';
    exit();
}
add_action( 'init', 'bwawwp_xmlrpc_getMediaLibrary', 999 );
?>
```

wp.getMediaItem

Calls the function `wp_getMediaItem($args)` and requires an array:

- $blog_id
- $username
- $password
- $attachment_id—A required integer of the attachment ID of the attachment you would like to retrieve.

This function returns an array of attachment data:

- date_created_gmt
- parent
- link

- thumbnail
- title
- caption
- description
- metadata

wp.uploadFile

Calls `mw_newMediaObject($args)` and requires an array:

- $blog_id
- $username
- $password
- $data—A required array of file data of the file you are uploading. The array must contain keys for `name`, `type`, and `bits`. The array can contain `post_id` if you want to attach to an uploaded file to a post and `overwrite` if you want to overwrite an existing file with the same name.

This function returns an array of file data:

```php
<?php
function bwawwp_xmlrpc_uploadFile() {
    global $xmlrpc_url, $xmlrpc_user, $xmlrpc_pass;
    $rpc = new IXR_CLIENT( $xmlrpc_url );
    // grab an image
    $args = array(
        'post_type' => 'attachment',
        'post_status' => 'any',
        'posts_per_page' => 1,
        'post_mime_type' => 'image/jpeg'
    );
    $posts = get_posts( $args );
    $name = basename( $posts[0]->post_title );
    $type = $posts[0]->post_mime_type;
    $bits = file_get_contents( $posts[0]->guid );
    $data = array(
        'name' => $name,
        'type' => $type,
        'bits' => new IXR_Base64( $bits ),
        'overwrite' => true
    );
    $rpc->query( 'wp.uploadFile', 0, $xmlrpc_user, $xmlrpc_pass, $data );
    echo '<h1>Uploaded File</h1>';
    echo '<pre>';
    print_r( $rpc->getResponse() );
```

```
        echo '</pre>';
        exit();
}
add_action( 'init', 'bwawwp_xmlrpc_uploadFile', 999 );
?>
```

wp.getPostFormats

Calls the function wp_getPostFormats($args) and requires an array:

- $blog_id
- $username
- $password

This function returns an array of post formats used by the site.

wp.getPostType

Calls the function wp_getPostType($args) and requires an array:

- $blog_id
- $username
- $password
- $post_type—A required string of the post type you would like to retrieve data for.
- $fields—An optional array of post type fields you would like to return. The array can contain keys for labels, description, capability_type, cap, map_meta_cap, hierarchical, menu_position, taxonomies, and/or supports.

This function returns an array of the post type fields you specified with the $fields parameter.

wp.getPostTypes

Calls the function wp_getPostTypes($args) and requires an array:

- $blog_id
- $username
- $password
- $filter—An optional array of filterable post type field values. The array can contain keys for any post type fields; see the function get_post_types(). The default is public → true.

- $fields—An optional array of post type fields you would like to return. The array can contain keys for labels, description, capability_type, cap, map_meta_cap, hierarchical, menu_position, taxonomies, and/or supports.

This function returns an array of the post types with the fields you specified with the $fields parameter:

```php
<?php
function bwawwp_xmlrpc_getPostTypes() {
        $rpc = new IXR_CLIENT( 'http://messenlehner.com/xmlrpc.php' );
        $filter = array( 'public' => 1 );
        $rpc->query( 'wp.getPostTypes', 0, $username, $password, $filter );
        $response = $rpc->getResponse();
        echo '<h1>Post Types</h1>';
        echo '<pre>';
        print_r( $response );
        echo '</pre>';
        exit();
}
add_action( 'init', 'bwawwp_xmlrpc_getPostTypes', 999 );
?>
```

The wp_xmlrpc_server class is located in */wp-includes/class-wp-xmlrpc-server.php*. If you take a look at the class, you can see all of the available functions for interacting with WordPress data.

## CHAPTER 11

Mobile Apps with WordPress

Native mobile applications with WordPress like iOS and Android applications? Well, sure, why not? We are going to explore building a very simple mobile application for both iOS and Android devices. We will leverage what we are already doing in WordPress to offer the most functionality in the least amount of time. How is this possible? With a native app wrapper.

App Wrapper

An app wrapper is basically a native mobile application with a webview. This means that the native app is really just a web browser embedded within the app itself. The URL of this embedded browser points to your WordPress application, hopefully using a responsive mobile design so it looks like it belongs on the device. You can always extend your hybrid app with more native functionality like accessing the camera, GPS device, contacts, and more. If you want a downloadable app in various mobile app marketplaces and don't have the time, money, or resources to build full-blown native apps, building a hybrid app may be the way to go. You will only have to build your web app once, and you can offer that same functionality in each mobile app. A hybrid mobile application like this is probably the fastest and most cost-effective way to get your app out there in the marketplace.

iOS Applications

To build a very basic iOS application and to deploy it in iTunes, you will need the following:

1. An Apple Computer running OS X 10.8.4 or later.

2. Xcode (*http://bit.ly/apple-xcode*), Apple's development environment for creating apps for Mac, iPhone, and iPad. Xcode is packed with an analysis tool, an iOS Simulator, and the latest SDKs for iOS.

3. Enrollment in the Apple Developer Program. You will need to do this if you want to distribute your apps in the App Store. It costs $99 per year for an active account, and once your account is activated, you can put as many apps in the App Store as you want.

Enrolling as an Apple Developer

You will want to start this process (*http://bit.ly/a-developer*) as soon as possible because it can take a while to get approved.

You will need to decide if you are going to enroll as an individual or a company/organization. If you register your company, the process will take a little bit longer because you will need to supply your company's D-U-N-S number. A D-U-N-S number is a unique identifying number for a company provided by Dun & Bradstreet (*http://dnb.com*).

Enrolling is a six-step process:

1. Enter account info—After choosing to enroll as an individual or a company, you will need to log in with your Apple ID. If you don't have an Apple ID, you will need to create one. Once logged in, you will need to read the Review Agreement and check off that you have read it and agree to its terms. You will then need to fill out a form with some basic information like what you will be developing and what other platforms you develop on. If you are enrolling your company or on behalf of a company, you will need to agree that you legally authorized to bind your company to Apple Developer Program legal agreements. Next you will need to submit basic information about you or about your company. When enrolling your company, you will need to enter your company's D-U-N-S number. If you don't have one, you will need to apply for one on the provided form. Getting a new D-U-N-S number is a separate process and can take several days.

2. Select program—You can also enroll in the Mac Developer Program, but make sure you enroll in the iOS Developer Program.

3. Review and submit—Once you have provided the required information, you can review and submit your enrollment application. Now the waiting begins, especially if you have to wait to get your D-U-N-S number from D&B. Apple will review your enrollment application and try to contact you to verify you are who you say you are.

4. Agree to license—Once Apple is able to verify your account, you will then have access to read and agree to its Licence Agreement. Make sure you read the entire thing because it is important to understand the Licence.

5. Purchase program—Get out your credit card. The time has come (finally) to where you can actually pay Apple for your iOS Developer Program Enrollment. Go ahead and do that. Once you pay, you will get an email receipt.

6. Activate program—In about a day after you make the program purchase, you will receive another email with an activation email in it. You are almost done; just click on the link to activate the program, and you are in. Welcome to the club!

Building Your App with Xcode

Go ahead and fire up Xcode and click on "Create a new Xcode project." You should be taken to a screen where you can choose a template to use. There are many templates you can start a native iOS app with; but in the basic example, we are going to choose the Single View Application. This template provides a starting point for an application that uses a single view. It provides a view controller to manage the view and a storyboard or nib file that contains the view.

Next you will see a screen where you can enter in basic project information. Fill out the fields and click next. You will then be prompted to save your new project to a location on your hard drive. Once your new project is created, Xcode will open it for you, and you can begin poking around.

Storyboard

By default, all the way on the left of Xcode are the files that make up your new project. You should notice two files called *Main_iPhone.storyboard* and *Main_iPad.storyboard*. Storyboards allow an iOS developer to visually create an application. If you click on *Main_iPhone.storyboard*, you should see a blank outline of an iPhone popup. This is basically an empty canvas that you can drag any objects onto. Notice the Object Library on the bottom right. Scroll through all of the objects to get an idea of what is available. When you see the Web View object, drag and drop it onto the iPhone outline. The UIWebview class displays embedded web content. You can set it to the URL of your responsive WordPress web application by adding Objective-C code to the *ViewController.h* and *ViewController.m* files, aka the UIViewController class.

View controller

The UIWebView Class is made up of two files, *ViewController.h* and *View-Controller.m*. The *ViewController.h* file is the view controller's header file. Your *ViewController.h* file should look something like the following code example:

```
//
//  XYZViewController.h
//  SchoolPress
//
//  Created by Brian Messenlehner on 6/16/13.
//  Copyright (c) 2013 Building Web Apps with WordPress. All rights reserved.
//

#import <UIKit/UIKit.h>

@interface XYZViewController : UIViewController
@property (weak, nonatomic) IBOutlet UIWebView *webView;

@end
```

Notice that the only real difference in the code you started with and the preceding code is that we added the line:

```
@property (weak, nonatomic) IBOutlet UIWebView *webView;
```

which is basically defining the webView variable.

Now open up the *ViewController.m* file, and add these lines of code:

```
NSString *fullURL = @"http://bwawwp.com";

NSURL *url = [NSURL URLWithString:fullURL];

NSURLRequest *requestObj = [NSURLRequest requestWithURL:url];

[_webView loadRequest:requestObj];
```

under the line of code:

```
[super viewDidLoad];
```

Your *ViewController.m* file should end up looking similar to the following code:

```
//
//  XYZViewController.m
//  SchoolPress
//
//  Created by Brian Messenlehner on 6/16/13.
//  Copyright (c) 2013 Building Web Apps with WordPress. All rights reserved.
//

#import "XYZViewController.h"

@interface XYZViewController ()

@end

@implementation XYZViewController

- (void)viewDidLoad
```

```
{
    [super viewDidLoad];
    // the following URL can be any URL you would like to point your webview to.
    NSString *fullURL = @"http://webdevstudios.com";
    NSURL *url = [NSURL URLWithString:fullURL];
    NSURLRequest *requestObj = [NSURLRequest requestWithURL:url];
    [_webView loadRequest:requestObj];
}

- (void)didReceiveMemoryWarning
{
    [super didReceiveMemoryWarning];
    // Dispose of any resources that can be recreated.
}

@end
```

Basically, the code we added is telling the webView to open the URL we specified. Now you will need to make a connection between your webView variable and the actual UIWebView on your storyboard (the screenshot shown in Figure 11-1).

Figure 11-1. View controller outlet

To do this, click your storyboard file *Main_iPhone.storyboard*, expand View Controller Scene, and Control-click on View Controller. Under Outlets, you should see webView; and to the right, you should see an empty circle. Click on that circle and drag and drop it on top of the UIWebView in the iPhone outline. Repeat this process for the iPad storyboard if you plan on making an iPad version of your app.

That should be it! Your first very basic iOS app WordPress hybrid is done and ready to be tested.

 Check out the UIWebView Class Reference (*http://bit.ly/uiwebview*) for more on the UIWebView class.

iOS simulator

Xcode comes packaged with an iOS simulator for both iPhones and iPads. You can test your iOS applications on this simulator at any time by clicking on the big play button at the top left of your Xcode screen. You can also toggle which iOS device you would like to run your app on. You can also test, run, and build your application builds from the Product menu. Go ahead and click Product → Run to fire up the simulator and run your new application. Figure 11-2 is a screenshot of the iPhone simulator displaying an app with a `webView` that is pointed to WebDevStudios.com.

App Distribution

So now that your app works runs in the iOS simulator, it's time to add it to the market-place. There are a few things you will need to do before you actually upload your app. Log in to *https://developer.apple.com/account/ios/* with your Apple ID. There are a few steps you need to take to make your application available for download on iTunes:

1. Create a production certificate.
2. Create a provisioning profile for distribution.
3. Enable code signing in Xcode.
4. Create a ZIP file of your app and upload it to iTunes.

I recommend watching Dani Arnaout's "How to upload an app to app store" video (*http://bit.ly/appstorevid*).

iOS Resources

- "Deploying iPhone Apps to Real Devices" (*http://bit.ly/apps-to-real*) on mobiForge

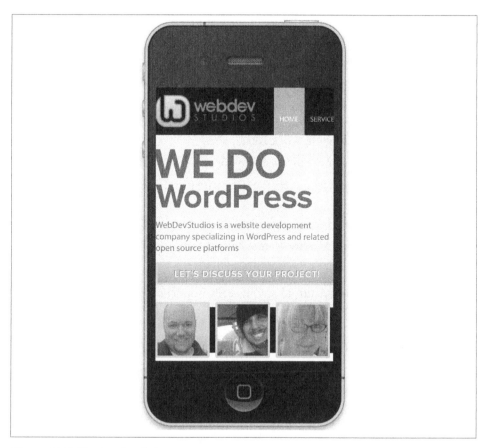

Figure 11-2. Device simulator

Android Applications

If you made a basic iOS app, deployed it, and thought to yourself, holy crap that was a lot of work, you will think deploying an Android app is a lot simpler.

To make a basic app, you will need:

1. Any computer that can run Eclipse (*http://eclipse.org*)
2. The Android SDK (*http://bit.ly/sdkandroid*)

You can download the ADT (Android Developer Tools) bundle. It comes with Eclipse and the ADT plugin, Android SDK Tools, Android Platform-tools, the latest Android platform, and the latest Android system image for the emulator. You can also choose to install Eclipse separately, then install the ADT Plugin and SDK Tools.

If you've installed the ADT Bundle, open up Eclipse, and you should have all of the Android tools already set up:

1. Go to File → New → Project and select Android Application Project. Then click Next.

2. Enter an Application Name, a Project Name, and a Package Name. Then choose your Minimum Required SDK, Target SDK, what API version you want to compile with, and the default theme. Click Next.

3. Choose a Workspace or the location of your project and click Next.

4. Select any of the default launcher icons (the icon people we will see for the app) and click Next.

5. Leave Create Activity checked and select Blank Activity. Then click Next.

6. Leave the defaults for Activity Name, Layout Name, and Navigation Type. Then click Finish.

That's it. You've got a basic Android app; it really doesn't do anything yet, but at least it's a start.

AndroidManifest.xml

This file is required for any Android application. It contains information about how your application is set up, what actions to take, what permissions it requires, what API version to use, and more. Think of this file as your WordPress *wp-config.php* file, since it is like a basic configuration file for your Android application. For more information on *AndroidManifest.xml*, check out Apple's Android guide (*http://bit.ly/android-manifest*).

You will need to add the following line of code to the *AndroidManifest.xml* file to tell your application that it will require permission to access the Internet:

```
<uses-permission android:name="android.permission.INTERNET" />
```

Your *AndroidManifest.xml* file should look something like the following code:

```
<?xml version="1.0" encoding="utf-8"?>
<manifest xmlns:android="http://schemas.android.com/apk/res/android"
    package="com.oreilly.bwawwp"
    android:versionCode="1"
    android:versionName="1.0" >

    <uses-permission android:name="android.permission.INTERNET" />

    <uses-sdk
        android:minSdkVersion="8"
        android:targetSdkVersion="18" />
```

```
<application
    android:allowBackup="true"
    android:icon="@drawable/ic_launcher"
    android:label="@string/app_name"
    android:theme="@style/AppTheme" >
    <activity
        android:name="com.oreilly.bwawwp.MainActivity"
        android:label="@string/app_name" >
        <intent-filter>
            <action android:name="android.intent.action.MAIN" />

            <category android:name="android.intent.category.LAUNCHER" />
        </intent-filter>
    </activity>
</application>

</manifest>
```

activity_main.xml

This file can have other names, and you can have multiple activity XML files, but this file basically stores the information about your main app screen. Your activity XML files are usually located in *res/layout* of your application project directory. If you used the default when creating your app, open up *activity_main.xml* and alter the code to look like this:

```
<RelativeLayout xmlns:android="http://schemas.android.com/apk/res/android"
    xmlns:tools="http://schemas.android.com/tools"
    android:layout_width="match_parent"
    android:layout_height="match_parent"
    tools:context=".MainActivity" >

    <WebView
        android:id="@+id/webView"
        android:layout_width="match_parent"
        android:layout_height="match_parent"
        android:layout_centerHorizontal="true" />

</RelativeLayout>
```

MainActivity.java

This file is the Java-based code behind for your main activity XML file. Your XML file is for the layout of your app screen, and this Java file is what makes it functional. In the last code example, you may have noticed the `tools:context` parameter set to `.MainActivity` in the `RelativeLayout` node of the XML. This directly references the public class in this Java file. Your Java files are going to be located in the *src* directory:

```
package com.oreilly.bwawwp;

// make these classes available
```

```
import android.os.Bundle;
import android.app.Activity;
import android.view.Window;
import android.view.WindowManager;
import android.webkit.WebView;
import android.webkit.WebViewClient;
// extend Activity class
public class MainActivity extends Activity {

        private WebView webView;

        @Override
        protected void onCreate(Bundle savedInstanceState) {
                super.onCreate(savedInstanceState);

                // make app full screen on device
                requestWindowFeature(Window.FEATURE_NO_TITLE);
                        getWindow().setFlags(
WindowManager.LayoutParams.FLAG_FULLSCREEN,
WindowManager.LayoutParams.FLAG_FULLSCREEN
);

                setContentView(R.layout.activity_main);

                        // set webView to the webView on activity_main.xml
                // by its id
                        webView = (WebView) findViewById(R.id.webView);
                        // enable javascript which is essential for slick
                //WP responsive designs
webView.getSettings().setJavaScriptEnabled(true);
                        // load any web url you like
webView.loadUrl("http://bwawwp.com");
                        // this makes sure that when links are clicked the user
        // stays in the app
                        webView.setWebViewClient(new WebViewClient());

}

}
```

Creating an APK file

An *.apk* file is a compiled Android Application. You should be able to run an *.apk* file on any Android device.

Every time you run the Android emulator, you actually create an *.apk* file; but if you want to eventually list your Android App in the Google Play store, you will need to follow these extra steps in Eclipse:

- Go to File → Export.

- Click Export Android Application and then the Next button.
- Choose the project you want to export and click the Next button.
- Check Create new keystore, choose a name and location, then enter a password and click the Next button.
- Fill out all of the Key Creation fields. Alias is the name people will see. For validity, put 25. When finished, click the Next button.
- Choose a name and destination for the actual .*apk* file that will be generated and click the Finished button.

You can manually copy the exported .*apk* file to any Android device and start using it!

Getting Your App on Google Play

If you are going through the trouble of creating a basic Android app, you probably want to put it up in Google's app store so people can download it. This process is easier and cheaper then getting an iOS app up on iTunes. You need to create an account online (*https://play.google.com/apps/publish/signup/*).

Android Resources

Here are some helpful links:

- The ADT Plugin page (*http://bit.ly/adt-plugin*)
- The Getting Started with Android Studio page (*http://bit.ly/gs-studio*)

Extend Your App

Now that your app is out in the wild, try to spend some time making it better. Maybe add some cool native functionality. If you are not an iOS or Android developer, you could certainly learn the basics by picking up an O'Reilly iOS and/or Android book.

Once you know the basics of building simple native apps, you can pull in specific data from your WordPress app. The most simple method of pulling WordPress data into your app is pulling in a RSS feed. You can also push and pull data via XML-RPC, as we went over in the last chapter. XML-RPC can be used to interact with any WordPress website or web application. You can manage pretty much any data stored in a WordPress MySQL database remotely using XML-RPC.

Wait, what? Both the WordPress iOS and Android apps are open source. Dig through the code in these apps and see how they are built and try to reuse what you can in your own app. If you're feeling up to it and already know how to build iOS (*http://bit.ly/wp-*

ios-github) and/or Android (*http://bit.ly/wp-android-github*) apps, try to contribute to these projects and make them better.

AppPresser

Want to easily build a hybrid mobile app for you or your client and don't want to write the code for it yourself? Check out AppPresser (*http://apppresser.com*); you can download a WordPress plugin that will allow you to build an iOS and/or Android app based off your own responsive mobile theme or a selected AppPresser theme. AppPresser is more than just a mobile theme; it can integrate with device hardware like the camera, geolocation, and more. AppPresser-created apps can be uploaded to iTunes and Google Play so you and your clients can have a real presence in the mobile app marketplace without touching a line of Objective-C or Java.

Mobile App Use Cases

OK, so we have mobile apps that can display content from my web app; how interactive can it really be? Hybrid WordPress mobile apps can be as interactive as you want them to be! Anything you can do with WordPress you can do in your hybrid mobile app.

You can force your app users to log into your app via Facebook, Twitter, or other social networks that allow single sign on.

Maybe your web app is an online store: your mobile app can give your customers the ability to browse and purchase products right from the app. Maybe your app allows multiple merchants to have their own stores on your network: your app can give them the ability to manage their inventory and upload photos of products in real time directly from their device.

Maybe you built a dating website with BuddyPress: making a branded mobile app for your dating service could really help boost your member base if you gain popularity in the marketplaces. You could utilize native device features like the camera to allow your social network members to take and upload selfies directly to their profile.

Maybe you are building a realtor site, and you want agents to be able to create new posts in a custom post type called "Homes" for a home they are trying to sell. You can give them the ability to snap some photos of the house and post them to the web application along with the longitude and latitude of the house so it will show up in Google Maps.

You could make a mobile app for construction contractors, plumbers, landscapers, electricians, or any other type of physical service–based business that could easily assist them in tracking jobs, accessing client details, uploading before-and-after photos or videos, tracking job locations via GPS, collaborating with coworkers, and more.

The possibilities of what you can build are limitless, especially the more you incorporate native functionality into your hybrid mobile application. If required, you could always build 100% native mobile apps and still make them access an online WordPress application so your content and user base is the same across all platforms.

CHAPTER 12
PHP Libraries, External APIs, and Web Services

Most programming languages, including PHP, have modularized collections of code, classes, and functions. These collections are usually referred to as a code library or extension. Don't recreate the wheel. There are PHP libraries that exist to perform very specific functionality that can be easily used to extend the applications you are building.

Most of WordPress is written in PHP, which means as a WordPress developer, you can utilize any PHP libraries available to you or even build your own! Check out the PHP.net Function Reference (*http://bit.ly/phpfunct-ref*) for an organized list of some PHP libraries.

An application programmable interface, or API, can be part of an application in which you have access to the source code, like the various WordPress APIs covered in this book. But an API can also enable you to use an application or service in which you don't have direct access to the source code. Many web-based applications and services offer some kind of API for accessing or manipulating their data from your application.

The WordPress plugin repository has more than a few plugins that interact with various web services, so any time you are looking for custom WordPress functionality, you might want to start at the WordPress plugin repository. Of course, if you don't find exactly what you are looking for in a plugin, you may need to write your own custom plugin or piggyback off of an existing one.

We mentioned GitHub more than a few times, but it is a great place to find functionality you may be looking for. Another good resource for code can be other PHP-based open source projects like Drupal or Joomla. If the functionality you are looking for doesn't exist as a WordPress plugin but does as a Drupal module, take the code and make it work with WordPress.

Depending on what your requirements are, you can interact with various libraries and APIs in many different ways. You can cache data from an API in a transient. You can create posts and post metadata. You can create users and user meta. You can sideload post attachments. You can push post data to a web service. These are just a few examples; the sky's the limit!

We are going to walk through some popular libraries and APIs that can be easily integrated into WordPress and talk about some use cases.

Imagick

Imagick is a powerful piece of software that allows you to resize and manipulate image files. It's like Photoshop for the command line, which can be useful for building mindless meme generators (*http://www.quickmeme.com/caption*) amongst other more productive things.

Imagick can be installed on your server and then run through the command line via the `shell_exec()` or `exec()` PHP functions or you can use the Imagick PHP library (*http://bit.ly/imagick-php*) as a wrapper for the underlying software. The Imagick library is not bundled with PHP and must be installed separately along with the Imagick software itself.

Imagick can be very useful if you require all of the images on your web application to be watermarked with your URL so if anybody hijacks your images at least they will have your web address embedded onto it. Justin Sternberg of WebDevStudios made some really easy-to-use methods for overlaying any text on any image and then saving the separate image as an attachment against a WordPress post. Check his code out at WordPress-Image-Watermark (*http://bit.ly/image-waterm*).

MaxMind GeoIP

MaxMind GeoIP (*http://bit.ly/geo-ip*) gets data from a users' IP address such as their location and Internet provider. There are many services out there like MaxMind, but we like to use this service because it has a very extensive API and a free downloadable database.

Maybe a school wants to add an extra layer of security for its web application and only wants to give access to the login page to people from within the same town or state that the school is in. This type of security feature might only be necessary if you want to lock down your application to a particular geographical location or locations, but it could greatly reduce the amount of potential hack attempts. Instead of only allowing access to your web application, you could also lock out particular locations, let's say China. Maybe depending on your application, you know that anyone visiting from China should not have access.

Maybe a state website using WordPress wants to be able to show its visitors schools in the area when the website first loads. Let's say "schools" are a CPT with address information stored as post meta. This can also be achieved by getting the end users' locations and doing a meta query to match schools in their area.

You can download the PHP library with all of the functionality from the MaxMind website. To utilize its API, download the code from GitHub (*http://bit.ly/geoip-github*).

In Example 12-1, we are assuming that you have signed up for MaxMind's Omni Service. The Omni service is MaxMind's most robust service and will return the most data for a supplied IP address.

Example 12-1. MaxMind GeoIP

```php
<?php
add_action( 'init', 'schoolpress_maxmind' );
function schoolpress_maxmind(){

    // Omni service code is 'e'
    $service = 'e';
    // MaxMind Licence Key
    $key = 'sELZl0ELZMrx97T'; // This is a fake key, get your own!

    // Build an array of the licence key and the ip address of the end user
    $params = getopt( 'l:i:' );
    if ( !isset( $params['l'] ) ) $params['l'] = $key;
    $ip = $_SERVER['REMOTE_ADDR'];
    if ( !isset( $params['i'] ) ) $params['i'] = $ip;

    /*
    $params should be an array siumlar to:
    Array
    (
        [l] => sELZl0ELZMrx97T
        [i] => 96.234.61.86
    )
    */

    // MaxMind request URL
    $query = 'https://geoip.maxmind.com/';
    $query.= $service . '?' . http_build_query( $params );
    // Get response from the URL
    $response = wp_remote_get( $query );
    $results = $response['body'];
    // Turn response into array to easily grab what we need
    $results = explode(',', $results);

    echo '<pre>';
    print_r($results);
    echo '</pre>';
    exit();
```

```
/*
$results should be an array simular to:
Array
(
    [0] => US
    [1] => "United States"
    [2] => NJ
    [3] => "New Jersey"
    [4] => Belmar
    [5] => 40.1784
    [6] => -74.0218
    [7] => 501
    [8] => 732
    [9] => America/New_York
    [10] => NA
    [11] =>
    [12] => "Verizon FiOS"
    [13] => "Verizon FiOS"
    [14] => verizon.net
    [15] => "AS701 MCI Communications Services
    [16] =>  Inc. d/b/a Verizon Business"
    [17] => Cable/DSL
    [18] => residential
    [19] => 7
    [20] => 99
    [21] => 31
    [22] => 93
    [23] =>
    [24] =>
)
*/
}
?>
```

 When working with MaxMind GeoIP data, it might be a good idea to utilize cookies to store a user's geolocation data so you don't have to keep querying MaxMind's API or querying the *.dat* file if you down-loaded the free database.

Google Maps JavaScript API v3

Everyone knows what Google Maps is, and I'm sure you have seen some WordPress plugins using it. Google offers a JavaScript-based API (*http://bit.ly/googlemaps-api*) for interacting with its maps, and you can build anything from a basic map zoomed into a specified location to a custom map with markers depicting various WordPress posts from a specific custom post type.

Besides all of the map functionality available via the Google Maps JavaScript API, Google also has some other API services related to its maps.

Directions

You can use this service to calculate directions between various locations and return step-by-step directions of what route(s) to follow. When creating a directions request, you can pass in an origin or a location for your directions to start and a destination or the end location. You can also specify the travel mode: driving (default), bicycling, transit, or walking.

Distance Matrix

The Google Distance Matrix API is a service that provides travel distance and time for a matrix of origins and destinations. The information returned is based on the recommended route between the start and endpoints, as calculated by the Google Maps API, and consists of rows containing duration and distance values for each pair.

Elevation

This API provides a way to query elevation data for provided locations.

Geocoding

This API will allow you to query geolocation data like latitude and longitude from a provided address. You can also use reverse geocoding to provide the closest address for a given latitude and longitude.

Street View Service

This API allows you to interact with Google Street View. This API is really cool because you can access all of the photos and locations available in Google Street View.

Practical App

In Example 12-2, we are going to create a custom meta box called Location that will allow a user to associate an address with a post. We will also display a Google Map in the meta box with a marker of a user-specified address. Sometimes the markers on a map don't line up exactly on the map where they should actually be. In our example code, you can drag and drop the marker to a new location, and when the post is updated, the marker will be saved in the location you moved it to.

Example 12-2. Creating a Location meta box

```php
<?php
// Only turn this on in the backend
add_action( 'admin_init', 'sp_register_meta_directions' );

// Add Directions Meta Box
```

```php
function sp_register_meta_directions() {
    add_meta_box(
        'sp-directions-meta',
        'Address Information',
        'sp_directions_meta_box',
        'post',
        'normal',
        'high'
    );
    add_action( 'save_post', 'sp_directions_save_meta' );
}

// Meta Box
function sp_directions_meta_box( $post='' ) {
    // Get curretn post ID
    $post_id = $post->ID;
    // Get pos meta data if exists
    $sp_directions_address = get_post_meta( $post_id,
        '_sp_directions_address',
        true
    );
    $sp_directions_latitude = get_post_meta( $post_id,
        '_sp_directions_latitude',
        true
    );
    $sp_directions_longitude = get_post_meta( $post_id,
        '_sp_directions_longitude',
        true
    );
    // Output text box to collect any address?>
    <input type="text"
        id="sp_directions_address"
        name="sp_directions_address"
        value="<?php echo $sp_directions_address;?>"
        size="60" />
    *123 Main St, New York, NY
    <input type="hidden"
        id="sp_directions_latitude"
        name="sp_directions_latitude"
        value="<?php echo $sp_directions_latitude;?>"/>
    <input type="hidden"
        id="sp_directions_longitude"
        name="sp_directions_longitude"
        value="<?php echo $sp_directions_longitude;?>"/>
    <?php // Javascript for the Map?>
    <script type="text/javascript"
        src="http://maps.google.com/maps/api/js?sensor=false"></script>
    <script type="text/javascript">
    // sets the hidden text boxes for lat & lng to the lat & lng of the dragged
    // and dropped marker
    function updateMarkerPosition(latLng) {
    document.getElementById('sp_directions_latitude').value = latLng.lat();
```

```php
        document.getElementById('sp_directions_longitude').value = latLng.lng();
    }

    // initialize the Google map
    function sp_map_initialize() {
    var map = new google.maps.Map(document.getElementById("map_canvas"), {
    scaleControl: true});
    var bounds = new google.maps.LatLngBounds();
    map.setMapTypeId(google.maps.MapTypeId.HYBRID);

    var myLatLng = new google.maps.LatLng(
        <?php echo $sp_directions_latitude;?>,
        <?php echo $sp_directions_longitude;?>
    );
    bounds.extend(myLatLng);

    var marker<?php echo $post_id;?> = new google.maps.Marker(
        {map: map, draggable: true, position:
    new google.maps.LatLng(
        <?php echo $sp_directions_latitude;?>,
        <?php echo $sp_directions_longitude;?>)}});

    google.maps.event.addListener(
      marker<?php echo $post_id;?>,
      'dragend',
      function(){
        updateMarkerPosition(
            marker<?php echo $post_id;?>.getPosition())
        ;
      }
    );

    map.fitBounds(bounds);
    }

    setTimeout("sp_map_initialize()",10);
    </script>
    <div id="map_canvas" style="height:300px;width:100%;"></div>
    <?php
}

// Save Data
function sp_directions_save_meta( $post_id ) {
    $address=strip_tags( $_POST['sp_directions_address'] );
    $lat=strip_tags( $_POST['sp_directions_latitude'] );
    $lng=strip_tags( $_POST['sp_directions_longitude'] );
    if ( $address != get_post_meta( $post_id, '_sp_directions_address', 1 ) ) {
        sp_get_lat_lng( $post_id, $address );
    }elseif ( $lat ) {
        update_post_meta( $post_id, '_sp_directions_latitude', $lat );
        update_post_meta( $post_id, '_sp_directions_longitude', $lng );
    }
```

```
        }

        // Get lat & lng from address and update post meta
        function sp_get_lat_lng( $post_id, $address ) {
            global $wpdb, $bp;
            if ( $address ) {
                // Get GeoLocattion data from Google by passin in an address
                $url = 'http://maps.googleapis.com/maps/api/geocode/json';
                $g_address = $url . '?sensor=true&address='.urlencode( $address );
                $g_address = wp_remote_get( $g_address );
                $g_address = $g_address["body"];
                $g_address = json_decode( $g_address );
                $lat = $g_address->results[0]->geometry->location->lat;
                $lng = $g_address->results[0]->geometry->location->lng;

                /*
                // Uncomment if you want to see the raw JSON response
                echo '<pre>';
                print_r($g_address);
                echo '</pre>';
                exit();
                */

                // update post meta for lat and lng
                update_post_meta( $post_id, '_sp_directions_latitude', $lat );
                update_post_meta( $post_id, '_sp_directions_longitude', $lng );
            }else {
                // if no address then delete post meta
                delete_post_meta( $post_id, '_sp_directions_latitude' );
                delete_post_meta( $post_id, '_sp_directions_longitude' );
            }
        }
        ?>
```

Google Translate

What if you wanted to auto-translate pieces of content into various languages? You can do this utilizing Google's translation API (*http://bit.ly/translate-api*). There are quite a few WordPress plugins that leverage this API; but depending on your scenario, you may want to translate various strings of text on the fly, and you can certainly use this API to do so.

This API is not free but can be well worth the cost depending on how important it is to you to automatically translate any of your content.

Google+

Google's social network, Google+, has a pretty extensive API (*http://bit.ly/goo-api*). Unlike Facebook's and Twitter's APIs, the Google+ API doesn't allow you to push data to it; it only allows you to pull data. Hopefully one day it will open it up to allow third-party developers to post data to it.

Google+ offers specific APIs for Android, iOS, Hangouts, and the Web via JavaScript and an extensive HTTP API. For integrating with WordPress, it is best to use the Java-Script and/or the HTTP API.

There are four main resource types within the HTTP API, and each resource type has a few methods. Each method returns its results in a JSON data structure.

People

The people resource type allows you to access information about Google+ members. You can return data from specific member's profiles, search profiles for particular keywords, and return data lists of members that have +1'd or shared activity.

Activities

The activity resource type allows you to access any activity or stream notes of a particular user in a list. You can return specific activity by ID, and you can search any public activity.

Comments

A comment is a reply to any activity. The comments resource allows you to access a list of all comments for a provided activity. You can also get a specific comment by its ID.

Moments

Moments describe activities that users engage within your app. The app activities comprise a moment type, a target, and many optional fields. The fields that are required when inserting moments depend on the type of moment. Your app can also list moments and delete moments that it previously wrote for the authenticated user.

 Most of Google's APIs are very similar, so once you learn one or two, you should be able to pick up most of them fairly quickly. For a complete reference of Google's APIs, go to their API Explorer (*http://bit.ly/api-explorer*).

Amazon Product Advertising API

Lots of people buy and sell products on Amazon.com, everything from golf balls to video games to kitchen sinks. Most of the product data is made available via Amazon's Product Advertising API (*http://bit.ly/api-list*). You can access basic product information, including a product's price, categories, customer reviews, similar products, and accessories. Most of the information that is available on any product on Amazon.com is also available via its API.

The first thing you will need to do to start using the API is to become an Amazon Associate (*http://bit.ly/amazon-affil*) and get your Associate Tag/Associate ID. This is a unique identifier you will need to make requests on the API. Once you sign up, you should receive an email with your Associate Tag in it. Along with an Associate Tag, you will also need an AWS Access Key ID and Secret Access Key. You can get those using your basic Amazon account information at *https://affiliate-program.amazon.com/gp/flex/advertising/api/sign-in.html*. Once you are signed in, click the Manage Your Account link, then click the Click Here link in the Access Identifiers box; this will take you to a page where you can generate/access both your Access Key ID and Secret Access Key.

Amazon.com is a great source of product information if you are looking to build any type of web application that has anything to do with various products and their data. You can bet that no matter what the product is, Amazon will most likely have data on it. In our example, we will be building a script to save various school supplies and their data from Amazon's API as individual WordPress posts.

Request Parameters

When creating a request to Amazon, you will need the following required parameters:

Service
> Specifies the Product Advertising API service. Amazon offers some other web services, but we will be focusing on the Product Advertising API, so the value should be "AWSECommerceService".

AssociateTag
> This is your Amazon Associate Tag/Associate ID.

AWSAccessKeyId
> This is your AWS Access Key ID.

Operation
> The operation you would like to perform.

Operations

Depending on what operation you use, you can pass in additional request parameters to help refine your results. The following is a list of the available operations and what additional request parameters can be passed in with them:

BrowseNodeLookup
> Given a browse node ID, BrowseNodeLookup returns the specified browse node's name, children, and ancestors. The names and browse node IDs of the children and ancestor browse nodes are also returned.

CartAdd
> The CartAdd operation enables you to add items to an existing remote shopping cart. CartAdd can only be used to place a new item in a shopping cart.

CartClear
> The CartClear operation enables you to remove all of the items in a remote shopping cart.

CartCreate
> The CartCreate operation enables you to create a remote shopping cart.

CartGet
> The CartGet operation enables you to retrieve the IDs, quantities, and prices of all of the items, including SavedForLater items, in a remote shopping cart.

CartModify
> The CartModify operation enables you to change the quantity of items that are already in a remote shopping cart and move items from the active area of a cart to the SaveForLater area or the reverse.

ItemLookup
> Given an Item identifier, the ItemLookup operation returns some or all of the item attributes, depending on the response group specified in the request. By default, ItemLookup returns an item's ASIN, Manufacturer, and ProductGroup, as well as the Title of the item.

ItemSearch
> The ItemSearch operation returns up to 10 search results per page. When condition equals "All," ItemSearch returns additional offers for those items, one offer per condition type.

SimilarityLookup
> The SimilarityLookup operation returns up to 10 products per page that are similar to one or more items specified in the request. This operation is typically used to pique a customer's interest in buying something similar to what she's already ordered.

Response Groups

A response group helps target the information returned by a query. Each operation has specific response groups that it can use. Some response groups utilize other response groups.

 Amazon keeps a full list of response groups (*http://bit.ly/response-groups*) in the AWS documentation.

In Example 12-3, we are going to query Amazon for any books about WordPress. This script can be used to import books into a CPT called Books. You could create post meta for all of the additional book information and even save the images as post attachments.

Example 12-3. Search for WordPress books

```php
<?php
add_action( 'init', 'wds_get_aws_products' );

function wds_get_aws_products() {

    //set our aws associate tag, access key id & secret access key
    $AssociateTag = 'webd167-423234';
    $AWSAccessKeyId = 'ACAJBDXQSKILGQDWZSNK';
    $AWSSecretAccessKey = '26AB/UhHl2kYu/YF8QokT1+078p5Ax/tgECtWbwug';

    //set up our search parameters
    $params = array(
        'AWSAccessKeyId' => $AWSAccessKeyId,
        'AssociateTag' => $AssociateTag,
        'Service' => 'AWSECommerceService',
        'ItemPage' => '10',
        'Operation' => 'ItemSearch',
        'SearchIndex' => 'Books',
        'Keywords' => "WordPress",
        'ResponseGroup' => 'Offers,ItemAttributes,OfferFull,Images' );

    $params['Timestamp'] = gmdate( "Y-m-d\TH:i:s.\\0\\0\\0\\Z", time() );
    $url_parts = array();
    foreach ( array_keys( $params ) as $key ) {
        $part = str_replace( '%7E', '~', rawurlencode( $params[ $key ] ) );
        $url_parts[] = $key . '=' . $part;
    }

    sort( $url_parts );
    $url_string = implode( "&", $url_parts );
    $string_to_sign = "GET\necs.amazonaws.com\n/onca/xml\n" . $url_string;
    $signature = hash_hmac( "sha256",
```

```php
        $string_to_sign,
        $AWSSecretAccessKey,
        TRUE
    );
    $signature = urlencode( base64_encode( $signature ) );
    $url = 'http://ecs.amazonaws.com/onca/xml?';
    $url.= $url_string . "&Signature=" . $signature;
    $response = file_get_contents( $url );

    $xml = simplexml_load_string( $response );

    echo '<pre>';
    print_r( $xml );
    echo '</pre>';
    exit();

}
?>
```

Twitter REST API v1.1

Twitter has an extensive API (*http://bit.ly/twitter-apis*) for publishing and getting tweets from its platform as well as allowing its users to sign in to any web application via a Twitter app. With the Twitter API, you can access data from and make updates to some of the following resources:

Timelines
  Timelines are collections of various tweets, ordered with the most recent first.

Tweets
  Tweets are what make up Twitter; they are 140-character status updates with additional associated metadata.

Search
  You can find tweets based on queries with provided keywords.

Direct Messages
  You can access these private messages sent back and forth between users of your application.

Friends and Followers
  You can access relationships between various users as well as manage some of those relationships for authenticated users.

Users
  You can access user data as well as update it for authenticated users.

Suggested Users
  You can access suggested users for authenticated users.

Favorites

> Users favorite tweets that they like. You can access favorited tweets as well as favorite specific tweets for authenticated users.

Lists

> Collections of tweets, called from a curated list of Twitter users. You can access lists as well as create lists for authenticated users.

Saved Searches

> Allows users to save their search criteria for reuse later.

Places and Geo

> Allows you to access geolocation data attached to tweets that have that data available. You can also attach location data to any tweets of authenticated users.

Trends

> The Trends methods allow you to explore what's trending on Twitter.

Spam Reporting

> Can be used to report spam to Twitter.

OAuth

> Twitter offers applications the ability to issue authenticated requests on behalf of the application itself (as opposed to on behalf of a specific user). Twitter's implementation is based on the Client Credentials Grant flow of the OAuth 2 specification.

The application-only auth flow follows these steps:

1. An application encodes its consumer key and secret into a specially encoded set of credentials.

2. An application makes a request to the POST oauth2/token endpoint to exchange these credentials for a bearer token.

3. When accessing the REST API, the application uses the bearer token to authenticate.

Set Up Your App on Twitter.com

To set up a new Twitter app, you must be signed in to Twitter and go to *https://dev.twitter.com/apps*. You can click the Create New App button to get started building your app. Fill out all of the required fields on the form and submit your app. On your app details page, you will find all of the information you will need for interacting with your app from within WordPress. Pay attention to the following:

- Consumer Key
- Consumer Secret

- Access Token
- Access Token Secret

You will need to copy these values later.

Leverage a PHP Library

There are several PHP libraries available out there for interacting with Twitter's API; we like to use twitteroauth (*http://bit.ly/awilliams-oauth*) by Abraham Williams. It's very simple to drop the necessary files you need in a subdirectory of a custom plugin and reference them.

You can download the ZIP file and extract the files into a *lib* directory in your custom plugin or theme. You will just need to reference the library in a manner like the following in your code: `require_once lib/twitteroauth.php;`.

In Example 12-4, we are going to search Twitter for any tweets that contain the keyword "bwawwp."

Example 12-4. Searching Twitter

```php
<?php
/*Plugin Name: BWAwWP - Twitter */

// reference the php library we downloaded from GitHub
require_once 'lib/twitteroauth.php';


// Copy over credentials from the Twitter app you created. Below are not real keys.
define( 'C_KEY', '0LU1wUibUKP3bccx2NFlK' );
define( 'C_SECRET', 'KGYQnbZlZaNPqdg2INldACazetPLwvprRqbo' );
define( 'A_TOKEN', '11018212-3qMnqt8D4HpCb2ACzyVoK1kAW' );
define( 'A_TOKEN_SECRET', 'jUMC3Ocy6Yx7JV4xRFhZ5eiCbiIyjc' );

add_action( 'init', 'sp_twitter_search' );
function sp_twitter_search() {
        // our search term
        $q = 'bwawwp';

        // call TwitterOAuth and pass in Twitter credentials.
        $toa = new TwitterOAuth( 'C_KEY', 'C_SECRET', 'A_TOKEN', 'A_TOKEN_SECRET' );

        // call the search tweets method
        $search = $toa->get( 'search/tweets', array( 'q' => $q ) );

        echo "<pre>";
        print_r( $search );
        echo "</pre>";
        exit();
```

```
}
?>
```

You can start to imagine the possible ways Twitter data can be integrated with Word-Press. Our example code could be useful for searching Twitter for any keywords and pulling those tweets into posts in a CPT. They could be saved as BuddyPress activities for a BuddyPress group. You could search for tweets having to do with various keywords and locations and plot them on a Google Map. The possibilities are really endless.

If you are utilizing Twitter's API to post data, like favoriting and retweeting tweets or following other users, make sure you comply with Twitter's usage terms and don't go over your rate limit (*http://bit.ly/rate-limiting*). You don't want to get your account banned, and you especially don't want to get a user of your application's account banned.

Facebook

Do you Facebook it up all the time? If you don't, there are millions of people who do. Facebook has a few different APIs available (*http://bit.ly/fb-javascript*), but its Graph API allows access to most of the data available to users. You can leverage WordPress to make native Facebook apps because a Facebook canvas page is basically an iframe. Why build something from scratch when you can link Facebook users to WordPress users and utilize WordPress as a Facebook app any way you see fit?

We are going to briefly go over Facebook's Graph API, the primary way that data is retrieved from or posted to Facebook.

Pictures

You can add */picture* to the end of most object URLs like people, events, groups, pages, applications, and photo albums. You can also add the following query strings to the end of a picture URL to change how the image is returned:

- type—Values can be square, small, normal, or large (type=square).
- width—A numerical value of the width you want the image to be (width=200).
- height—A numerical value of the height you want the image to be (height=200).
- return_ssl_resources—If set to 1, the image will be returned over a secure connection.

For example, if you go to the URL *https://graph.facebook.com/bmess/picture?type=large*, you will see my latest Facebook profile picture in a large view. Try this out with your Facebook profile name and some of the query string arguments you can use.

Search

All Graph API search queries require an access token passed in with the `access_to ken=<token>` parameter. The type of access token you need depends on the type of search you're running. Searches across page and place objects require an app access token, while all other endpoints require a user access token.

Facebook supports searching the following objects:

- Public Posts
- People
- Pages
- Events
- Groups
- Places
- Checkins

Permissions

Your application may need to interact with Facebook users in various ways, and you may need permission from end users to access some of their information via the Graph API:

Email Permissions
> Email is a protected property and must be specifically asked for and granted.

Extended Permissions
> Because these permissions give access to more sensitive info and the ability to pub-lish and delete data, they are optional when presented to users in the login dialog. They can also be removed by a user through privacy settings. Apps should be built to handle revoked permissions without reducing the user experience.

Extended Profile Properties
> These permissions cannot be revoked in the login dialog during the login flow, meaning they are nonoptional for users when logging in to your app. If you want them to be optional, you should structure your app to only request them when absolutely necessary and not upon initial login.

Open Graph Permissions
> These permissions allow your app to publish actions to the Open Graph and also to retrieve actions published by other apps.

Page Permissions
> Permissions related to management of Facebook Pages.

Public Profile and Friend List
> The Public Profile and Friend List is the basic information available to an app. All other permissions and content must be explicitly asked for.

Building an Application

To build a basic Facebook app and/or to use Facebook to log in users to your web app, you will need to create an app on Facebook. Go to the UI (*https://developers.face book.com/apps*) and click on the Create New App button. Follow the instructions. If you need help, search online; we don't want to walk through all the ins and outs of creating a basic app. Once you have created an app, you will have access to the App ID/API Key and the App Secret Key. You now have a very basic Facebook app.

Leverage What's Out There

You could build your own login process for Facebook, but why? Use what is already out there. We like to leverage the plugin WordPress Social Login (*http://bit.ly/wp-social-login*). This plugin provides you with a nice UI for managing logins to your WordPress site for Facebook and a number of other social networks. This plugin only really authenticates users: what if we need to do more than that? What if we need to access specific users' posts and friends or even post to a user's wall using the Graph API (*http://bit.ly/fb-g-api*)? We can build an add-on plugin that uses an already authenticated user from the WordPress Social Login to handle whatever functionality we may require.

You may need to alter the WordPress Social Login plugin a little, depending on what you want to to do. The has all of the Facebook permissions that we need. If you were building something that requires additional permissions, you would need to alter the plugin itself.

If you download the plugin and open up */plugins/wordpress-social-login/hybridauth/Hybrid/Providers/Facebook.php*, you will see a `Hybrid_Providers_Facebook` class with a variable named `scope` that looks like this:

```
public $scope = "email, user_about_me, user_birthday, user_hometown,
user_website, read_stream, offline_access, publish_stream, read_friendlists";
```

You can alter the `scope` string to the exact permissions you need for your application.

Twilio

Need to be able to send customized SMS alert messages to members? Maybe your application needs an additional layer of security and you need to verify user accounts via random activation codes text messaged to mobile phones. Twilio (*http://*

www.twilio.com/sms/api) has a great web service that lets you send and receive SMS messages back and forth between users' cell phones and your account(s) with them.

Maybe a school would like to verify the contact numbers of parents so they can later send text message alerts with import information like if their child is playing hooky and has cut a class. The first thing you should do is download the Twilio PHP library from GitHub (*http://bit.ly/twilio-php*). If you are building a custom plugin, drop *Twilio.php* and the Twilio directory into a lib directory in your plugin. Your directory structure should look something like */wp-content/plugins/your-plugin/lib/Twilio*.

We recommend interacting with the Twilio API over SSL.

Microsoft Sharepoint

Microsoft? A lot of people in the open source world like to bash Microsoft. The fact of the matter is governments and big businesses across the world use many Microsoft products; and although we think that open source will one day change this, it isn't going to happen anytime soon. SharePoint (*http://msdn.microsoft.com/*) is Microsoft's flagship collaboration product these days; it's web based and super powerful. If you have ever seen a large-scale SharePoint deployment, then you know how useful and integrated into a business's workflow it can be. One of SharePoint's most impressive features is its integration with the entire Microsoft Office suite.

SharePoint has a web service available for almost every feature it offers. You can actually push and pull almost any data available in a SharePoint deployment via these web services:

Administration Web service
> Provides methods for managing a deployment of Microsoft Windows SharePoint Services, such as for creating or deleting site collections.

Alerts Web Service
> List and delete alert subscriptions. Alert subscriptions specify when and how notifications are sent to users when changes are made to content stored on the server. The protocol does not specify the creation or editing of alert subscriptions.

Authentication Web Service
> Provides classes for logging on to a SharePoint site that is using forms-based authentication.

Copy Web Service
> Provides services for copying files within a SharePoint site and between SharePoint sites.

Document Workspace Web Service
> Exposes methods for managing Document Workspace sites and the data they contain.

Forms Web Service
> Provides methods for returning forms that are used in the user interface when working with the contents of a list.

Imaging Web Service
> Provides methods that enable you to create and manage picture libraries.

List Data Retrieval Web Service
> An adapter service that provides a method for performing queries against SharePoint lists.

Lists Web Service
> The Lists Web service provides methods for working with SharePoint lists, content types, list items, and files.

Meetings Web Service
> Enables the creation and management of Meeting Workspace sites.

People Web Service
> Provides classes that can be used to associate user identifiers with security groups for Windows SharePoint Services website permissions. User IDs are validated against Active Directory Domain Services as well as various role or membership providers. SPGroup security information may also be stored in a collection of cross-site groups for the site collection.

Permissions Web Service
> The Permissions Web service provides methods for working with list and site permissions in Windows SharePoint Services.

SharePoint Directory Management Web Service
> Provides classes that enable requests for various management operations for email distribution groups.

Site Data Web Service
> The Site Data web service supports site indexing by external indexing services. Indexing is the process of building an external index of the website, facilitating search, auditing, or cataloging of the site content.

Sites Web Service
> The Sites Web service provides methods and properties that support export and import operations using SOAP calls against Windows SharePoint Services websites (SPWeb instances) to allow migrating site content from one location to another.

The Sites Web service provides one of three ways to migrate content from one Windows SharePoint Services website to another.

Search Web Service

Enterprise Search in Microsoft Office SharePoint Server exposes its search functionalities through the Query web service. This allows you to access Enterprise Search results from client applications and web applications outside of the context of a SharePoint site.

Users and Groups Web Service

The Users and Groups Web service provides methods for working with users and groups in Windows SharePoint Services.

Versions Web Service

The Versions Web service provides methods for working with file versions in SharePoint document libraries.

Views Web Service

The Views Web service provides methods for creating, deleting, or updating list views in Windows SharePoint Services.

Web Part Pages Web Service

Provides methods for working with Web Parts.

Webs Web Service

Provides methods for working with sites and subsites.

For more information, check out the Microsoft Developer Network (*http://msdn.micro soft.com/*).

You can imagine how useful it might be pushing and pulling data to and from a document library. Think of document libraries or lists in SharePoint as custom post types in WordPress. You can create custom fields and custom forms to store metadata, attach documents, interact with other lists, and more when building document libraries. If you needed a custom web app built with WordPress and needed to sync it with specific data stored in a SharePoint site, you could use these web services. Also, if you need to completely manage data in a SharePoint site and you don't know the first thing about developing in .NET, you could use these web services.

We Missed a Few

We have just mentioned a few available PHP libraries, web services, and APIs you could leverage, depending on what you are trying to accomplish. These are some of the more popular ones, but they are really just the tip of the iceberg of what's available across the Internet.

Don't reinvent the wheel. Before you build anything, look to see what resources are available to you. Leverage data from external data sources, and integrate your data with external social networks and directories. Work smarter, not harder!

The following are some other popular web services you might want to mess around with:

- FourSquare (*https://developer.foursquare.com/*)
- Instagram (*http://instagram.com/developer/*)
- Salesforce (*http://bit.ly/soap-api*)
- flickr (*http://www.flickr.com/services/api/*)
- YouTube (*https://developers.google.com/youtube/*)
- eBay (*http://developer.ebay.com/common/api/*)
- Dropbox (*https://www.dropbox.com/developers*)
- LinkedIn (*http://developer.linkedin.com/apis*)
- MailChimp (*http://apidocs.mailchimp.com/*)
- Constant Contact (*https://developer.constantcontact.com/*)

## CHAPTER 13

Building WordPress Multisite Networks

With the release of WordPress version 3.0 came WordPress Multisite. WordPress Multisite was known as WordPress Multiuser or WPMU prior to v3.0 because it was a separate open source project. Since WordPress and WPMU share most of the same code, it made sense to roll it all into one project. Multisite gives WordPress administrators the ability to create their own network with multiple sites. All of the sites on a Multisite network share the same database and the same source files. When Multisite is set up, new tables are created in the database for each new website created on the network.

Why Multisite?

If you are running more than one install of WordPress, you should consider using Multisite. Some of the benefits include:

- Logging into one network and making any changes you need to any of your WordPress sites with one administrator account.

- Making updates to WordPress and installed plugins and/or themes one time in one place instead of multiple websites.

- Managing all of the users on your network in one location.

- Easily deploying a new website with a few clicks.

- If you are using a theme framework for all of the sites on your network, you could make updates to all of your themes at the same time utilizing an available hook in your theme.

Setting Up a Multisite Network

Although setting up Multisite is not as easy as enabling it in a WordPress setting, it is fairly straightforward. The first thing you should do if you are not setting up a brand-new WordPress install is to make a backup of your database and file directory.

Open your *wp-config.php* file in the root of your WordPress directory and add the following piece of code right under the line that says /* That's all, stop editing! Happy blogging. */:

```
define( 'WP_ALLOW_MULTISITE', true );
```

Refresh your WordPress admin dashboard and go to Tools → Network Setup. Here you should see a few form fields asking you for the following information:

Subdomain or Subdirectory
> How do you want to build the subsites on your Multisite network? If you want subdomains like sub.domain.com, then choose subdomain. If you want domain.com/sub, then choose subdirectory. You could always use a domain mapping plugin to map any domain you want to either a subdomain or subdirectory.

Network Title
> The name of your Multisite network.

Admin Email Address
> The email of the network administrator, most likely your email address.

Once you have filled out the required information, click the Install button.

You should now see two text area boxes. The first text area box is going to contain code that you will need to copy and paste into your *wp-config.php* file right under the line of code you just previously added under the line that says /* That's all, stop editing! Happy blogging. */:

```
define( 'MULTISITE', true );
define( 'SUBDOMAIN_INSTALL', false );
define( 'DOMAIN_CURRENT_SITE', 'whatever.com' );
define( 'PATH_CURRENT_SITE', '/' );
define( 'SITE_ID_CURRENT_SITE', 1 );
define( 'BLOG_ID_CURRENT_SITE', 1 );
```

In this example, we chose to use subdirectories, which is why we are defining SUBDOMAIN_INSTALL to false. If we chose subdomains, SUBDOMAIN_INSTALL would be set to true.

The second text area box contains code that you will need to copy and paste into your *.htaccess* file, which should also be in the root directory of your WordPress install:

```
RewriteEngine On
RewriteBase /
```

```
RewriteRule ^index\.php$ - [L]

# add a trailing slash to /wp-admin
RewriteRule ^([_0-9a-zA-Z-]+/)?wp-admin$ $1wp-admin/ [R=301,L]

RewriteCond %{REQUEST_FILENAME} -f [OR]
RewriteCond %{REQUEST_FILENAME} -d
RewriteRule ^ - [L]
RewriteRule ^([_0-9a-zA-Z-]+/)?(wp-(content|admin|includes).*) $2 [L]
RewriteRule ^([_0-9a-zA-Z-]+/)?(.*\.php)$ $2 [L]
RewriteRule . index.php [L]
```

Once you have copied and pasted the code from each text area box into the appropriate files and saved them on your web server, you can refresh your browser.

You should now be prompted to log in again. Log in with your administrator account username and password. Boom! You should now be running WordPress Multisite as a Super Administrator. A Super Administrator has full access to all of the sites on your network, while regular administrators only have full access to the sites they are administrators of.

If you decided to use subdomains instead of subdirectories, there are a couple extra steps you should take to save you time in the long run. You should set up a subdomain wildcard record on your domain registrar DNS settings page. Remember when first installing WordPress, you set the A (Host) record to the IP address of your hosting account? Well, in the same place you did that, you should be able to add a host name of "*" instead of "@" and point it to the same IP address as the "@" record. This acts as a catchall for any subdomains on your main domain. In short, whatever.whatever.com or somethingelse.whatever.com will both be mapped to the same IP address as the main domain.

Depending on your hosting account, you may also need to set up a wildcard subdomain entry to point to the same directory that your main domain is pointing to. So register a new subdomain like *.whatever.com and point it to the same folder of whatever.com.

So why are we doing all of this? We set up a wildcard for subdomains so when we create new sites on the Multisite network they will automatically work. If we didn't set up a wildcard for subdomains, we would have to manually add each subdomain we create to the domain registrar and to the host. If we set up the subdomain wildcard once, it will automatically work for any subdomain sites we create on our Multisite network.

Managing a Multisite Network

In your WordPress Admin Menu Bar, go to My Sites → Network Admin to administer your new Multisite network. You can also go to *whatever.com/wp-admin/network/* to get to the network dashboard. The network admin area looks very similar to any other site admin area on the network. To help keep track of where you are, just look for the /

network/ at the end of the address bar in your browser because it can be easy to get confused.

Dashboard

Your network dashboard is set up very similarly to the default dashboard you are used to seeing on a standard WordPress install except the Right Now widget displays links to quickly add new network sites or users. It also has two text boxes to search for specific users or sites. Just like the regular WordPress dashboard, this network dashboard can be completely customized using plugins or custom code.

Sites

Under Sites, you will manage all of the sites on your network. You can add any number of sites you like and even give access to your network users to create their own sites.

Adding a new site is pretty straightforward; click the Add New button at the top of the sites page or click Add New Link on the Sites submenu to get to the Add New Site page, where you will see the following fields:

Site Address
Depending on how you set up your network, the address you enter will either be a subdomain or a subdirectory.

Site Title
The title or name of your new site.

Admin Email
The email address of the administrator of your new site. This does not have to be your email address; it could be a client or a user that you are setting up a new WordPress site for.

Click the Add Site button, and voila, instant WordPress website. That sure saves a lot of time setting up a brand new install of WordPress.

Users

All of the sites you create on your network will pull from the same users pool. Technically, all users are stored in the wp_users table, and they each have user metadata tying them to one or more sites on your network. From the network users page, you can manage all of the users on any of your sites, set any user to be a Super Admin where the user would have rights to manage the entire WordPress Multisite network, and see what sites each user is a member of.

You can click the Add New button at the top of the Users page or the Add New Link on the Users submenu to get to the Add New User page, where you will see the following fields:

Username
> The username of the new user you are creating. Remember, all lowercase and no spaces or special characters.

Email
> The email address of the new user you are adding.

Once you click the Add User button, the user you added should receive an email with her username and password, which she can use to log in to the default top-level website with a default role of whatever you set a new user's role to be. Adding users this way may not be ideal, as you will have to take another step to add them to specific subsites on your network. Depending on your situation, it might be easier for you to add new users to subsites directly from within that subsite, where you can add a new user the same way you would on a typical install of WordPress. If you try to add a user to a site and that username already exists on the network, you will receive a message indicating that the username already exists. At that point, you can add the user to the site by adding her username to the Add Existing User section and choosing a role and whether to send a confirmation email to that user.

Themes

These are all of the themes available in the */wp-content/themes/* directory. You can control all of the themes any of the sites on your network can use. You must network activate a theme first before any site on your network can use it. If you don't network activate a theme, it won't even show up as an option to activate on a site's Appearance → Themes page.

Plugins

These are all of the plugins available in the */wp-content/plugins/directory*. You can network activate plugins so that they will automatically run on all sites on your network, including new sites. Network-activated plugins will not show up on the individual site's plugins page. In fact, unless you specifically enable the plugins menu on the network settings page (see next section), individual site administrators won't even see the plugins page. If you allow each site administrator to manage their own plugins, he will only be able to activate plugins that are already installed; he will not be able to install his own plugins. This is good because you want to know what plugins are available to all of the sites on your network. You don't want a site administrator to be able to install any plugin he wants or a custom plugin that could potentially have a negative effect on other sites on your network.

To add a new plugin at the network level, you would add it the same way you would on a normal install of WordPress.

Settings

These settings are unlike the typical WordPress settings you can update for a standard WordPress site; these are network-wide settings. If you click the Settings link on the left admin navigation menu, you should see the following settings:

Operational Settings

- Network Name
- Network Admin Email

Registration Settings

- Allow new registrations
- Registration notification
- Add New Users
- Banned Names
- Limited Email Registrations
- Banned Email Domains

New Site Settings

- Welcome Email
- Welcome User Email
- First Post
- First Page
- First Comment Author
- First Comment URL

Upload Settings

- Site upload space
- Upload file types
- Max upload file size

Menu Settings

- Enable administration menus

Updates

Just like in a standard WordPress installation, you can update core WordPress or any outdated plugins and/or themes all from this page. The beauty of a Multisite network is update everything once and they are updated across all of the sites on your network. This is way more efficient than running updates on multiple WordPress installs. Update WordPress, plugins, and themes…done and done!

Multisite Database Structure

All sites on a Multisite network share the same database. Enabling WordPress Multisite creates a few new tables in your existing database.

Network-Wide Tables

wp_blogs

The wp_blogs table stores information about each site created on the Multisite network. Table 13-1 shows the structure of the wp_blogs table.

Table 13-1. DB schema for wp_blogs table

Column	Type	Collation	Null	Default	Extra
blog_id	bigint(20)		No	None	AUTO_INCREMENT
site_id	bigint(20)		No	0	
domain	varchar(200)	utf8_general_ci	No		
path	varchar(100)	utf8_general_ci	No		
registered	datetime		No	0000-00-00 00:00:00	
last_updated	datetime		No	0000-00-00 00:00:00	
public	tinyint(2)		No	1	
archived	enum(0, 1)	utf8_general_ci	No	0	
mature	tinyint(2)		No	0	
spam	tinyint(2)		No	0	
deleted	tinyint(2)		No	0	
lang_id	int(11)		No	0	

wp_blog_versions

The `wp_blog_versions` table stores which database schema each site on the network is using. Table 13-2 shows the structure of the `wp_blog_versions` table.

Table 13-2. DB schema for `wp_blog_versions` table

Column	Type	Collation	Null	Default	Extra
blog_id	bigint(20)		No	0	
db_version	varchar(20)	utf8_general_ci	No		
last_updated	datetime		No	0000-00-00 00:00:00	

wp_registration_log

The `wp_registration_log` table stores information about each user that registers on your network like user ID, email address, IP address, and blog ID. Table 13-3 shows the structure of the `wp_registration_log` table.

Table 13-3. DB schema for `wp_registration_log` table

Column	Type	Collation	Null	Default	Extra
ID	bigint(20)		No	None	AUTO_INCREMENT
email	varchar(255)	utf8_general_ci	No		
IP	varchar(30)	utf8_general_ci	No		
blog_id	bigint(20)		No	0	
date_registered	datetime		No	0000-00-00 00:00:00	

wp_signups

The `wp_signups` table also stores information about each user that registers on your network. Table 13-4 shows the structure of the `wp_signups` table.

Table 13-4. DB schema for the `wp_signups` table

Column	Type	Collation	Null	Default	Extra
domain	varchar(200)	utf8_general_ci	No		
path	varchar(100)	utf8_general_ci	No		
title	longtext	utf8_general_ci	No	None	
user_login	varchar(60)	utf8_general_ci	No		
user_email	varchar(100)	utf8_general_ci	No		
registered	datetime		No	0000-00-00 00:00:00	
activated	datetime		No	0000-00-00 00:00:00	
active	tinyint(1)		No	0	
activation_key	varchar(50)	utf8_general_ci	No		

Column	Type	Collation	Null	Default	Extra
meta	longtext	utf8_general_ci	Yes	NULL	

wp_site

The wp_site table stores basic information about your Multisite network like the ID, domain, and path. This table will usually only ever have one record in it. Table 13-5 shows the structure of the wp_site table.

Table 13-5. DB schema for wp_site table

Column	Type	Collation	Null	Default	Extra
id	bigint(20)		No	None	AUTO_INCREMENT
domain	varchar(200)	utf8_general_ci	No		
path	varchar(100)	utf8_general_ci	No		

wp_sitemeta

The wp_sitemeta table stores all of the network-wide options or settings. Table 13-6 shows the structure of the wp_sitemeta table.

Table 13-6. DB schema for wp_sitemeta table

Column	Type	Collation	Null	Default	Extra
meta_id	bigint(20)		No	None	AUTO_INCREMENT
site_id	bigint(20)		No	0	
meta_key	varchar(255)	utf8_general_ci	Yes	NULL	
meta_value	longtext	utf8_general_ci	Yes	NULL	

Individual Site Tables

Every site added to your network is automatically given a blog_id when it is created. Each site also creates its own tables, adding its blog_id to each table name. Let's say we are creating the first additional site on our network besides our main site. It would be given a blog_id of 2, and the following tables would be created in the database:

- wp_$blog_id_options
- wp_$blog_id_posts
- wp_$blog_id_postmeta
- wp_$blog_id_comments
- wp_$blog_id_commentsmeta
- wp_$blog_id_links

- `wp_$blog_id_term_taxonomy`
- `wp_$blog_id_terms`
- `wp_$blog_id_term_relationships`

As you can see, these are the same exact tables included in a standard install of Word-Press, except they have a `blog_id` in the name. For every new site you create on your Multisite network, these tables will be duplicated with that new site's `blog_id`.

Shared Site Tables

All users on your Multisite network share the same `wp_users` and `wp_usermeta` tables.

Users are associated with various sites on the network by a few user meta keys in the `wp_usermeta table`. If we added a new user to our second site on the network, these meta keys would be created:

- `primary_blog`
- `wp_2_capabilities`
- `wp_2_user_level`

A user can only have one `primary_blog` but can be tied to multiple sites with the `capabilities` and `user_level` meta keys. In a default install of WordPress and on the top-level site on a Multisite network, these meta keys are stored as `wp_capabilities` and `wp_user_level`. When you add users to sites on the network, new meta key records are created for each user for the `blog_id` you are adding them to with whatever role you added them as.

Multisite Plugins

If a regular WordPress plugin is built correctly, then it should work the way it was intended on one or more sites on your network. Developers can also build WordPress plugins specifically for Multisite. The following are a few of the more popular Multisite plugins and what they are built to accomplish.

WordPress MU Domain Mapping

This plugin (*http://bit.ly/wp-mumap*) allows you to map your blog or site on the Multisite network to an external domain. This does require manual installation, and complete instructions can be found with the plugin.

Blog Copier

This plugin (*http://bit.ly/wp-blogcopy*) is very useful for anyone who needs to duplicate the content from one site for another site on the network. However, it only allows copying from one subsite to another subsite and does not allow you to copy the top-level site.

More Privacy Options

Once installed, this plugin (*http://bit.ly/wp-privacy*) adds additional levels of privacy to the Reading settings. These new levels are Network Users Only, Blog Members Only, and Admins Only, which makes your site visible only to whichever of these groups you choose.

Multisite Global Search

This allows you to search across the multiple sites on your network and receive results from all those sites. This plugin (*http://bit.ly/wp-globalsearch*) also comes with a built-in widget that can be used to display the search bar in the sidebar. Both the widget and the results page come with a customizable stylesheet. The plugin uses shortcodes, enabling you to insert the search in any templates you choose.

Multisite Robots.txt Manager

This plugin (*http://bit.ly/wp-robotstxt*) allows you to create custom *robots.txt* files for each website on the network and then quickly publish those files to the network or a website. This plugin will also instantly add sitemap URLs to all the *robots.txt* files. It will also automatically detect 404 or old *robots.txt* files and allows for easy correction once identified.

Basic Multisite Functionality

When you activate WordPress Multisite, you can utilize Multisite-specific functionality that was sitting there dormant in WordPress core just waiting to be used.

$blog_id

After reviewing the tables Multisite creates, we know that each site has a unique `blog_id`. You can use this ID to tell WordPress what site you want to retrieve data from or push data to.

The global variable `$blog_id` will automatically be set to the site you are on unless changed with the `switch_to_blog()` function. This variable will be useful when writing custom Multisite functionality:

```php
<?php
function wds_show_blog_id(){
    global $blog_id;
        echo 'current site id: ' . $blog_id;
}
add_action( 'init', 'wds_show_blog_id' );
?>
```

If you are on the top-level site or original site on your network, you should see 1. If you are on the second site you created on your network, you should see 2.

is_multisite()

This function checks to see if WordPress Multisite is enabled. You should only run Multisite-specific functionality if you are running Multisite. If you are not running Multisite and try to use a Multisite function, you may get an error. Always do a check to see if Multisite is enabled before executing any Multisite-specific code:

```php
<?php
function wds_run_multisite_functions(){
        if ( is_multisite() )
                echo 'Run whatever WordPress Multisite functionality you want!';
}
add_action( 'init' , 'wds_run_multisite_functions' );
?>
```

get_current_blog_id()

This function returns the blog_id that your are currently on. The function itself is literally two lines of code:

```php
<?php
// core function get_current_blog_id
function get_current_blog_id() {
        global $blog_id;
        return absint($blog_id);
}
?>
```

get_current_blog_id() is located *in wp-includes/load.php.*

switch_to_blog($new_blog)

This function switches the current blog to any blog you specify. This function is useful if you need to pull posts or other information from other sites on your network. You can switch back afterward using restore_current_blog(). Autoloaded options and plugins are not switched with this function. This function accepts one parameter, $new_blog, which is a required integer of the ID of the site to which you want to switch.

If we wanted to switch the current site we are on, we could run the following code in any plugin function or theme file:

```php
<?php
echo 'current site id: ' . get_current_blog_id() . '<br>';
switch_to_blog(2);
echo 'new current site id: ' . get_current_blog_id();
?>
```

The code should output something like:

```
current site id: 1
new current site id: 2
```

switch_to_blog() is located in *wp-includes/ms-blogs.php*.

restore_current_blog()

With this function we can restore the current site, after calling the switch_to_blog() function. This function doesn't accept any parameters.

If we wanted to restore a switched site, we could run the following code:

```php
<?php
echo 'current site id: ' . get_current_blog_id() . '<br>';
switch_to_blog(2);
echo 'new current site id: ' . get_current_blog_id() . '<br>';
restore_current_blog();
echo 'original site id: ' . get_current_blog_id();
?>
```

The code should output something like:

```
current site id: 1
new current site id: 2
original site id: 1
```

restore_current_blog() is located in *wp-includes/ms-blogs.php*.

get_blog_details($fields = null, $get_all = true)

This function gets all of the available details of a site/blog and accepts two parameters:

- $fields—The ID or name of a specific blog, or an array of blog IDs or blog names. Defaults to the current blog ID.

- $getall—Default is set to true to return all available data in the object.

This function returns an object of the following variables:

- *blog_id*—The ID of the blog being queried.
- *site_id*—The ID of the site this blog ID is attached to.

- *domain*—The domain used to access the blog.
- *path*—The path used to access the site.
- *registered*—Timestamp of when the blog was registered.
- *last_updated*—Timestamp of when the blog was last updated.
- *public*—1 or 0 indicating whether the blog is public or not.
- *archived*—1 or 0 indicating whether the blog is achieved or not.
- *mature*—1 or 0 indicating whether the blog has adult content or not.
- *spam*—1 or 0 indicating whether the blog has been marked as spam or not.
- *deleted*—1 or 0 indicating whether the blog has been deleted or not.
- *lang_id*—ID of the language the blog is written in.
- *blogname*—The name of the blog.
- *siteurl*—The URL of the site the blog belongs to.
- *post_content*—The number of posts in the blog.

If we wanted to display the entire object returned by this function, we would run the following code:

```php
<?php
$details = get_blog_details( 1 );
echo '<pre>';
print_r($details);
echo '</pre>';
echo 'Site URL:' . $details->siteurl;
echo 'Post Count:' . $details->post_count;
?>
```

The code should return a similar object and string:

```
stdClass Object
(
    [blog_id] => 1
    [site_id] => 1
    [domain] => schoolpress.me
    [path] => /
    [registered] => 2013-03-01 00:23:26
    [last_updated] => 2013-04-01 14:18:59
    [public] => 1
    [archived] => 0
    [mature] => 0
    [spam] => 0
    [deleted] => 0
    [lang_id] => 0
    [blogname] => School Press
    [siteurl] => http://schoolpress.me
```

```
    [post_count] => 10
)
```

This site URL is *http://schoolpress.me* and has 10 posts.

get_blog_details() is located in *wp-includes/ms-blogs.php*.

update_blog_details($blog_id, $details = array())

This function updates the details for a blog and accepts two parameters:

- $blog_id—A required integer of the ID of the blog you want to update.
- $details—A required array of any of the fields from the blog's table as keys with any values you want to update.

If we wanted to mark a particular site as deleted, we could run the following code:

```php
<?php
update_blog_details( 2, array( 'deleted' => '0' ) );
?>
```

update_blog_details() is located in *wp-includes/ms-blogs.php*.

get_blog_status($id, $pref)

This function is similar to the get_blog_details() function, except instead of returning an object of all of the fields in the wp_blogs table, it returns the value of one specific field:

- $id—A required integer of the ID of the site you want to return a wp_blogs field from.
- $pref—A required string of the field name from the wp_blogs table.

If we wanted to show when the current site was registered, we could run the following code:

```php
<?php
echo get_blog_status( get_current_blog_id(), 'registered' );
?>
```

get_blog_status() is located in *wp-includes/ms-blogs.php*.

update_blog_status($blog_id, $pref, $value)

This function is similar to the update_blog_details() function, except instead of updating an array of fields in the wp_blogs table, it updates one specific field:

- $blog_id—A required integer of the ID of the site you want to update a `wp_blogs` field for.

- $pref—A required string of the field name from the `wp_blogs` table you want to update.

- $value—A required string of the field value you want to update.

If we wanted to mark the current site as deleted, we could run the following code:

```php
<?php
update_blog_status( get_current_blog_id(), 'deleted', '1' );
?>
```

`update_blog_status()` is located in *wp-includes/ms-blogs.php*.

get_blog_option($id, $option, $default = false)

This function saves you the hassle of using `switch_to_blog()` and then using the regular WordPress `get_option()` function or writing a custom SQL query if you wanted to grab an option from a specific site. This function will return an option value from any site on your network by passing in the following parameters:

- $id—A required integer of the ID of the site you want to get an option from. You can pass in `null` if you want to get an option from the current site.

- $option—A required string of the option name you want to get.

- $default—Optional string to return if the function does not find a matching option.

If we wanted to get the `admin_email` of a particular site, we could run the following code:

```php
<?php
echo 'The admin email for site id 2 is ' . get_blog_option( 2, 'admin_email' );
?>
```

`get_blog_option()` is located in *wp-includes/ms-blogs.php*.

update_blog_option($id, $option, $value)

This function updates any option for a particular site and accepts three parameters:

- $id—A required integer of the ID of the site you want to update an option on.

- $option—A required string of the option name you want to update.

- $value—A required string of the option value you want to update.

If we wanted to update the `admin_email` of a particular site, we could run the following code:

```php
<?php
update_blog_option( 2, 'admin_email', 'brian@webdevstudios.com' );
?>
```

`update_blog_option()` is located in *wp-includes/ms-blogs.php*.

delete_blog_option($id, $option)

This function deletes any option from a particular site and accepts two parameters:

- $id—A required integer of the ID of the site you want to delete an option on.
- $option—A required string of the option name you want to delete.

If we wanted to delete a custom site option from a particular site, we could run the following code:

```php
<?php
delete_blog_option( 2, 'wds_custom_option' );
?>
```

`delete_blog_option()` is located in *wp-includes/ms-blogs.php*.

get_blog_post($blog_id, $post_id)

This function gets a post from any site on the network and accepts two parameters:

- $blog_id—A required integer of the blog ID of the site you want to get a post from.
- $post_id—A required integer of the post ID of the post that you want to get.

If we wanted to get the post title of the third post from the second site on our network, we could run the following code:

```php
<?php
$post = get_blog_post( 2, 3 );
echo $post->post_title;
?>
```

`get_blog_post()` is located in *wp-includes/ms-functions.php*.

add_user_to_blog($blog_id, $user_id, $role)

This function adds a user to any site on the network with a specified user role and accepts three parameters:

- $blog_id—A required integer of the blog ID of the site you want to add the user to.
- $user_id—A required integer of the user ID of the user that you want to add to the site.

- $role—A required string of the role you want the user to have.

This function will return `true` if a user was added successfully; and if not, it will return a `WP_Error`.

If we wanted to add a specific user to the second site on our network with a role of Administrator, we could run the following code:

```php
<?php
add_user_to_blog( 2, 5, 'administrator' );
?>
```

`add_user_to_blog()` is located in *wp-includes/ms-functions.php*.

create_empty_blog($domain, $path, $weblog_title, $site_id = 1)

This function creates a new site on the network after making sure it doesn't already exist. The UI for adding new sites in the network admin uses this function. This function accepts four parameters:

- $domain—A required string of the domain of the new blog.
- $path—A required string of the path of the new blog.
- $weblog_title—A required string of the title or name of the new blog.
- $site_id—An optional integer of the site ID associated with the new blog. The default is 1.

If we wanted to add a new site to our network we could run the following code:

```php
<?php
create_empty_blog( 'someteacher.schoolpress.me', '/', 'Mr. Some Teacher' );
?>
```

`create_empty_blog()` is located in *wp-includes/ms-functions.php*.

Functions We Didn't Mention

We didn't cover all of the Multisite functions available, but we did cover most of the important ones. Well I guess that depends on what you are trying to accomplish. To find all of the available Multisite functions, look in the code! You can find WordPress Multisite functions in the following files:

- *wp-admin/includes/ms.php*
- *wp-includes/ms-blogs.php*
- *wp-includes/ms-functions.php*

## CHAPTER 14

Localizing WordPress Apps

Localization (or internationalization) is the process of translating your app for use in different locales and languages. This chapter will go over the tools and methods available to WordPress developers to localize their apps, themes, and plugins.

You will sometimes see localization abbreviated as l10n and internationalization sometimes abbreviated as i18n.

Do You Even Need to Localize Your App?

The market for web apps is increasingly global. Offering your app in other languages can be a strong competitive advantage to help you gain market share against competition within your own locale/language and will also help to stave off competition in other locales/languages.

If you plan to release any of your code under an open source license, localizing it first is a good way to increase the number of developers who can get involved in your project. If your plugin or theme is localized, developers speaking other languages will be more likely to contribute to your project directly instead of forking it to get it working in their language.

If you plan to distribute a commercial plugin or theme, localizing your code increases your number of potential customers.

If your target market is the United States only and you don't have any immediate plans to expand into other regions or languages, then you may not want to spend the time preparing your code to be localized. Also, remember that each language or regional version of your app will likely require its own hosting, support, customer service, and maintenance. For many businesses, this will be too high a cost to take on in the early days of an application. On the other hand, you will find that the basics of preparing your code for localization (wrapping string output in a _(), _e(), or _x() function) is simple to do and often has other uses outside of localization.

Finally, it's important to note that sometimes localization means more than just translating your code. If your code interfaces with other services, you will need to make sure that those services work in different regions or be prepared to develop alternatives. For example, an important component of the Paid Memberships Pro plugin is integration with payment gateways. Before localizing Paid Memberships Pro, Jason made sure that the plugin integrated well with international payment gateways. Otherwise, people would have been able to use Paid Memberships Pro in their language, but it wouldn't have worked with a viable payment gateway for their region.

How Localization Is Done in WordPress

WordPress uses the gettext translation system developed for the GNU translation project. The gettext system inside of WordPress includes the following components:

- A way to define a locale/language
- A way to translate strings in your code
- *.pot* files containing all of the words and phrases to be translated
- *.po* files for each language containing the translations
- *.mo* files for each language containing a compiled version of the *.po* translations

Each of these components must be in place for your translations to work. The following sections explain each step in detail. At the end, you should have all of the tools needed to create a localized plugin and translated locale files.

Defining Your Locale in WordPress

To define your locale in WordPress, simply set the WPLANG constant in your *wp-config.php* files:

```php
<?php
// use the Spanish/Spain locale and language files.
define('WPLANG', 'es_ES');
?>
```

 The term "locale" is used instead of language because you can have multiple translations for the same language. For example, British English is different from United States English. And Mexican Spanish is different from Spanish Spanish.

Prepping Your Strings with Translation Functions

The first step in localizing your code is to make sure that every displayed string is wrapped in one of the translation functions provided by WordPress. They all work pretty much the same way: some default text is passed into the function along with a *domain* and/or some other information to let translators know what context to use when translating the text.

We'll go over the most useful functions in detail.

__($text, $domain = "default")

This function expects two parameters: the $text to be translated and the $domain for your plugin or theme. It will return the translated text based on the domain and the language set in *wp-config.php*.

The $domain is a string set by you with the load_theme_textdomain() or load_plu gin_textdomain() function (explained later). For example, the domain for our School-Press app is "schoolpress." The domain for the Paid Memberships Pro plugin is "pmpro." You can use anything as long as it is unique and consistent.

> The __() function is really an alias for the translate() function used in the background by WordPress. There's no real reason you couldn't call translate() directly, but __() is shorter and you'll be using this function *a lot*.

Here is an example of how you would wrap some strings using the __() function:

```php
<?php
// setting a variable to a string without localization
$title = 'Assignments';

// setting a variable to a string with localization
$title = __( 'Assignments', 'schoolpress' );
?>
```

_e($text, $domain = "default")

This function expects two parameters: the $text to be translated and the $domain for your plugin or theme. It will echo the translated text based on the domain and the language set in *wp-config.php*.

This function is identical to the __() function except that it echoes the output to the screen instead of returning it.

Here is an example of how you would wrap some strings using the _e() function:

```
<?php
// echoing a var without localization
?>
<h2><?php echo $title; ?></h2>
<?php
// echoing a var with localization
?>
<h2><?php _e( $title, 'schoolpress' ); ?></h2>
```

In practice, you will use the __() function when setting a variable and the _e() function when echoing a variable.

_x($text, $context, $domain = "default")

This function expects three parameters: the $text to be translated, a $context to use during translation, and the $domain for your plugin or theme. It will return the translated text based on the context, the domain, and the language set in *wp-config.php*.

The _x() function acts the same as the __() but gives you an extra $context parameter to help the translators figure out how to translate your text. This is required if your code uses the same word or phrase in multiple locations, which might require different translations.

For example, the word "title" in English can refer both to the title of a book and also a person's title, like Mr. or Mrs. In other languages, different words might be used in each context. You can differentiate between each context using the _x() function.

In the following slightly convoluted example, we are setting a couple of variables to use on a class creation screen in SchoolPress:

```
<?php
$class_title_field_label = _x( 'Title', 'class title', 'schoolpress' );
$class_professor_title_field_label = _x( 'Title', 'name prefix', 'schoolpress' );
?>
<h3>Class Description</h3>
<label><?php echo $class_title_field_label; ?></label>
<input type="text" name="title" value="" />

<h3>Professor</h3>
<label><?php echo $class_professor_title_field_label; ?></label>
<input type="text" name="professor_title" value="" />
```

 The _x() and _ex() functions are sometimes referred to as "*ex*plain" functions because you use the context parameter to further explain how the text should be translated.

_ex($title, $context, $domain = "default")

The _ex() function works the same as the _x() function but echoes the translated text instead of returning it.

Escaping and Translating at the Same Time

In Chapter 7, we talked about the importance of escaping strings that are displayed within HTML attributes or in other sensitive areas. When also translating these strings, instead of calling two functions, WordPress offers a few functions to combine two functions into one. These functions work exactly as you would expect them to by first translating and then escaping the text:

- esc_attr__()
- esc_attr_e()
- esc_attr_x()
- esc_html__()
- esc_html_e()
- esc_html_x()

Creating and Loading Translation Files

Once your code is marked up to use the translation functions, you'll need to generate a *.pot* file for translators to use to translate your app. The *.pot* file will include a section like the following for each string that shows up in your code:

```
#: schoolpress.php:108
#: schoolpress.php:188
#: pages/courses.php:10
msgid "School"
msgstr ""
```

The preceding section says that on lines 108 and 188 of *schoolpress.php* and line 10 of *pages/courses.php*, the word "School" is used.

To create a Spanish-language translation of your plugin, you would then copy the *schoolpress.pot* file to *schoolpress-es_ES.po* and fill in the msgstr for each phrase. It would look like:

```
#: schoolpress.php:108
#: schoolpress.php:188
#: pages/courses.php:10
msgid "School"
msgstr "Escuela"
```

Those *.po* files must then be compiled into the *.mo* format, which is optimized for processing the translations.

For large plugins and apps, it is impractical to locate the line numbers for each string by hand and keep that up to date every time you update the plugin. In the next section, we'll walk you through using the xgettext command-line tool for Linux to generate your *.pot* file and the msgfmt command-line tool to compile *.po* files into *.mo* files. Alternatively, the free program Poedit (*http://www.poedit.net*) has a nice GUI to scan code and generate *.pot*, *.po*, and *.mo* files and is available for Windows, Max OS X, and Linux.

Our File Structure for Localization

Before getting into the specifics of how to generate these files, let's go over how we typically store these files in our plugins.

For our SchoolPress app, we'll store the localization files in a folder called *languages* inside of the main app plugin. Each language will also have a directory to store other language-specific assets. We'll add all of our localization code, including the call to load_plugin_textdomain(), in a file in the *includes* directory called *localization.php*. So our file structure looks something like this:

1. *../plugins/schoolpress/schoolpress.php* (includes *localization.php*)
2. *../plugins/schoolpress/includes/localization.php* (loads text domain and other localization functions)
3. *../plugins/schoolpress/languages/schoolpress.pot* (list of strings to translate)
4. *../plugins/schoolpress/languages/schoolpress.po* (default/English translations)
5. *../plugins/schoolpress/languages/schoolpress.mo* (compiled default/English translations)
6. *../plugins/schoolpress/languages/en_US/* (folder for English/US language assets)
7. *../plugins/schoolpress/languages/schoolpress-es_ES.po* (Spanish/Spain translations)
8. *../plugins/schoolpress/languages/schoolpress-es_ES.mo* (compiled Spanish/Spain translations)
9. *../plugins/schoolpress/languages/es_ES/* (folder for Spanish/Spain language assets)

When building a larger app with multiple custom plugins and a custom theme, localization is easier to manage if you localize each individual plugin and theme separately instead of trying to build one translation file to work across everything. If your plugins are only going to be used for this one project, they can probably be built as includes or module *.php* files in your main app plugin. If the plugins are something that you might use on another project, then they should be localized separately so the localization files can be ported along with the plugin.

Generating a .pot File

We'll use the xgettext tool, which is installed on most Linux systems,[1] to generate a *.pot* file for our plugin.

To generate a *.pot* file for our SchoolPress app, we would open up the command line and cd to the main app plugin directory at *wp-content/plugins/schoolpress*. Then execute the following command:

```
xgettext -o languages/schoolpress.pot \
--default-domain=schoolpress \
--language=PHP \
--keyword=_ \
--keyword=__ \
--keyword=_e \
--keyword=_ex \
--keyword=_x \
--keyword=_n \
--sort-by-file \
--copyright-holder="SchoolPress" \
--package-name=schoolpress \
--package-version=1.0 \
--msgid-bugs-address="info@schoolpress.me" \
--directory=. \
$(find . -name "*.php")
```

Let's break this down.

-o languages/schoolpress.pot
Defines where the output file will go.

--default-domain=schoolpress
Defines the text domain as schoolpress.

--language=PHP
Tells xgettext that we are using PHP.

--keyword=…
Sets xgettext up to retrieve any string used within these functions. Be sure to include a similar parameter for any of the other translation functions (like esc_attr__) you might be using.

--sort-by-file
Helps organize the output by file when possible.

---

1. If not, locate and install the "gettext" package for your Linux distro.

--copyright-holder="SchoolPress"
> Sets the copyright holder stated in the header of the .pot file. This should be whatever person or organization owns the copyright to the application, plugin, or theme being built.

 From the GNU.org website (*http://bit.ly/gnu-gettext*):
> Translators are expected to transfer or disclaim the copyright for their translations, so that package maintainers can distribute them without legal risk. If [the copyright holder value] is empty, the output files are marked as being in the public domain; in this case, the translators are expected to disclaim their copyright, again so that package maintainers can distribute them without legal risk.

--package-name=schoolpress
> Sets the package name stated in the header of the .*pot* file. This is typically the same as the domain.

--package-version=1.0
> Sets the package version stated in the header of the .*pot* file. This should be updated with every release version of your app, plugin, or theme.

––msgid-bugs-address="info@schoolpress.me"
> Sets the email stated in the header of the .*pot* file to use to report any bugs in the .*pot* file.

--directory=.
> Tells xgettext to start scannging from the current directory.

$(find . -name "*.php")
> This appears at the end, and is a Linux command to find all .*php* files under the current directory.

Creating a .po File

Again, the Poedit tool has a nice graphical interface for generating .*po* files from .*pot* files and providing a translation for each string. Hacking it yourself is fairly straightforward though: simply copy the .*pot* file to a .*po* file (e.g., es_ES.po) in your languages directory and then edit the .*po* file and enter your translations on each msgstr line of the file.

Creating a .mo File

Once your *.po* files are updated for your locale, they need to be compiled into *.mo* files. The msgfmt program for Linux can be used to generate the *.mo* files using the command msgfmt es_ES.po --output-file es_ES.mo.

Loading the Textdomain

For each localized plugin or theme in your site, WordPress needs to know how to locate your localization files. This is done via the load_plugin_textdomain(), load_textdo main(), or load_theme_textdomain() function. All three functions are similar, but take different parameters and make sense in different situations.

Whichever function you use, it should be called as early as possible in your app because any strings used or echoed through translation functions before the textdomain is loaded will not be translated.

Here are a few ways we could load our textdomain in *includes/localization.php*.

load_plugin_textdomain($domain, $abs_rel_path, $plugin_rel_path)
> This function takes three parameters. The first is the *domain* of your plugin or app ("schoolpress" in our case). You then use either the second or third parameter to point to the languages folder where the *.mo* file should be loaded from. The $abs_rel_path is deprecated, but still here for reverse-compatibility reasons. Just pass FALSE for this and use the $plugin_rel_path parameter:
>
> ```php
> <?php
> function schoolpress_load_textdomain(){
>     //load textdomain from /plugins/schoolpress/languages/
>     load_plugin_textdomain(
>         'schoolpress',
>         FALSE,
>         dirname( plugin_basename(__FILE__) ) . '/languages/'
>     );
> }
> add_action( 'init', 'schoolpress_load_textdomain', 1 );
> ?>
> ```
>
> The preceding code will load the correct language file from our languages folder based on the WPLANG setting in *wp-config.php*. We use plugin_base name(__FILE__) to get the path to the current file and dirname(...) to get the path to the root plugin folder since we are in the *includes* subfolder of our school press plugin folder.

load_textdomain($domain, $path)
> This function can also be used to load the textdomain, but you'll need to get the locale setting yourself.

Calling `load_textdomain()` directly is useful if you want to allow others to easily replace or extend your language files. You can use code like the following to load any *.mo* file found in the global WP languages directory (usually *wp-content/languages/*) first and then load the *.mo* file from your plugin's local languages directory second. This allows developers to override your translations by adding their own *.mo* files to the global languages directory:

```php
<?php
function schoolpress_load_textdomain() {
    // get the locale
    $locale = apply_filters( 'plugin_locale', get_locale(), 'schoolpress' );
        $mofile = 'schoolpress-' . $locale . '.mo';

        /*
    Paths to local (plugin) and global (WP) language files.
        Note: dirname(__FILE__) here changes if this code
    is placed outside the base plugin file.
    */
        $mofile_local  = dirname( __FILE__ ).'/languages/' . $mofile;
        $mofile_global = WP_LANG_DIR . '/schoolpress/' . $mofile;

        // load global first
        load_textdomain( 'schoolpress', $mofile_global );

        // load local second
        load_textdomain( 'schoolpress', $mofile_local );
}
add_action( 'init', 'schoolpress_load_textdomain', 1 );
?>
```

This version gets the local via the `get_locale()` function, applies the `plugin_locale` filter, and then looks for a *.mo* file in both the global languages folder (typically */wp-content/languages/*) and the languages folder of our plugin.

load_theme_textdomain($domain, $path)

If you have language files for your theme in particular, you can load them through the `load_theme_textdomain()` function like so:

```php
<?php
function schoolpress_load_textdomain() {
        load_theme_textdomain(
        'schoolpress', get_template_directory() . '/languages/'
        );
}
add_action( 'init', 'schoolpress_load_textdomain', 1 );
?>
```

Localizing Nonstring Assets

If you've gone through the previous steps, you will have everything you need to make sure any string used by your plugin, theme, or app is properly translated. However, you will sometimes have nonstring assets that still need to be swapped out depending on the locale being used.

For example, you might have images with words in them that should be swapped for alternative images with those words translated. Maybe your localized app uses different colors for different countries; you can swap CSS files based on the detected locale.

We often use *.html* email templates in our plugins that need to be translated. We could wrap the entire email in one big __() function, or we could create a directory of templates for each language. The latter option might mean more work for your translators because they'll have to generate *.html* templates along with the *.mo* files, but it will give developers using your code a bit more flexibility.

Below we'll write some code to load images and email templates for our plugin based on the local. Assume we have folders like this:

- *schoolpress/images/* (default images)
- *schoolpress/emails/* (default email templates)
- *schoolpress/languages/es_ES/*
- *schoolpress/languages/es_ES/images/* (Spanish-version images)
- *schoolpress/languages/es_ES/emails/* (Spanish-version email templates)

We'll make sure that the functions that load these assets have hooks that will allow us to override which directory is used to get them.

In the following code, we assume that the constant SCHOOLPRESS_URL points to the relative URL for the SchoolPress plugin folder, for example, */wp-content/plugins/school-press/*:

```php
<?php
// Gets the full URL for an image given the image filename.
function schoolpress_get_image( $image ) {
$dir = apply_filters(
    'schoolpress_images_url',
    SCHOOLPRESS_URL . '/images/'
);
        return $dir . $image;
}
?>
```

Now in our *includes/localization.php* folder, we can put some code in place that will filter schoolpress_images_url if a nondefault locale is used:

```php
<?php
function localize_schoolpress_images_url( $url ) {
        $locale = apply_filters( 'plugin_locale', get_locale(), 'schoolpress' );
        if ( $locale != 'en_US' )
                $url = SCHOOLPRESS_URL . '/languages/' . $locale . '/images/';

        return $url;
}
add_filter( 'schoolpress_images_url', 'localize_schoolpress_images_url' );
?>
```

You could do the same thing for loading emails. In the following code, we assume the constant SCHOOLPRESS_PATH points to the server pathname for the SchoolPress plugin, for example, */var/vhosts/schoolpress.com/httpdocs/wp-content/plugins/schoolpress/*:

```php
<?php
// Gets the full path for an email template given the email filename.
function schoolpress_get_email( $email ) {
    $dir = apply_filters(
        'schoolpress_emails_path', SCHOOLPRESS_PATH . '/emails/'
        );
        return $dir . $image;
}

// Filters the schoolpress_emails_path value based on locale.
// Put this in includes/localization.php
function localize_schoolpress_emails_path( $path ) {
        $locale = apply_filters( 'plugin_locale', get_locale(), 'schoolpress' );
        if ( $locale != 'en_US' )
                $path = SCHOOLPRESS_PATH . '/languages/' . $locale . '/emails/';

        return $path;
}
add_filter( 'schoolpress_emails_path', 'localize_schoolpress_emails_path' );
?>
```

Depending on the use case of your web application, translating your app may be essential to its success. When building any custom theme or plugin, it's good practice to write all of your code with localization in mind!

## CHAPTER 15

Ecommerce

At some point, you may want to charge for access to your app or otherwise accept payments on your site. In this chapter, we'll go over the best ecommerce and membership plugins available and give you a few pointers for choosing between them. We'll also go through setting up a typical paywall in the software as a service (SaaS) model.

Choosing a Plugin

There are many different plugins that will allow you to accept payments on your site. Each has its strengths and weaknesses. Choosing between the various plugins can be daunting, but we're here to help.

WordPress ecommerce plugins generally fall into two main categories: shopping cart plugins and membership plugins. We'll also cover a couple of plugins that don't fall inside these categories exactly.

All plugins in this section have these features in common:

- Integration with multiple payment gateways
- Secure checkout forms
- Saved order information
- Products (or membership levels) with pricing

Shopping Cart Plugins

The plugins we'll cover in this section focus around offering products for sale on your site.

Features of these plugins include:

- A products custom post type
- The ability to browse products
- The ability to search through products
- The ability to purchase multiple products at once
- Support for shipping addresses and shipping price calculations
- Support for custom tax rules

Our favorite: Jigoshop

Why: the Jigoshop ecommerce plugin (*http://jigoshop.com*) is released under the GPL license and available in the WordPress plugin repository. Dozens of extensions exist for Jigoshop that do everything from add support for different payment gateways to customize your emails to conform to Norwegian tax rules.

The base plugin, which includes all of the functionality to add products and process orders, is free. Most of the extensions are available for under $50 each, or you can purchase a membership to gain access to all of the extensions sold through the main Jigoshop store.

Jigoshop works well with any WordPress theme you might be using. There are Jigoshop-specific themes, and you can also easily customize the default CSS that Jigoshop provides with the plugin itself.

The code behind Jigoshop includes a lot of hooks and filters you can use to override the default behavior. And the source code for the base Jigoshop plugin is managed on GitHub, making it easy to do a pull request to add your own hooks and filters or to get involved in the development of the plugin. The Jigoshop developers are very responsive with merging in new code that is clean and improves the plugin.

Notable runner-up: WooCommerce

WooCommerce (*http://woocommerce.com*), which was forked from Jigoshop, has improved both the underlying code and the number and quality of extensions. The community is definitely behind WooCommerce in a big way as WooCommerce is quickly eclipsing Jigoshop (and ecommerce platforms in general) in terms of both user and developer adoption.

WooCommerce extensions are pricier than Jigoshop extensions. They run about $50–$200 each, with no membership with access to all extensions. More important for many app developers is the fact that licenses for each individual extension must be maintained to ensure updates. In practice this isn't so bad, but we worry about the added overhead around using the licensed extensions versus a system like Jigoshop's where you simply pay for access to GPL code and get it.

Other shopping cart plugins include WP e-Commerce, Shopp Plugin, and Cart 66.

Membership Plugins

Plugins in this section focus around accepting payment for a membership access to a WordPress site or app.

Features of these plugins include:

- Recurring pricing for subscriptions
- Tools for locking down content based on membership level

Our favorite: Paid Memberships Pro

Why: Besides being developed by our coauthor Jason Coleman, Paid Memberships Pro (*http://www.paidmembershipspro.com*) is the only WordPress membership plugin that is 100% GPL and available for free in the WordPress repository. Other plugins have either paid modules or upgraded versions that are necessary to gain access to all of the plugin's features.

All of the Paid Memberships Pro code is managed on GitHub and open to developer input. Like Jigoshop, there are a lot of hooks and filters available to change the default behavior of the plugin.

Nearly every membership site has a slightly different way of calculating upgrades or special offers, or exactly how and when to lock down content. Instead of offering an extra long settings page, Paid Memberships Pro carefully designed its hooks and filters to make it easy to setup nearly any pricing model with just a few lines of code.

Another key difference between Paid Memberships Pro and some other membership plugins is that Paid Memberships Pro uses its own table to define membership levels and their relationships to users and orders. Some membership plugins use the built-in WordPress user roles so that each membership level is also a user role. User roles are very important in some membership sites (see Chapter 6), but in general, it's better to separate the concept of a membership level and a user role, allowing you for example to have members who are admins *and* members who are subscribers. If you *do* need to assign roles based on membership level, that is easy to do with Paid Memberships Pro, and we have an example later in this chapter.

Other membership plugins include s2Members, Restrict Content Pro, Members, WPMU Membership, and MemberPress.

Digital Downloads

Our favorite: Easy Digital Downloads

All of the ecommerce and membership plugins mentioned so far can be used for digital products and downloads as well as physical goods. However, if you are only planning on selling digital goods, you should consider Easy Digital Downloads (*http://easydigitaldownloads.com*), which was developed specifically for this use case.

Like Jigoshop, the core Easy Digital Downloads plugin is available for free in the WordPress repository, while extensions are available for purchase at the plugin's website. Extension prices range from $6–$83. There is a core extensions bundle that includes many of the most popular extensions at a reduced price.

Notable extensions that could be useful to app developers include the Software Licensing and Product Support add-ons. The core plugin and all of the extensions are well coded and well supported.

Payment Gateways

A payment gateway is a service that processes and sometime stores customer credit cards and makes sure that the money winds up in your bank account.[1] Popular gateways in the United States include Stripe, PayPal, Authorize.net, and Braintree Payments. There are dozens of gateways, many specializing in particular parts of the world or in particular markets.

These are the important things to look out for when choosing a gateway:

- Does the gateway support the country and currency you do business in?
- Does the gateway integrate with the plugin you are using for ecommerce?
- Does the gateway work with the type of business you are in? Some gateways will not work with adult sites, gambling sites, or other "high-risk merchants."
- Does the gateway offer the features you need like recurring billing or stored credit cards?
- How does the gateway handle Payment Card Industry (PCI) compliance?[2]
- Will the gateway work with my merchant account? (See the merchant account section below.)

---

1. Minus any fees.

2. At the high end, PCI compliance requires more expensive server setups and full-time resources to maintain and document them properly. Some gateways have technology and processes to help you avoid those costs while still keeping your customer data secure.

- Finally, what are the fees? 1% of $10 million is a lot of money, and it is worth fighting for lower fees. However, in general, the fees are fairly standard across gateways, and you should first look for a gateway that will work with your business setup. As your business grows in revenue and volume, it becomes very easy to negotiate lowering your fees to the standard minimums in your industry.

Merchant Accounts

Merchant accounts are often confused with payment gateways, but are actually a separate thing you need to process payments on your website. Part of the confusion comes from the fact that some gateways use their own merchant accounts.

In any case, both a payment gateway and merchant account are required to make money online, and both kinds of providers will help you secure the other service. That is, you can shop for a payment gateway and have it help you find a merchant account, or you can shop for a merchant account and have it help you find a payment gateway. We find that younger companies typically get better fees when they start with a payment gateway and get a merchant account with their help, rather than going to their bank to open a merchant account.

Here is how the credit card information and money flows from a customer on your website into your checking account: WordPress → Ecommerce Plugin → Payment Gateway → Merchant Account → Your Checking Account.

One way to think of the difference between gateways and merchant accounts is that the payment gateway is largely technology related, and the merchant account is largely business related.

The payment gateway provides the technology to validate and charge a credit card and setup recurring payments, and some can store customer information for later billing.

The merchant account is a kind of bank account that stores incoming money until it can be moved to your bank account. Why not just put the money directly into your bank account? The delay is kind of like waiting for a check to clear. If for some reason the credit card company needs to request the money back, because of an error or a customer request, it can pull it out of your merchant account.

These are the important things to look out for when choosing a merchant account:

- Will my gateway work with this merchant account?
- Will this merchant account underwrite my type of business? Some merchant accounts will not work with adult sites, gambling sites, or other "high-risk merchants."

- Will this merchant account underwrite my size of business? Some merchant accounts will not approve new businesses that sell high-priced (thousands of dollars) goods.

- Finally, what are the fees? Sometimes these fees are bundled into the payment gateway fees, and sometimes they are separate.

The best route to accepting credit cards online is usually to choose a plugin first, then choose a payment gateway that works with that plugin, and then work with the gateway to find a merchant account.

SSL Certificates and HTTPS

When accepting sensitive information through a web form, for example, a credit card number, you should encrypt that information by loading and submitting the form over SSL or HTTPS.

First some definitions: *SSL* stands for "Secure Sockets Layer" and is the technology that encrypts data that is transferred to and from a web page. *HTTP* stands for "Hypertext Transfer Protocol." This is the standard *protocol* for serving web pages without encryption. *HTTPS* stands for "HTTP Secure." This is the protocol for serving web pages with SSL encryption.

Installing an SSL Certificate on Your Server

First make sure that you have SSL enabled on your web server. How to do that will depend on your specific host and web server. O'Reilly's ONLamp has great instructions for setting up SSL on a server running Apache (*http://bit.ly/config-ssl-apache*).

When setting up SSL, you'll need an SSL certificate. You can use self-signed certificates for testing purposes, but modern-day browsers will show some fairly dire warnings when browsing to a site using a self-signed certificate. Figure 15-1 shows the warning shown to Chrome users.

For production environments, you'll want to use a public key certificate from a certificate authority or CA. Public key certificates must be purchased, and are usually bundled or offered as an add-on to your web hosting package. You can also use public key certificates (SSL certificates) purchased from third parties; visit this book's website (*http://bwawwp.com/ssl/*) for a list of vendors we like. A good CA certificate will be trusted by all modern web browsers, which is what gives you the green or golden padlock icon on your website instead of a broken or red padlock.

What you're really doing is paying for the confirmation that you really own the domain you are using the certificate on. Ownership of the domain is usually confirmed via email to an address on the domain.

Internet consumers are trained to look for that padlock (see Figure 15-2). Both savvy and nonsavvy users will feel better seeing it. So even if you aren't accepting credit card information directly on your page (e.g., if you are sending users to PayPal to pay), it's still a good idea to purchase a CA certificate and serve your checkout page over SSL.

Besides using a CA certificate, the other thing to do when setting up SSL is to have your HTTPS directory point to your HTTP directory through a symbolic link, or symlink for short. A symlink is like a shortcut in a Windows PC. The symlink points to another directory rather than being a directory of its own.

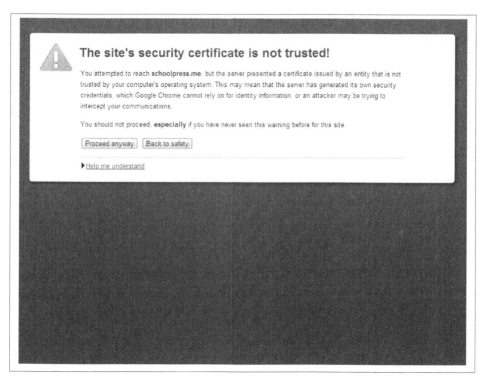

Figure 15-1. Chrome SSL warning

The end result of using a symlink for your HTTPS directory is that the same *.php* source files will be loaded when people visit *https://yoursite.com* as when they visit *http://yoursite.com*. Your server will make sure that the traffic through the HTTPS link is encrypted and both WordPress and your ecommerce plugin will make sure that the correct secure page is shown to the user when being served over SSL.

Assuming your HTTP directory is called "html" and you want your HTTPS directory to be called "ssl_html," you would issue the following Linux command to create a symlink to that directory: `ln -s http ssl_http`.

Next you'll need to tell your ecommerce plugin to use SSL on your checkout page.

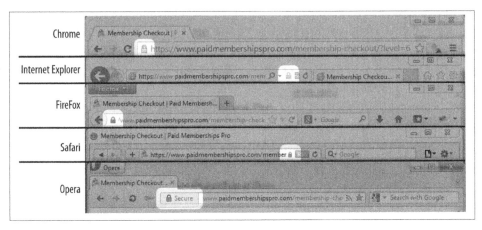

Figure 15-2. Various padlocks across browsers

SSL with Paid Memberships Pro

Figure 15-3 shows the Payment Settings tab of the Membership settings in your Word-Press dashboard.

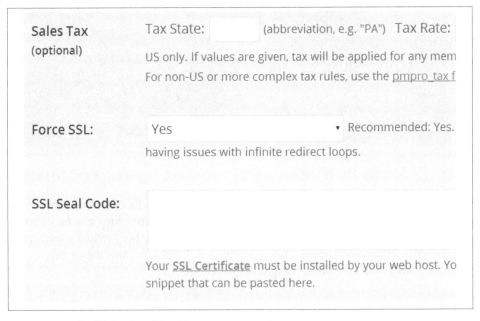

Figure 15-3. Paid Memberships Pro payment settings

To get Paid Memberships Pro to serve your checkout page over SSL, set the Force SSL option to Yes. Depending on which payment gateway you are using, this option will either be forced to Yes or will give you the option to choose Yes or No. Set to Yes and click the Save Settings button.

When this setting is enabled, a user browsing to the HTTP version of the page will be redirected to the HTTPS version of the page. Conversely, users browsing to an HTTPS version of a noncheckout page will be redirected to the HTTP version.

SSL with Jigoshop

To get Jigoshop to serve your checkout page over HTTPS, go to Jigoshop → Settings in your WordPress dashboard, click the General tab, then check the "Force SSL on checkout" option (Figure 15-4) and click the Save General Changes button.

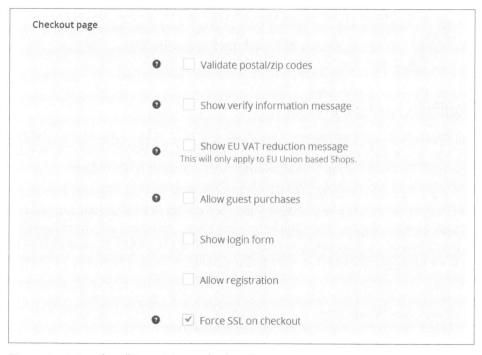

Figure 15-4. Jigoshop "Force SSL on checkout" option

Other ecommerce plugins will have similar settings.

WordPress Login and WordPress Admin over SSL

Serving your checkout page over SSL is the minimum you can do to secure the private data passed to and from your site. You can also set up WordPress to use SSL on the login page, in the admin dashboard, across the entire site, or only on select pages.

SSL logins in WordPress are done by setting the FORCE_SSL_LOGIN constant to true in your *wp-config.php* file. Place the following line of code above the "That's all, stop editing! Happy blogging." comment at the end of the file:

```
define('FORCE_SSL_LOGIN', true);
```

To use SSL on the login page *and* in the admin dashboard, use the following FORCE_SSL_ADMIN constant instead:

```
define('FORCE_SSL_ADMIN', true);
```

 The FORCE_SSL_ADMIN constant supersedes the FORCE_SSL_LOGIN constant. You should only set one or the other constant to true. If FORCE_SSL_LOGIN is false and FORCE_SSL_ADMIN is true, your login page will still be served over SSL.

WordPress Frontend over SSL

You might think, "Why not serve my entire site over SSL?" The reason not to is that the SSL encryption adds a small bit of CPU computation and a few microseconds to each page load. This may not matter, but on larger sites at scale, it could add up.

There are occasions when you may need to use SSL across the entire frontend and backend of your site. Maybe you don't mind the extra bit of CPU use and just want to set your members at ease. Maybe you have secure forms and information on many pages in your frontend. In these cases, you can set the FORCE_SSL_ADMIN constant to true in your *wp-config.php* file and then include this plugin:

```
<?php
/*
Plugin Name: Always HTTPS
Plugin URI: http://www.strangerstudios.com/wp/always-https
Description: Redirect all URLs to the HTTPS version.
Version: .1
Author: strangerstudios
*/

/*
    Make sure to set FORCE_SSL_ADMIN to true.
        Add the following to your wp-config.php:

define('FORCE_SSL_ADMIN', true);
*/
```

```
//redirect to https
function always_https_redirect()
{
        //if FORCE_SSL_ADMIN is true and we're not over HTTPS
        if(force_ssl_admin() && !is_ssl())
        {
                //redirect to https version of the page
                wp_redirect("https://" . $_SERVER['HTTP_HOST'] .
            $_SERVER['REQUEST_URI']);
                exit;
        }
}
add_action('wp', 'always_https_redirect', 2);

//(optional) Tell Paid Memberships Pro to get on board with the HTTPS redirect.
add_filter("pmpro_besecure", "__return_true");
?>
```

If FORCE_SSL_ADMIN is on, but the current page is not already being served over HTTPS, the user is redirected to the HTTPS version of the page.

This code can cause an infinite redirect loop in a few situations. Sometimes plugins, like Paid Memberships Pro, will have their own idea on which pages should and shouldn't be served over HTTPS. In the preceding code, we use a filter in Paid Memberships Pro to tell it that all pages should be served over HTTPS. Other plugins should have similar filters.

Another situation that comes up is that certain server setups, particularly those that are using a proxy like the Varnish caching system (covered in Chapter 16), will fail to properly set the $_SERVER['HTTPS'] global, which the is_ssl() function checks to see if the current page is being served over HTTPS. These conflicts are harder to handle. Sometimes, you can update your *wp-config.php* to set the $_SERVER['HTTPS'] global based on some other global being set by the proxy. Or you can adjust the check in the Always HTTPS plugin to check for the particular values set by your proxy.

We're going to go through two more techniques, which we've bundled into the Paid Memberships Pro plugin. We'll show you how to use these features in Paid Memberships Pro and also how to set them up yourself if you aren't using the Paid Memberships Pro plugin.

SSL on Select Pages

Sometimes you will want to serve only certain pages over SSL. Paid Memberships Pro does this, where by default only the checkout page is served over SSL, and all other pages are served over regular HTTP.

If you're using the Paid Memberships Pro plugin, and there are other pages you'd like to serve over SSL, you can add a custom field to the post, page, or CPT called "besecure" and set the value to "1" or "true." Paid Memberships Pro will then make sure that the page is served over SSL.

Let's see how Paid Memberships Pro does this so you can understand what's going on and potentially use the same method for your site that isn't running the Paid Memberships Pro plugin.

 The code in this section is similar to the code found in the Paid Memberships Pro plugin, but is slightly altered for clarity.

To serve certain pages over SSL, we'll need a few things:

- A way to detect if the user is on the login page, so we can respect the FORCE_SSL_LOGIN or FORCE_SSL_ADMIN constants
- A way to set which pages should be served over SSL and a function to redirect pages to either the HTTP or HTTPS version of a page depending on that setting
- A way to filter URLs used on a page to use the correct protocol (HTTP or HTTPS)

First up, our function to detect if the user is on the login page. This function checks if we're on the /wp-login.php or /wp-register.php pages or if the current page has the slug "login":

```
function my_is_login_page()
{
    return (in_array(
                $GLOBALS['pagenow'], array('wp-login.php', 'wp-register.php')) ||
                is_page("login")
            );
}
```

WordPress sets the pagenow global to the filename of the PHP script loaded. Typically this is *index.php*, but the login page will be accessed via *wp-login.php*.

 Fresh installs of WordPress will not have a *wp-register.php* file, but we're still checking for it here. WordPress sites set up before version 3.4 included a *wp-register.php* file. A redirect from *wp-register.php* to the actual registration page at *wp-login.php?action=register* was added in WP 3.4, but the old *wp-register.php* file wasn't deleted if you upgraded. Since it doesn't hurt anything, we can check for *wp-register.php* too just in case the WordPress site includes it.

The is_page() function can take a post ID or slug as a parameter and will return true if the current page has that ID or slug. If you use a plugin like Theme My Login or a similar method to place your login page within your theme on the frontend, you'll have a WordPress page for your login page. Tweak the code to check for whatever you set the slug to on your login page.

Next up is a function to redirect the user to the correct version of a page (HTTP or HTTPS), depending on if the page is set to be served over SSL or not:

```
function my_besecure()
{
    global $besecure, $post;

    //check the post meta for a besecure custom field
    if(!empty($post->ID) && !$besecure)
        $besecure = get_post_meta($post->ID, "besecure", true);

    //if forcing ssl on admin, be secure in admin and login page
    if(!$besecure && force_ssl_admin() && (is_admin() || my_is_login_page()))
        $besecure = true;

    //if forcing ssl on login, be secure on the login page
    if(!$besecure && force_ssl_login() && my_is_login_page())
        $besecure = true;

    //a hook so we can filter this setting if need be
    $besecure = apply_filters("my_besecure", $besecure);

    if($besecure && (!is_ssl()))
    {
      //need to be secure
      wp_redirect("https://" . $_SERVER['HTTP_HOST'] . $_SERVER['REQUEST_URI']);
        exit;
      }
      elseif(!$besecure && is_ssl())
      {
      //don't need to be secure
      wp_redirect("http://" . $_SERVER['HTTP_HOST'] . $_SERVER['REQUEST_URI']);
            exit;
      }
}
add_action('wp', 'my_besecure', 2);
add_action('login_init', 'my_besecure', 2);
```

Stepping through the preceding code, first we check for a "besecure" custom field in the current post's post meta. If this custom field is set, we'll want to serve over SSL.

Then we check if we're on the login page and if either the FORCE_SSL_LOGIN or FORCE_SSL_ADMIN constant is set to true. If so, we'll want to serve over SSL.

We add a hook in there to allow other code throughout our application to override the $besecure variable at this point.

Then we figure out if we need to redirect. We're using WP's built-in is_ssl() function, which will return true if $_SERVER['HTTPS'] is turned on or if $_SERVER['SERVER_PORT'] is set to 443 (the typical port number for SSL).

 As explained above, some server setups with proxies may not properly set the $_SERVER globals. You can add a check to your *wp-config.php* for the value they do set and set $_SERVER['HTTPS'] to true if you are over HTTPS.

If $besecure is true, but we're not serving over SSL, we redirect the browser to the HTTPS version of the page.

Similarly, if $besecure is false, but we *are* serving over HTTPS, we redirect the browser to the HTTP version of the page.

We're rebuilding the current URL by appending the appropriate protocol to the $_SERVER['HTTP_HOST'] and $_SERVER['REQUEST_URI'] globals set up by PHP.

The two lines at the bottom of the previous code block set up this function to fire during the wp and login_init events in WordPress. The wp hook is activated on the frontend of WordPress after loading the theme, but before generating any output. The login_init hook is found in the *wp-login.php* file. We're setting the priority to 2 here so this will fire before any actions set up using the default priority (10), but after any action that may be set up with a priority 1 or lower. You may need to tweak this depending on the other plugins and custom code you are running using these hooks.

Finally, we're going to write a quick little function to filter URLs generated by WordPress to use the same protocol as the current page. Remember earlier we talked about how URLs like *http://yoursite.com/some-page/* (HTTP) that show up on a page like *https://yoursite.com/checkout/* (HTTPS) will cause your browser to show a security warning:

```
function my_https_filter($s)
{
    global $besecure;
        if($besecure)
                return str_replace("http:", "https:", $s);
        else
                return str_replace("https:", "http:", $s);
}
add_filter('bloginfo_url', 'my_https_filter');
add_filter('wp_list_pages', 'my_https_filter');
add_filter('option_home', 'my_https_filter');
add_filter('option_siteurl', 'my_https_filter');
add_filter('logout_url', 'my_https_filter');
```

```
add_filter('login_url', 'my_https_filter');
add_filter('home_url', 'my_https_filter');
```

Since we saved $besecure to a global variable in the my_besecure() function, we don't need to recalculate it. Then we use the str_replace function to swap "http:" for "https:" or vice versa. We set this filter to run on a number of built in WordPress hooks used at various places throughout the WordPress code base where URLs are generated.

When you output URLs in other places of your custom application code, be sure to use the home_url() function to make sure the URL is generated correctly and the my_https_filter is run on it.

Avoiding SSL Errors with the "Nuclear Option"

The my_https_filter function will make sure links that show up on a page use the correct protocol. However, sometimes raw *http://...* URLs may be hardcoded into your posts, or maybe a plugin you use doesn't use the built-in WordPress functions like it should when outputting same site URLs or loading JavaScript or CSS files. Figure 15-5 shows the Chrome Developer Tools Console, which can help locate errors.

Figure 15-5. An SSL error in the Chrome Developer Tools Console. Use the Chrome Developer Tools Console to find SSL errors, or use the Nuclear Option to avoid them.

In these cases, you can try to find each case of a bad URL and fix the link in your posts or code to use a relative URL or the proper WordPress function to make sure it will output on the frontend using the proper protocol. However, it's sometimes easier to use what we call the Nuclear Option:

```
constant('MY_SITE_DOMAIN', 'yoursite.com');

function my_NuclearHTTPS()
{
        ob_start("my_replaceURLsInBuffer");
}
add_action("init", "my_NuclearHTTPS");

function my_replaceURLsInBuffer($buffer)
{
    global $besecure;

        //only swap URLs if this page is secure
        if($besecure)
        {
/*
okay swap out all links like these:
* http://yoursite.com
* http://anysubdomain.yoursite.com
* http://any.number.of.sub.domains.yoursite.com
*/
$buffer = preg_replace(
        '/http\:\/\/([a-zA-Z0-9\.\-]*'.str_replace('.','\.',MY_SITE_DOMAIN).')/i',
        'https://$1',
$buffer
        );
        }

        return $buffer;
}
```

First we need to make sure we define a constant MY_SITE_DOMAIN and set it to the second-level domain (SLD) for your site. Your site_url() set in WordPress may be *www.your-site.com*, but we are interested here in just the *yoursite.com* part of that.

Then my_NuclearHTTPS() fires on the init hook and uses the PHP function ob_start() to turn on output buffering. Output buffering means that all output generated by PHP (e.g., via echo function calls or inline HTML) goes into a buffer string instead of straight to the browser. Then, when PHP is finished generating all output (or if you call the ob_end_flush() function first), the buffer string is passed to a callback function, which is my_replaceURLsInBuffer() in this case.

The my_replaceURLsInBuffer() function filters the buffer string, swapping out "http:" for "https:" on *every* link. The regular expression magic we're doing in the preg_re `place()` call there makes sure that links to any subdomain using the same domain (why we needed to set the `MY_SITE_DOMAIN` constant) will also be filtered.

So you might have caught on by now why we call this the "Nuclear Option." Instead of finding the source of bad URLs in your app and fixing them, we just fix all of the URLs at once before sending the output to the browser. There will be a small performance hit here, depending on how large your HTML output is. But this method can be useful in a pinch, especially if you are using many third-party plugins that you can't or don't want to fix to output site URLs properly.

Setting Up Software as a Service (SaaS) with Paid Memberships Pro

The model of charging for access to a web app is called software as a service, or SaaS (pronounced "sass") for short.

In this section, we will go through setting up Paid Memberships Pro on our SchoolPress app, with a $10/month membership.

The Software as a Service Model

The software as a service model (of SaaS) basically means that instead of purchasing your software in a shrink-wrapped box and installing it on your computer, you pay—typically a monthly or annual fee—for access to a cloud-enabled web app.

Examples of companies using the SaaS model are GitHub, Dropbox, Evernote, and Google Apps, and now even Microsoft Office can be purchased under a SaaS plan.

SaaS is popular because it generates relatively predictable recurring revenue. But SaaS is also an important way to make money off of open source software like WordPress. Because WordPress is GPL, if you were to sell and distribute the code for your software, your customers would be entitled under the GPL to redistribute that code…potentially for free. So using the SaaS service model allows your customers to use your software without having to distribute your source code to them.

The following instructions will help you if you want to charge a one-time, monthly, or annual fee for access to your app.

Step 0: Figure Out How You Want to Charge for Your App

Is it a lifetime fee, or a monthly subscription? Is it an annual subscription? Does the subscription automatically bill every year, or does the customer have to renew?

These are questions you will want to answer as best as you can before you start integrating Paid Memberships Pro or coding up customizations. Jason has a good series for how to price your web apps and premium content sites (*http://bit.ly/pmp-pricing*).

For our SchoolPress app, we will be charging each school account a $1,000 annual fee. When a school signs up, we will create a WordPress network site for it (e.g., *myschool.schoolpress.com*) and give it admin access to that site so it can start adding teachers and other content.

We will set the membership level to automatically bill the schools each year.

Step 1: Installing and Activating Paid Memberships Pro

Paid Memberships Pro is available in the WordPress plugin repository, which makes installing and activating the plugin a breeze (Figure 15-6).

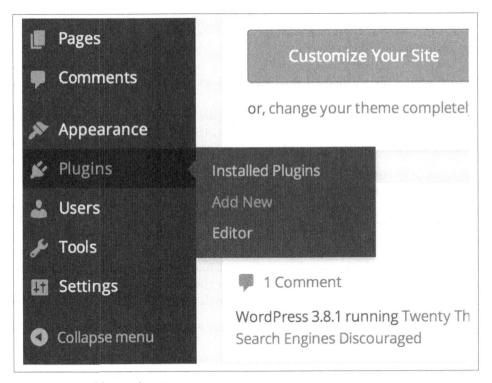

Figure 15-6. Add new plugin

1. From your WordPress dashboard, go to Plugins → Add New.
2. Search for Paid Memberships Pro.
3. Find Paid Memberships Pro and click the Install link.

4. Optionally enter your FTP information here. (Some hosting setups will not require this.)

5. When the plugin installs successfully, click the Activate link.

Step 2: Setting Up the Level

1. From your WordPress dashboard, go to the newly created Memberships page.

2. Click the "Add new level" link or button.

3. Enter the membership information in the boxes, as shown in Figure 15-7. For our level, that will be:

   a. Name:

   b. Description: School administrators should sign up here to create and gain access to your SchoolPress site.

   c. Confirmation Message: (can leave it blank)

   d. Initial Payment: 1000

   e. Recurring Subscription: Checked

      i. Billing Amount: 1000

      ii. Per: 1

      iii. Days/Weeks/Years: Years

      iv. Billing Cycle Limit: 0

      v. Custom Trial: Unchecked

   f. Disable New Signups: Unchecked

   g. Membership Expiration: Unchecked

   h. Categories: All Unchecked

4. Click Save Level.

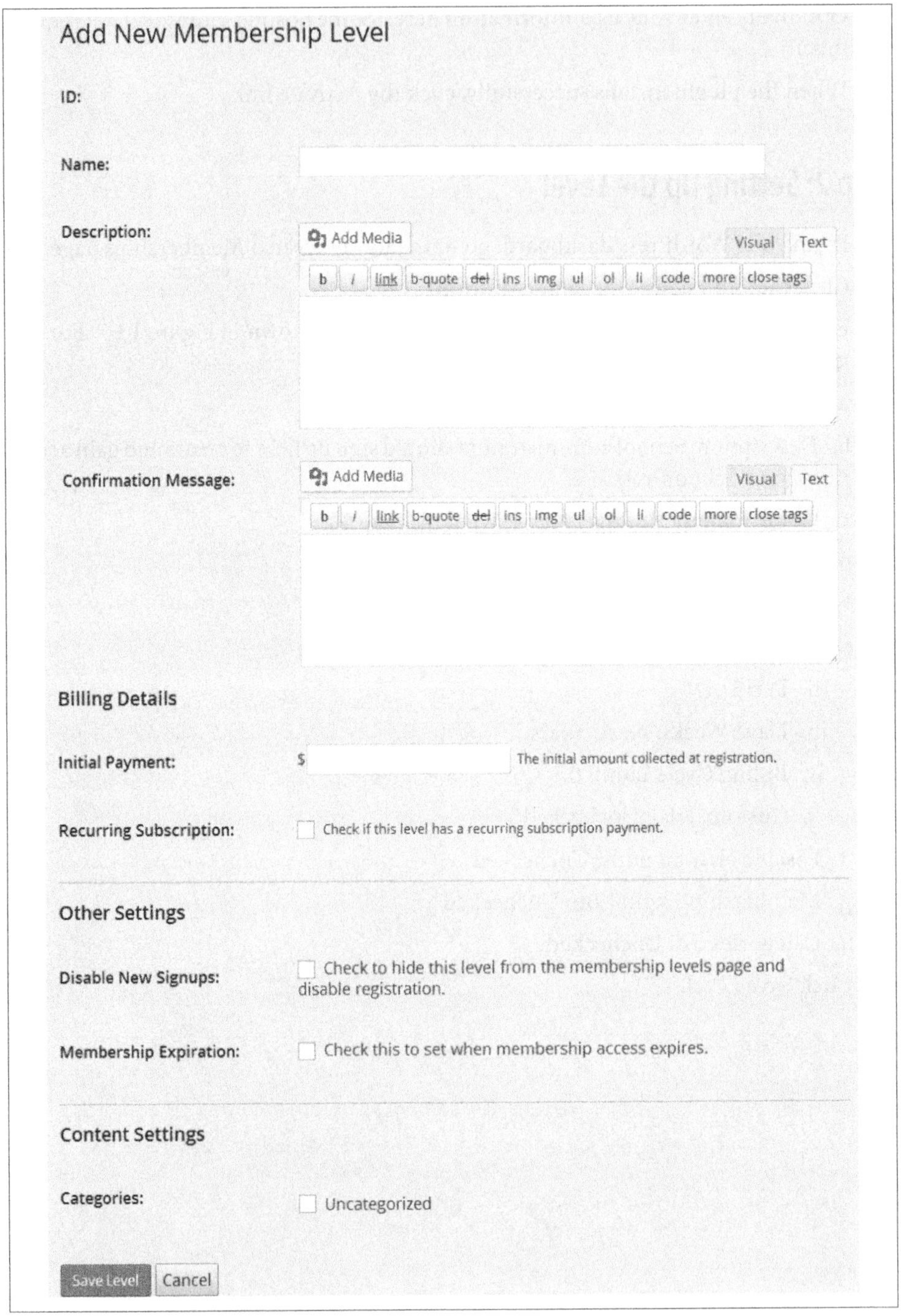

Add New Membership Level

ID:

Name:

Description:

> **Add Media**   Visual | Text
>
> b | *i* | link | b-quote | del | ins | img | ul | ol | li | code | more | close tags

Confirmation Message:

> **Add Media**   Visual | Text
>
> b | *i* | link | b-quote | del | ins | img | ul | ol | li | code | more | close tags

Billing Details

Initial Payment:

$ _____   The initial amount collected at registration.

Recurring Subscription:

☐ Check if this level has a recurring subscription payment.

Other Settings

Disable New Signups:

☐ Check to hide this level from the membership levels page and disable registration.

Membership Expiration:

☐ Check this to set when membership access expires.

Content Settings

Categories:

☐ Uncategorized

[Save Level] [Cancel]

Figure 15-7. Paid Memberships Pro New Level screen

Step 3: Setting Up Pages

Paid Memberships Pro needs several pages to facilitate checkout and other member-related functions. When you click on the "Page" tab of the PMPro settings, you will see a form like the one shown in Figure 15-8.

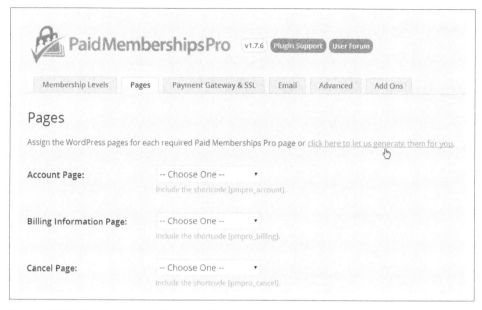

Figure 15-8. Generate pages for Paid Memberships Pro

If you already have pages dedicated to describing your levels or for a user account, you can choose those pages through the dropdowns on the Pages tab of the Paid Membership Pro settings. In most cases though, you will just want to click the "click here to let us generate them for you" link and pages will be created for the Account, Billing Information, Cancel, Checkout, Confirmation, Invoice, and Levels pages. Figure 15-9 shows what this page looks like once the script has generated these pages for you.

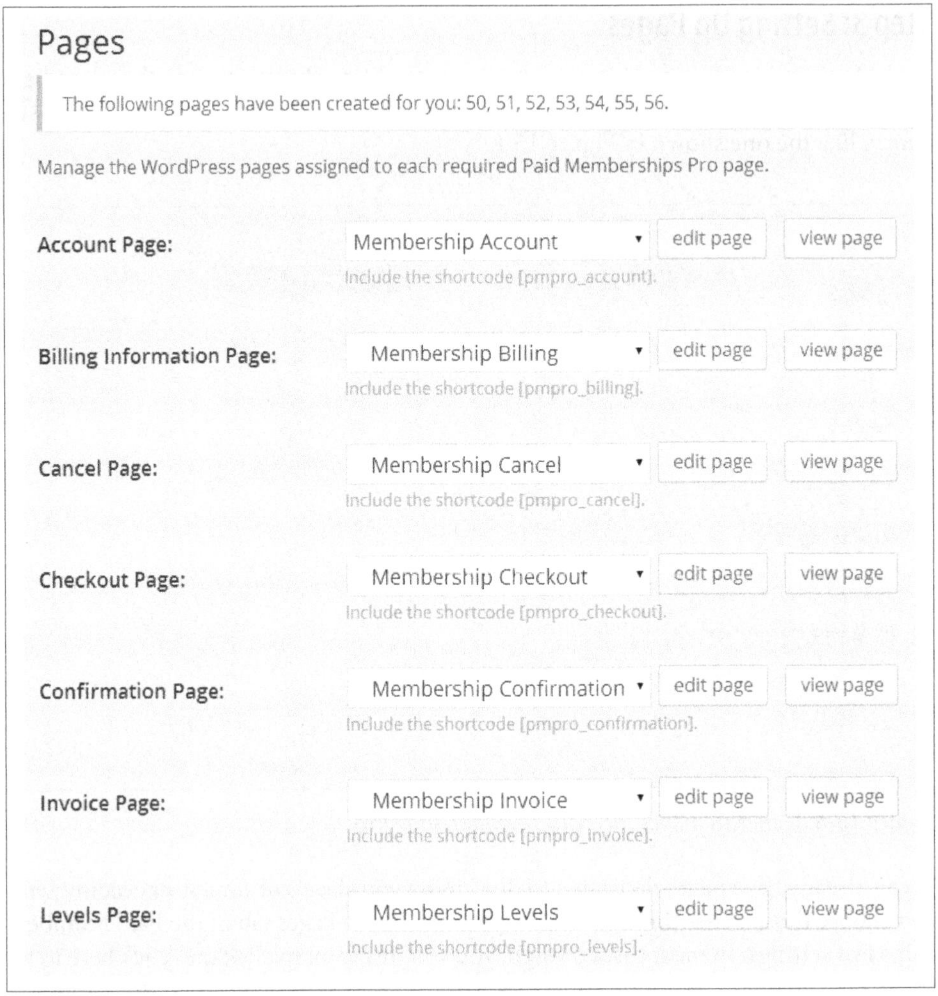

Pages

The following pages have been created for you: 50, 51, 52, 53, 54, 55, 56.

Manage the WordPress pages assigned to each required Paid Memberships Pro page.

Account Page:	Membership Account ▾	edit page	view page
	Include the shortcode [pmpro_account].		
Billing Information Page:	Membership Billing ▾	edit page	view page
	Include the shortcode [pmpro_billing].		
Cancel Page:	Membership Cancel ▾	edit page	view page
	Include the shortcode [pmpro_cancel].		
Checkout Page:	Membership Checkout ▾	edit page	view page
	Include the shortcode [pmpro_checkout].		
Confirmation Page:	Membership Confirmation ▾	edit page	view page
	Include the shortcode [pmpro_confirmation].		
Invoice Page:	Membership Invoice ▾	edit page	view page
	Include the shortcode [pmpro_invoice].		
Levels Page:	Membership Levels ▾	edit page	view page
	Include the shortcode [pmpro_levels].		

Figure 15-9. Default pages generated by Paid Memberships Pro

Step 4: Payment Settings

Figure 15-10 shows the Payment Gateway & SSL tab of the PMPro settings. Here you will choose your gateway and then fill out of corresponding user and/or API values. Depending on which gateway option you choose, this page will also allow you to change the currency used, which credit cards are available, whether to use SSL or not (remember you should always install SSL unless it is a test site), and whether to use the Nuclear Option for SSL or not.

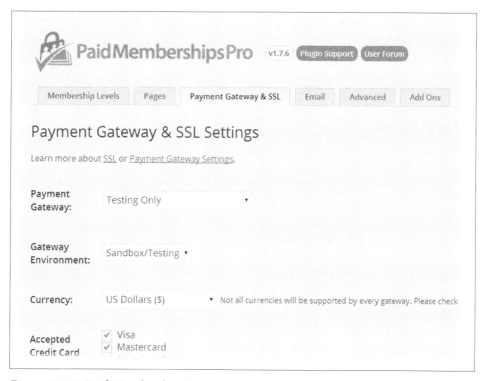

Figure 15-10. Paid Memberships Pro payment settings

The payment settings page will also give you a place to paste in your SSL Seal Code and enter a tax state and percentage. The tax calculation can also be done programmatically through the `pmpro_tax` filter (described below).

The payment settings page will also show you the URL you should share with your gateway to enable behind-the-scenes communication from the gateway to your site. This function has various names depending on the gateway: PayPal calls it an "IPN handler"; Authorize.net calls it a "silent post URL"; and Stripe and Braintree will call it a "webhook."

Step 5: Email Settings

By default, WordPress will send emails from your site from "WordPress" at *word-press@yoursite.com*. This doesn't look nice and is often not a real email address. The Email tab of the Paid Memberships Pro settings, shown below in Figure 15-11, allows you to override these values and also check or uncheck which membership-related admin emails you would like to receive.

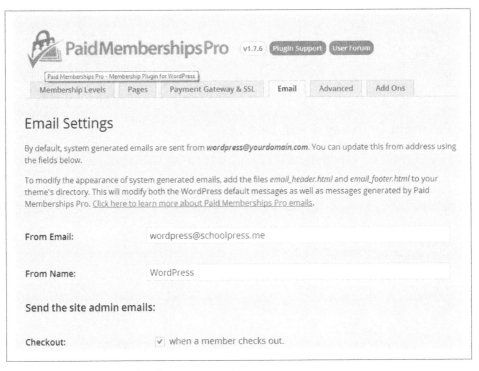

Figure 15-11. Paid Memberships Pro email settings

Step 6: Advanced Settings

Figure 15-12 shows the Advanced Settings tab, which has a few built-in options for running Paid Memberships Pro. Of particular interest may be the option to choose a Terms of Service page to show users on sign up. They will see a scrollable text box with the TOS page content shown within it and will have to check a box to agree to the Terms of Service.

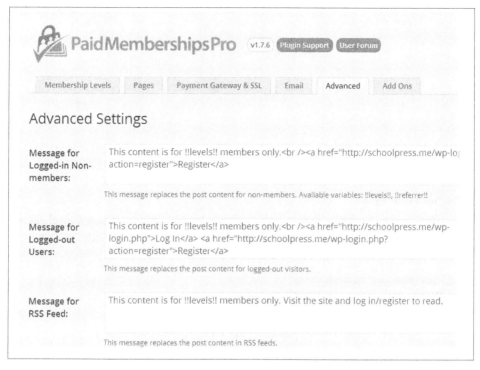

Figure 15-12. Paid Memberships Pro advanced settings

Step 7: Locking Down Pages

Besides generating a checkout page and integrating with your payment gateway, the main functionality added by Paid Memberships Pro is the ability to lock down certain pages or portions of pages based on a user's membership level. There are a few different ways to do this.

Lock down a specific page

Paid Memberships Pro adds a Require Membership box to the sidebar of the edit post and edit page pages in the WordPress dashboard. An example of the Require Membership box is shown in Figure 15-13. To lock down a page for a certain membership level, check the box next to that level.

If more than one level is checked, members of *either* level will be able to view that page. If no levels are checked, anyone (including nonusers) will be able to view that page.

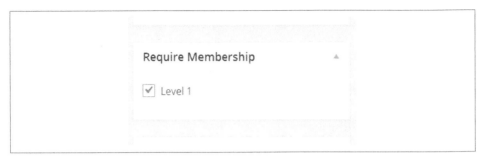

Figure 15-13. Check which levels are required to view this page

Lock down a page by URL

Sometimes it may be easier to restrict access to a page or group of pages by checking the page's URL. For example, to keep nonmembers out of certain BuddyPress groups, you could add the following code to a custom plugin:

```
//lock down our members group
function my_buddy_press_members_group()
{
    $uri = $_SERVER['REQUEST_URI'];
        if(strtolower(substr($uri, 0, 16)) == "/groups/members/")
        {
                //make sure they are a member
                if(!pmpro_hasMembershipLevel())
                {
                        wp_redirect(pmpro_url("levels"));
                        exit;
                }
        }
}
add_action("init", "my_buddy_press_members_group");
```

The workhorse here is the pmpro_hasMembershipLevel() function. This function can take two parameters. The first is the ID or name of a membership level to check for. The second parameter is the user ID of the user you want to check. If no parameters are set, the function will check if the current user has *any* membership level.

You can also do negative checks by passing, for example, "-1" as the level ID. pmpro_hasMembershipLevel(-1) will return true if the current user *doesn't* have level 1. If you pass a zero specifically, the function will check that the user has *no* level at all. So pmpro_hasMembershipLevel(0) will return true if the current user does not have a membership level. (You could also do !pmpro_hasMembershipLevel().)

Multiple level IDs and names can be passed in an array. For example, to check for members with level 1 or 2, use this code:

```
if(pmpro_hasMembershipLevel(array(1,2)))
{
```

```
        //do something for level 1 and 2 members here
    }
```

Lock down a portion of a page by shortcode

Another way to restrict access to content is to use shortcodes in your post body content. The following is an example of some page content that will show different messages to different membership levels:

```
Welcome to SchoolPress!

[membership level="1"]Thanks for your continuing membership.[/membership]

[membership level="-1"]Sign up your school now![/membership]
```

The [membership] shortcode is fairly simple. It takes one parameter level that, similar to the parameter for the pmpro_hasMembershipLevel() function, can take a level ID, name, or a zero or negative level ID. Any content within the shortcode will be shown based on the stated level. Multiple level IDs can be passed separated by commas.

Lock down a portion of a page by PHP code using the pmpro_hasMembershipLevel() function

When locking down the BuddyPress members group, we used the pmpro_hasMember shipLevel() function. You can also use this function within your page templates or other code to restrict access to content or portions of code. For example, you might find code like this in your header:

```php
<?php if(is_user_logged_in()) { ?>
<div class="user-welcome">
  Welcome
  <?php if(function_exists("pmpro_hasMembershipLevel")
    && pmpro_hasMembershipLevel()) { ?>
      <a href="<?php echo pmpro_url("account"); ?>">
    <?php echo $current_user->display_name;?>
    </a>
  <?php } else { ?>
      <a href="<?php echo home_url("/wp-admin/profile.php"); ?>">
    <?php echo $current_user->display_name;?>
    </a>
  <?php } ?>
</div> <!-- end user-welcome -->
<?php } ?>
```

The preceding code will show members a link to the PMPro account page. Users without a membership level are shown a link to their WP profile page.

Step 8: Customizing Paid Memberships Pro

Below are a few common customizations for Paid Memberships Pro. The general process for customizing a plugin like Paid Memberships Pro is to:

1. Figure out what you want to change.

2. Find out where the default behavior for your change is coded.

3. Locate or add a hook to support the customization you want.

4. Write an action or filter to use the hook.

Restricting nonmembers to the homepage

By default, Paid Memberships Pro does not lock down any part of your site unless you specifically tell it to. For some sites, you will want very limited public access (just the sales, about, and contact pages). You can do this by redirecting nonmembers away from any nonapproved page. Use the following code:

```
function my_template_redirect()
{
        $okay_pages = array(
        pmpro_getOption('billing_page_id'),
        pmpro_getOption('account_page_id'),
        pmpro_getOption('levels_page_id'),
        pmpro_getOption('checkout_page_id'),
        pmpro_getOption('confirmation_page_id')
    );

        //if the user doesn't have a membership, send them home
        if(!is_user_logged_in()
                && !is_home()
                && !is_page($okay_pages)
                && !strpos($_SERVER['REQUEST_URI'], "login"))
        {
            wp_redirect(home_url('wp-login.php?redirect_to='.
            urlencode($_SERVER['REQUEST_URI'])));
        }
        elseif(is_page()
                        && !is_home()
                        && !is_page($okay_pages)
                        && !pmpro_hasMembershipLevel())
        {
                wp_redirect(home_url());
        }
}
add_action('template_redirect', 'my_template_redirect');
```

In the preceding code, we set up an array of post IDs for pages that nonmembers should be able to see. We use the pmpro_getOption() function to get the IDs of the pages generated by PMPro and also allow access to the home page by using the WordPress is_home() function. We also allow access to any page with the word "login" in the URL, which on our setup will just the login page.

Locking down files

Some of the pages you are locking down may have images or other files attached to them. If the page is locked down, the link or image will not show up on the site for your users. However, users who know the direct URL to the file will be able to download to the file without first being logged in as a member.

This is because when Apache processes a URL like *http://schoolpress.me/wp-content/uploads/logo.png*, it serves the file directly to the user without checking with PHP or WordPress first.

You can change this behavior by adding a rule to your site's *.htaccess* file that will redirect any URL like the preceding one through a special script bundled with Paid Memberships Pro. Add the following code to the top of your *.htaccess* file, above the other rewrite rules:

```
RewriteEngine On
RewriteBase /
RewriteRule ^wp-content/uploads/(.*)$ \
    /wp-content/plugins/paid-memberships-pro/services/getfile.php [L]
```

How does this work? In WordPress, images and files can be uploaded to a post or page. These files, called attachments by WordPress, are all stored in the */wp-content/uploads/* folder, but they are also associated with the post they were attached to via an entry in the wp_posts table.

Attachments are stored in the wp_posts table with the post_status set to "attachment" and the post_parent set to the ID of the post they are attached to.

The *getfile.php* script will find the corresponding entry in the wp_posts table for the requested file; and if the attachment's parent requires membership, it will check to make sure a valid member is logged in before serving the file.

Change user roles based on membership levels

For most of the examples in this section, we assume that members only have access to the frontend application of your site. However, sometimes you may want to give members access to the WordPress dashboard, give them the "author" role so they can post to the blog, or otherwise assign a role other than "subscriber" to them.

This code will add the author role to any new member of a particular level. It will also downgrade the member to a subscriber role if her membership level is removed:

```
function my_pmpro_after_change_membership_level($level_id, $user_id)
{
    if($level_id == 1)
        {
                //New member of level #1.
        //If they are a subscriber, make them an author.
                $wp_user_object = new WP_User($user_id);
```

```
                    if(in_array("subscriber", $wp_user_object->roles))
                            $wp_user_object->set_role('author');
            }
            else
            {
                    //Not a member of level #1.
            //If they are an author, make them a subscriber.
                    $wp_user_object = new WP_User($user_id);
                    if(in_array("author", $wp_user_object->roles))
                            $wp_user_object->set_role('subscriber');
            }
    }
    add_action(
        "pmpro_after_change_membership_level",
        "my_pmpro_after_change_membership_level",
        10,
        2
    );
```

More information on users and roles is in Chapter 6.

International and long-form addresses

By default, the Paid Memberships Pro checkout form will show address fields with the city, state, and zip code formatted on one line and the country hidden and assumed to be "US." The default Paid Memberships Pro billing address form is shown in Figure 15-14.

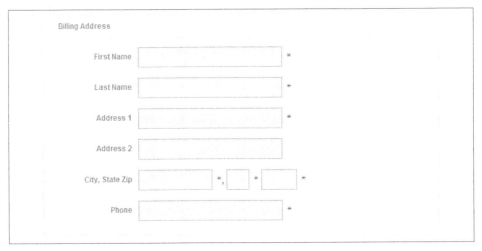

Figure 15-14. Paid Memberships Pro billing address

If you anticipate international users, you will want to show a long-form address with a dropdown to select your country. This is done with the following code:

```
add_filter("pmpro_international_addresses", "__return_true");
add_filter("pmpro_longform_address", "__return_true");
```

That's it, two lines. The `pmpro_international_addresses` hook/setting will show a country dropdown if `true`. The `pmpro_longform_address` hook/setting will show each address field on its own line if `true`.

Figure 15-15 shows the updated billing address fields.

Figure 15-15. Paid Memberships Pro international billing address

You may also want to change the default country, change the list of countries, or make some of the address fields not required. Here is some example code doing that:

```
/*
    Change the Default Country from US to GB (Great Britain)
*/
function my_pmpro_default_country($default)
{
        return "GB";
}
add_filter("pmpro_default_country", "my_pmpro_default_country");

/*
        Add/remove some countries from the default list.
*/
function my_pmpro_countries($countries)
```

```
{
        //remove the US
        unset($countries["US"]);

        //add The Moon (LN short for Lunar?)
        $countries["LN"] = "The Moon";

        //You could also rebuild the array from scratch.
        //$countries = array("CA" => "Canada", "US" => "United States",
    //  "GB" => "United Kingdom");

        return $countries;
}
add_filter("pmpro_countries", "my_pmpro_countries");

/*
        (optional) You may want to add/remove certain countries from the list.
    The pmpro_countries filter allows you to do this.
        The array is formatted like
    array("US"=>"United States", "GB"=>"United Kingdom");
    with the acronym as the key and the full
        country name as the value.
*/
function my_pmpro_countries($countries)
{
        //remove the US
        unset($countries["US"]);

        //add The Moon (LN short for Lunar?)
        $countries["LN"] = "The Moon";

        //You could also rebuild the array from scratch.
        //$countries = array("CA" => "Canada", "US" => "United States",
    //  "GB" => "United Kingdom");

        return $countries;
}
add_filter("pmpro_countries", "my_pmpro_countries");

/*
        Change some of the billing fields to be not required.
        Default fields are: bfirstname, blastname, baddress1, bcity, bstate,
    bzipcode, bphone, bemail, bcountry, CardType, AccountNumber,
    ExpirationMonth, ExpirationYear, CVV
*/
function my_pmpro_required_billing_fields($fields)
{
        //remove state and zip
        unset($fields['bstate']);
        unset($fields['bzipcode']);

        return $fields;
```

```
    }
add_filter("pmpro_required_billing_fields", "my_pmpro_required_billing_fields");
```

Upgrade/downgrade pricing

By default, when an existing member checks out for a new membership level, the member's old level is cancelled immediately and he's charged full price for the new membership level starting on the day he is checking out.

This works for some setups, but sometimes you might want to either (1) keep your member's payment date the same or (2) give him some credit from his old membership level toward his new membership level. In other words, you want to prorate his payment.

You can do the math in many different ways, but the following code will show the idea behind overriding the subscription start date and the checkout price based on factors like old membership level:

```
/*
    Calculate the prorated membership cost.
*/
function my_pmpro_checkout_level($level)
{
    //does the user have a level already?
        if(pmpro_hasMembershipLevel())
        {
                //get current level
                global $current_user;
                $clevel = $current_user->membership_level;

                //get the difference in amount
                $diff = $level->billing_amount - $clevel->billing_amount;

                //only prorate if the difference is positive (upgrading)
                if($diff > 0)
                {
                        //what day is it?
                        $now = time();
                        $today = intval(date("j", $now));

                        //get their payment date
                        $morder = new MemberOrder();
                        $morder->getLastMemberOrder();

                        $payment_day = intval(date("j", $morder->timestamp));

                        //how many days in that month?
                //either 1 for months with 31 days or -2 for Feb
                        $days_in_month = date("t", $morder->timestamp);
                        $extra_days = $days_in_month - 30;

                        //how many days are left in this payment period?
                        $days_left = $payment_day - $today + $extra_days;
```

```
                //if negative, we need to "flip it"
                if($days_left < 0) $days_left = 30 + $days_left;

                //as a % (decimal)
                $per_left = $days_left / $days_in_month;

                        //how many days have passed
                        $days_passed = $days_in_month - $days_left;

                //as a % (decimal)
                        $per_passed = $days_passed / $days_in_month;

                        /*
                        Now figure out how to adjust the price.
                        (a) What they should pay for new level
                = $level->billing_amount * $per_left.
                        (b) What they should have paid for current level
                = $clevel->billing_amount * $per_passed.
                        What they need to pay = (a) + (b) - (already paid)
                        */
                        $new_level_cost = $level->billing_amount * $per_left;
                        $old_level_cost = $clevel->billing_amount * $per_passed;

                        $level->initial_payment = round($new_level_cost +
                $old_level_cost - $morder->total, 2);

                        //just in case we have a negative payment
                        if($level->initial_payment < 0)
                                $level->initial_payment = 0;
                }
                else
                {
                        //let's just zero out the initial payment for
                //downgrades or you could figure out how to do a credit
                        $level->initial_payment = 0;
                }
        }

        return $level;
}
add_filter("pmpro_checkout_level", "my_pmpro_checkout_level");

/*
        If you have an old membership level, keep your startdate.
*/
function my_pmpro_checkout_start_date_keep_startdate($startdate, $user_id,
  $level)
{
        if(pmpro_hasMembershipLevel())
        {
          global $wpdb;
```

```
            $sqlQuery = "SELECT startdate FROM $wpdb->pmpro_memberships_users
            WHERE user_id = '" . $wpdb->escape($user_id) . "'
                AND membership_id = '" . $wpdb->escape($level->id) . "'
                AND status = 'active'
            ORDER BY id DESC
            LIMIT 1";
        $old_startdate = $wpdb->get_var($sqlQuery);

            if(!empty($old_startdate))
                    $startdate = "'" . $old_startdate . "'";
        }

        return $startdate;
}
//remove the default PMPro filter
remove_filter("pmpro_checkout_start_date",
    "pmpro_checkout_start_date_keep_startdate", 10, 3);

//our filter works with ANY level
add_filter("pmpro_checkout_start_date",
    "my_pmpro_checkout_start_date_keep_startdate", 10, 3);
```

The integration with Paid Memberships Pro here is pretty straightforward. We are filtering the initial (first month) cost of a membership level using the `pmpro_check` `out_level` `filter`. We also filter the subscription start date (or payment date) using the `pmpro_checkout_start_date` filter.

In both cases, we check if the user checking out already has a membership, meaning this is an upgrade or downgrade.

The rest of the code is simply math to figure out what percentage of a payment period has passed or what the user's next payment date was going to be.

## CHAPTER 16

WordPress Optimization and Scaling

This chapter is all about squeezing the most performance possible out of WordPress through optimal server configuration, caching, and clever programming.

WordPress often gets knocked for not scaling as well as other PHP frameworks or other programming languages. The idea that WordPress doesn't work at scale mostly comes from the fact that WordPress has traditionally been used to run small blogs on shared hosting accounts. Decisions are made by the WordPress core team (including supporting deprecated functionality and older versions of PHP and MySQL) to make sure that WordPress will boot up easily on as many hosting setups as possible, including underpowered shared hosting accounts.

So there are a lot of really slow WordPress sites out in the wild that help to give the impression that WordPress itself is slow. However, *WordPress is pretty darn fast on the right setup and can be scaled using the same techniques any PHP/MySQL-based app can use*. We will cover many of those techniques in this chapter, introducing you to a number of tools and concepts that can be applied to your own WordPress apps.

Terms

In this chapter, and throughout this book, we'll throw around terms like "optimization" and "scaling." It's important to understand exactly what we mean by these terms.

Optimization generally refers to getting your app and scripts to run as fast as possible. In some cases, we will be optimizing for memory use or something other than speed. But for the most part, when we say "optimize," we are talking about making things fast.

Scaling means building an app that can handle *more stuff*. More page views. More visits. More users. More posts. More files. More subsites. More computations.

Scaling can also mean building an app to handle *bigger stuff*. Bigger pages. Bigger posts. Bigger files.

The truth is that sometimes an app or specific parts of an app will run fine under light use or when database tables are smaller, etc. But once the number of users and objects being worked on gets larger in number or size, the performance of the app falls off or locks up completely.

Scalability is a subjective measure of how well your code and application handles more and bigger stuff. Generally, you want to build your app to handle the amount of growth you expect and then some more just in case. On the other hand, you want to always weigh the pros and cons of any platform or coding decision made for the sake of scalability. These decisions usually come at a cost, both in money and also in technical debt or added complexity to your codebase. Also, some techniques that make handling many, big transactions as fast as possible actually slow things down when working with fewer, smaller transactions. So it's always important to make sure that you are building your app toward your real-world expectations and aren't programing for scalability for the sake of it.

Scaling and optimization are closely related because applications that are fast scale better. There is more to scaling than having fast components, but fast components will make scaling easier. And having a slow application can make scaling harder. For this reason, it always makes sense to optimize your application from the inside out. In "The Truth About WordPress Performance," (*http://bit.ly/truth-wp-per*) a great whitepaper by Copyblogger Media and W3 Edge, the authors refer to optimizing the "origin" versus optimizing the "edge."

Origin refers to your WordPress application, which is the source of all of the data coming out of your app. Optimizing the origin involves making your WordPress app and the server it runs on faster.

Edge refers to services outside of your WordPress application, which are further from the origin but potentially closer to your users. These services include content delivery networks (CDNs) as well as things like browser caching. Optimizing the edge involves using these services in a smart way to make the end user experience better.

Origin Versus Edge

Again, we advocate optimizing from the inside out, or from the origin to the edge. Improvements in the core WordPress performance will always trickle through the edge to the end user. On the other hand, performance increases based on outside services, while improving the user experience, will sometimes hide bigger issues in the origin that need to be addressed.

A typical example to illustrate this point is when a proxy server like Varnish (covered in more detail later in this chapter) is used to speed up load times on a slowly loading site. Varnish will make a copy of your fully rendered WordPress pages. If a visitor is requests a page that is available in the Varnish cache, that copy is served to the visitor rather than generating a new one through WordPress.

Serving flat files is much faster than running dynamic PHP code, and so Varnish can greatly speed up a website. A page that takes 10 seconds to load on a slow WordPress setup might load in 1 second using Varnish when a copy is fetched. However, 10-second load times are unacceptable, and they are still going to happen. The first time each page is loaded, it will take 10 seconds. Page loads in your admin dashboard are going to take 10 seconds. If a page copy is cleaned out of the Varnish cache for any reason, either because it has been updated or because Varnish needed to make room, it's going to take 10 seconds to load a fresh copy of that page.

Varnish and tools like it are great at what they do and can be a valuable part of your application platform. At the same time, you want to make sure that these edge services aren't hiding issues in your origin.

Testing

For this chapter, part of our definition of performance will be tied to how fast certain pages load in the web browser. We will use a few different tools to test page loads for a single user and also for many simultaneous concurrent users.

For all of the tests in this chapter, we used a fresh install of WordPress, running the Twenty Thirteen theme and no other plugins. The site was hosted on a dedicated server running CENTOS 6 with the following specs:

- Intel® Xeon® E3-1220 processor
- 4 Cores x 3.1 GHz
- 12 GB DDR3 ECC RAM
- 2 TB SATA hard drives in software RAID

When not otherwise specified, the server was running a minimal setup with only Apache, MySQL, and PHP installed.

What to Test

Before getting into *how to test*, let's spend a little bit of time thinking about *what to test*. The testing tools described below primarily work by pointing your browser or another tool at a specific URL or a group of URLs for testing. But how do you choose which URLs to test?

The easy answer is to test everything, but that's not very helpful. As important as knowing which pages to test is why those pages should be tested and what you are looking for. So here are a few things to think about when testing your app's pages for performance.

Test a "static" page to use as a benchmark

By static here, we don't mean a static *.html* file. The page should be one generated by WordPress, but choose one, like your "about" page or contact form, that has few moving parts. The results for page load on your more static pages will represent a sort of best-case scenario for how fast you can get pages to load on your app. If static pages are loading slowly, fix that first before moving on to your more complicated pages.

Test your pages with all outside page caches and accelerators turned off

You first want to make sure that your core WordPress app is running well before testing your entire platform including CDNs, reverse proxies, and any other accelerators you are using to speed up the end user experience. If you send 100 concurrent connections a page with a full page cache setup, the first page load might take 10 seconds, then the following 99 may take 1 second. Your average load time will be 1.09 seconds! However, as we discussed earlier that first 10-second load time is really unacceptable and hints at larger problems with your setup.

Test your pages with all outside page caches and accelerators turned on

Turning off the outside accelerators will help you locate issues with your core app. However, you want to run tests with the services on as well. This will help you locate issues with those services. Sometimes they will *slow down* your app.

Test prototypical pages

Whichever *kind* of page your users are most likely to be interacting with are pages you will want to test. If your app revolves around a custom post type, make sure that the CPT pages perform well. If your app revolves around a search of some kind, test the search form and search results pages.

Test atypical pages

While you should spend the most time focusing on the common uses of your app, it is a good idea to test the atypical or longtail uses of your app as well, especially if you have some reason to expect a performance issue there.

Test URLs in groups

Some of the following tools (like Siege and Blitz.io) allow you to specify a list of URLs. By including a list of all of the different types of pages your users will interact with, you get a better idea of what kind of traffic your site can handle. If you expect (or know from analytics) that 80% of your site traffic is on static pages and 20% is on your search pages, you can build a list of URLs with eight static pages and two search results pages, which will simulate that same 80/20 split during testing. If the test shows your site can handle 1,000 visitors per minute this way, it's a pretty good indication that your site will be able to handle 1,000 visitors in a real-world scenario.

Test URLs by themselves

Testing URLs in groups will make the topline results more realistic, but it will make tracking down certain performance issues harder. If your static pages load in under 1 second, but your search results pages load in 10 seconds, doing the 80/20 split test described would result in an average load time of 2.8 seconds. However, the 10-second load time on the search results page may be unacceptable. If you test a single search result page or a group of similar search results pages, you'll be better able to diagnose and fix performance issues with the search functionality on your site.

Test your app from locations outside your web server

The command-line tools described below can be run from the same server serving your website. It's a good idea to run the tools from a different server outside that network so you can get a more realistic idea of what your page loads are when including network traffic to and from the server.

Test your app from inside your web server

It also makes sense to run performance tests from within your web server. This way you remove any effect the outside network traffic will have on the numbers and can better diagnose performance issues that are happening within your server.

Each preceding example has a good counterexample, which is another way of saying you really do have to test everything page of your site under multiple conditions if you want the best chances of finding any performance issues with your site. The important part is to have an idea of what you are trying to test and to try as much as possible to reduce outside influences on the one piece you are focusing on.

Chrome Debug Bar

The Google Chrome Debug Bar is a popular tool with web developers that can be used to analyze and debug HTML, JavaScript, and CSS on websites. The Network tab also allows you to view all requests to a website, their responses, and the time each request took.

Similar tabs exist in the Firebug plugin for Firefox and in Internet Explorer's Developers Tools.

To test your site's page load time using the Chrome Debug Bar:

1. Open Chrome.
2. Click the Chrome menu and go to Tools → Developer Tools.
3. Click the Network tab of the debug bar that shows in the bottom pane.
4. Navigate to the page you want to test.
5. You will get a report of all of the requests made to the server.

6. Scroll to the bottom to see the total number of requests and final page load time.

Figure 16-1 shows an example of the Chrome Debug Bar running on a website.

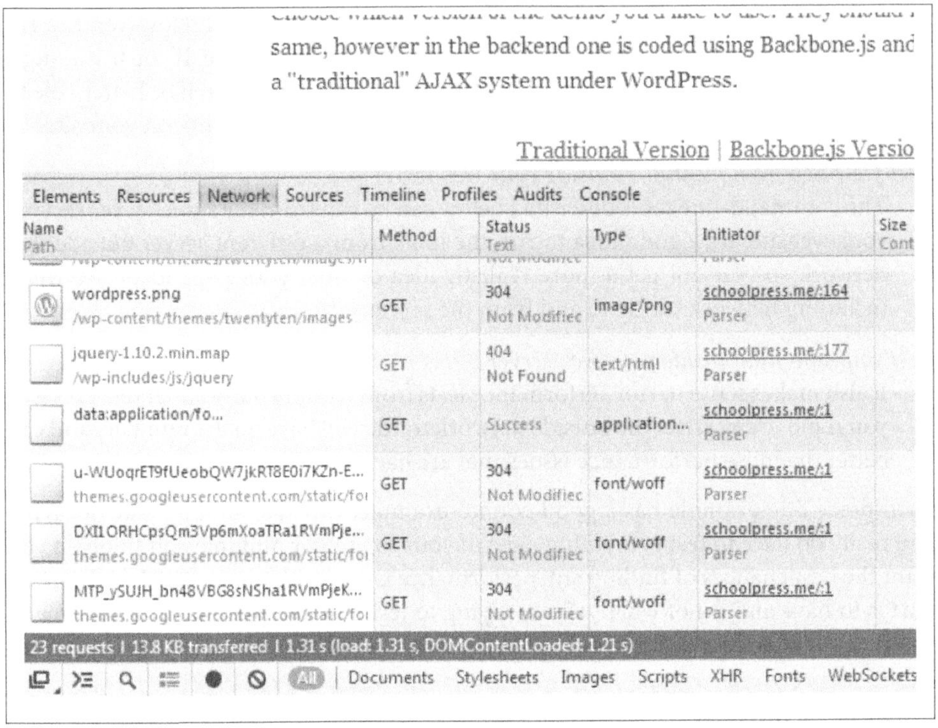

Figure 16-1. A shot of the Network tab of the Chrome Debug Bar

The final report will look something like the following:

```
19 requests  |  35.7 KB transferred  |  1.42 s (load: 1.16 s, DOMContentLoaded: 1.10 s)
```

This line is telling us the number of requests, the total amount of data transferred to and from the server, the final load time, and also the amount of time it took to load the DOM.

A DOMContentLoaded action is fired once all of the HTML of a given site has been loaded, but before any images, JavaScript, or CSS may have finished loading. For this reason the "DOMContentLoaded" time will be smaller than the total load time reported by the debug bar.

The Chrome Debug Bar is a crude way to test load times. You have to do multiple loads manually and keep track of the load times to get a good average. However, the debug bar does give you useful information about individual file and script load times, which can be used to find bottlenecks in your site images or scripts.

When testing page load times with the Google Chrome Debug Bar, the first time you visit a web page will typically be much slower than subsequent loads. This is because CSS, JavaScript, and images will be cached by the browser. Additional server-side caching may also affect load times. Keep this in mind when testing load times. Unless you are trying to test page loads with caching enabled, you may want to disable caching in your browser and on the server.

You can also use the Audit tab of the Chrome Debug Bar (or the PageSpeed Tools by Google (*http://bit.ly/pagespeed-tool*)) to get recommendations for how to make your website faster. Figure 16-2 shows an example of the report generated by the Audit tab. This chapter will cover the main tools and methods for carrying out the kinds of recommendations made by the PageSpeed audit.

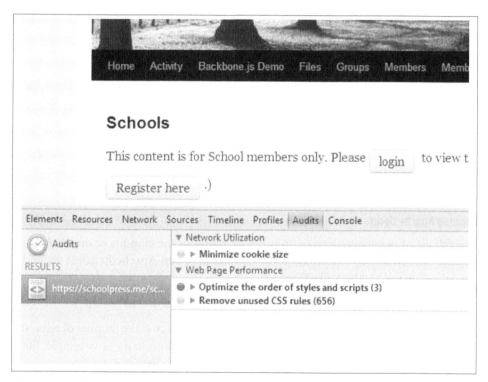

Figure 16-2. The Audit tab of the Chrome Debug Bar

 There is also a PageSpeed Server offered by Google that is in beta at the time of this writing. In the future, this may be a useful tool for speeding up websites through caching, but in our experience, the tool is not flexible enough to work with complicated web apps (that can't simply cache everything). We recommend the other tools covered in this chapter instead.

Apache Bench

Using your web browser, you can get an idea of load times for a single user under whatever load your server happens to be under at the time of testing. To get an idea of how well your server will respond under constant heavy load, you need to use a benchmarking tool like Apache Bench.

Despite the name, Apache Bench can be used to test other HTTP servers besides Apache. What is basically does is spawn the specified number of dummy connections against a website and records the average load times along with other information.

Installing Apache Bench

Apache Bench is available for all Linux distributions. On CENTOS and RedHat servers, you can install it via the httpd-tools package. If you have the yum package manager installed, you can use this command:

```
yum install httpd-tools
```

On Ubuntu servers, Apache Bench will be part of the apache2-utils package. If you have apt-get installed, you can use this command:

```
apt-get install apache2-utils
```

Apache Bench is also available for Windows and should have been installed alongside your Apache installation. Information on how to install and run Apache Bench on Windows can be found in the Apache docs (*http://bit.ly/apache-http*).

Running Apache Bench

The full list of parameters and options can be found in the man file or on the Apache website (*http://bit.ly/apacheparam*). The command to run Apache Bench is ab, and a typical command will look like this:

```
ab -n 1000 -c 100 http://yourdomain.com/index.php
```

The two main parameters for the ab command are n and c. n is the number of requests. c is the number of concurrent requests to perform at one time. In the last example, 1,000 total requests will be made in batches of 100 simultaneous requests at a time.

 If you leave off the trailing slash on your domain or don't specify a *.php* file to load, Apache Bench may fail with an error.

The output will look something like this (The report shows the results for 100 concurrent requests against the homepage of a default WordPress install running on our test server).

```
#ab -n 1000 -c 100 http://yourdomain.com/index.php
This is ApacheBench, Version 2.3 <$Revision: 655654 $>
Copyright 1996 Adam Twiss, Zeus Technology Ltd, http://www.zeustech.net/
Licensed to The Apache Software Foundation, http://www.apache.org/

Benchmarking yourdomain.com (be patient)


Server Software:        Apache/2.2.15
Server Hostname:        yourdomain.com
Server Port:            80

Document Path:          /
Document Length:        251 bytes

Concurrency Level:      100
Time taken for tests:   8.167 seconds
Complete requests:      1000
Failed requests:        993
   (Connect: 0, Receive: 0, Length: 993, Exceptions: 0)
Write errors:           0
Non-2xx responses:      7
Total transferred:      9738397 bytes
HTML transferred:       9516683 bytes
Requests per second:    122.44 [#/sec] (mean)
Time per request:       816.740 [ms] (mean)
Time per request:       8.167 [ms] (mean, across all concurrent requests)
Transfer rate:          1164.40 [Kbytes/sec] received

Connection Times (ms)
              min  mean[+/-sd] median   max
Connect:        0    0   0.4      0       2
Processing:     3  799 127.4    826    1164
Waiting:        2  714 113.7    729    1091
Total:          3  799 127.4    826    1164

Percentage of the requests served within a certain time (ms)
  50%    826
  66%    854
  75%    867
  80%    876
  90%    904
  95%    936
  98%    968
  99%    987
 100%   1164 (longest request)
```

The main stat to track here is the first "Time per request". In the test, the mean is shown as 816.740 milliseconds (ms) or about 0.817 seconds. What this number means [1] is that

---

1. Pun intended.

when there are 100 people hitting the site at the same time, it takes about 0.817 seconds for the server to originate the HTML for the home page

There is a second "Time per request" stat under the first labeled "mean, across all concurrent requests." This is simply the mean divided by the number of concurrent connections. In the example it shows 8.167 ms or about 1 hundredth of a second. It's important to realize that the second "Time per request" number is *not* the load time for a single request. However, across multiple tests, this ratio (average request time / number of concurrent requests) does give you an idea of how well your server handles larger numbers of concurrent users. If the mean across concurrent requests stays the same as you increase -c, it means that your server is scaling well. If it goes up drastically, it means that your server is not scaling well.

Another important stat in this report is "requests per second." This number sometimes maps more directly to your load estimates. You can get real-life "requests per day" or "requests per hour" numbers from your site stats and convert these to requests per second and compare that to the numbers showing up in your reports and then tweak the n and c inputs to match your desired conditions.

Testing with Apache Bench

There are a few tips that will help you when testing a website with Apache Bench.

First, run Apache Bench from somewhere other than the server you are testing since Apache Bench itself will be using up resources required for your web server to run. Running your benchmarks from outside locations will also give you a more realistic idea of page generation times, including network transfer times.

On the other hand, running Apache Bench from the same server the site is hosted on will take the network latency out of the equation and give you an idea of the performance of your stack irrespective of the greater Internet.

Second, start with a small number of simultaneous connections and build up to larger numbers. If you try to test 100,000 simultaneous connections right out the door, you can fry your web server, your testing server, or both. Try 100 connections, then 200, then 500, then 1,000, then more. Large errors or bottlenecks in your server and app performance can come out with as few as 100 connections. Once you pass those tests, try throwing more connections at the app.

Third, run multiple tests. There are a lot of factors that will affect the results of your benchmarks. No two tests will be exactly the same, so try to run a few tests on different pages of your site, at different times, under different conditions, and from different servers and geographical locations. This will give you a more realistic results.

Graphing Apache Bench results with gnuplot

The -g parameter of Apache Bench can be used to specify an output file of the result data in the gnuplot format. This data file can be fed into a gnuplot script to generate a graph image.

> You can also use the -e parameter to specify an output file in CSV (Excel) format.

You can run the following commands to set up some space for your testing and save the gnuplot data:

```
# mkdir benchmarks
# mkdir benchmarks/data
# mkdir benchmarks/graphs
# ab -n 5000 -c 200 -g benchmarks/data/testing.tsv "http://yourdomain.com/"
```

The summary report for this benchmark includes:

```
Requests per second:    95.00 [#/sec] (mean)
Time per request:       2105.187 [ms] (mean)
```

Then you'll need to install gnuplot.[2] Once installed, you can create a couple of gnuplot scripts to generate your graphs. Here are a couple scripts modified from the examples in a blog post by Brad Landers (*http://bit.ly/landersgnu*). Put these in your */benchmark/* folder.

This first graph will draw a line chart showing the distribution of load times. This chart is good at showing how many of your requests loaded under certain times. You can save this script as *plot1.gp*:

```
# Let's output to a png file
set terminal png size 1024,768
# This sets the aspect ratio of the graph
set size 1, 1
# The file we'll write to
set output "graphs/sequence.png"
# The graph title
set title "Benchmark testing"
# Where to place the legend/key
set key left top
# Draw gridlines oriented on the y axis
set grid y
# Label the x-axis
```

---

2. Run yum install gnuplot on CENTOS/Redhat systems. More information can be found at the gnuplot homepage (*http://www.gnuplot.info/*).

```
set xlabel 'requests'
# Label the y-axis
set ylabel "response time (ms)"
# Tell gnuplot to use tabs as the delimiter instead of spaces (default)
set datafile separator '\t'
# Plot the data
plot "data/testing.tsv" every ::2 using 5 title 'response time' with lines
exit
```

This second graph will draw a scatterplot showing the request times throughout the tests. This chart is good at showing the distribution of load times throughout the tests. You can save this script as *plot2.gp.*:

```
# Let's output to a png file
set terminal png size 1024,768
# This sets the aspect ratio of the graph
set size 1, 1
# The file we'll write to
set output "graphs/timeseries.png"
# The graph title
set title "Benchmark testing"
# Where to place the legend/key
set key left top
# Draw gridlines oriented on the y axis
set grid y
# Specify that the x-series data is time data
set xdata time
# Specify the *input* format of the time data
set timefmt "%s"
# Specify the *output* format for the x-axis tick labels
set format x "%S"
# Label the x-axis
set xlabel 'seconds'
# Label the y-axis
set ylabel "response time (ms)"
# Tell gnuplot to use tabs as the delimiter instead of spaces (default)
set datafile separator '\t'
# Plot the data
plot "data/testing.tsv" every ::2 using 2:5 title 'response time' with points
exit
```

To turn your benchmark data into graphs then, run these commands:

```
# cd benchmark
# gnuplot plot1.gp
# gnuplot plot2.gp
```

The resulting charts should look like Figure 16-3 and Figure 16-4.

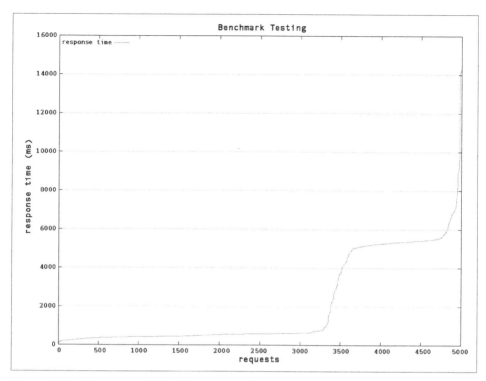

Figure 16-3. The output of the plot1.gp gnuplot script

Seeing the data in graphical form can help a lot. For example, while the summary showed a mean load time of 2,105 ms, the graphs above show us that a little over half of our requests were processed in under 1 second, and the remaining requests took over 4.5 seconds.

You might think that a two-second load time is acceptable, but a four-second load time is not. Based on the summary report, you'd think you were in the clear, when really something like 30%+ of your users would be experiencing load times over four seconds.

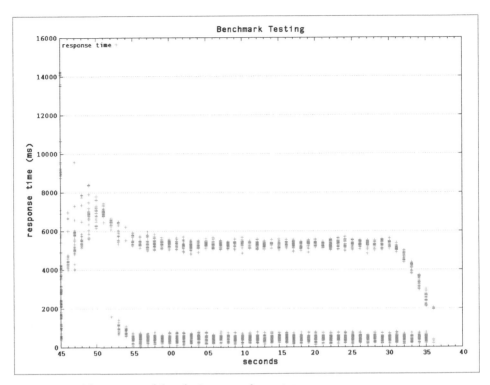

Figure 16-4. The output of the plot2.gp gnuplot script

Siege

Siege is a tool like Apache Benchmark that will hit your site with multiple simultaneous connections and record response times. The report generated by Siege does a good job of showing just the most interesting information.

Siege will need to be installed from source. You can get the latest source files at the Joe Dog software site (*http://www.joedog.org/siege-home/*).

A sample Siege command will look like this:

```
siege -b -c100 -d20 -t2M http://yourdomain.com
```

The -b parameter tells Siege to run a benchmark. The -c100 parameter says to use 100 concurrent users. The -d20 parameter sets the average sleep time between page loads for each user to 20 seconds. And the -t2M parameter says to run the benchmark for two minutes. You can also use -t30S to set a time in seconds or -t1H to set a time in hours.

The output will look like this:

```
** Preparing 100 concurrent users for battle.
The server is now under siege...
```

```
Lifting the server siege...      done.

Transactions:              1160 hits
Availability:              100.00 %
Elapsed time:              119.29 secs
Data transferred:            9.53 MB
Response time:               0.11 secs
Transaction rate:            9.72 trans/sec
Throughput:                  0.08 MB/sec
Concurrency:                 1.05
Successful transactions:     1160
Failed transactions:            0
Longest transaction:         0.26
Shortest transaction:        0.09
```

The server was hit 1,160 times by the 100 users, with an average response time of 0.11 seconds. The server was up 100% of the time, and the longest response time was just 0.26 seconds.

Blitz.io

Blitz.io is a web server for running benchmarks against your websites and web apps. Blitz.io offers a nice GUI for starting a benchmark and generates some beautiful graphical reports showing your app's response times. More importantly, Blitz.io can generate traffic coming from different areas of the world using different user agents to simulate a more realistic traffic scenario.

The service can get a little costly, but can be useful for easily generating final reports that represent a more realistic estimate of how your site will perform in the wild.

W3 Total Cache

There are a few plugins for WordPress that will help you set up various tools to increase the performance of a WordPress site. One plugin in particular, W3 Total Cache, offers just about every performance-increasing method out there.

Frederick Townes, founder of Mashable and the lead developer of W3 Total Cache, shares our belief that WordPress optimization should be done as close to the core WordPress app (the origin) as possible:

> Mileage varies, but one thing we know for certain is that user experience sits right next to content in terms of importance - they go hand in hand. In order for a site or app to actually reach its potential, it's critical that the stack, app and browser are all working in harmony. For WordPress, I try to make that easier than it was in the past with W3 Total Cache.

For many sites with low traffic or little dynamic content, setting up the most common settings in W3 Total Cache is all you will need to scale your app. For other sites, you may want to implement some of the methods bundled with W3 Total Cache individually so you can customize them to your specific app. In general, W3 Total Cache does a great job of making sure that all of the bundled techniques play nice together. For this reason, it's a good idea to work *with* W3 Total Cache to customize things rather than use a solution outside of the plugin that could conflict with it. We'll go over a typical configuration for W3 Total Cache, and also describe briefly how some of the techniques work in general.

W3 Total Cache is available for download from the WordPress.org plugin repository. Once the plugin is installed, a Performance menu item will be added to the admin dashboard. You'll usually have to update permissions on various folders and files on your WordPress install to allow W3 Total Cache to work. The plugin will give you very specific messages to get things set up. Once this is done, you're ready to start enabling the various tools bundled with the plugin.

 The W3 Total Cache plugin is available in its entirety for free through the WordPress plugin repository. You will need to purchase a plan through a content delivery network provider (CDN) to take advantage of the CDN features of W3 Total Cache. And finally, the makers of W3 Total Cache (*http://bit.ly/wpo-w3cache*) offer various support and configuration services through their website.

To enable the tools we want to use, go to the General Settings page of the W3 Total Cache Performance Menu. Find the Enable checkbox for the Page Cache, Minify, Database Cache, Object Cache, and Browser Cache sections, check the box, and then click one of the Save All Settings (see Figure 16-5).

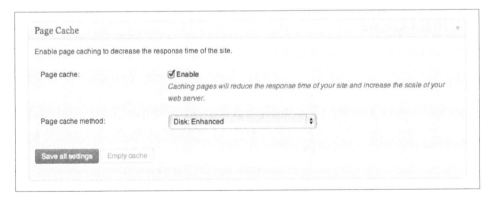

Figure 16-5. Check Enable in the box for each performance technique that you want to use

You can typically get by using the default and recommended settings for all of the W3 Total Cache tools. Your exact settings will depend on the specifics of your app, your hosting setup, and how your users use your app. There are a lot of settings, and we won't go over all of them, but we'll cover a few of the more important settings in the following sections.

Page Cache Settings

A page cache is exactly what it sounds like: the caching of entire web pages after they've been generated. When a new user visits your site, if a cache of the page is available, that static HTML file is served instead of loading the page through PHP and WordPress. If there is no cache or the cache has expired, the page is loaded as it normally would through WordPress.

For a web server like Nginx or Apache, serving a static HTML file is much faster than serving a dynamic PHP file. Serving stacking files avoids all of the database calls and calculations that are required in your dynamic PHP scripts, but it also plays to the strengths of your web stack, which is architected from the OS level up to the web server level primarily to push files around quickly.

Every visit that is served a static HTML file instead of generating a dynamic page in PHP is going to save you some RAM and CPU time. With more resources available, even noncached or noncachable pages are going to load faster. So page caching can greatly speed up page loads on your site, and is one of the primary focuses of web hosts and others trying to serve WordPress sites quickly.

On the Page Cache page under the Performance menu, you'll usually want to enable the following options in the General box: Cache front page, Cache feeds, Cache SSL (https) requests, Cache 404 (not found) pages, and "Don't cache pages for logged in users." See Figure 16-6 for an example.

The "Don't cache pages for logged in users" checkbox is an important option to check because logged-in users will often have access to private account information, and you don't want that stuff getting into the cache. At the very least, you might accidentally show a cached "Howdy, Jason" in the upper right of your website for users who aren't Jason. In the worst-case scenario, you might share Jason's personal email address or account numbers.

For these reasons, full page caching is typically going to cause problems for logged-in members. Other types of caching can still help speed up page load speeds for logged-in members, and we'll cover a few methods later in this chapter.

Figure 16-6. W3 Total Cache page cache general settings

Another important option to get familiar with is the ability to exclude certain pages, paths, and URLs from the page cache. Inside of the Advanced box is a text area labeled "Never cache the following pages." This text area is shown in Figure 16-7.Pages, paths, and URLs added to this setting are going to be ignored by the page cache, and so will be generated fresh on every page load. Place one URL string per line, and regular expressions are allowed.

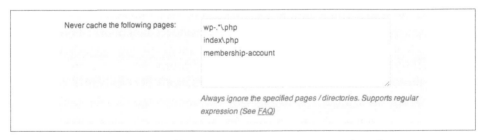

Figure 16-7. Never cache the following pages section in W3 Total Cache Page settings

Some common pages that you will want to exclude from the page cache include checkout pages, login pages, non-JavaScript-based contact forms, API URLs, and any other pages that should be generated dynamically on each load.

Minify

Minifying is the process of both combining and removing excess whitespace and unnecessary characters from source files, typically JavaScript and CSS files, to reduce the file size of those files when served to the web browser. Smaller file sizes means faster load times.

You are probably familiar with files like *jquery.min.js*, which is a minimized version of the jQuery library. W3 Total Cache will automatically minify all of your CSS and JS files for you. You can also enable the minification of HTML files (most notably from the page cache), which can save a bit on page loads as well.

In general, minification is a good idea on production sites. On development sites, you will want to leave minification off so you can better debug CSS and scripting issues.

Database Caching

W3 Total Cache offers database caching. This will store the results of SELECT queries inside of a cache file (or in a memory backend). Repeated calls to the same DB query will pull results from the cache instead of querying the database, which may be on an entirely different service that is part of the slowdown.

If your database server is running on solid state drives (SSDs) or have some kind of caching enabled at the MySQL layer, database caching with W3 Total Cache may not improve performance and can negatively impact it, relatively speaking. So be sure to run benchmarks before and after enabling database caching to see if it helps your site and analyze your slow query log to identify queries that can be manually tuned. Remember, caching scales servers; it doesn't magically resolve fundamentally slow performing queries or code.

If you find that specific queries are taking a long time, you can cache them individually using WP transients or other fragment caching techniques, which are covered later in this chapter.

Object Cache

Object caching is similar to database caching, but the PHP representations of the objects are stored in cache instead of raw MySQL results. Like database caching, object caching can sometimes slow your site down instead of speeding it up; your mileage may vary. Using a persistent object cache (covered later in this chapter) will make it more likely that the object cache will speed up your site. Be sure to benchmark your site before and after configuring object caching.

Object caching is also known to cause issues with some WordPress plugins or activities in WordPress. Object caching is a powerful tool for speeding up your site, but you may have to spend time tweaking the lower levels of the scripts you use to make them work with the plugins and application code for your specific app.

CDNs

A content delivery network or CDN is a service that can serve static files for you—typically images, JavaScript files, and CSS files—on one or many colocated servers that are optimized for serving static files. So instead of loading an image off the same server that is generating the PHP pages for your site, your images will be loaded from whichever CDN server is closest to you. Even if you use your own server as a CDN, you can decrease load times because the browser will be able to load the static files and PHP page at the same time because a separate browser connection will be used for both.

W3 Total Cache can help you integrate with many of the most popular CDNs. The plugin will handle uploading all of your media files, static script files, and page cache files to the CDN, automatically redirect URLs on your site to the CDN and, most importantly, purge modified files for those CDNs that support it.

GZIP Compression

GZIP compression is another neat trick that will often speed up your site. In effect, you trade processing time (when the files are zipped up) for download time (since the files will be smaller). The browser will unzip the files on the receiving end. The time saved by downloading smaller files usually makes up for the time spent zipping and unzipping them. Of course, when using W3 Total Cache, the compression happens once when the cache is built.

But again, like everything else, run a benchmark before and after enabling GZIP compression to make sure that your site is benefiting from the feature.

Hosting

Upgrading your hosting is one of the best things you can do to improve performance for your WordPress app. More CPU and RAM will speed up PHP, MySQL, and your underlying web server. This may be sound obvious, but many people can get caught up in the excitement of optimizing code or using caching techniques to speed up part of their web app while ignoring a simple hosting upgrade that will improve performance across the board.

Of course, we advocate using all of the techniques in this chapter if applicable and within budget. However, one of the earliest decisions you are likely to make, possibly before you even start coding, is where you are going to host your finished web app.

You can find our specific recommendations for hosting WordPress apps on this book's website (*http://bwawwp.com/hosting/*). In this section, we'll cover the different types of hosting to consider.

WordPress-Specific Hosts

As WordPress has become more popular for building websites, hosting companies have cropped up that are configured specifically for running WordPress sites. The earliest of these were Page.ly, Zippykid, WP Engine, and SiteGround.

The WordPress-specific hosts offer managed environments with server-side caching and a support staff that is more knowledgeable about WordPress than a typical hosting company.

The control panels for these hosts are similar to shared hosting plans, with limited flexibility in adjusting the underlying configuration. On the plus side, these hosts typically handle a lot of your caching setup, do a great job managing spam and denial of service attacks, and can quickly scale your app as load increases. On the downside, the limited configurability can be an issue with certain apps and plans can get pricey for larger sites.

Rolling Your Own Server

The alternative to WordPress-specific managed hosting is to roll your own server, either on dedicated hardware or in a cloud environment.

On the dedicated side, Rackspace is a popular choice, and 1and1 provides powerful hardware at wholesale prices. On the cloud side, Amazon EC2 is very popular, and Digital Ocean is a cost-effective alternative.

No matter which route you go, you will have to set up your own web server, install PHP and MySQL yourself, and manage all of the DNS and other server maintenance yourself. Depending on your needs and situation, this could be a good thing or a bad thing. If you need a more specific configuration for your app, you have to roll your own server. On the other hand, you'll have to spend time or money on server administration that might be better spent elsewhere.

It's important to know where your limits are in terms of server administration. For example, Jason is very experienced setting up web servers like Apache and configuring and maintaining PHP and MySQL. On the other hand, he has little experience managing a firewall against denial of service attacks or load balancing across multiple servers. You'll want to choose a hosting company and option that works to your strengths and makes up for your weaknesses.

Rolling your own server and getting 10 times the raw performance for 1/10th the cost of a shared hosting plan can feel pretty good. But when you find yourself up at 3 a.m., wasting time struggling to keep your server alive against automated hacking attempts from foreign countries, the monthly fee of the managed options may not seem so steep.

Below, we'll go quickly over a few common setups for Linux-based servers running WordPress. Details on how to set up each individual configuration are constantly evolving. We will try to always have links to the most recent instructions and reviews online at the book's website (*http://bwawwp.com/servers/*).

 Best practices for setting up and running web servers and the various caching tools that speed them up are changing all the time. Also, instructions will depend on your particular server, which version of Linux it is running, which other tools you are using, and the specifics of the app itself. The proper way to use the information in the rest of this chapter is to go over the instructions provided here and in the linked to articles to get an idea of how the technique being covered works. If you decide to implement the technique on your own server, do some research (Google) to find a tutorial or instructions that are up to date and more specific to your situation.

Apache server setup

As the most popular web server software in use today, it is usually fairly painless to install Apache on any flavor of Linux server.

Once set up, there are a few things you can do to optimize the performance of Apache for your WordPress app:

- Disable unnecessary modules loaded by default.
- Set up Apache to use prefork or worker multi-processing, depending on your need. A good overview of each option can be found at Understanding Apache 2 MPM (worker vs prefork) (*http://bit.ly/apache2mpm*). Prefork is the default and what is usually best for running WordPress.
- If using the Apache Prefork Multi-Processing Module (default), configure the StartServers, MinSpareServers, MaxSpareServers, ServerLimit, MaxClients, and MaxRequestsPerChild values.
- If using the worker Multi-Processing Module, configure the StartServers, MaxClients, MinSpareThreads, MaxSpareThreads, ThreadsPerChild, and MaxRequestsPerChild values.

There are a couple settings in particular to pay attention to when optimizing Apache for your hardware and the app it's running. These settings typically have counterparts in other web servers as well. The concepts behind them should be applicable to any web server running WordPress.

The following settings and instructions assume you are using the more common prefork module for Apache:

MaxClients

When Apache is processing a request to serve a file or PHP script, the server creates a child process to handle that request. The MaxClients setting in your Apache configuration tells Apache the maximum number of child processes to create.

After reaching the MaxClients number, Apache will queue up any other incoming requests. So if MaxClients is set too low, your visitors will experience long load times as they wait for Apache to even start to process their requests.

If MaxClients is set to high, Apache will use up all of your RAM and will start to use swap memory, which is stored on the hard drive and much much slower than physical RAM. When this happens, your visitors will experience long load times since their requests will be handled using the slower swap memory.

Besides simply being slower, using swap memory also requires more CPU as the memory is swapped from hard disks to RAM and back again, which can lead to lower performance overall. When your server backs up like this, it's called thrashing and can quickly spiral out of control and eventually will lock up your server.

So it's important to pick a good value for your MaxClients setting. To determine an appropriate value for MaxClients for your Apache server, take the amount of server memory you want to dedicate to Apache (typically as much as possible after you subtract the amount that MySQL and any other services on your server use) and then divide that by the average memory footprint of your Apache processes.

There is no exact way to figure out how much memory your services are using or how much memory each Apache process takes. It's best to start conservatively and to tweak the values as you watch in real time.

Using the command top -M we can see the total memory on our server, how much is free, and how much active processes are currently using. On our test server, which is under no load, I see that we have 11.7 GB of memory and 10.25 GB of that free. If we want to do a 50/50 split between Apache and MySQL (another assumption you should test out and adjust to your specific app), we can dedicate about 4.5 GB to Apache, 4.5 GB to MySQL, and leave the rest (up to 2.7 GB in this case) for padding and other services running on the server.

Figure 16-8 shows an example of the output from running the top command.

```
 root@u17134797:~                                                    _  □  X
top - 19:16:27 up 88 days,  4:00,  2 users,  load average: 2.97, 0.68, 0.22
Tasks: 149 total,   9 running, 140 sleeping,   0 stopped,   0 zombie
Cpu(s): 96.2%us,  3.5%sy,  0.0%ni,  0.0%id,  0.0%wa,  0.0%hi,  0.3%si,  0.0%st
Mem:    11.731G total, 1652.238M used,   10.117G free,  179.586M buffers
Swap: 4095.984M total,    0.000k used, 4095.984M free,  999.453M cached

  PID USER      PR  NI  VIRT  RES  SHR S %CPU %MEM    TIME+  COMMAND
29098 apache    20   0  285m  28m  17m R 26.0  0.2  0:04.08 httpd
28891 apache    20   0  285m  27m  17m R 25.3  0.2  0:04.44 httpd
29304 apache    20   0  285m  28m  17m R 25.3  0.2  0:03.77 httpd
15956 apache    20   0  289m  42m  29m S 25.0  0.4  0:05.69 httpd
15957 apache    20   0  297m  50m  35m S 25.0  0.4  0:06.05 httpd
15959 apache    20   0  288m  42m  31m R 25.0  0.4  0:06.16 httpd
29303 apache    20   0  286m  28m  17m S 25.0  0.2  0:03.76 httpd
15962 apache    20   0  287m  39m  29m R 24.3  0.3  0:05.82 httpd
28036 apache    20   0  317m  67m  34m S 24.3  0.6  0:04.91 httpd
29305 apache    20   0  286m  28m  17m S 24.3  0.2  0:03.75 httpd
29301 apache    20   0  285m  28m  17m S 24.0  0.2  0:03.64 httpd
15963 apache    20   0  289m  37m  26m R 23.6  0.3  0:05.56 httpd
15965 apache    20   0  307m  54m  23m S 23.6  0.5  0:05.46 httpd
29097 apache    20   0  286m  28m  17m R 23.6  0.2  0:04.12 httpd
15954 apache    20   0  299m  57m  35m S 23.0  0.5  0:05.78 httpd
15960 apache    20   0  298m  47m  32m R 22.6  0.4  0:05.54 httpd
28799 root      20   0  772m 7624  940 S  5.3  0.1  0:00.90 siege
```

Figure 16-8. Using the top command to figure out how much memory is available

To figure out how much memory Apache needs for each process, you can use top -M again, when the server is under normal loads. Look for processes running the httpd command. If we see our app using about 20 MB of memory for each process, we would divide 4.5 GB (~4600 MB) by 20 MB and get 230, meaning our server should be able to support 230 MaxClients in 4.5 GB of memory.

When setting the MaxClients value, set the ServerLimit value to the same number. ServerLimit is a kind of MaxMaxClients that can only be changed when Apache is restarted. The MaxClients setting can be changed by other scripts while Apache is running, although this isn't commonly done. So theoretically ServerLimit could be set higher than MaxClients and some process could change the MaxClients value up or down while Apache was running.

MaxRequestsPerChild
Each child process or client spun up by Apache will handle multiple requests one after another. If MaxRequestsPerChild is set to 0, these child processes are never shut down, which is good since it lowers the overhead of spinning up a new child process but can be bad if there is a memory leak in your app. Setting MaxRequestsPerChild to a very high number like 1,000 or 2,000 is a nice compromise so that new processes aren't shut down and restarted too often but if a memory leak does occur it will be cleaned up when the child process is eventually shut down.

KeepAlive

By default, the KeepAlive setting of Apache is turned off, meaning that after serving a file to a client browser, the connection is closed. A separate connection is opened and closed for each file request from that browser. Since a single page may have several files associated with it in the form of images, JavaScript, and CSS, this can lead to a lot of unnecessary opening and closing of connections.

With KeepAlive turned on, Apache will keep the first connection from a web browser open and serve all subsequent requests from the same browser session through that connection. After sitting idle with no requests from the same browser session, Apache will close the connection. Using a single connection instead of many can lead to great performance gains for some sites, especially if there are a lot of images or separate CSS and JavaScript on each page (you should probably be minimizing your CSS and JavaScript into one file for each anyway).

On the other hand, turning KeepAlive on requires more RAM since each connection will hold onto the memory for each request as it keeps a connection open.

It's useful to experiment with turning KeepAlive on. If you do, you should change the KeepAliveTimeout value from the default 15 seconds to something smaller like 2-3 seconds—or something closer to the real load times of a single page visit on your site. This will free up the memory faster.

Also, if you turn KeepAlive on, you should probably adjust the MaxClients and MaxRequestsPerChild settings. Since each child process will be using more memory as it keeps the connection open, you may need to adjust your MaxClients value lower to avoid running out of memory. Since each connection counts as one request with respect to MaxRequestsPerChild, you may want to adjust your MaxRequestsPerChild value lower since there will be fewer requests overall per visit.

Some other good articles on optimizing Apache include:

- "Apache Performance Tuning" (*http://bit.ly/apache-tuning*)
- "Apache MPM Prefork" (*http://bit.ly/apache-prefork*)
- "Apache MPM Worker" (*http://bit.ly/apache-worker*)
- "How to Set MaxClients in Apache/Prefork" at Fuscata (*http://bit.ly/set-maxclients*)
- "Optimize Apache for WordPress" by Drew Strojny (*http://bit.ly/optimize-apache*)
- "Apache Optimization: KeepAlive On or Off?" by Abdussamad (*http://bit.ly/apache-keepalive*)

Nginx server setup

A popular alternative to Apache that is gaining a lot of momentum right now is Nginx. The main advantage of Nginx is that it is an *asynchronous* web server whereas Apache is a *process-based* web server. What this means in practice is that when many simultaneous clients hit an Apache-based server, a new thread is created for each connection. With Nginx, all connections are handled by a single thread or a small group of threads. Since each thread requires a block of memory, Nginx is more memory efficient and so can process a higher number of simultaneous requests than Apache can.

Some good articles about installing and configuring Nginx include:

- "Nginx," an article from the WordPress Codex (*http://bit.ly/codex-nginx*)
- "How to Install WordPress with nginx on Ubuntu 12.04" by Etel Sverdlov (*http://bit.ly/wp-nginx*)

Nginx in front of Apache

The trade-off in using Nginx over Apache is that Nginx has fewer module extensions than Apache. Some modules like `mod_rewrite` for "pretty permalinks" will have to be ported over to the Nginx way of doing things. Other modules may not have Nginx equivalents.

For this reason, it is becoming popular to set up a dual web server configuration where Nginx serves cached web pages and static content and Apache serves dynamically generated content. One article explaining how to configure this setup is "How To Configure Nginx as a Front End Proxy for Apache" by Etel Sverdlov (*http://bit.ly/nginx-frontend*).

The main advantage of this setup is that static files will be served from Nginxk, which is configured to serve static files quickly; this will ease the memory burden of Apache. If you are already using a CDN for your static files, then using Nginx for static files would be redundant. Also, because you are still serving PHP files through Apache, you won't gain the memory benefits of Nginx on dynamically generated pages. For these reasons, it is probably better to use Nginx for both static files and PHP or Apache with a CDN for static files.

MySQL optimization

To get the best performance out of WordPress, you will want to make sure that you've configured MySQL properly for your hardware and site use and that you've optimized the database queries in your app.

Optimizing MySQL configuration

The MySQL configuration file is typically found at */etc/my.cnf* or */etc/mysql/my.cnf* and can be tweaked to improve performance on your site. There are several interelated settings. The best way to figure out a good configuration for your hardware and site is to use the MySQLTuner Perl script (*http://mysqltuner.com*).

After downloading the MySQLTuner script, you will also need to have Perl installed on your server. Then run `perl mysqltuner.pl` and follow the recommendations given. The output will look like the following:

```
-------- General Statistics ----------------------------------------------
[--] Skipped version check for MySQLTuner script
[OK] Currently running supported MySQL version 5.5.32
[OK] Operating on 64-bit architecture

-------- Storage Engine Statistics ---------------------------------------
[--] Status: +Archive -BDB -Federated +InnoDB -ISAM -NDBCluster
[--] Data in MyISAM tables: 35M (Tables: 395)
[--] Data in InnoDB tables: 16M (Tables: 316)
[--] Data in PERFORMANCE_SCHEMA tables: 0B (Tables: 17)
[!!] Total fragmented tables: 327

-------- Security Recommendations  ---------------------------------------
[OK] All database users have passwords assigned

-------- Performance Metrics ---------------------------------------------
[--] Up for: 26d 22h 6m 21s (8M q [3.755 qps], 393K conn, TX: 15B, RX: 1B)
[--] Reads / Writes: 95% / 5%
[--] Total buffers: 168.0M global + 2.8M per thread (151 max threads)
[OK] Maximum possible memory usage: 583.2M (7% of installed RAM)
[OK] Slow queries: 0% (0/8M)
[OK] Highest usage of available connections: 21% (33/151)
[OK] Key buffer size / total MyISAM indexes: 8.0M/21.1M
[OK] Key buffer hit rate: 100.0% (84M cached / 40K reads)
[!!] Query cache is disabled
[OK] Sorts requiring temporary tables: 0% (3 temp sorts / 1M sorts)
[!!] Joins performed without indexes: 23544
[!!] Temporary tables created on disk: 26% (359K on disk / 1M total)
[!!] Thread cache is disabled
[OK] Table cache hit rate: 34% (400 open / 1K opened)
[OK] Open file limit used: 68% (697/1K)
[OK] Table locks acquired immediately: 99% (8M immediate / 8M locks)
[OK] InnoDB data size / buffer pool: 16.1M/128.0M

-------- Recommendations -------------------------------------------------
General recommendations:
    Run OPTIMIZE TABLE to defragment tables for better performance
    Enable the slow query log to troubleshoot bad queries
    Adjust your join queries to always utilize indexes
    When making adjustments, make tmp_table_size/max_heap_table_size equal
    Reduce your SELECT DISTINCT queries without LIMIT clauses
    Set thread_cache_size to 4 as a starting value
Variables to adjust:
    query_cache_size (>= 8M)
    join_buffer_size (> 128.0K, or always use indexes with joins)
```

```
tmp_table_size (> 16M)
max_heap_table_size (> 16M)
thread_cache_size (start at 4)
```

One thing to note is that MySQLTuner will give better recommendations if it has at least one day's worth of log data to process. For this reason, it should be run 24 hours after MySQL has been restarted. You'll want to follow the recommendations given, wait 24 hours, and run the script again, then rinse and repeat over a few days to narrow in on optimal settings for your MySQL setup.

Optimizing DB queries

A large source of load-time-draining process cycles is unoptimized, unnecessary, or otherwise slow MySQL queries. Finding and optimizing these slow SQL queries will speed up your site. Caching database queries, either at the database level or through the use of transients for specific queries, will help with slow queries, but you definitely want the original SQL as optimized as possible.

The first step in optimizing your database queries is to find out which queries are slow or otherwise undeeded. A great tool to do this is the Black Box Debug Bar (*http://bit.ly/blackboxdebug*) plugin.

The Black Box Debug Bar, shown in Figure 16-9, adds a bar to the top of your website that will show you a page's load time in milliseconds, the number of SQL queries made and how long they took, and the number of PHP errors, warnings, and notices on the page.

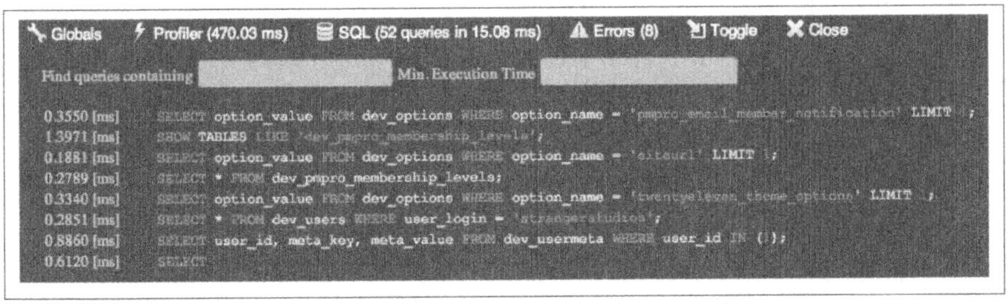

Figure 16-9. The Black Box Debug Bar added to the top of all pages on your site while active

If you click on the SQL icon in the debug bar, you will also see all of the SQL queries made and the individual query times.

Viewing the final generated SQL query is especially useful for queries that might be constructed across several PHP functions or with a lot of branching logic. For example, the final query to load posts on the blog homepage of WordPress is generated using many variables stored in the $wp_query object depending on if a search is being made, what page of the archive you are on, etc.

With the debug bar turned on, you can browse around your site looking for queries that are slow or outright unnecessary.

Another way to find slow SQL queries is to enable slow query logging in your MySQL configuration file. This will help find slow queries that come up in real use. You don't want to rely on the slow query log, but it can catch some real-world use cases that won't come up in testing.

To enable slow query logging in MySQL, find your *my.cnf* or *my.ini* file and add the following lines:

```
slow-query-log = 1;
slow-query-log-file = /path/to/a/log/file;
```

After updating your MySQL configuration file, you will need to restart MySQL.

When trying to optimize your DB queries, you should always be on the lookout for:

- Cases where the same SQL query is being run more than once per page load. Store the result in a global variable or somewhere else to access it later in the page load.

- Cases where one SQL query can be used instead of many. For example, plugins can load all of their options at once instead of using a separate query or getOp tion() call for each option.

- Cases where a SQL query is being run, but the result is not being used. Some queries may only need to be run in the dashboard or only on the frontend or only on a specific page. Change the WordPress hook being used or add PHP logic around these calls so they are only executed when needed.

If you find a necessary query that is taking a particularly long time, how you go about optimizing it will be very specific to the query itself. Here are some things to try:

- Adjust queries to use only indexed columns in WHERE, ON, ORDER BY, and GROUP BY clauses.

- Add WHERE clauses to your JOINs so you are joining smaller subtables.

- Use a different table to store your data, for example, using taxonomies versus post meta, which is covered in Chapter 5.

- Add indexes to columns that are used in WHERE, ON, ORDER BY, and GROUP BY clauses.

advanced-cache.php and object-cache.php

The keystones[3] that enable all of these caching techniques, including the ones used by the W3 Total Cache plugin, are the *advanced-cache.php* and/or *object-cache.php* files, which can be added to the */wp-content/* directory.

To tell WordPress to check for the *advanced-cache.php* and *object-cache.php* files, add the line define('WP_CACHE', true); to your *wp-config.php* file.

The *advanced-cache.php* file is loaded by *wp-settings.php* before the majority of the WordPress source files are loaded. Because of this, you can execute certain code (e.g., to look for a cache file on the server) and then stop PHP execution with an exit; command before the rest of WordPress loads.

If a *object-cache.php* file is present, it will be used to define the WP Cache API functions instead of the built-in functions found in *wp-includes/cache.php*. By default, WordPress will cache all options in an array during each page load. Transients are stored in the database. If you write your own *object-cache.php* file, you can tell WordPress to store options and transients in a RAM-based memory that is persisted between page loads.

Plugins like W3 Total Cache are mostly a frontend for generating an *advanced-cache.php* file based on the settings you choose. You can also choose to roll your own *advanced-cached.php* or *object-cache.php* file or use one configured already for a specific caching tool or technique. Most of the caching techniques that follow involve using a specific *advanced-cache.php* or *object-cache.php* file to interact with another service for caching.

If you add a header comment to the top of your *.php* files dropped into the *wp-content* directory with the same structure as a plugin (plugin name, description, etc), then that information will show up on the Drop-ins tab of the plugins page in the WordPress dashboard.

Alternative PHP Cache (APC)

Alternative PHP Cache is an extension for PHP that acts as an opcode cache and can be used to store key-value pairs for object caching.

---

3. I suppose there can only be one keystone. You'll have to forgive me this time.

Opcode caching

When a PHP script is executed, it is compiled to opcodes that are ready to be executed by the server. With an opcode cache, part of the compiling is cached until the underlying PHP scripts are updated.

Key-value cache

APC also adds the `apc_store()` and `apc_fetch()` functions, which can be used to store and retrieve bits of information from memory. A value stored in memory can typically be loaded faster than a value stored on a hard disk or in a database, especially if that value requires some computation. Plugins like W3 Total Cache or APC Object Cache Backend (*http://wordpress.org/plugins/apc/*) can be used to store the WordPress object cache inside of RAM using APC.

These are the rough steps to set up APC:

1. Install APC on your server, configure PHP to use it, and restart your web server.
2. Configure WordPress to use APC using W3 Total Cache, APC Object Cache Backend, or another plugin or custom *object-cache.php* script.

Here are some good links for information on using APC in general and with WordPress:

- "Alternative PHP Cache" at PHP.net (*http://bit.ly/php-apc-manual*)
- "How to Install Alternative PHP Cache (APC) on a Cloud Server Running Ubuntu 12.04" by Danny Sipos (*http://bit.ly/install-php-cache*)

 PHP versions 5.5 and higher come compiled with OPCache, which is an alternative to APC for opcode caching. However OPCache does not have the same store and fetch functionality that APC has for object caching. For this reason, you need to either disable OPCache and use APC or run an updated version of APC called APCu alongside OPCache. APCu offers the store and fetch functionality but leaves the opcode caching to OPCache.

Memcached

Memcached is a system that allows you to store key-value pairs in RAM that can be used as a backend for an object cache in WordPress. Memcached is similar to APC, minus the opcode caching.

You can store your full-page caches inside of Memcached instead of files on the server for faster load times, although the performance gain will be slower for modern servers with faster solid-state drives. Memcached can be run on both Apache- and Nginx-based servers.

One of the advantages of Memcached over other object caching techniques (including Redis and APC) is that a Memcached cache can be distributed over multiple servers. So if you have multiple servers hosting your app, they can all use the one Memcached instance to store a common cache instead of having their own (often redundant) cache stores on each server. Interesting note: the enterprise version of W3 Total Cache allows you to use APC across multiple servers seamlessly.

These are the rough steps to set up Memcached:

1. Install the Memcached service on your server, give it some memory, and run it.
2. Use W3 Total Cache or the Memcached Object Cache (*http://bit.ly/wp-memcached*) plugin to update the WordPress object cache to use Memcached.

Here are some good links for information on using Memcached in general and with WordPress:

- "Memcached" at PHP.net (*http://bit.ly/php-mem*)
- the Memcached website (*http://memcached.org/*)
- "WordPress + Memcached" by Scott Taylor (*http://bit.ly/scott-taylor*)

Redis

Redis is another system for storing key-value pairs in memory on your Apache- or Nginx-based web server. Like Memcached, it can be used as a backend for your WordPress object cache or page cache.

Unlike Memcached, Redis can store data in lists, sets, and sorted sets in addition to simple key-value hashes. These data structures are always useful for your apps, and the maturity of Memcached, which was created a few years before Redis, is appreciated by some developers.

These are the rough steps to setup Redis:

1. Install Redis on your server, give it some memory, and run it.
2. Use a replacement for the WordPress *index.php* that searches the Redis cache and serves pages from there if found. A popular version is wp-redis-cache.
3. Run a plugin or other script to clear the Redis cache on post updates/etc.

Here are some good links for information on using Redis in general and with WordPress:

- The Redis website (*http://redis.io*)
- WP-Redis-Cache (*http://bit.ly/wp-redis-cache*)

- "WordPress with Redis as a Frontend Cache" by Jim Westergren (*http://bit.ly/wp-with-redis*)

Varnish

Varnish is a reverse proxy that can sit in front of your Apache or Nginx setup and serve cached versions of complete web pages to your visitors. Because your web server and PHP are never even loaded for cached pages, Varnish will outperform Memcached and Redis for full page caching. On the other hand, Varnish is not meant to do object caching and so will only work for static pages on your site.

These are the rough steps for setting up Varnish with WordPress:

1. Install Varnish on your server.
2. Configure Varnish to ignore the dashboard at */wp-admin/* and other sections of your site which shouldn't be cached.
3. Use a plugin to purge the Varnish cache when posts are updated and other updates are done to WordPress. Some popular plugins to do this are WP-Varnish (*http://bit.ly/wp-varnish*) and Varnish HTTP Purge (*http://bit.ly/varnish-http*).

Here are some good links for information on using Varnish in general and with WordPress.

- The Varnish website (*https://www.varnish-cache.org/*)
- "How to Install and Customize Varnish for WordPress" by Austin Gunter (*http://bit.ly/custom-varnish*)
- Varnish 3.0 Configuration Templates (*http://bit.ly/varnish30*)

Batcache

Batcache uses APC or Memcached as a backend for full-page caching in WordPress. The end result should be similar to using W3 Total Cache or another plugin integrated with APC or Memcached for full-page caching.

One thing unique to Batcache is that the caching is only enabled if a page has been loaded two times within 120 seconds. A cache is then generated and used for the next 300 seconds. These values can be tweaked to fit your purposes, but the basic idea here is that Batcache is meant primarily as a defense against traffic spikes like those that happen when a website is "slashdotted," "techcrunched," "reddited," or linked to by any of the other websites large enough to warrant its own verb. Another benefit to caching only pages under heavy load is that a lower amount of RAM is required to store the cache.

If you tweak the default settings, you can set up Batcache to work as an always-on full page caching system.

These are the rough steps for setting up Batcache with WordPress:

1. Set up Memcached or APC to be used as the in-memory key-value store for Batcache.

2. Download the Batcache plugin from the WordPress repository.

3. Move the *advanced-cache.php* file to the *wp-content* folder of your WordPress install.

Batcache has an interesting pedigree since it was developed specifically for WordPress. It was first used on WordPress VIP sites and WordPress.com. Batcache was originally called Supercache, but the popular caching plugin WP Super Cache was released around the same time and the Supercache/Batcache authors changed the name from one famous DC Comics caped crusader to another. Here are some good links for information on using Batcache with WordPress.

- The Batcache plugin (*http://bit.ly/wp-batcache*)
- "WordPress Caching using APC and Batcache" by Jonathan D. Johnson (*http://bit.ly/cache-apc*)
- Original Batcache announcement and overview by Andy Skelton (*http://bit.ly/batcache-app*)

Selective Caching

The caching methods described so far have either been full page caches or otherwise "dumb" caches storing every WordPress object in cache. Rules could then be added to tell the cache to avoid certain URLs or conditions, but basically you were caching all of the things.

Sometimes you will want to do things the other way around. You'll want to cache specific pages and objects. This is typically done by storing information within a WordPress *transient*. If you have a persistent object enabled like APC, that stored object will load that much faster.

What we're calling *selective caching* here is being commonly referred to as *fragment caching*. No matter the term, the concept is the same: caching parts of a rendered web page instead of the full page.

For example, you might have a full-page cache enabled through W3 Total Cache or Varnish, but you'll need to exclude logged-in users from seeing the cache because member-specific information could get cached. Mary could end up seeing "Welcome, Bob" in the upper right of the page. Still, some portion of each page might be the same for each user or certain kinds of users. We can selectively cache that information if it takes excessive database calls or computation to compile.

Good candidates for selective caching include reports, complicated post queries, and other bits of content that require a lot of time or memory to compute.

The Transient API

Transients are the preferred way for WordPress apps to set and get values out of the object cache. If no persistent caching system is installed, the transients are stored inside of the wp_options table of the WordPress database. If an object caching system like APC, APCu, Memcached, or Redis is installed, then that system is used to store the transients.

At any time, the server could be rebooted or the object cache memory could be cleared, wiping out your stored transients. For this reason, when storing transients, you should always assume that the storage is temporary and unreliable. If the information to be stored needs to be saved, you can still store it inside of a transient redundantly for performance reasons, but make sure you also store it in another way—most likely by saving an option through update_option().

In the SchoolPress app, we need to get an average homework score across all assignments a single student has submitted. The query for this would involve running the average function against the meta_value column of the wp_usermeta table. Running an average for one student with say 10 to 100 assignments wouldn't be too intense; however, if you had a page showing the average score for 20-80 students within one class, that series of computations might take a while to run. To speed this up, we can cache the results of the full class report within a transient, as illustrated in Example 16-1.

This is a perfect use case for using transients because having access to the computed results inside of a transient will speed up repeated loads of the report, but it's OK if the transient suddenly disappears because we can always compute the averages from scratch.

Example 16-1. SPClass

```
class SPClass()
{
        /* ... constructor and other methods ... */

        function getStudents()
        {
                /* gets all users within the BuddyPress group for this class */
```

```
                return $this->students; //array of student objects
        }

        function getAssignmentAverages()
        {
                //check for transient
        $this->assignment_averages =
            get_transient('class_assignment_averages_' . $this->ID);

                //no transient found? compute the averages
                if(empty($this->assignment_averages))
                {
                        $this->assignment_averages = array();
                        $this->getStudents();

                        foreach($this->students as $student)
                        {
                                $this->assignment_averages[$student->ID] =
                        $student->getAssignmentAverages();
                        }

                        //save in transient
                        set_transient('class_assignment_averages_' .
                $this->ID, $this->assignment_averages);
                }

                //return the averages
                return $this->assignment_averages;
        }
}

//clear assignment averages transients when an assignment is graded
public function clear_assignment_averages_transient($assignment_id)
{
    //class id is stored as postmeta on the assignment post
        $assignment = new Assignment($assignment_id);
    $class_id = $assignment->class_id;

        //clear any assignment averages transient for this class
    delete_transient('class_assignment_averages_' . $class_id);
}
add_action('sp_update_assignment_score', array('SPClass',
    'clear_assignment_averages_transient'));
```

The example includes a lot of snipped code and makes some assumptions about the SPClass and Student classes. However, you should get the idea of how this report uses transients to store the computed averages, retrieve them, and clear them out on updates.

In the preceding example, we store the array stored in `$this->assignment_averages` in the transient. Alternatively, we could have stored the generated HTML, but storing the array saves us most of the complex database calls and is more flexible.

The function to store a value inside of a transient is `set_transient($transient, $value, $expiration)`, and attributes are as follows:

- $transient—Unique name for the transient, 45 characters or less.
- $value—The value to store. Objects and arrays are automatically serialized and unserialized for you.
- $expiration – An optional parameter to set an expiration for the transient in seconds. Expired transients are deleted by a WordPress garbage collection script. By default, this value is 0 and doesn't expire until deleted.

Notice that we use a descriptive key (`class_assignment_averages_`) followed by the ID of the class group. This way all classes will have their own transient for storing assignment averages.

To retrieve the transient, we simply call `get_transient($transient)`, passing one parameter with the unique name of the transient. If the transient is available and not past expiration, the value is returned. Otherwise the call returns `false`.

To delete the transient before expiration, we simply call `delete_transient($transient)` passing one parameter with the unique name of the transient. Notice that in the example, we hook into the `sp_update_assignment_score` that is fired when any assignment gets scored. We pass an array as the callback for the hook since the method is part of the SPClass class. The "sp_update_assignment_score" hook passes the `$assignment_id` as a parameter. The callback method uses this ID to find the assignment and the associated class ID, then deletes the corresponding `class_assignment_averages_{ID}` transient.

If you were storing transients related to posts or users, you may want to clear them out on "save_post" or "profile_update," respectively.

 The transient functions are fairly simple wrappers for the functions defined in the default *wp-includes/cache.php* or your drop-in *object-cache.php* file: `wp_cache_set()`, `wp_cache_get()`, and `wp_cache_delete()`. If you wanted, you could call these functions directly. Information on these functions can be found in the WordPress Codex (*http://bit.ly/class-ref*).

Multisite Transients

In network installs, the transients set with `set_transient()` are specific to the current network site. So our "class_assignment_averages_1" set on one network site won't be available on another network site. (This makes sense in the assignment scores example.)

If you'd like to set a transient network-wide, WordPress offers variants of the transient functions:

- `set_site_transient($transient, $value, $expiration)`
- `get_site_transient($transient)`
- `delete_site_transient($transient)`

These functions work the same as the basic transient functions; however, the `_site_transients` are stored in `wp_site_options` instead of the individual network site `wp_options` tables.

Because the transients set with `set_site_transient()` prefix the string `_site` to the front of the transient name, you only have 40 characters to work with for the name versus the usual 45.

Finally, it should be noted that a different set of hooks fire before and after a network-wide transient is set versus a single network site transient. If you've written code that hooks into `pre_set_transient`, `set_transient`, or `setted_transient`, you may need to have that code also hook into `pre_set_site_transient`, `pre_set_transient`, and `pre_setted_site_transient`.

Using JavaScript to Increase Performance

A useful tactic for speeding up page loads is to load certain parts of a web page through JavaScript instead of generating the same output through dynamic PHP.

This technique can make pages appear to load faster since the frame of the web page can be loaded quickly while the time-intensive portion of the site can loaded over time while a "loading…" icon flashes on the screen or a progress bar fills up. Your users will get immediate feedback that the page has loaded along with an indication to sit tight for a few seconds while the page renders.

Using JavaScript can also literally speed up your page loads. If you load all of the dynamic content of a page through JavaScript, you can then use a page cache to serve the rest of the page without hitting PHP.

For example, on many blogs, the only piece of dynamic content is the comments. Using the built-in WordPress comments and a full page cache means that recent comments won't show up on the site until the cache clears. However, if you use a JavaScript-based commenting system like those provided through the JetPack plugin or a service like Disqus or Facebook, then your comments section is simply a bit of static JavaScript code that loads the dynamic comments from another server.

Example 16-2 shows a bare-bones example of how you can go about loading specific content through JavaScript on an otherwise static page.

Example 16-2. JS Display Name plugin

```php
<?php
/*
Plugin Name: JS Display Name
Plugin URI: http://bwawwp.com/js-display-name/
Description: A way to load the display name of a logged-in user through JS
Version: .1
Author: Jason Coleman
Author URI: http://bwawwp.com
*/


/*
        use this function to place the JavaScript in your theme
        if(function_exists("jsdn_show_display_name"))
        {
                jsdn_show_display_name();
        }
*/
function jsdn_show_display_name($prefix = "Welcome, ")
{
?>
<p>
        <script src="<?php echo admin_url(
        "/admin-ajax.php?action=jsdn_show_display_name&prefix=" .
            urlencode($prefix)
        );?>"></script>
</p>
<?php
}


/*
This function detects the JavaScript call and returns the user's display name
*/
function jsdn_wp_ajax()
{
        global $current_user;
        if(!empty($current_user->display_name))
        {
                $prefix = sanitize_text_field($_REQUEST['prefix']);
                $text = $prefix . $current_user->display_name;

                header('Content-Type: text/javascript');
        ?>
```

```
            document.write(<?php echo json_encode($text);?>);
            <?php
            }

            exit;
}
add_action('wp_ajax_jsdn_show_display_name', 'jsdn_wp_ajax');
add_action('wp_ajax_nopriv_jsdn_show_display_name', 'jsdn_wp_ajax');
```

Custom Tables

Another tool you will definitely need in your toolbox when building WordPress apps
in general, but specifically when trying to optimize performance, is to build a custom
database table or view to make certain lookups and queries faster.

With SchoolPress, we may need to do lots of queries on the assignment objects. We'll
want to sort by score, class, teacher, student, assignment date, and submission date.
Maybe we need to sort by some combination of those. If those values are stored in the
wp_postmeta table, queries on that data will be slow because (1) the wp_postmeta table
will be large with other nonassignment posts and post meta and (2) the meta_value
column is not indexed.

Indexing the meta_value column would be overkill because we would be indexing a lot
of post meta that we don't need indexed. Inserts into the wp_postmeta table would take
forever and use up a lot of memory.

Switching some of the post meta over to taxonomies wouldn't make much sense, would
be pretty hard to manage, and wouldn't necessarily give us the speed increase that we
need.

The following code is a bit contrived, but at some point you will come across a case
where it is better for you to store your data in a custom table rather than some combination of posts, post meta, and taxonomies.

Our assignments table might look like the following:

```
CREATE TABLE `wp_sp_assignments` (
  `id` bigint(20) unsigned NOT NULL AUTO_INCREMENT,
  `post_id` bigint(20) unsigned,
  `class_id` bigint(20) unsigned,
  `student_id` bigint(20) unsigned,
  `score` int(10),
  `assignment_date` DATETIME,
  `due_date` DATETIME,
  `submission_date` DATETIE
  PRIMARY KEY (`id`),
  UNIQUE KEY `post_id` (`post_id`),
  KEY `class_id` (`class_id`),
  KEY `student_id` (`student_id`),
```

```
    KEY `score` (`score`),
    KEY `asignment_date` (`assignment_date`),
    KEY `due_date` (`due_date`),
    KEY `submission_date` (`submission_date`)
);
```

This is a rather extreme example; every column has an index. It's probably overkill here, but it does allow us to make extremely fast queries against this table joined with the wp_posts table or wp_users table.

If you had a table like this, you would need to hook into the save_post hook to update the corresponding row in wp_sp_assignments like this:

```
function sp_update_assignments_table($post_id)
{
  //get the post
  $post = get_post($post_id);

  //we only care about assignments
  if($post->post_type != "assignment")
    return false;

  //get data ready for insert or replace
  $assignment_data = array(
    "post_id" => $post_id,
    "student_id" => $post->post_author,
    "teacher_id" => $post->teacher_id,
    "score" => $post->score,
    "assignment_date" => $post->assignment_date,
    "due_date" => $post->due_date
    "submission_date" => $post->submission_date
  );

  //look for an existing assignment
  $assignment_id = $wpdb->get_var("SELECT id
                                   FROM wp_sp_assignments
                                   WHERE post_id = '" . $post_id . "'
                                   LIMIT 1");

  //if no assignment id, this is a new assignment
  if(empty($assignment_id))
  {
    $assignment_id = $wpdb->insert("wp_sp_assignments", $assignment_data);
  }
  else
  {
    $assignment_data['id'] = $assignment_id;
    $wpdb->replace("wp_sp_assignments", $assignment_data);
  }

  return $assignment_id;
```

```
}
add_action('save_post', 'sp_update_assignments_table');
```

Bypassing WordPress

Finally, one last technique to help you scale your WordPress app: you don't have to use WordPress for every part of your app.

We've already gone over a few variants of this advice earlier in this chapter. When you use Varnish, you are bypassing WordPress and loading static HTML files instead. When you use *advanced-cache.php*, you are bypassing part of WordPress. When you use JavaScript to load comments from Facebook, you are bypassing WordPress. When you store some of your data in a custom database table, you are bypassing the WordPress framework.

We use WordPress to build our apps because of the benefits of its security, its functionality, and the large community of plugins and solutions. Having your code written with the WordPress platform makes it easy for you to hook into the WordPress CMS and user management. It makes it easy to add hooks into your own code.

However, sometimes the performance downside will outweigh all of the benefits. You don't have to scrap WordPress altogether, but you can bypass WordPress for specific functions.

For example, our last script to get the display name of a user through JavaScript could be written as a simple PHP script that runs a simple SELECT query to get the `dis play_name` column of the user specified in the WordPress user cookie. Doing so could save a few milliseconds off of each page load in your website. If you multiply this across several dynamic bits across your app, the savings can add up.

In most cases, cutting out WordPress like this should be used as a last resort. The speed savings are there but at the cost of complicating your code. Running scripts like this through *admin-ajax.php* like we did cuts out a lot of the overhead of WordPress and still allows your code to interact with other plugins and use built-in WordPress classes and APIs if it need to.

If you are loading a script to export CSV, which is going to take 10 seconds to run anyway, it's not as important to cut off that extra 0.5 seconds.

You should always program things as straightforwardly as possible, in this case through traditional WordPress methods, and only optimize at this level when a bottleneck is found that is worth optimizing. At that point, explore all of the options presented in this chapter to figure out which works best for the specific feature you are optimizing, considering your needs and the team and tools you have at your disposal.

Index

Symbols

$authordata global variable, 68
$blog_id global variable, 321
$current_user object, 76
$post global variable, 68, 239
$shortcode_tags global variable, 180
$styles object, 123
$template variable, 105
$temp_content` function, 65
$text variable, 181
$wpdb class, 72
    SELECT queries with, 73
$wpdb object, 227
$wpdb->get_col() method, 72, 73
$wpdb->get_results() method, 73
$wpdb->get_row() method, 74
$wpdb->insert() method, 74
$wpdb->prefix property, 69
$wpdb->prepare() function, 227
$wpdb->prepare() method, 71
$wpdb->query() method, 70
$wpdb->replace() method, 75
$wpdb->update() method, 75
$wpdb` class, 68
$wpdb→query() method, 68
$wp_query object, 76
$wp_query→query_vars[subject] global variable, 199
$_REQUEST values, checking, 239

$_SERVER[HTTPS] global variable, 351
$_SERVER[HTTP_USER_AGENT] global variable, 118
% (percent sign), escaping in SQL queries, 72
@import_url, 111
_ (underscore)
    meta data keys starting with, 38
    _s theme framework, 109
    __ (double underscore), class methods starting with, 157
    __() function, 331
_e() function, 331
_ex() function, 332
_x() function, 332
→ (arrow) operator, 157

A

action hooks, 77
actions available to users, controlling, 4
active_sidebar() function, 187
activity_main.xml file, 283
add-ons to existing plugins, 66
add-user_meta() function, 31
add_action() function, 77, 183
add_cap() method, 165
add_comment_meta() function, 47
add_feed() function, 200
add_filter() function, 78, 196
add_meta_box() function, 146

We'd like to hear your suggestions for improving our indexes. Send email to index@oreilly.com.

add_option() function, 24
add_post_meta() function, 39
add_rewrite_endpoint() function, 200
add_rewrite_rule() function, 198, 202
add_rewrite_tag() function, 200
add_role() function, 164
add_user_to_blog() function, 327
admin bar, hiding from non-admins, 174
admin dashboard
    settings for plugins, 193
    SSL login, 350
Admin role, 162
admin username, importance of changing, 216
admin-ajax.php file, 22
admin.css files, 62
admin.js files, 63
/adminpages/ directory, 61
admin_enqueue_scripts hook, 238
ADT (Android Developer Tools), 281
advanced-cache.php, 406
AJAX
    admin-ajax.php file, 22
    calls triggered through Heartbeat API, 246–251
    calls with WordPress and jQuery, 240–244
    check_ajax_referer() function, 236
    defined, 237
    managing multiple AJAX requests, 244
    PHP code for calls in /services/ directory, 65
Akismet plugin, 57, 223
All in One SEO Pack plugin, 79
ALTER TABLE statement, 70
Alternative PHP Cache (APC), 406
Amazon Product Advertising API, 298
    operations, 299
    request parameters, 298
    response groups, 300
    search for WordPress books, 300
Android applications, 281–285
    activity_main.xml, 283
    AndroidManifest.xml, 282
    creating an APK file, 284
    extending, 285
    getting your app on Google Play, 285
    MainActivity.java, 283
    resources, 285
Android SDK, 281
anonymous functions, 196
Antivirus-Once plugin, 225

Apache Bench, 384–389
    graphing results with gnuplot, 387
    installing, 384
    running, 384
    testing with, 386
Apache server
    Nginx server in front of, 402
    setup, 398
.apk file, 284
app wrapper, 275
Apple developer, enrolling as, 276
apply_filters() function, 78, 179
AppPresser.com, 286
apps
    admin, using global of settings, 194
    defined, 1
    developing, themes versus plugins, 95
archives
    for registered CPTs, 142
    specifying if post type has archive page, 131
arrays, storing in user meta, 160
arrow operator (→), 157
Ask Apache Password Protect plugin, 225
Asynchronous JavaScript and XML (see AJAX)
asynchronous processing, WordPress limitations with, 251
attachments, 126
attributes
    HTML, escaping, 229
    shortcode, 178
authenticating users, 159
Author role, 162
    upgrading Subscriber to, 164
Authorize.net, 344

B

Backbone.js framework, 252
Backup Buddy plugin, 82, 224
backups, 222
    plugins for, 224
Bad Behavior plugin, 223
BadgeOS Community Add-on plugin, 94
BadgeOS plugin, 79
Batcache, 409
bbPress plugin, 16
BBQ (Block Bad Queries) plugin, 225
Blitz.io, 391
Block Bad Queries (BBQ) plugin, 225
Blog Copier plugin, 321

blogs, WordPress and, 7
bookmarks, 49
Bootstrap framework, 110
  including in StartBox theme, 111
  responsive stylesheet adjusting CSS rules for
    screen width, 115
Braintree Payments, 344
browscap.ini file, 122
Browser Capabilities Project website, 122
browser detection
  in PHP, 118
  in WordPress core , 119
  reasons for sparing use of, 122
  with PHP get_browser(), 121
browsers
  CSS stylesheet caching, 106
  padlocks, 347
brute-force attacks, 215
  plugin protecting against, 225
BuddyMobile plugin, 94
BuddyPress FollowMe plugin, 93
BuddyPress Media plugin, 93
BuddyPress plugin, 82–94
  components, setting up, 88
  configuring additonal settings, 91
  groups, SchoolPress classes as, 16
  pages, mapping to components used, 90
  plugins to extend BuddyPress, 93
  profile fields, 92
  tables created in WordPress database, 84
  Toolbar, 93
BuddyPress Registration Options plugin, 94
buffering output, 65
_builtin, 134

C

caching, 391
  (see also W3 Total Cache)
  advanced-cache.php and object-cache.php,
    406
  Alternative PHP Cache (APC), 406
  Batcache, 409
  Memcached, 407
  Redis, 408
  selective, 410
    multisite transients, 414
    Transient API, 411–413
  Varnish, 409
  W3 Total Cache plugin, 81

can_export, 133
capabilities
  custom post types (CPTs), 128
  taxonomy, 140
  user, 162
    adding new, 165
    checking, 163, 226
    removing, 165
capability_type, 128
CDNs (content delivery networks), 396
checkUsername() function, 242
check_admin_referer() function, 234
check_ajax_referer() function, 236
Chrome Debug Bar, 381
Chrome Developer Tools Console, SSL error in,
  355
/classes/_ directory, 61
closures, 196
CMS (content management system), WordPress
  as, 4, 21
code examples from this book, xvii
Codex
  Dashboard Widgets API page, 189
  menu position values, 133
  Rewrite API and WP_Rewrite class pages,
    202
  widgets page, 182
comment meta data, in wp_commentmeta table,
  46
comments on posts, in wp_comments table, 42
community plugins, 82–94
compression, 396
content delivery networks (CDNs), 396
content sites, WordPress and, 8
content-focused web apps, 3
Contributor role, 162
cost advantages of WordPress for web app development, 6
CPTs (see customm post types)
CREATE TABLE statement, 68
create_empty_blog() function, 328
create_function() function, 183
cron jobs, 202–207
  adding to an app, 202
  PHP code for, 65
  scheduling, 203
  using server crons only, 206
crontab -e command, 205
cron_schedules hook, 204

cross-site scripting attacks, 101
CSRF (cross-site request forgery) attacks, 232
CSS
    device and display detection in, 115
    files for an app plugin, 62
    style.css file for themes, 106
    using to show/hide menu items, 114
    versioning files used in themes, 123
current_user_can() function, 163, 226
Custom Post Type UI plugin, 80, 135
custom post types (CPTs), 4, 125
    custom wrapper classes for, 148–154
        extending WP_Post vs. wrapping it, 150
        keeping CPT functionality in wrapper
           class, 152
        keeping CPTs and taxonomies together,
           151
        making code easier to read, 154
        reasons for using wrapper clases, 151
    defining and registering, 126–135
    in SchoolPress sample app, 16
    metadata with, 145–148
    themes and, 108
    using in themes and plugins, 141–145
        looping through CPTs, 142
        theme archive and single template files,
           142

D

dashboard
    customizing users table in, 172
    WordPress Multisite network, 314
dashboard widgets, 188
    adding your own, 191
    removing, 189
database caching, 395
database, WordPress
    $wpdb class, 68
    changing default tables prefix, 218
    custom tables for performance optimization,
        416
    escaping in values passed to query() method,
        71
    Multisite network database, 317–320
        individual site tables, 319
        network-wide tables, 317
        shared site tables, 320
    structure of, 23–55
        functions in /wp-includes/option.php, 24

functions in /wp-includes/pluggable.php
    file, 27
    wp_comments table, 42
    wp_commentsmeta table, 46
    wp_links table, 49
    wp_options table, 23
    wp_postmeta table, 38
    wp_posts table, 34
    wp_terms table, 50
    wp_term_relationships table, 54
    wp_term_taxonomy table, 53
    wp_usermeta table, 30
    wp_users table, 26
   tables created by BuddyPress, 84
   using custom tables, 68
   wp_p2p and wp_p2pmeta tables, 80
datatypes, jQuery.ajax() output, 243
dbDelta() function, 68
db_version, 69
delete_blog_option() function, 327
delete_comment_meta() function, 48
delete_option() function, 25
delete_post_meta() function, 40
delete_user and deleted_User hooks, 162
delete_user_meta() function, 32
delete_with_user, 134
deleting users, 161
denial of service (DoS) attacks, 215
description (CPTs), 128
device capabilities, web apps, 3
device detection
    in CSS, 115
    in JavaScript, 116
    in PHP, 118
directions, map, 293
directory structure, WordPress, 21
    /wp-admim directory, 22
    /wp-content directory, 22
    /wp-content/plugins directory, 22
    /wp-includes directory, 22
    /wp/content/mu/plugins directory, 23
    /wp/content/themes directory, 23
    /wp/content/uploads directory, 23
    root directory, 22
DISABLE_WP_CRON, 205
DISALLOW_FILE_EDIT, 218
displays, detection using CSS media queries, 115
Distance Matrix API, 293
distributed (source code), 58

do_action() function, 77
do_shortcode() function, 179
dynamic_sidebar() function, 187

E

Easy Digital Downloads plugin, 344
Eclipse, 281
ecommerce, 341–375
  choosing a plugin, 341–344
    digital downloads, 344
    membership plugins, 343
    shopping cart plugins, 341
  installing SSL certificates on your server, 346
  merchant accounts, 345
  payment gateways, 344
  setting up SaaS with Paid Memberships Pro, 357–375
  SSL certificates and HTTPS, 346–357
    avoiding SSL errors with nuclear option, 355
    SSL on select pages, 351
    SSL with Jigoshop, 349
    SSL with Paid Memberships Pro, 348
    WordPress frontend over SSL, 350
    WordPress login and admin over SSL, 350
edge, 378
  origin versus, 378
Editor role, 162
  removing edit_pages capabilities, 165
_edit_link, 134
edit_user_profile, hooking into, 171
Elevation API, 293
email addresses
  sanitizing, 230
  validating and sanitizing, 231
endpoint mask constants, 202
escaping data, 228
  while translating strings, 333
esc_attr() function, 101, 229
esc_html() function, 229
esc_js() function, 229
esc_sql() function, 71, 227
esc_textarea() function, 101, 229
esc_url() function, 228
esc_url_raw() function, 229
exclude_from_search (CPTs), 128
Exploit Scanner plugin, 225
extending WordPress, 55

external APIs, 289
  Google Maps JavaScript API v3, 292
external IP address, 222
extract() function, 179

F

Facebook, 304–307
  building an app, 306
  leveraging existing plugin, 306
  permissions, 305
  pictures, 304
  search, 305
feature detection in JavaScript, 117
File Header API, 209
  adding file headers to your files, 211
file structure for an app plugin, 60–65
  /adminpages/ directory, 61
  /classes/ directory, 61
  /css/ directory, 62
  /images/ directory, 63
  /js/ directory, 63
  /scheduled/ directory, 65
  /services/ directory, 65
  main plugin file, 65
__FILE__, 239
filters
  in plugins, 66
  using in WordPress core, plugins, or themes, 78
  using instead of settings page, 195
  wp_default_styles, 107
flexibility of WordPress, 5
flexibility, importance of, 11
flush_rewrite_rules() function, 199
FORCE_SSL_ADMIN constant, 350, 351
FORCE_SSL_LOGIN constant, 350
forms
  Gravity Forms plugin, 81
  page template features for, 101
Foundation framework, 110
frameworks
  importing into themes, 111
  popular theme frameworks, 108
    non-WP frameworks, 110
frontend pages added by plugins, 64
frontend.css files, 62
frontend.js files, 63
functions to register custom post types, 135

functions.php file
    for themes, 111
    of the active theme, 108

G

Genesis theme framework, 110
Geocoding API, 293
__get() method, WP_User class, 157, 158, 167
get_blog_details() function, 323
get_blog_option() function, 326
get_blog_post() function, 327
get_blog_status() function, 325
get_browser() function, 121
get_comment() function, 42
get_comments() function, 43
get_comment_meta() function, 47
get_current_blog_id() function, 322
get_file_data() function, 211
get_locale() function, 338
get_object_taxonomies() function, 54
get_option() function, 24
get_plugin_data() function, 209
get_post() function, 35
get_posts() function, 36, 142
get_post_meta() function, 38
get_taxonomies() function, 53
get_taxonomy() function, 53
get_template_part() function, 103
get_term() function, 51
get_terms() function, 50
get_userdata() function, 28
get_user_by() function, 28
get_user_meta() function, 30, 157
    looping through all meta data for a user, 158
GitHub, 289
    SchoolPress source code, 15
global variables, 67
    in wp-includes/vars.php, 119
    using to store array of options for plugin or
        app, 194
GNU General Public License, version 2
    (GPLv2), 10, 58
gnuplot, 387
Google Maps JavaScript API v3, 292–296
    creating a practical app, 293–296
    Distance Matrix, 293
    Elevation, 293
    Geocoding, 293
    Street View service, 293

Google Play, getting your Android app on, 285
Google Translate, 296
Google+, 297
    activities, 297
    comments, 297
    moments, 297
    people, 297
Gravity Forms plugin, 81
Gumby framework, 110
GZIP compression, 396

H

has_archive, 131
has_shortcode() function, 180
have_posts() function, 67
header.php file, 238
Heartbeat API, 246–251
    JavaScript events triggered by, 247
    speeding up or slowing down heartbeat, 250
heartbeat_received hook, 248
Hello Dolly plugin, 57
hidden fields in forms, 101
Hide Admin Bar from Non-Admins plugin, 174
hierarchical option
    posts, 130
    taxonomies, 139
hooks
    action hooks, 77
    admin_enqueue_scripts, 238
    apply_filters(), 79
    cron_schedules, 204
    delete_user and deleted_User, 162
    in custom profile field, 171
    in plugins, 66
    user_register, 161
    using for settings, 194
    using to copy page templates, 102
    wp_dashboard_setup, 190, 193
    wp_enqueue_scripts, 238
    wp_network_dashboard_setup, 190
hosting, 396–410
    rolling your own server, 397–410
        Apache server setup, 398
        Nginx in front of Apache, 402
        Nginx server setup, 402
    WordPress-specific hosts, 397
.htaccess file, 197, 221
HTML
    detecting HTML5 features, 117

escaping, 229
validating and sanitizing with wp_kses()
function, 231
HTTPS, 346, 349
(see also SSL)
URLs, 354
using symlink for HTTPS directory, 347

I

/images/ directory, 63
Imagick, 290
importing data
frameworks and libraries into themes, 111
parent theme's stylesheet to child themes,
111
WP All Import plugin, 82
/includes/ directory, 63
/includes/lib/ directory, 64
includes/settings.php file, 194
index.php file, 98
rendering of custom post types, 108
init() method, CPT wrapper class, 152
INSERT queries, $wpdb command for, 74
interactive elements of web apps, 2
internationalization, 329
intervals, custom, for cron schedules, 204
iOS applications, 275–281
app distribution, 280
building your app with Xcode, 277
iOS simulator, 280
storyboards, 277
View Controller, 277
enrolling as Apple developer, 276
extending, 285
iOS resources, 280
iOS simulator, 280
IP addresses
blocking access for, 222
external IP address, 222
is_multisite() function, 322
is_ssl() function, 354
iThemes Security plugin, 221

J

Java, MainActivity.java file, 283
JavaScript, 5, 237
Backbone.js framework, 252
deciding where to put custom code, 239

device and feature detection, 116
enqueuing jQuery library, 238
enqueuing other libraries, 238
escaping strings in, 229
events triggered by Heartbeat API, 247
feature detection, 117
files for app plugin in /js/ directory, 63
Google Maps API, 292–296
heartbeat.js file, 247
in WordPress, 251
using to increase performance, 414–416
versioning files used in themes, 123
JavaScript Object Notation (see JSON)
Jigoshop ecommerce plugin, 342
SSL with, 349
jQuery, 237
AJAX calls with WordPress and, 240–244
and WordPress, 238
detecting window and screen sizes and other
informaton about browsers, 116
feature detection, 118
jQuery(document).ready(), 242, 247
jQuery.ajax(), 242, 245
jQuery.bind(), 242
/js/ directory, 63
JSON (JavaScript Object Notation)
data returned from AJAX calls in Word-
Press, 240
defined, 237
json_encode() and json_decode() functions, 237

L

label
custom post types (CPTs), 127
taxonomy, 138
labels array
for CPTs, 127
for taxonomies, 138
libraries
feature detection, 118
importing into themes, 111
third-party libraries for app plugin, 64
licensing
GNU General Public License, version 2
(GPLv2), 10
WordPress plugins, 58
Limit Login Attempts plugin, 225
link manager plugin, 49
links/blogroll manager UI, 49

lname field in forms, 101
load_plugin_textdomain() function, 334, 337
load_template() function, 104
load_textdomain() function, 337
load_theme_textdomain() function, 337, 338
locale, 330
localization, 329
localizing WordPress apps, 329–340
    creating and loading translation files, 333–339
        creating a .mo file, 337
        creating a .po file, 336
        file structure for localization, 334
        generating a .pot file, 335
        loading the textdomain, 337
    defining your locale, 330
    determining need for, 329
    how it's done in WordPress, 330
    nonstring assets, 339–340
    prepping strings with translation functions, 331
        escaping and translating simultaneously, 333
Location meta box, creating, 293–296
login error messages, hiding, 220
logins, 3, 159
    disallowing logins via wp-login.php, 221
    plugins for protection of, 225
    SSL logins in WordPress, 350
    Theme My Login plugin, 174
    WordPress Social Login plugin, 306

M

magic methods, 157
mail() function, 207
malware, protecting web applications against, 223
manage_users_columns filter, 172
manage_users_custom_column filter, 172
manage_users_sortable_columns filter, 173
map_meta_cap, 129
mashups, 3
MaxMind GeoIP, 290
media queries, 115
Members plugin, 81, 175
membership levels, SchoolPress sample app, 16
membership plugins, 343
Memcached, 407

menus, 113
    dynamic, 114
    navigation, 113
    storing posts with information for, 126
menu_icon, 133
menu_name, 128
menu_position, 132
merchant accounts, 345
meta boxes
    creating Location meta box, 293–296
    default, removing from dashboard pages, 190
meta capabilities, 128
metadata, 38
    (see also post meta)
    with CPTs, 145–148
    wp_usermeta table, 30
meta_key, 160
meta_value, querying wp_usermeta by, 160
Microsoft Sharepoint, 307
minifying, 395
.mo files, 337, 338
mobile apps, 275–287
    Android applications, 281–285
        activity_main.xml, 283
        AndroidManifest.xml, 282
        creating an APK file, 284
        getting your app on Google Play, 285
        MainActivity.java, 283
    app wrapper, 275
    AppPresser.com, 286
    extending, 285
    iOS applications, 275–281
        app distribution, 280
        building your app with Xcode, 277
        enrolling as Apple developer, 276
    use cases, 286
Modernizr.js library, 118
More Privacy Options plugin, 321
msg shortcode (example), 178
mu (must use) plugins directory, 23
Mullenweg, Matt, 8, 11
Multisite Global Search plugin, 321
multisite network dashboard, removing widgets, 190
Multisite networks (see WordPress Multisite networks)
Multisite Robots.txt Manager plugin, 321
multisite transients, 414

MVC frameworks
  controllers as template loader, 14
  how MVC works, 12
  models as plugins, 13
  plugins for WordPress, 13
  views as themes, 14
MySQL, 5
  optimization, 402–406
MySQL Workbench, 219
MY_SITE_DOMAIN constant, 356

N

navigation menus, 113
nav_menu_css_class filter, 114
nested shortcodes, 179
.NET web applications, cost of building, 6
Nginx server
  in front of Apache server, 402
  setup, 402
nonces, 232
  check_ajax_referer() function, 236
  wp_create_nonce() function, 233
  wp_nonce_field() function, 235
  wp_nonce_url() function, 234
  wp_verify_nonce() function, 233
note widget, 183
Nuclear Option, avoiding SSL errors with, 356

O

object caching, 395
object-cache.php, 406
offline work, 3
optimization and scaling, 377–418
  bypassing WordPress, 418
  custom tables, 416
  definitions of terms, 377
  hosting, 396–410
  MySQL optimization, 402–406
  origin versus edge, 378
  selective caching, 410–414
  testing, 379
    using Apache Bench, 384–389
    using Blitz.io, 391
    using Chrome Debug Bar, 381
    using Siege, 390
    what to test, 379
  using JavaScript for increased performance,
    414–416

W3 Total Cache, 391–396
origin, 378
  versus edge, 378
output buffering, 65, 144

P

P2P plugin, 80
padlocks, 347
page templates, 99–103
  copying using hooks, 102
  loading, 101
  sample, 99
  when to use for themes, 103
pages, 125
  caching with W3 Total Cache, 393
  mapping BuddyPress components to new or
    existing pages, 90
  SSL on, 351
/pages/ directory, 64
Paid Memberships Pro plugin, 9, 165, 174, 343
  custom settings pages, 197
  in SchoolPress sample app, 15
  SaaS (software as a service), 357–375
  SSL with, 348
passwords
  encrypted, 222
  examples of bad passwords, 217
  examples of good passwords, 217
  plugins for protection of, 225
payment gateways, 344
  versus merchant accounts, 345
PayPal, 344
performance, 377
  (see also optimization and scaling)
  limitations of WordPress web apps, 11
permalink redirects, 198
permalink structure of a post, customizing, 130
permalink_epmask, 132
PHP, 5
  classes in SchoolPress sample app, 17
  device detection, 118
  output buffering, functions for, 65
  server-side, in Heartbeat API, 248
  versus JavaScript in WordPress, 251
PHP libraries, 289
  Imagick, 290
  interacting with Twitter REST API, 303
php.ini file, 122
phpMyAdmin, 219

plugins, WordPress, 4, 5, 57–94
  /wp-content/plugins directory, 22
  /wp/content/mu/plugins directory, 23
  add-ons to existing plugins, 66
  building your own, 59
  community plugins, 82
    BuddyPress, 82–94
  criticisms concerning quality of, 9
  favorites, 5
  file headers, 209
    adding, 212
  file structure, 60–65
  for custom settings pages, 197
  for ecommerce, 341
    digital downloads, 344
    membership plugins, 343
    shopping cart plugins, 341
  for Multisite networks, 315, 320–321
  for security, 221, 223
    backup plugins, 224
    login and password protection, 225
    scanner plugins, 224
    spam blocking plugins, 223
  free plugins, 79
  installing, 58
  JavaScript code in, 239
  licensing, 58
  loop for displaying posts, 66
  MVC framework models as plugins, 13
  not allowing admins to edit, 218
  plugin repository, 57
  premium plugins, 81
  themes versus, 95–97
  user management, 174
  using action hooks, 77
  using custom database tables, 68
  using custom post types and taxonomies,
    141–145
  using filters, 78
  using global variables, 67
    $wpdb, 68
  using locate_template() in, 104
plugins_url() function, 239
plugin_locale filter, 338
PMPro Network plugin, 15
PMPro Register Helper plugin, 15, 168, 174
.po files, 336
post meta
  functions for manipulation of, 38

storage in wp_postmeta table, 38
taxonomies versus, 135
with CPTs, 145–148
posts, 126
  (see also custom post types)
  custom post types and taxonomies, plugin
    for, 80
  default post types and custom post types,
    125–126
    attachments, 126
    definition of posts, 125
    navigation menu item, 126
    revisions, 126
  display by WordPress loop, 66
  relating taxonomies to, 54
  storage in wp_posts table, 34
  themes and custom post types, 108
Posts 2 Posts plugin, 80
post_type_supports, 134
.pot file, 335
prepare() method, 227
pre_user_query filter, 173
primitive capabilities, 128
  default, 129
profile fields
  adding, 168–172
    manually, 171
  creating for BuddyPress, 92
public
  post, 130
  taxonomy, 139
publicly_queryable, 128

Q

query() method, escaping in values passed to, 71
query_var
  post, 131
  taxonomies, 139

R

Random.org, 217
Redis, 408
register_activation_hook() function, 203
  functions adding new roles and capabilities,
    165
register_deactivation_hook() function, 203
register_meta_box_cb, 132
register_nav_menu() function, 113

register_nav_menus() function, 113
register_post_type() function, 127–135
    examples of registering custom post types, 134
register_sidebar() function, 186
register_taxonomy() function, 54, 137–141
register_taxonomy_for_object_type() function, 141
registration
    adding fields to registration page, 168–172
    PMPro Register Helper plugin, 174
remote procedure call (RPC), 255
    (see also XML-RPC)
remove_cap() method, 165
remove_meta_box() function, 189
remove_role() function, 165
remove_shortcode() function, 180
REPLACE command (MySQL), 75
resizing page elements, 117
responsive design, 115
    browser detection and, 122
    browser detection in PHP's get_browser(), 121
    browser detection in WordPress core, 119
    device and display detection in CSS, 115
    device and feature detection in JavaScript, 116
    device detection in PHP, 118
restore_current_blog() function, 323
Retina displays, 116
revisions, 126
rewrite
    post, 130
    taxonomy, 139
Rewrite API, 197–202
    adding rewrite rules, 198
    flushing rewrite rules, 199
    other rewrite functions, 200
robots.txt files, 321
roles, 162
    checking for a user, 163
    creating custom roles, 164
    in SchoolPress sample app, 16
    Roles and Capabilities system, 4
    upgrading Subscribers to Authors, 164
root directory (WordPress), 22

S

SaaS (software as a service), 357
    setting up on Paid Memberships Pro, 358–375
sanitize_email() function, 101, 230
sanitize_file_name() function, 230
sanitize_option() function, 229
sanitize_text_field() function, 101, 230
sanitize_title() function, 230
sanitize_user() function, 230
sanitizing data, 228
scalability, 378
scaling, 377
    (see also optimization and scaling)
    criticism of WordPress about, 8
    defined, 377
scanner plugins, 224
/scheduled/ directory, 65
SchoolPress sample web app, xvii, 2
    anatomy of, 15
        business model, 15
        classes as BuddyPress groups, 16
        CPTs (custom post types), 16
        main custom plugin, 17
        membership levels and user roles, 16
        multisite version of WordPress, 15
        other custom plugins, 18
        StartBox theme framework, 18
    note widget, 183
screens
    checking widths using CSS media query, 115
    detecting size with JavaScript and jQuery, 116
search engine optimization (see SEO)
Secure Sockets Layer (see SSL)
security, 215–236
    backing up everything, 222
    criticisms of WordPress about, 9
    frequent security updates for WordPress, 6
    frequent updates of WordPress and plugins/themes, 216
    hardening your WordPress install, 218
        adding custom .htaccess rules to lock down wp-admin, 221
        changing default database tables prefix, 218
        hiding login error messages, 220
        hiding WordPress version, 220
        moving wp-config.php, 219

not allowing admins to edit plugins or themes, 218

not allowing logins via wp-login.php, 221

not using username admin, 216

plugins for, 223

backup plugins, 224

login and password protection, 225

scanner plugins, 224

spam blocking plugins, 223

scanning or monitoring for attacks, 223

using strong password, 217

writing secure code, 225

checking user capabilities, 226

custom SQL statements, 227

data validation, sanitation, and escaping, 227

nonces, 232

SELECT queries, $wpdb object methods for, 73

SEO (search engine optimization), 5

All in One SEO Pack plugin, 79

theme development and, 97

servers

detection in WordPress core, 120

kicking off cron jobs from web server, 205

rolling your own, 397–410

sending email from, 209

URL rewriting systems, 197

/services/ directory, 65

__set() method, WP_User class, 158

settings

configuring BuddyPress settings, 91

for Multisite networks, 316

Settings API, 193–197

deciding if you really need a settings page, 194

ignoring standards when adding settings, 196

using hook or filter instead of settings page, 194

using standards when adding settings, 196

set_transient() function, 414

Sharepoint, 307

shopping cart plugins, 341

shortcodes, 177–181

attributes, 178

creating, with attributes and enclosed content, 178

nested, 179

other useful functions for, 180

removing, 180

using in widgets, 182

shortcode_atts() function, 178

shortcode_parse_atts() function, 181

show_admin_column, 140

show_in_admin_bar, 134

show_in_menu, 133

show_in_nav_menus, 133

taxonomy, 140

show_tagcloud, 140

show_ui

custom post type (CPT), 132

taxonomy, 140

show_user_profile, hooking into, 171

sidebars, 187

(see also widgets)

embedding widget outside of dynamic sidebar, 188

Siege, 390

single events, scheduling, 204

single.php file, 108

creating for registered CPTs, 142

site_url() function, 356

slug-name.php file, 104

SMS messages, 306

software as as service (see SaaS)

source code, distributed, 58

spam blocking plugins, 223

sp_assignments_dashboard_widget() function, 193

sp_assignments_dashboard_widget_configuration() function, 193

sp_manage_users_custom_column() function, 173

sp_stub, 65

SQL (Structured Query Language)

CREATE TABLE statement, 68

updating existing table nemes in database with new prefix, 219

writing custom statements, 227

SQL clients, 219

SQL injection attacks, 218

SSL (Secure Sockets Layer), 346

avoiding SSL errors, 355

installing SSL certificate on your server, 346

on select pages, 351

with Jigoshop, 349

with Paid Memberships Pro, 348

WordPress frontend over SSL, 350

WordPress login and admin over SSL, 350
StartBox theme framework, 109
 creating child theme, 111
 in SchoolPress app, 18
State of WordPress presentation (Mullenweg), 8
Street View Service API, 293
Stripe, 344
strip_shortcodes() function, 181
strong passwords, 217
str_replace() function, 355
style.css file, 98
 for themes, 106
  child themes, 111
  versioning, 106
styling, 187
 (see also CSS; themes)
 for widgets and titles, 187
subdirectories, 312
subdomains, 312
 setting up, 313
SUBDOMAIN_INSTALL, 312
Subscriber role, 162
 upgrading to Author, 164
Sucuri, 223
Super Admin role, 162, 314
supports array (CPTs), 131
switch_to_blog() function, 322
symlinks, 347

T

Tag Cloud Widget, taxonomy's inclusion in, 140
task focus in web apps, 3
taxonomies, 135–141
 creating custom taxonomies, 137
  register_taxonomy() function, 137–141
  register_taxonomy_for_object_type()
   function, 141
 custom post type (CPT), 132
 custom, plugin for, 80
 defined, 135
 keeping together with CPTs, 151
 relating taxonomy terms to posts, 54
 terms and, 50
 using custom taxonomies in themes and
  plugins, 141–145
 versus post meta, 135
 wp-term_taxonomy table, 53
Template Hierarchy, 14, 97
 documentation, 99

template loader, MVC controllers versus, 14
templates
 locating in plugins, 104
 page templates, 99–103
template_content function, 103
terms, 50, 136
 wp_term_relationships table, 54
text widgets, 181
 uses of, 182
<textarea> element, encoding text for, 229
Theme My Login, 174
themes, 95–124
 /wp/content/themes directory, 23
 and custom post types, 108
 creating child theme for StartBox, 111
 embedding widget area into, 187
 embedding widget directly into using
  the_widget(), 188
 file header information, getting, 210
 files containing the WordPress loop, 67
 for WordPress Multisite networks, 315
 functions for, 103
  using locate_template() in your plugins,
   104
 functions.php file, 108
 including Bootstrap in app's theme, 111
 JavaScript code in, 239
 JavaScript files supporting, 63
 licensing, 58
 menus, 113
  dynamic menus, 114
  navigation menus, 113
 MVC views and, 14
 not allowing admins to edit, 218
 page templates, 99–103
  using hooks to copy templates, 102
  when to use theme template, 103
 registering sidebar for, 186
 responsive design, 115
  browser detection in PHP's get_brows-
   er(), 121
  browser detection in WordPress core,
   119
  device and display detection in CSS, 115
  device and feature detection in Java-
   Script, 116
  device detection in PHP, 118
 StartBox theme framework in SchoolPress
  app, 18

style.css file, 106
versioning, 106
template hierarchy, 97
theme frameworks, 108
Genesis, 110
non-WP frameworks, 110
StartBox, 109
_s, 109
using custom post types and taxonomies in, 141–145
theme archive and single template files, 142
versioning CSS and JS files, 123
versus plugins, 95–97
when developing apps, 95
when developing plugins, 96
when developing themes, 97
the_content filter, 179
the_post() function, 67
the_widget() function, 188
transients, 411–414
multisite, 414
translate() function, 331
translation files, creating and loading, 333–339
translation functions, 331
Twenty Thirteen theme, 187
Twenty Twelve theme, 99
Twilio, 306
Twitter REST API v1.1, 301–304
leveraging a PHP library, 303
twitteroauth library, 303

U

UI frameworks, 110
UIViewController class, 277
UIWebview class, 277
UPDATE queries, 75
updates, managing for Multisite networks, 317
update_blog_details() function, 325
update_blog_option() function, 326
update_blog_status() function, 325
update_comment_meta() function, 47
update_count_callback, 139
update_option() function, 24
update_post_meta() function, 38, 137
update_user_meta() function, 30, 160
updating users, 159
uploads, /wp/content/uploads directory, 23
URL rewriting (see Rewrite API)

URLs
adding nonces to, 234
escaping, 228
for AJAX queries, 240
plugins_url() function, 239
user agent strings, 118
User class (see WP_User class)
user management, 4, 155
adding registration and profile fields, 168–172
adding, updating, and deleting users, 158
customizing users table in dashboard, 172
getting user data, 156
hooks and filters, 161
plugins for, 174
roles and capabilities, 162
checking, 163, 226
WordPress Multisite networks, 314
user meta
accessing in wp_usermeta table, 157
updating, 160
user roles (see roles)
usernames
admin username, not using, 216
sanitizing, 230
users
extending WP_User class, 166
not trusting, 227
user_can() function, 163, 226
user_login, 159
user_register, 161

V

validation of data, 228
email addresses, 231
wp_kses() function, 231
Varnish, 409
VaultPress plugin, 224
versions
hiding your WordPress version, 220
updating for WordPress and plugins, 216
ViewController.h file, 277
ViewController.m file, 278

W

W3 Total Cache, 391
CDNs (content delivery networks), 396
database caching, 395

GZIP compression, 396
minifying, 395
object cache, 395
Page Cache settings, 393
W3 Total Cache plugin, 81
web apps
defined, 1
features of, 2
scanning or monitoring for attacks, 223
web services, 289
MaxMind GeoIP, 290
Microsoft SharePoint, 307
other popular web services, 310
websites
defined, 1
typical progression for lean startup running
on WordPress, 5
WHERE clause, UPDATE statement, 75
widgets, 181–193
adding, 182
defining a widget area, 186
embedding widget outside of dynamic
sidebar, 188
checking out existing widgets, 182
dashboard, 188
adding your own, 191
removing, 189
windows, browser, detecting size of, 116
WooCommerce plugin, 342
custom settings pages, 197
WordPress
anatomy of a WordPress app, 15–19
as application framework, 11
MVC frameworks versus, 12
building web apps with, 1
reasons to use WordPress, 3
responses to common criticisms, 7
when not to use WordPress, 10
cost of building web applications, .NET versus, 6
database structure, 23–55
directory structure, 21–23
JavaScript and PHP in, 251
jQuery, 238
limitations with asynchronous processing,
251
optimization and scaling (see optimization
and scaling)
plugin repository, 57

theme frameworks, 109
WordPress MU Domain Mapping plugin, 320
WordPress Multisite networks, 311–328
basic functionality, 321–328
$blog_id, 321
add_user_to_blog(), 327
create_empty_blog(), 328
delete_blog_option(), 327
get_blog_details(), 323
get_blog_option(), 326
get_blog_post(), 327
get_blog_status(), 325
get_current_blog_id(), 322
is_multisite(), 322
restore_current_blog(), 323
switch_to_blog(), 322
update_blog_details(), 325
update_blog_option(), 326
update_blog_status(), 325
database structure, 317–320
individual site tables, 319
network-wide tables, 317
shared site tables, 320
managing, 313
dashboard, 314
plugins, 315
settings, 316
sites, 314
themes, 315
updates, 317
users, 314
plugins, 320–321
setting up a network, 312
WordPress Social Login, 306
work, offline, 3
WP Admin plugin, 221
WP All Import plugin, 82
WP Mail, 207–209
sending nicer emails with, 208
WP Security Scan plugin, 224
wp-admin directory, 22
locking down, 221
wp-config.php file, 22
moving for security reasons, 219
/wp-content directory, 22
/wp-content/plugins directory, 22
WP-Cron, 202–207
kicking off cron jobs from the server, 205
schduling single events, 204

using server crons only, 206
wp-cron.php file, 205
WP-Doc plugin, 195
/wp-includes directory, 22
/wp-includes/comment.php file, functions in, 42, 47
/wp-includes/option.php file, functions in, 24
/wp-includes/pluggable.php file, 27
/wp-includes/post.php file, 34, 38
/wp-includes/taxonomy.php file, functions in, 50, 53
wp-includes/vars.php file, 119
wp-login.php file, 174
    (see also logins)
    not allowing logins via, 221
/wp/content/mu/plugins directory, 23
/wp/content/themes directory, 23
/wp/content/uploads directory, 23
wpdoc_caps, 195
wpdoc_template_redirect() function, 195
wpmu_delete_user() function, 161
wp_add_dashboard_widget() function, 191
WP_ALLOW_MULTISITE, 312
wp_blog_versions table, 318
wp_comments table, 42
    functions for interactions with, 42
wp_commentsmeta table, 46
    functions for interactions with, 47
wp_create_user() function, 27
wp_dashboard_setup, 190, 193
wp_default_styles action, 123
wp_default_styles filter, 107
wp_deleteComment() function, 269
wp_deletePost() function, 260
wp_deleteTerm() function, 263
wp_delete_post() function, 36
wp_delete_term() function, 52
wp_delete_user() function, 28, 161
wp_editComment() function, 270
wp_editPost() function, 259
wp_editProfile() function, 266
wp_editTerm() function, 263
wp_email filter, 208
wp_enqueue_script() function, 238
wp_enqueue_scripts hook, 238
wp_enqueue_style() function, 106
    media query in, 115
wp_getComment() function, 268
wp_getCommentCount() function, 266

wp_getComments() function, 269
wp_getMediaItem() function, 271
wp_getMediaLibrary() function, 271
wp_getOptions() function, 267
wp_getPageTemplates() function, 267
wp_getPost() function, 257
wp_getPostFormats() function, 273
wp_getPosts() function, 256
wp_getPostTypes() function, 273
wp_getProfile() function, 265
wp_getTaxonomies() function, 263
wp_getTaxonomy() function, 264
wp_getTerm() function, 261
wp_getTerms() function, 261
wp_getUser() function, 265
wp_getUsers() function, 264
wp_getUsersBlogs() function, 255
wp_get_object_terms() function, 54
wp_get_theme() function, 210
wp_head hook, 238
wp_insert_comment function, 44
wp_insert_post() function, 35
wp_insert_term() function, 52
wp_insert_user() function, 27, 159
wp_is_mobile() function, 120
wp_kses() function, 231
wp_links table, 49
wp_mail() function, 207
    sending nicer emails, 208
wp_mail_content_type filter, 208
wp_mail_from filter, 208
wp_mail_from_name filter, 208
wp_nav_menu() function, 113
wp_network_dashboard_setup, 190
wp_newComment() function, 270
wp_newMediaObject() function, 272
wp_newPost() function, 259
wp_newTerm() function, 262
wp_nonce_field() function, 235
wp_nonce_url() function, 234
wp_options table, 23
    functions for interactions with, 24
    wp_user_roles option, 165
wp_p2p table, 80
wp_p2pmeta table, 81
WP_Post class, 148
    (see also custom post types; posts)
    extending versus wrapping, 150

wp_postmeta table, 38, 136
    functions for interactions with, 38
wp_posts table, 34
    limiting number of revisions stored in, 126
WP_POST_REVISIONS, 126
WP_Query class, 36, 142
wp_registration_log table, 318
WP_Rewrite class, 202
wp_schedule_event() function, 203
    intervals, 204
wp_schedule_single_event() function, 204
wp_setOptions() function, 267
wp_set_object_terms() function, 55
wp_signon() function, 159
wp_signups table, 318
wp_site table, 319
wp_sitemeta table, 319
wp_specialchars() function, 229
wp_terms table, 50, 136
    functions for interactions with, 50
wp_terms_relationships table, 136
wp_terms_taxonomy table, 136
wp_term_relationships table, 54
wp_term_taxonomy table, 53
wp_update_comment() function, 44
wp_update_post() function, 35
wp_update_term() function, 52
wp_update_user() function, 28, 159
WP_User class, 28
    extending, 166
        Teacher and Student classes, 166–168
    getting a WP_User object to work with, 156
    getting user data from WP_User object, 156
    using overloaded properties or __get() magic method, 157
wp_usermeta table, 30, 320
    accessing data stored in, 157
    functions for interactions with, 30
    storing arrays in, different methods, 160
wp_users table, 26
    accessing data stored in, 157
    demonstration of functions interacting with, 29
wp_user_roles option, 165
wp_verify_nonce() function, 233
WP_Widget class, 182
wp_xmlrpc_server class, 255, 274

wrapper classes for CPTs, 148–154
    extending WP_Post vs. wrapping it, 150
    keeping CPT functionality together, 152
    keeping CPTs and taxonomies together, 151
    making code easier to read, 154
    reasons for using, 151
WYSIWYG editor, 4

X

Xcode, 277–280
    iOS simulator, 280
    storyboards, 277
    View Controller, 277
XML-RPC, 255–274, 285
    wp_deleteComment() function, 269
    wp_deletePost() function, 260
    wp_deleteTerm() function, 263
    wp_editComment() function, 270
    wp_editPost() function, 259
    wp_editProfile() function, 266
    wp_editTerm() function, 263
    wp_getComment() function, 268
    wp_getCommentCount() function, 266
    wp_getComments() function, 269
    wp_getMediaItem() function, 271
    wp_getMediaLibrary() function, 271
    wp_getOptions() function, 267
    wp_getPageTemplates() function, 267
    wp_getPost() function, 257
    wp_getPostFormats() function, 273
    wp_getPosts() function, 256
    wp_getPostTypes() function, 273
    wp_getProfile() function, 265
    wp_getTaxonomies() function, 263
    wp_getTaxonomy() function, 264
    wp_getTerm() function, 261
    wp_getTerms() function, 261
    wp_getUser() function, 265
    wp_getUsers() function, 264
    wp_getUsersBlogs() function, 255
    wp_newComment() function, 270
    wp_newMediaObject() function, 272
    wp_newPost() function, 259
    wp_newTerm() function, 262
    wp_setOptions() function, 267

About the Authors

Brian Messenlehner is the cofounder of WebDevStudios.com, a WordPress development shop. Brian is also the cofounder of AppPresser, a mobile application framework for WordPress. Since he comes from a background of building large-scale web applications for the US Marine Corps, he has always looked at utilizing WordPress for more than a blogging system or basic CMS. Brian and the team at WDS have built several nontraditional websites using WordPress as an application framework. Brian enjoys learning about new technology and believes open source software like WordPress is the key to successful, cost-effective web solutions in any situation. You can find Brian on Twitter @bmess.

Jason Coleman is the CEO of Stranger Studios and lead developer of Paid Memberships Pro, a membership platform for WordPress. He has been developing applications in PHP and on top of WordPress for over five years. Jason enjoys helping his customers GET PAID through Paid Memberships Pro, enabling them to start new businesses and expand current ones. You can find Jason at *http://therealjasoncoleman.com* or on Twitter @jason_coleman.

Colophon

The animal on the cover of *Building Web Apps with Wordpress* is a common iguana (*Iguana iguana*). This reptile is native to Central and South America, and its range encompasses parts of Mexico and extends all the way down to southern Brazil. There are also populations in South Florida, Hawaii, and the Rio Grande Valley in Texas that arose from the escape or disposal of captive individuals. In some South American countries, iguana eggs are sold as a novelty food; they are boiled in salt and can fetch twice the price of a chicken egg.

The word *iguana* is derived from the language of the Taíno people, who called the lizard *iwana*. Despite being commonly known as the green iguana, this species can be many different colors, depending on their area of origin. In the more southern countries of their range, iguanas appear more bluish in color, with bright blue markings. On islands like Aruba and Grenada, their skin can be lavender or black; individuals from the western side of Costa Rica are red, and Mexican iguanas tend to be a light orange.

Iguanas are excellent climbers and can fall for about 50 feet without being hurt. Their strong back legs and claws allow them to grasp branches and make long leaps from tree to tree. As well as being at home in the canopy, iguanas are natural swimmers who use their powerful tails to propel them through the water. Their tails are also used as weapons to protect the iguanas from predators or to incapacitate a rival. If the tail gets caught in something, the iguana will allow it to break in order to escape; a new tail eventually grows out to replace the old one.

Because of their dramatic looks and laid-back nature, green iguanas are popular pets. However, they require specialized care, and it is sadly very common for iguanas to be abandoned or disposed of because an owner could not provide the correct environment. They need to be provided with varied leafy vegetables and access to fresh water, and should be kept at a constant temperature of 79°F and given access to UVA and UVB lighting. An iguana can live up to 20 years if cared for properly, so the decision to keep one as a pet should be given much consideration.

The cover image is from Wood's *Animate Creation*. The cover fonts are URW Typewriter and Guardian Sans. The text font is Adobe Minion Pro; the heading font is Adobe Myriad Condensed; and the code font is Dalton Maag's Ubuntu Mono.

Get even more for your money.

Join the O'Reilly Community, and register the O'Reilly books you own. It's free, and you'll get:

- $4.99 ebook upgrade offer
- 40% upgrade offer on O'Reilly print books
- Membership discounts on books and events
- Free lifetime updates to ebooks and videos
- Multiple ebook formats, DRM FREE
- Participation in the O'Reilly community
- Newsletters
- Account management
- 100% Satisfaction Guarantee

Signing up is easy:

1. Go to: oreilly.com/go/register
2. Create an O'Reilly login.
3. Provide your address.
4. Register your books.

Note: English-language books only

To order books online:
oreilly.com/store

For questions about products or an order:
orders@oreilly.com

To sign up to get topic-specific email announcements and/or news about upcoming books, conferences, special offers, and new technologies:
elists@oreilly.com

For technical questions about book content:
booktech@oreilly.com

To submit new book proposals to our editors:
proposals@oreilly.com

O'Reilly books are available in multiple DRM-free ebook formats. For more information:
oreilly.com/ebooks

Spreading the knowledge of innovators   oreilly.com

Have it your way.

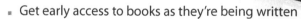

Lightning Source UK Ltd.
Milton Keynes UK
UKOW06f0905100414

229700UK00002B/6/P